Asian/Oceanian Historical Dictionaries
Edited by Jon Woronoff

Asia

1. *Vietnam*, by William J. Duiker. 1989
2. *Bangladesh*, by Craig Baxter and Syedur Rahman, second edition. 1996
3. *Pakistan*, by Shahid Javed Burki. 1991
4. *Jordan*, by Peter Gubser. 1991
5. *Afghanistan*, by Ludwig W. Adamec. 1991
6. *Laos*, by Martin Stuart-Fox and Mary Kooyman. 1992
7. *Singapore*, by K. Mulliner and Lian The-Mulliner. 1991
8. *Israel*, by Bernard Reich. 1992
9. *Indonesia*, by Robert Cribb. 1992
10. *Hong Kong and Macau*, by Elfed Vaughan Roberts, Sum Ngai Ling, and Peter Bradshaw. 1992
11. *Korea*, by Andrew C. Nahm. 1993
12. *Taiwan*, by John F. Copper. 1993
13. *Malaysia*, by Amarjit Kaur. 1993
14. *Saudi Arabia*, by J. E. Peterson. 1993
15. *Myanmar*, by Jan Becka. 1995
16. *Iran*, by John H. Lorentz. 1995
17. *Yemen*, by Robert D. Burrowes. 1995
18. *Thailand*, by May Kyi Win and Harold Smith. 1995
19. *Mongolia*, by Alan J. K. Sanders. 1996
20. *India*, by Surjit Mansingh. 1996
21. *Gulf Arab States*, by Malcolm C. Peck. 1996
22. *Syria*, by David Commins. 1996
23. *Palestine*, by Nafez Y. Nazzal and Laila A. Nazzal. 1997
24. *Philippines,* by Artemio R. Guillermo and May Kyi Win. 1997

Oceania

1. *Australia*, by James C. Docherty. 1992
2. *Polynesia*, by Robert D. Craig. 1993
3. *Guam and Micronesia*, by William Wuerch and Dirk Ballendorf 1994
4. *Papua New Guinea*, by Ann Turner. 1994
5. *New Zealand*, by Keith Jackson and Alan McRobie, 1996

New Combined Series (July 1996)

Historical Dictionary of Bangladesh

Second Edition

Craig Baxter
and
Syedur Rahman

Asian Historical Dictionaries, No. 2

The Scarecrow Press, Inc.
Lanham, Md., & London
1996

SCARECROW PRESS, INC.

Published in the United States of America
by Scarecrow Press, Inc.
4720 Boston Way
Lanham, Maryland 20706

4 Pleydell Gardens, Folkestone
Kent CT20 2DN, England

British Cataloguing-in-Publication Information Available

Library of Congress Cataloging-in-Publication Data

Baxter, Craig.
Historical dictionary of Bangladesh / by Craig Baxter and Syedur Rahman. — 2nd ed.
p. cm. — (Asian historical dictionaries ; no. 2)
Includes bibliographical references.
ISBN 0–8108–3187–2 (alk. paper)
1. Bangladesh—History—Dictionaries. I. Rahman, Syedur. II. Title. III. Series.
DS394.5.B39 1996
954.92'003—dc20 96–15454

ISBN 0-8108-3187-2 (cloth : alk.paper)

The paper used in this publication meets the minimum requirements of American National Standard for Information Sciences—Permanence of Paper for Printed Library Materials, ANSI Z39.48–1984.
Manufactured in the United States of America.

CONTENTS

EDITOR'S FOREWORD

Bangladesh is certainly not one of the best-known Asian countries. And what is "known" about it is not always very favorable. It is usually presented in stories that stress its overpopulation and underdevelopment. But there is much more to it than that. Bengal has a long and oftentimes proud tradition. It has produced writers and artists of genius. It is an important outpost of Islam. And, with a population of over a hundred million, it is one of the larger countries in the world. It therefore deserves to be known better by more people.

That is the purpose of this volume. But it was not easy to achieve, given the great length and considerable complexity of the history of a place now called Bangladesh, but previously just East Pakistan, and before that part of British India, and so on into the past. It has been inhabited by different people, of different religions and ruled over by different leaders who imposed different regimes. Yet, despite the difficulty of writing a "historical" dictionary, the effort has succeeded. With its many entries, an enlightening introduction, and an ample bibliography, we trust that this book will serve as an accessible point of entry for those new to the country, and still a source of useful information for the more experienced.

This Asian historical dictionary was produced by two leading authorities. One is Craig Baxter, a retired foreign service officer and now professor of politics and history at Juniata College, whose long familiarity with the country and the region was refreshed by a recent trip. He is the author of one of the few topical works, *Bangladesh: A New Nation in an Old Setting.* The other is Syedur Rahman, born in Bangladesh and educated there and in the United States, who has taught at the University of Dhaka and is now at the Pennsylvania State University. He has written, *inter alia*, on regional cooperation in South Asia.

Jon Woronoff
Series Editor

ACKNOWLEDGMENTS

The authors wish to acknowledge the assistance of several persons in the preparation of the second edition of this work.

Abby Wertzberger and Julie Elvey, both students at Juniata College, worked extensively on the preparation of the bibliography. Syed Omar Ahmed Karimushan, also a student at Juniata College, assisted in the translation of materials originally in Bangla. Kenneth Miller and Matt Sherer, other Juniata students, were of great assistance in formatting the book. Arif ibne Mizan of the Centre for Development Research Bangladesh assisted in obtaining material available only in Bangladesh and in translation. Dr. Mumtaz Ahmad of Hampton University and Dr. Tony K. Stewart of North Carolina State University assisted on certain entries. The process of scanning the first edition into a form that could be edited was aided by Dr. Joe Vasey and Sally Crandell of the Pennsylvania State University.

The authors greatly appreciate this assistance.

Craig Baxter
Syedur Rahman

ACRONYMS

ASA	Association for Social Advancement
BAKSAL	Bangladesh Krishak Sramik Awami League
BARD	Bangladesh Academy for Rural Development
BNP	Bangladesh Nationalist Party
BRAC	Bangladesh Rural Advancement Committee
CML	Council Muslim League
COP	Combined Opposition Parties
CPI	Communist Party of India
EBDO	Electoral Bodies (Disqualification) Order
HYV	High Yield Varieties
JAGODAL	Jatiyatabadi Gonotantrik Dal
JSD	Jatiya Samajtantrik Dal
KSP	Krishak Shramik Party
KPP	Krishak Praja Party
NAP	National Awami Party
NAP(B)	National Awami Party (Bhashani)
NAP(W)	National Awami Party (Wali)
OIC	Organization of the Islamic Conference
PPP	People's Party of Pakistan
PRODA	Public & Representative Offices Disqualification Act
SAARC	South Asian Association for Regional Cooperation
UF	United Front

CHRONOLOGY OF IMPORTANT EVENTS

1500 B.C.	Approximate date of arrival of Indo-Aryans in the Indus valley.
1000 B.C.	Approximate date of arrival of Bang tribe in the lower Ganges valley.
273-232 B.C.	Reign of Maurya emperor Asoka.
320-510 A.D.	Gupta dynasty.
606-647	Reign of Harsha.
750	Founding of Pala dynasty.
1095	Beginning of Sena dynasty.
1155	Fall of Pala dynasty.
1202	Fall of Sena capital, Nadia, to Khalji general representing Ghurid dynasty.
1336	Rebellion against Tughluq dynasty of Delhi sultanate led by Fakhruddin Mubarak Shah.
1346	After decade of turmoil, Shamsuddin Ilyas Shah founds Ilyas Shahi dynasty.
1490	Overthrow of Ilyas Shahi dynasty. Founding of Husain Shahi dynasty.
1517	Arrival of Portuguese in Chittagong.
1538	Conquest of Bengal by troops of the Mughal emperor Humayun.
1539	Rebels under Sher Shah Suri, an Afghan, take Bengal and rule to 1564.
1564	Rival Afghan dynasty wins control of Bengal.
1576	Conquest of Bengal by Mughal emperor Akbar.
1608	Dhaka becomes capital of Mughal's Bengal province.
1650	Arrival of British in Bengal.

1690	British found Calcutta.
1704	Murshidabad replaces Dhaka as capital.
1756	Mughal governor Sirajuddaulah attacks Calcutta. Incident of the "Black Hole."
1757	British under Robert Clive defeats Sirajuddaulah at Battle of Plassey.
1765	Clive becomes governor of Bengal
1772	Warren Hastings becomes governor. Becomes governor-general in 1773.
1793	Permanent Settlement decreed by Cornwallis.
1857	Sepoy Mutiny.
1858	Transfer of power from British East India Company to the Crown. Queen Victoria's proclamation that all subjects are equal under the law.
1861	India Councils Act permits inclusion of Indians in legislative councils of lieutenant governors and the governor-general.
1883	Local Councils Act permits limited election to local government boards.
1885	Indian National Congress founded at Bombay.
1894	India Councils Act expands rights given in 1861 act.
1905	Partition of Bengal.
1906	Muslim delegation meets Lord Minto at Simla. Muslim League founded in Dhaka.
1909	Government of India Act (Morley-Minto Act) grants Muslim demand of separate electorates and further expanded powers of legislative councils.

1911	Annulment of partition of Bengal. Capital of India transferred from Calcutta to New Delhi.
1917	Montagu Declaration proposing ultimate "self-government" for India.
1919	Government of India Act (Montagu-Chelmsford Act) creates system of dyarchy at provincial level.
1935	Government of India Act provides for provincial autonomy and responsible government. Proposed changes at federal level are not fully implemented as Indian princes would not accept subordination to dyarchical system at that level.
1937	Provincial elections held. Fazlul Haq becomes first prime minister of Bengal.
1940	March 23. Muslim League passes at Lahore proposing that partition of India may be necessary (often referred to as the "Pakistan Resolution" although the word "Pakistan" does not appear). It is seconded by Fazlul Haq.
1941	Fazlul Haq leaves Muslim League but his prime ministership continues.
1943	Muslim League ministry headed by Nazimuddin is formed.
1945	Nazimuddin government falls; governor assumes rule.
1946	New elections held. Muslim League forms ministry headed by Suhrawardy.
1947	August 15. Partition of India and independence of dominions of India and Pakistan. Muslim League forms ministry in East Bengal headed by Nazimuddin.
1951	Nazimuddin becomes governor-general of Pakistan. Nurul Amin heads East Bengal ministry.

1952	February 21. Martyrs' day in memory of students killed in pro-Bengali language demonstrations in Dhaka.
1954	Muslim League trounced by United Front of Awami League (Suhrawardy) and Krishak Sramik Party (KSP) (Fazlul Haq). Fazlul Haq becomes chief minister briefly, but central government imposes governor's rule (to 1956).
1955	East Bengal renamed East Pakistan.
1956	First Pakistani constitution effective on March 23.
1956-1958	United Front having broken apart, Awami League and KSP alternate leadership of government during increasingly tumultuous period.
1958	President Mirza declares martial law on October 7. General Muhammad Ayub Khan dismisses Mirza on October 28 and assumes presidency.
1962	Ayub proclaims second constitution including formalization of system of basic democracies (operative since 1959). Martial law ends.
1965	September War between Pakistan and India.
1966	Sheikh Mujibur Rahman announces Awami League Six-Point Program.
1969	March 25. Ayub resigns and turns presidency over to General Yahya Khan. Martial law reimposed.
1970	December. Elections held in Pakistan. Awami League wins 160 of 162 national assembly seats from East Pakistan, but none of 138 from West Pakistan.
1971	Constitutional talks among Yahya, Mujib, and Bhutto fail. On evening of March 24, Pakistan army moves against Bengalis. Civil war breaks out. Indian forces enter

conflict in late November. Pakistan surrender of Dhaka to allied forces December 16.

1972 Mujib, who had been in captivity in West Pakistan, returns to Dhaka January 10. On December 16, Bangladesh constitution promulgated.

1973 Elections to Bangladesh parliament give Awami League 292 of 300 seats.

1975 Mujib assassinated on August 15. Khondakar Mushtaque Ahmad becomes president. Insurrection November 3-5 led by Khalid Musharaf fails. Ziaur Rahman emerges as key figure. A. S. M. Sayem is named president.

1977 Zia replaces Sayem as president on April 21. Wins referendum to hold office on May 30.

1978 Zia elected president and Abdus Sattar appointed vice president on June 3.

1979 Parliamentary election gives Zia's party 207 of 300 seats.

1981 Zia assassinated on May 30. Sattar becomes acting president. Sattar elected president on November 15.

1982 Sattar overthrown in military coup led by H. M. Ershad on March 24.

1986 Parliamentary election gives Ershad's party a slight majority. Awami League and its allies win about one-third of the seats. Bangladesh Nationalist Party boycott the poll.

1987 Awami League withdraws from parliament. In November, major demonstrations against Ershad take place, causing him to declare a state of emergency and dissolve parliament.

1988 New elections to parliament are held and are boycotted by both the Awami League and the Bangladesh Nationalist Party. Ershad's Jatiya Party wins about 250 of 300 seats.

1990 Demonstrations against Ershad continue in 1989 and 1990 at a relatively low level, but in November 1990 grow to major proportions. Two major parties, Bangladesh Nationalist Party and Awami League,

	agree on ousting Ershad and holding "free and fair" elections under a neutral government. Ershad resign December 4, turning over reins of government to Chief Justice Shahabuddin Ahmed.
1991	Elections held in March give Bangladesh Nationalist Party a small majority; its leader, Begum Khaleda Zia, is sworn in as prime minister. Parliament approves constitutional amendment ending presidential system and establishing parliamentary system of government. Parliament elects Abdur Rahman Biswas as president with mainly ceremonial duties.
1994	Endemic opposition to Khaleda Zia in parliament and elsewhere leads opposition to withdraw from parliament unless its demand for future elections to be held under neutral caretaker governments is met. Opposition resigned from parliament December 28.
1995	Opposition seats are declared vacant on June 20 as opposition members had not attended parliamentary sittings for ninety consecutive days. By-elections can not be held as opposition declares it will boycott them. Parliament is dissolved on November 24 by the president on the advice of the prime minister.
1996	A new election is held on February 15, resulting in an overwhelming BNP majority as the opposition boycotts amid increasing violence. The new parliament passes a constitutional amendment providing for future elections under a neutral caretaker government. The election on June 16 results in a plurality for the Awami League, which forms an alliance with the Jatiya Party. A new government led by Sheikh Hasina Wajid of the Awami League is formed on June 23.

MAP of BANGLADESH

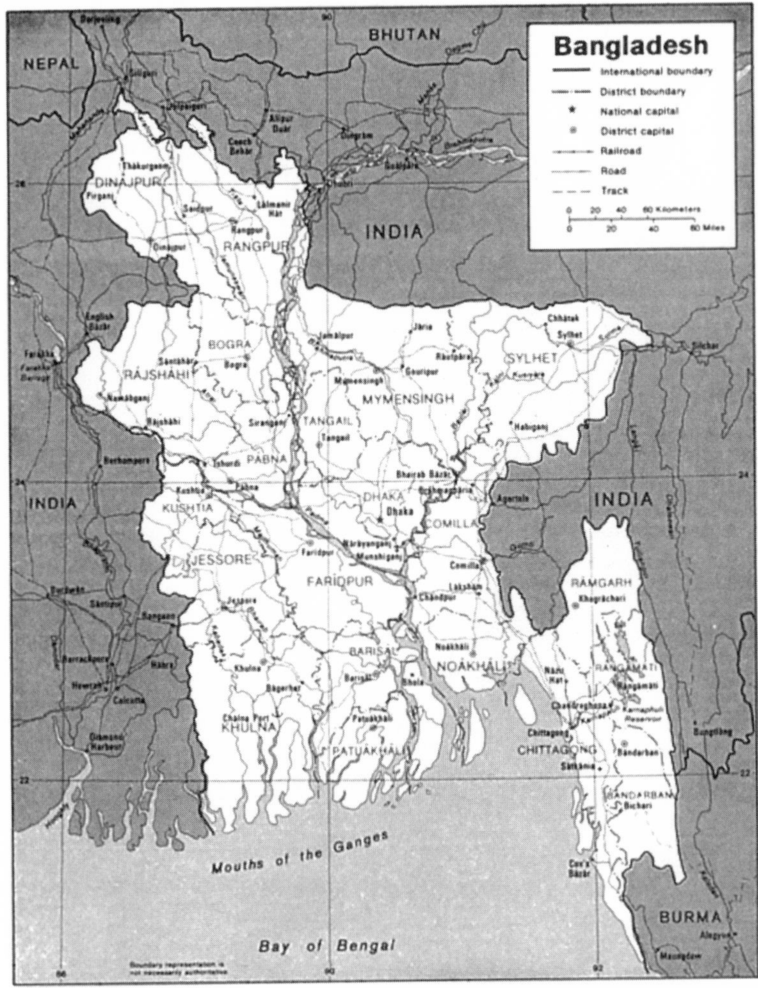

INTRODUCTION

Bangladesh (literally, the land of the Bengalis) is the most recent addition (in 1971) to the independent nations of South Asia. The term "South Asia" is usually defined now as including the seven states that are members of the South Asian Association for Regional Cooperation (SAARC): Bangladesh, Bhutan, India, the Maldives, Nepal, Pakistan, and Sri Lanka. In academic usage the term may also include Afghanistan. These states are ones that were under British control or influence throughout much of the nineteenth and early twentieth centuries. Those controlled directly by the British attained independence in 1947 (India and Pakistan), 1948 (Sri Lanka, then Ceylon), and 1971 (Bangladesh, but from Pakistan not Britain). They therefore share a heritage in such areas as administration, legal systems, and many political structures. They also share a traditional background, although Hinduism, which still dominates in India (and Nepal), has long since been superseded by Islam in Pakistan and Bangladesh, and by Buddhism in Sri Lanka.

The separation of Bangladesh from Pakistan in 1971 and the partition of India in 1947 make it evident that there will be much overlap among the works in this series on the three countries. A further complication is that the term "Bangladesh" itself is a misnomer. While Bangladesh contains a majority of the speakers of the Bengali language, there are many more who live in and give their name to the Indian state of West Bengal and others in fair numbers in the state of Assam and in the smaller hill states of northeastern India.

Geography

Bangladesh is a compact country, comprising mainly the deltaic area formed by the mouths of the combined Ganges (Ganga) and Brahmaputra Rivers that rise respectively in Indai and Tibet. To these rivers is added another major stream, the Meghna, which rises in the northeastern part of Bangladesh itself. The region is thus an alluvial plain with but few exceptions. These include the hills in the northeastern protion (Sylhet Region), where rainfall occurs at one of the highest rates in the world, and the southeastern area (Chittagong Hill Tracts Region) with lower but still substantial rainfall. (It should be noted that the political units once known as "districts" have now been reclassified as "regions," and those formerly known as "subdivision" as "districts," although no structure or functions have been assigned to the "regions.")

The combination of the usually heavy monsoon rainfall and the flow from the rivers resulting from upstream snowmelt provides Bangladesh with a quantity of water that can be both a blessing and a curse. On the positive side, the annual flooding provides water for the growing of such water-demanding crops as rice and jute and also replenishes the fertile soil with deposits of silt brought from the Himalaya and the Tibetan plateau. The streams also provide an intricate network of routes for domestic travel and commerce, but, of course, at the same time they act as formidable barriers to the development of roads and rail transport. The continued migration of the rivers and streams makes bridging a difficult task, and the major rivers have also inhibited the distribution of electricity and of the natural gas that is abundant in the country. A major bridge to cross the Jamuna is under construction and will be a combination road and rail bridge and will carry gas and electricity lines. Another serious "curse" is the frequent extensive flooding that, rather than contributing to agriculture, washes away crops, kills animals and often people, and destroys villages.

Although there are dangers from an excess of water, Bangladesh is clearly heavily dependent on the flow of the rivers. The withdrawals of water from the Ganges by the upper riparian, India, has diminished the flow into Bangladesh. This has been demonstrated most clearly in the building of a barrage at Farraka, just upstream from the border, by India with the purpose of diverting Ganges water through the Bhagirathi and Hooghly Rivers to assist the city of Calcutta. In effect, the Farraka diversion would restore the Bhagirathi-Hooghly system as the principal distributary of the Ganges, which it was prior to the natural diversion in the sixteenth and seventeenth centuries that made the Padma, which flows through Bangladesh, the principal distributary. An important and unresolved political dispute between India and Bangladesh has resulted, although there has been a temporary agreement to divide the water roughly evenly during the low-flow period in April, May, and June. India has proposed a link canal to move water from the Brahmaputra (which usually carries more water than is needed for irrigation and navigation downstream) to a point on the Ganges upstream from Farraka to augment the low season flow. Bangladesh has objected, as the canal would have both its intake and outflow under Indian control but would flow for most of its length in Bangladesh. Bangladesh has proposed a tripartite arrangement that would include Nepal and result in additional storage dams on Nepali territory to regulate the flow of the Ganges and at the same time add to hydroelectric generation in Nepal and northern India. India opposes any multilateral agreement.

The rivers flow slowly through Bangladesh. Dhaka, for example, is only twenty-four feet above sea level. Therefore there is but limited potential for hydroelectric generation. The only exception, so far, is the harnessing of the Karnaphuli River upstream from Chittagong for power.

Bangladesh is also subject to another climatic phenomenon that can only be destructive: the cyclones that arise in the Bay of Bengal and cause damage in Bangladesh as well as in eastern India. The great cyclone of 1970 may have killed as many as half a million people along the coastal areas and left countless more injured and homeless. Construction of homes from more permanent materials and the development of extensive early warning programs are helping to ameliorate such widespread damage. The building of polders, with Dutch assistance, has also been effective in some areas. Major cyclones have struck as recently as 1991 and 1993.

Bangladesh's borders are neither traditional nor natural. The land boundary is almost entirely with India, the exception being in the very southeastern end of the country where it borders on the Arakan area of Myanmar (Burma). As will be discussed below, the border with India was set in 1947 as part of the process of partitioning British India. The result has been the leaving of enclaves on one side or the other and another political problem between the two countries.

The southern boundary is the Bay of Bengal, but the exact location of that boundary is still a matter of dispute between India and Bangladesh. The appearance of new islands in the bay has complicated the negotiations, as has the law of the sea agreement. Bangladesh, as a state at the end of an indenture in the sea, is not accorded an economic zone of 200 miles, as this zone must be plotted on a line that respects also the rights of Myanmar and India. The determination of the ownership of new islands would affect the base points from which the economic zone is determined.

The People

The 115 million people of Bangladesh are crowded into an area of 55,126 square miles (about the size of Wisconsin). This gives the country a population density of more than 2,000 per square mile, higher than any state except for such city-states as Singapore and Hong Kong. There has been much progress in the family planning program; the growth rate, which was 2.5 percent (1960-1992), is expected to drop to 2.2 percent (1992-2000). Nonetheless, a population of 134.4 million is forecast for the end of the century. Such overcrowding has, of course, important economic and social implications, which will be noted in the next section.

The rate of urbanization has been lower in Bangladesh than in most third-world countries. More than 80 percent of the population is classified as rural. Dhaka, with 5.7 million (1990), is the largest city. Only two other cities have a population higher than one million, Chittagong with 2.1 million and Khulna, 1.0 million (1990).

The vast majority of the people are Bengalis, a branch of the Indo-Aryans who migrated to the eastern areas of the subcontinent after the earlier movement of the group from Central Asia to the region of the Indus River in the second millennium before Christ. Prior to their arrival, the region seems to have been populated by Dravidian groups, whose physical characteristics of shorter stature and darker skin are seen in the mixed population of Bangladesh. Evidence of some Mongoloid background can also be seen in eastern Bangladesh, especially in the regions of Sylhet and Chittagong.

About 88 percent of the Bangladeshis are Muslim, almost all of the Sunni branch. These include a small proportion who are descendants of Muslims who migrated from north India to serve as officers and soldiers of the Delhi sultanate or the Mughal empire and remained in Bengal. The bulk, however, were converted, usually through Sufi preachers, from among the population already resident in the area. For reasons that are not clear, the rate of conversion was higher in the eastern parts of Bengal than the western, and this was recognized when the united province of Bengal was partitioned in 1947.

Most of the remaining population (10.5 percent) is Hindu. Among them, the majority belong to the Scheduled Castes (a legal term for those formerly known as Untouchables). The bulk of the upper-caste Hindus fled to India by the early 1950s or later, at the time of the civil war in 1971. Generally, the western districts of Bangladesh have a higher percentage of Hindus than the eastern.

The other Bangladeshis are Christian (a few hundred thousand) or Buddhist. Many of each group are tribals. Christian tribals (e.g., Garos, Khasis) are often southern extensions of groups whose main territory is in the Indian state of Meghalaya, north of Bangladesh. Buddhist tribals are most often found in the Chittagong Hill Tracts (e.g., Chakmas, Tripuras). Many of the latter group have been in rebellion against the Bangladesh government, asserting that "flatlanders" have moved into the reserved hill areas. Some tribals, however, are Hindus or animists.

A special group among the Muslims are known as Biharis, who numbered about 600,000 in 1971. These are Urdu-speaking Muslims who fled India in 1947 eastward to what was then East Bengal, rather than westward as most Muslim refugees did. Unable and perhaps unwilling to integrate with their Bengali-speaking co-religionists, the group strongly supported the retention of a united Pakistan. They were therefore looked upon as a kind of fifth column by the Bangladeshi nationalists. Since 1971, some (usually younger persons) have been able to integrate, some have been sent to Pakistan or have made their own way there, but others remain in camps awaiting transportation to Pakistan.

Bangladesh is the only South Asia state that is unilingual; almost all Bangladeshis have Bengali as their mother tongue. The language is derived from Sanskrit, the most eastern of the Indo-European languages. It is written in a script that is a modification of the Sanskrit writing system and is akin to the script of Hindi. Early modern contributions to the rich Bengali literature have been mainly the product of Hindu writers, including the Nobelist Rabindranath Tagore. More recently, Muslims have also added to the literary tradition with the works of such writers as Kazi Nazrul Islam. During the period of Sheikh Mujibur Rahman, great emphasis was placed on Bengalization of all activity, but since then English has revived as a key language of international communications and commerce, although it is often neglected in the educational system.

The Economy

In terms of per capita gross national product (GNP), Bangladesh is among the poorest nations in the world. According to data collected by the World Bank for 1992, GNP per capita was $220. Equity, as measured by income distribution, was badly skewed in 1988-89, the latest year for which figures are available: the highest 20 percent of the population received about 39 percent of the income, while the lowest 20 percent received but 9.5 percent. It has been said with good reason that 60 to 75 percent of the population of Bangladesh lives below the poverty line. The rural population probably has a higher rate of poverty than the urban. Agriculture, which employed about 75 percent of the working labor force, produced only 34 percent of the GNP. The share of industry in the GNP was only 17 percent.

The economy of Bangladesh, therefore, is based almost entirely on agricultural products. For domestic consumption the key is rice; for international trade it is jute, a fiber used in such products as burlap and carpeting (as backing) but one which has a diminishing market, partly as the result of the development of synthetic fibers. These products are grown on very small plots of land. There is a land ceiling, but this means little to most Bangladeshis, as the average landholding among those with land was 3.5 acres in 1977. If the rural landless family units are factored into the calculation, the average drops to 2.3 acres. In addition, owing to inheritance patterns, a holding may be divided into as many as twenty or more fragments. Offsetting this to a limited degree is the ability in some areas to till the land two or three times a year; 38 percent of the land is double-cropped and 7 percent triple-cropped.

Campaigns to intensify production, especially of rice, have had a major effect. Production of this cereal did not reach pre-independence levels of just more than 10 million tons until the 1973-74 crop year, but by 1992-93 the production surpassed 18 million tons. Nonetheless, the production of this staple is less than one pound per person per day, and, even assuming equitable distribution, this means a nutritional deficiency. Bangladesh must receive additional supplies (often wheat rather than the preferred rice) either through purchase or through international assistance programs. In 1992, about 1.3 million tons of cereals were imported.

Industrial growth has been inhibited by a lack of raw materials, a shortage of investment capital, an untrained labor force, an early policy of nationalization, and frequent periods of political instability. More recently, the government has privatized many industrial units and has enacted a more liberal investment policy for both domestic and foreign investors, but, at this writing, this has had little effect on investment patterns. One sector that has shown remarkable growth is the manufacture of garments primarily for export; garments are a significant element in the export pattern of Bangladesh. An offsetting factor has been the migration of Bangladeshi workers to the Middle East. While this has accentuated shortages of trained labor in several fields, it has resulted in remittances by overseas workers of more than $800 million a year. However, with the decline in world oil prices, this amount has also declined, although not as sharply as once anticipated.

The infrastructure is weak. The division of the country by the rivers has made the linking of the electrical grids impossible so far. This is also true of gas transmission lines from the fields in the east to the west. Projects are now under way to overcome both these deficiencies. The use of the abundant domestic natural gas would help to offset the growing cost of imported petroleum. As mentioned earlier, highway and railway networks are also hindered by the rivers, and the use of small boats for industrial traffic is not entirely satisfactory.

The future of the Bangladesh economy, particularly in view of the steadily growing population, is not bright. Bangladesh will need the assistance of international aid donors for many years to come.

Early History

One of the leading British historians of India said in the early part of this century: "No definite affirmation of any kind can be made about specific events in . . . Bengal before 300 B.C." Since he wrote there have been no discoveries that would change that statement. Unlike in the Indus valley in the western part of the subcontinent, where a developed civilization existed prior to the arrival of the Indo-Aryans, no archaeological remains have been found to suggest the existence of a similar civilization in the lower Ganges valley. There are references to *Vanga* in early Sanskrit literature (the "b" and "v" are interchanged), and it is thought that an Indo-Aryan tribe, the Bang (or Vang), moved to the Bengal area in the beginning of the first millennium before Christ. The tribe, it is believed, gave its name to the area.

Bengal formed the eastern extremity of the empire built by Chandragupta Maurya in the fourth century B.C. and expanded by his grandson, Asoka, in the third century B.C. A seaport (near

Tamluk in West Bengal) was developed, and, in addition to trade, it may have served as the point from which Buddhism was spread to Myanmar, Sri Lanka, and Southeast Asia.

When the Mauryan empire collapsed shortly after the death of Asoka, Bengal was left very much on its own. Local rulers presumably held sway, although Bengal paid tribute to the Gupta empire in the fourth and fifth centuries A.D. During this period, eastern Bengal was dominated by the kingdom of Samatata (located near the present city of Chandpur). In the seventh century, Samatata was drawn briefly into the short-lived Gupta revival empire of Harsha. In any event, during the long period from the Mauryas to Harsha, Bengal was very much a backwater as far as the rulers who dominated the heartland of India were concerned.

In 750 Bengal produced a dynasty that would spread its control over areas outside Bengal itself. This was the Pala dynasty, which ruled, at times with difficulty, until 1155. As its power moved westward, it faced challenges from other kingdoms in India that had the same goal of reconstructing the empire of Harsha. Also as it expanded, its base moved westward from Bengal and its capital became what is the present city of Monghyr in Bihar. The Pala capital within Bengal was Vikrampur in the neighborhood of Dhaka. The Palas were ardent Buddhists, descendants perhaps of those who had been converted from lower castes to Buddhism during the time of Asoka.

As Pala power began to decline in the eleventh and twelfth centuries, it appeared that another group would inherit at least the Bengali portion of the empire. This came in 1155 when the last Pala (and Buddhist) ruler was overthrown by a tributary principality ruled by the Senas, a Hindu dynasty. In their brief career, the Senas worked to revive Brahmanism as the religion of Bengal, a task that alienated many of the common people who had welcomed casteless Buddhism and who would soon welcome equally casteless Islam in their aversion to the Brahmanical Hinduism of the Senas. In 1202 the last major Sena ruler was expelled from his capital at Nadia (now in West Bengal) by Muslims. Collateral branches of the Senas continued to rule for a short time in eastern Bengal, but the period of Islamic rule had begun in eastern India and would last until 1757.

Islamic Rule

The Muslims had entered India in the eighth century in Sindh, but the major invasion that would change the political complexion of most of the subcontinent came at the beginning of the eleventh century. Then Mahmud of Ghazni, a Turk, began a series of incursions from what is now Afghanistan. The Slave (Mamluk) dynasty was the first to rule from Delhi (1206-1290).

Ikhtiyaruddin Muhammad Bakhtiyar Khalji, representing the Ghurids (who had succeeded the Ghaznavids), attacked Bengal between 1198 and 1201, conquering Nadia in 1202. During the next fifty years, eastern Bengal would also come under control of the Slave dynasty of the Delhi sultanate, and the surviving Sena rulers would be eliminated. He established the capital of the region at Gaur, now a ruin site near Malda in West Bengal. Until Dhaka was established as the capital in 1608, Gaur and its neighbors Pandua and Tanda would serve almost continuously as the seat of government of Bengal.

Under the Khalji dynasty (1290-1320) in Delhi, Bengal remained a province of the sultanate. The sultanate reached its greatest power under the Tughluq dynasty (1320-1413), but the period also saw the beginnings of the disintegration of the sultanate. During the early years of the reign of Muhammad bin Tughluq (1325-1351), the territory ruled by the sultanate reached its greatest extent, but by the time his reign ended much had been lost. Independent kingdoms were established in a number of areas including Gujarat, the Deccan, Malwa, and Bengal.

The Bengal rebellion was begun in 1336 by Fakhruddin Mubarak Shah, who ruled the area somewhat tentatively for about ten years. In the confused condition of Bengal, Shamsuddin Ilyas Shah came out the winner and established the Ilyas Shahi dynasty as independent rulers of Bengal. This dynasty was overthrown in 1490 by Alauddin Husain Shah. The Husain Shahi dynasty founded by him ruled until 1538.

A new force had arrived in Delhi that sought to reassemble the territories of the Delhi sultanate and expand them. The decaying Lodhi dynasty in Delhi was defeated on April 21, 1526, at Panipat, north of Delhi, by Babar, the leader of the group that would found the Mughal empire. Troops of his son, Humayun (reigned 1530-1540 and 1555-1556), conquered Bengal in 1538. However, Humayun faced a revolt from the Afghan Sher Shah Suri, whose troops took Bengal in 1539. Although Humayun regained the throne shortly before his death, the region of Bengal remained under the rule of the successors of Sher Shah until 1564. Bengal continued to remain separate from Delhi under a new Afghan dynasty founded by Sulaiman Karrani.

The Mughal emperor Akbar (1556-1605) brought Bengal under imperial control in 1576 when his troops defeated Daud Khan, the second and last sultan of Bengal in the Afghan dynasty. From then until 1971, when a portion of Bengal became independent, Bengal would be under the control of non-Bengal-based rulers.

Bengal became a province (*suba*) of the Mughal empire and was ruled by a governor (*naib nazim*; later the governor was termed *nawab*) appointed from Delhi. The power exercised by the governor was dependent on the strength of the Mughal court. After the death of the emperor Aurangzeb in 1707, the empire steadily declined in power; conversely, the relative independence of the governors in Dhaka (where the capital had moved in 1608) tended to increase. Furthermore, the governorship became hereditary. The capital was moved from Dhaka to Murshidabad (now in West Bengal) in 1704.

In the sixteenthth century, Europeans began to arrive in Bengal. The Portuguese made their first settlement in Chittagong in 1517 and added a station at Hooghly, on the river of the same name, in 1579. The Dutch arrived in 1602, followed by the British in 1650. The French and the Danes would follow. The British founded Calcutta in 1690.

So long as the governors were backed by some measure of Mughal strength, they were able to keep the Europeans in check and to regulate their activities reasonably well. In the early eighteenth century the system began to break down. A rebellion by Alivardi Khan, the deputy for Bihar to the governor, displaced the incumbent, and Alivardi became governor until his death in 1756. His grandson and successor, Sirajuddaulah, would see his brief rule bring the British into effective power.

The British Period

The British had become the dominant European power in India, in the south through their defeat of the French and in Bengal with the decline of the Portuguese and the evident relative weakness of the French, the Dutch and the Danes. The British expanded their station at Calcutta and built trading networks with the local merchants. Sirajuddaulah then attacked Calcutta on June 20, 1756, and took Fort William. According to British reports, the captured British were placed in a room (the "Black Hole") in the fort and 123 of the 146 prisoners died of suffocation. The British were determined to avenge the defeat and the deaths.

They were able to find persons in Sirajuddaulah's court, including a close relative, Mir Jafar, who would work with them. On June 23, 1757, at Plassey (Pilasi), a British force under the command of Robert Clive defeated Sirajuddaulah with the help of the treachery of Mir Jafar. Sirajuddaulah was executed on July 2, 1757; four days earlier the British recognized Mir Jafar as governor. In 1760 Mir Jafar was replaced by his son-in-law, Mir Qasim, but the latter was displaced in 1763 and Mir Jafar returned to office until his death in 1765.

In that same year, the British were granted the *diwani* (the right to collect and expend revenue) for Bengal, Bihar, and Orissa by the Mughal emperor. The Bengal government was not well organized until Warren Hastings was appointed governor in 1772. The following year, Hastings became the first governor-general of India, retaining the office of governor of Bengal and subordinating the other two major settlements, Bombay and Madras, to Calcutta. Calcutta would remain the capital of British India until 1911.

The dominance of Calcutta, however, tended to make the eastern portion of the province (the area that is now Bangladesh) a backwater. The Permanent Settlement initiated by Lord Cornwallis (governor-general, 1786-1793, and again briefly in 1805) also contributed to the slower development of eastern Bengal. Bengal under the Mughals and under the British had used a system of tax collectors (*zamindar*s) who collected land tax from the *ryot*s (tillers) and remitted an amount to the government after keeping a share for their services. Under the new system introduced by Cornwallis in 1793, the zamindar was recognized as owner of the land from which he had collected taxes. The ryots then, for all practical purposes, became his tenants. The system would not be fully abolished in East Bengal until after the independence of Pakistan. Most, but by no means all, of the zamindars in eastern Bengal were Hindus and most of the ryots Muslims. Gradually the zamindars became absentee landlords, and most migrated to Calcutta to participate in the development of that city, to the detriment of the rural areas of eastern Bengal.

Calcutta did indeed flourish. It became a center not only of government and commerce but also of the arts and literature and of reformist movements leading eventually to the demand for Indian independence. Dhaka, which had ceased to be the capital in 1704, languished and saw much of its industry, especially the manufacture of Dhaka muslin, decline. Calcutta became the seat of a university in 1857; Dhaka not until 1921. As we shall see, there was a brief revival when Dhaka became a capital again after the first partition of Bengal in 1905.

The British Indian army (actually that of the British East India Company) was composed of three separate armies: Bengal, Bombay, and Madras. The troops (*sepoys*) were Indian; the officers British. There were also units of the British army stationed in India, but these were separate from the British Indian army. The British Indian army had faced several outbreaks of mutiny in the early nineteenth century, but these were relatively small affairs and were put down quickly.

In 1857, however, the British faced a large-scale mutiny by the Bengal army (Madras and Bombay did not join the mutineers). It broke out in Meerut on May 10, 1857, although there had been unrest elsewhere before. Delhi fell to the sepoys and eventually was recaptured. By early 1858, the mutiny was over but two subsequent decisions would affect Bengal.

The British East India Company was formally wound up in 1858. It had been severely circumscribed by a series of acts passed by the British parliament beginning with the act that created the office of governor-general in 1773. In 1858, control of British India passed from the company to the Crown. Queen Victoria (she would be designated Empress of India in 1877), in her proclamation, stated that all of her subjects wouldbe treated equally before the law. Although this declaration was never fully implemented, it served as one step along the path of opening the system of governance to Indian participation. The governor-general would now also hold the title of viceroy.

A second outcome was the determination that India was populated by martial races and nonmartial races. The Bengalis were in the latter category, as the British believed that the Bengalis were a major element among the mutineers. This meant that recruitment for the military was barred for Bengalis (except for some specialized personnel) and that the recruiting grounds moved to the northwest, primarily to the Sikhs and the Punjabi Muslims. One of the grievances of the East Pakistanis against the central government of Pakistan after independence in 1947 would be the small share of Bengalis in the military as Pakistan continued the policy of the British with but small change.

Bengal itself would be in the forefront of administrative changes made by the British. It and some other provinces saw Indians appointed to the legislative councils of the lieutenant governors under the provisions of the India Councils Act of 1861 and more under the next edition of the act in 1894. The viceroyalty of Lord Ripon (1880-1884), a liberal associate of Gladstone, saw several changes (implemented first in Bengal), including the establishment of local boards at the subdivision level and district boards above them. Membership was elective, subject to rather strict franchise requirements. The bodies were permitted to raise and expend funds for such purposes as education and public works. Ripon also repealed the act that limited free expression in local-language newspapers and gave those newspapers equal status with those published in English. He attempted, but failed, to reform the judicial system so that Indian judges would have the same right to try Europeans as British judges did.

The Indian National Congress was founded in Bombay on December 28, 1885. The first president was a Bengali Hindu from Calcutta. For several reasons, Muslims did not associate with the Congress in large numbers. Part of this abstention came from the appeal of a leading Muslim educationist, Sir Syed Ahmad Khan, who sowed the seeds for the "Two Nation Theory" that would eventually be a source for the partition of India in 1947. Sir Syed and others who further developed the theory maintained that there was sufficient difference between the Hindus of India and the Muslims of India that they should be considered separate nations even though they inhabited the same territory. Sir Syed also feared that the departure of the British would result in a Hindu *raj* in which the Muslims would play a minor, if any, role and in which values held important by Muslims could be violated by a form of dictatorship of the majority. This theme, too, would be replayed as Indian independence approached.

The introduction of the elective principle by Ripon through his act on local government also concerned the Muslims. Even in areas where Muslims might be in a majority in the population, they could be outvoted as a result of the stringent franchise rules, which generally involved either property ownership or educational attainments. Perhaps in no place more than eastern Bengal would the Muslims find meeting franchise qualifications so difficult.

Muslims throughout India recognized this problem. It was brought to a head when it became apparent that the viceroy, Lord Minto (viceroy, 1905-1910), and the secretary of state for India in the British cabinet, Lord Morley, were determined that further constitutional advance for India should be enacted. The Muslims would take two steps, a meeting with Minto at Simla and the formation of the Muslim League.

Before these two events occurred, however, another event of great importance for eastern Bengal took place. The governor-general/viceroy had been relieved of the direct administration of Bengal in 1854, when the province was placed under separate administration (the title for the head of the provincial government throughout India was then lieutenant governor, later to be changed to governor by the Government of India Act of 1909). Lord Curzon (viceroy, 1899-1905) determined that the large province of Bengal, which included Bihar and Orissa, was too unwieldy to be managed effectively. He partitioned the province so that Bengal itself was divided. The eastern portion of the province (roughly Bangladesh today) was joined with Assam into the province of Eastern Bengal and Assam; the remaining area became the province of (western) Bengal, Bihar, and Orissa; each had a lieutenant governor.

Bengali Hindus objected to the change. In the first place, it created a Muslim majority province in the east (only one other, the Punjab in the northwest, existed at that time). With a view toward future elected governments at the provincial level, Hindus saw the danger of a Muslim raj much as Muslims saw the reverse on an all-India level. Second, those who spoke Bengali became a minority in the western province, being outnumbered by the total of the Hindi speakers of Bihar and the Oriya speakers of Orissa. Hindus reacted with measures that included violence and terrorism as well as less violent means such as a boycott of British goods. Noted Hindu Bengalis, including the poet Tagore and the future religious leader but then revolutionary, Aurobindo Ghose lent their voices and pens to the protest. The Muslims supported the partition, and Dhaka temporarily revived from its backwater status to become a provincial capital.

The British eventually heeded the Hindu opposition and, to the great disappointment of the Muslims, revoked the partition of Bengal in 1911. The announcement was made during the imperial visit to India of King George V and Queen Mary. However, the annulment of the partition was coupled with an imperial decree transferring the capital of India from Calcutta to New Delhi. Under the new arrangement of provinces, Assam reverted to a separate status, eastern and western Bengal became the province of Bengal, and the remainder became the province of Bihar and Orissa (these two were later separated under the Government of India Act of 1935).

During the partition period, as noted earlier, the Muslims were active politically. A delegation led by the Aga Khan met Lord Minto at Simla in 1906 and proposed a system of separate electorates under which seats would be apportioned in legislative bodies between Muslims and "others" in proportion to the two groups' shares in the population. In the election, Muslims and "others" would vote separately and only for representatives of their own community. (As the system developed later, other religious groups such as Sikhs and Indian Christians would also gain separate representation and electorates.) The Muslim demand, a natural culmination of the Two Nation Theory, was incorporated into the Government of India Act of 1909 (the "Morley-Minto Act"). Separate electorates would continue in East Pakistan through the election of 1954.

In December 1906 a group of leading Muslims met in Dhaka at the invitation of Nawab Salimullah of Dhaka and of the Aga Khan. There they founded the All-India Muslim League. The basic goals of the League were to support the Crown and to work for the interests of Muslims in India but not to act against the interests of any other community. The League would have an occasionally rocky path, but it would eventually lead the movement for the partition of India.

The act of 1909 established the elective principle for a portion of the provincial and national legislatures but retained most of the power in the hands of the governors and the officials. Indians began to enter the latter group as members of the Indian Civil Service; Bengali Hindus were well represented but the Muslims of the province were not. In education they continued to lag behind the Hindus.

In 1917, Secretary of State for India Edwin Montagu declared that the ultimate goal of British rule in India was self-governance. After the war, this led to the act of 1919 (also called the Montagu-Chelmsford Act after the secretary of state and the viceroy). It expanded the Indian membership of the legislatures and set up a system of "dyarchy" at the provincial level. Under this system, the departments (ministries) that were related to development, such as education, health, agriculture, and public works, were placed under ministers who were responsible individually to the legislature. Departments that served the "steel-frame" method of rule (home, finance, and revenue) were headed by executive councilors who were appointed by and responsible to the governor. Several Bengali Muslims gained important experience during the period of dyarchy by serving as ministers. These included Fazlul Haq and Khwaja Nazimuddin.

The Muslim League in Bengal became more and more dominated by a group that would later be called the "national elite." This group was concerned primarily with the problems of

Muslims on the broad canvas of India as a whole. Many of the group were descendants of Delhi sultanate and Mughal empire officials and used Urdu as a family language. Nazimuddin (a member of the family of the Nawab of Dhaka) and the younger Husain Shahid Suhrawardy were among these, although the latter would later change his course. On the other hand, there were those of the "vernacular elite," individuals whose primary concern was the improvement of the status of the largely impoverished Muslims of Bengal, notably in the eastern region. They worked in Bengali rather than Urdu. Chief among these was Fazlul Haq, who prior to the 1937 election would form the Krishak Praja Party (KPP, "Farmers', People's Party") to oppose the Muslim League in the Muslim seats and to try, with little success, to enlist peasants from the Hindu community as well. Fazlul Haq's platform was based on economic and social issues; the League's on communal matters.

The Government of India Act of 1935 confirmed the separate electorates despite strong opposition from the Indian National Congress led by Mahatma Gandhi. It also provided for fully responsible ministries in the provinces, although emergency powers were retained by the governors. Following the election of 1937, a coalition government was formed in Bengal under the prime ministership (this term was used until the independence of Pakistan and India, after which the title became chief minister) of Fazlul Haq but with support of the Muslim League and its leader, Nazimuddin.

Fazlul Haq and his fellow Muslim prime ministers from the Punjab and Assam, who were also not from the Muslim League, pledged their support to the Muslim League and Muhammad Ali Jinnah on national issues with the understanding that provincial matters were to remain in their hands. This pledge, at Lucknow in 1937, was a boost to Jinnah, as the Muslim League had fared poorly in the 1937 election, especially in the Muslim-majority provinces. Fazlul Haq was also the author of one of several reports that condemned the behavior of Congress governments toward Muslims in the Muslim-minority provinces.

On March 23, 1940, in Lahore, the Muslim League passed a resolution often called the "Pakistan resolution" although the word Pakistan does not appear in it. The resolution stated that if conditions for Muslims in India, especially in the Muslim minority provinces, did not improve, the Muslims would have no choice but to demand that separate states (plural, *sic*) be established as homelands for the Muslims of India. Fazlul Haq, who was a member of the Muslim League as well as leader of the KPP, was among the movers of the resolution. The acronym PAKISTAN, it should be noted, does not contain a letter for Bengal; all of the letters are derived from the northwest of India, present-day Pakistan. Fazlul Haq broke with Jinnah in 1941 over the former's membership in the viceroy's war advisory council. Haq resigned from the council but also from the League. The

League withdrew its support from Haq's ministry, but he was able to continue until 1943 with Hindu assistance. In 1943, Nazimuddin set up a Muslim League ministry, which fell in early 1945 and was followed by a short period of governor's rule.

In the 1945-1946 election, Bengali Muslims voted overwhelmingly for the Muslim League, although Fazlul Haq was able to retain his own seat. Among Muslims, the League received 82 percent of the votes, the highest of any of the Muslim-majority provinces. Nazimuddin was not selected again as prime minister; the position went to Suhrawardy. At his initiative, a meeting of Muslim legislators in New Delhi in 1945 decided that a single state of Pakistan should be formed rather than the two states contemplated in the Lahore resolution.

Suhrawardy waffled later and worked with some Hindus for the creation of a separate "united" Bengal as a third dominion on the subcontinent. He was prime minister during the Great Calcutta Killing in August 1946 but later worked with Gandhi to pacify the city as partition and independence approached. With almost undue haste the new viceroy, Lord Mountbatten, worked toward the end of British rule. This came on August 15, 1947—and the problems of Bengal would continue.

The Pakistan Period

The first independence day of the people of Bangladesh found them as residents of a province, East Bengal, of the Dominion of Pakistan. Jinnah and the central leaders, angered at Suhrawardy's brief espousal of a united Bengal, managed his ouster from the prime ministership and replaced him with Nazimuddin, who became chief minister.

The boundaries of the new province were settled in two ways. The Assamese district of Sylhet contained a majority of Muslims. A plebiscite at the level of subdivision was held there, and most of the district voted to join Pakistan. For the division of Bengal itself, a commission headed by a British judge was appointed to determine the contiguous areas of Muslim majority. Some latitude was allowed and the final boundary did not follow precisely the contiguous area formula, but a boundary was established that was workable, with one major exception: the land boundary between the West Bengal district of Cooch Behar and the adjoining areas of Bangladesh remains in dispute.

It took little time for the disputes with West Pakistan that would lead to the dissolution of united Pakistan to appear. Before the political history is resumed, it is best to look at these grievances.

The government in Karachi seemed to Bengalis to be dominated by persons whose political activity had been either in the areas that remained in India (including Jinnah and the prime minister, Liaquat Ali Khan) or in the provinces included in West

Pakistan. Originally only one Bengali, a Scheduled Caste Hindu, was included in the nine-member cabinet, although he was shortly joined by Khwaja Shahabuddin, a younger brother of Nazimuddin. His selection was clearly not from among the vernacular elite. In that group, Fazlul Haq was relegated to the post of advocate general, and Suhrawardy, who would soon join the group, remained in India, temporarily avoiding the wrath of Jinnah. With Jinnah's death in September 1948, Nazimuddin was appointed governor-general but clearly with much less influence than Jinnah. Later another person with remote connections with Bengal, Iskandar Mirza, would become in 1955 the last governor-general and in 1956 the first president of Pakistan. His connection, however, was with the family of Sirajuddaulah and Mir Jafar—the latter, of course, not held in high esteem.

It was not only in the political positions in government that the Bengalis had grievances. There were very few Muslim Bengalis in the higher civil service under the British. Consequently, few were taken into the central administration and many posts in the East Bengal provincial administration were filled by Muslims from India or West Pakistan or by reemployed British officers. Pakistan would make arrangements through preferences and quotas to attempt to redress the imbalance, but these had not resulted in equality by 1971.

This imbalance was even greater in the military. As already noted, the British had practiced the doctrine of the martial races, which all but excluded Bengalis from military service. The practice, however, was continued by the independent Pakistan government: recruits still were very largely drawn from the Punjab and some districts of the Northwest Frontier Province (NWFP). An answer often given by West Pakistanis to the problem was that there was indeed no martial tradition in Bengal and there were few applicants for military positions. At the time of Bangladeshi independence there were but two Bengalis of general officer rank in the army.

Economic development in the newly independent Pakistan was also uneven. The lack of natural resources in East Bengal made the region a less attractive place for investment than the Punjab and the Karachi area of the west wing. Furthermore, the foreign exchange earnings gained from the export of east-wing jute was often invested in the west wing. Moreover, such investment as occurred in the east wing was usually from industrialists based in West Pakistan, and this often resulted in an outflow of funds as profits moved to the west wing. For example, the largest jute mill in the world, located in Narayanganj near Dhaka, was owned by a Karachi-based firm, the Adamjees. When a study was done in the 1960s, of the major industrial and financial groups in Pakistan, only one of these was owned by a native Bengali family, the A. K. Khan group of Chittagong, with investments mainly in textiles and jute. Those in the east wing of Pakistan felt that their agreement to parity in government and in the legislature (see below) would be accompanied by parity in economic development. It must be said that the central government did make efforts to expand the economy of the east wing. However, while the East Pakistani economy grew, it grew at a lower rate than that of West Pakistan, and the gap increased rather than narrowed.

The issues that have been mentioned were important, but the one that aroused the highest emotional response was that of language. Jinnah and the other key persons in the government had determined that Urdu would be the national language of Pakistan. This decision was taken in spite of Bengali being the language spoken by the majority of the people of Pakistan. Urdu is, furthermore, a language that is not native to Pakistan, its literary home being in Uttar Pradesh and Delhi in India. In addition, many of the contributors to the rich literary heritage of Urdu have been Hindus and Sikhs.

Jinnah, in March 1948, on his only visit to East Bengal after independence, declared that anyone opposing Urdu as the national language was an "enemy" of Pakistan. His views were supported by the chief minister, Nazimuddin, but were widely rejected by the Bengalis. The eventual downfall of the Muslim League can, in large measure, be attributed to the position of Nazimuddin and his ministry. The agitation continued and culminated in the demonstrations held in Dhaka in February 1952. On February 21, several students were killed by the police. The day is still remembered as Martyrs' Day in Bangladesh. Eventually, in September 1954, the constituent assembly of Pakistan decided that "Urdu and Bengali and such other languages as may be declared" shall be the "official languages of the Republic." They added that English would also be used as long as necessary.

Although the language issue was decided in a manner acceptable to the Bengalis, it and the other grievances left a record that would fester and grow into the autonomy and then independence movements that would destroy the unity of Pakistan.

Pakistan took an inordinately long time in framing its constitution, being governed in the meantime by the Government of India Act of 1935 as amended by the India Independence Act of 1947. These were acts that continued and preserved a viceregal form of government, one in which the governor-general would have ultimate power, as the viceroy had before 1947. That is, this would be the system unless the governor-general were a Bengali. During Nazimuddin's tenure (1948-1951), the locus of power moved to the prime minister, Liaquat Ali Khan. When Liaquat was assassinated in 1951, Nazimuddin stepped down from the governor-generalship to become prime minister himself. The new governor-general, Ghulam Muhammad, a civil servant before independence, dismissed Nazimuddin in 1953 without permitting the prime minister to test his support in the constituent assembly.

Other Bengalis (Muhammad Ali Bogra, 1953-1955, and Suhrawardy, (1956-1957) would be prime ministers but their power was subject to the whim of the governor-general.

A constitution for Pakistan was finally passed and became effective on March 23, 1956. However, it required the Bengalis to sacrifice their numerical majority in the population and agree to parity in the national parliament. There would be 300 members, 150 from each wing of Pakistan. The votes of Bengalis therefore counted for less than the votes of West Pakistanis. In an act passed prior to the constitution, West Pakistan (a term we have been using) was formally created by the merger of the provinces in the west wing. (The name of the east wing was changed from East Bengal to East Pakistan at the same time.) The creation of two provinces with equality in the parliament was the outcome of these actions. Bengal, led by Suhrawardy, was willing at the time to pay that price if similar parity could be achieved in other areas, including economic development and government employment. They were to be posappointed.

Before the constitution was passed, an election had been held in aast Bengal. The position on the language issue was one factor in the growing discontent with the Muslim League. In 1949, Suhrawardy, returning from India, launched a new political party, which would become the Awami League. It was to be a noncommunal party open to all residents of Pakistan. Meanwhile, Fazlul Haq had revived his earlier party under a slightly different name, the Krishak Sramik Party (KSP, peasants' and workers' party, but non-Marxist, unlike some other parties that have used a similar name). These two parties represented the vernacular elite. They decided to contest the 1954 election to the East Bengal legislative assembly as a United Front. The Muslim League was trounced; even Chief Minister Nurul Amin lost his seat.

The twenty-one-point platform of the United Front was directed largely at provincial issues. A key matter was the recognition of Bengali as a national language of Pakistan. Foreshadowing the later Six-Point Program of Mujibur Rahman was a demand for provincial autonomy except in matters of foreign affairs, defense, and currency. There were also points regarding free trade with and travel to India, a newly and directly elected constituent assembly, and freedom of trade in jute.

Suhrawardy directed his attention to national affairs. He departed for Karachi and joined the cabinet of Muhammad Ali Bogra, who was then prime minister, also from East Bengal, but a Muslim Leaguer. Suhrawardy became prime minister in 1956. He had key lieutenants in Dhaka, notably Ataur Rahman Khan, who eventually became chief minister, and Sheikh Mujibur Rahman, the key party organizer. He also associated with Maulana Abdul Hamid Khan Bhashani, a leftist religious leader with whom he would split in 1957. Fazlul Haq and his KSP tended to look more toward the provincial arena. He became chief minister briefly in 1954, but the central government intervened and there was a period of governor's rule. Fazlul Haq had made some remarks during a visit to Calcutta that were interpreted by Karachi as being treasonous in the sense that Fazlul Haq had referred generally to the unity of Bengalis.

By the time parliamentary government was restored in East Pakistan in 1956, the United Front had split, and the KSP held a slight edge in the provincial assembly. KSP leader Abu Husain Sarkar became chief minister. Fazlul Haq was named governor. The next two years saw the provincial assembly serve as a battleground between the Awami League and the KSP for control of the East Pakistan government. In 1956 Ataur Rahman Khan became chief minister over the opposition of Governor Fazlul Haq but with the support of the central government, now headed by Prime Minister Suhrawardy. By 1958, the tussle became more complicated with a split in the Awami League (see below) and changes in both the governorship and the prime ministership. As Pakistan moved toward military intervention, both Sarkar and Abdur Rahman Khan held the chief ministership in 1958. Turmoil on the streets moved into the assembly house itself to the extent that the deputy speaker died from wounds received on the floor of the assembly.

Meanwhile, as noted earlier, the language issue had been settled, West Pakistan had been unified, and a constitution had become effective on March 23, 1956. It was expected that elections would be held in 1958. Here again, the differences between East and West Pakistan were evident. West Pakistan favored the continuance of separate electorates (which Pakistan under Zia ul-Haq reinstated) on the grounds that these would reinforce the Two Nation Theory. East Pakistan—and here the Awami League and the KSP agreed—favored joint electorates in which there would be no distinction among communities. Their reasoning was fairly straightforward: Muslim votes might be split, but Hindus (then about 20 percent of East Pakistan) would surely not vote for the Muslim League, a party they were not even permitted to join, and would therefore be likely to support one of the members of the United Front, ensuring victory for the Front. It was decided in Karachi that each province could frame its own election law. It mattered little, for the elections were not held.

It has been mentioned earlier that Suhrawardy and Bhashani split. Bhashani disagreed with what he believed was a pro-West and pro-market economy stance by Suhrawardy. Bhashani withdrew from the Awami League in 1957 to form the National Awami Party with his followers and with some groups from West Pakistan. Several members of the provincial assembly followed him, and these would hold the balance in the body (as they did also in West Pakistan). The jockeying between Sarkar and Abdur Rahman Khan was complicated by the presence of this small but critical group.

On October 7, 1958, President Mirza dismissed the parliament and the two provincial assemblies and the cabinets of Firoz Khan Noon at the center and those in the provinces and proclaimed martial law. Named as chief martial law administrator was General Muhammad Ayub Khan, the army commander in chief. On October 28, Ayub dismissed Mirza and assumed the presidency himself.

Although the ending of the parliamentary era was initially welcomed as a relief from the tumultuous politics preceding martial law, it soon became a burden for East Pakistan. Many key oppositionists, including Suhrawardy, Mujib, and Fazlul Haq, were deprived of their political rights or were jailed. Suhrawardy died in 1963, and the leadership of the Awami League in East Pakistan was taken by Mujibur Rahman. Ataur Rahman Khan eventually left the Awami League to form a splinter party. Fazlul Haq died in 1962, and his party has not since been a factor in East Pakistan or Bangladesh. Nazimuddin returned to politics to lead the Council Muslim League (CML) and the Combined Opposition Parties (COP) group, but he died in 1964. The COP opposed Ayub's reelection in 1965, nominating Jinnah's sister, Fatima, but Ayub won handily in West Pakistan and by a small majority in East Pakistan.

Ayub's newly proclaimed constitution of 1962 changed the electoral system. His form of local government, basic democracy, was based on earlier systems in that locally and directly elected members of the councils were given local administrative and development duties. The new element was that the union councilors would also serve as members of an electoral college for election of the president and the members of the national and provincial assemblies. There were 80,000 councilors, 40,000 in each province. It was clearly easier to control such a small number rather than the entire electorate. The electoral college function came under constant attack from the opposition, which favored a system of direct elections by the entire electorate at all levels of government.

Ayub also envisaged a system that would be nonparty. The first elections in 1962 to the national and provincial assemblies were held on this basis. But no sooner had the assemblies convened than parties were formed in them. Ayub, yielding to the inevitable, then convened a session of a party that would support him. This party became the Pakistan Muslim League (Convention). Other Muslim Leaguers formed an opposition group, the Council Muslim League (CML). Still other parties began to function again, including, in East Pakistan, the Awami League led by Mujib, and the National Awami Party led by Bhashani.

After his reelection in 1965, Ayub's stock began to fall, for a number of reasons. Bengalis objected to the war with India in 1965 over Kashmir as, in their view, it left East Pakistan defenseless. The economy also turned downward and Ayub's health deteriorated. The upshot was a strong opposition move against him spearheaded by the newly formed People's Party of Pakistan (PPP) headed by Zulfiqar Ali Bhutto in West Pakistan and the Awami League in East Pakistan.

In early 1966, Mujib had proclaimed a platform of Six Points. These were: (1) a federal government, parliamentary in form, with free and regular elections; (2) federal government control over only foreign affairs and defense; (3) a separate currency or separate accounts for each wing to prevent the movement of capital from the east to the west; (4) taxation only at the provincial level, with grants from the provinces to support the federal government; (5) the right of each province to enter into international trade agreements on its own initiative; and (6) each province could raise a militia. The key provision was not the last but the fourth: without a source of revenue under its own control, the federal government would be subject to the whim of either provincial government.

In the face of increasing demonstrations, Ayub resigned on March 25, 1969, and turned the government over to the commander in chief of the army, General Agha Muhammad Yahya Khan, who proclaimed martial law. Yahya promised to hold elections and did so in December 1970. The election rules for the national assembly scrapped both the system of separate electorates and the system of parity: of the 300 directly elected seats, East Pakistan would have 162 and West Pakistan 138. The result displayed the polarity between the two wings. In East Pakistan, the Awami League won 160 of the 162; in West Pakistan, the PPP won 81 of 138. Neither party won seats in the other wing.

Yahya opened talks with both Bhutto and Mujib with a view toward forming a government agreeable to each and toward cooperation in the framing of a new constitution. With mounting pressure from his supporters, Mujib was forced to stand firmly on the Six Points as a basis for the constitution. This was adamantly opposed by both Yahya and Bhutto. Violent demonstrations began in East Pakistan. At the same time, Yahya increased greatly the number of troops (almost all of West Pakistani origin) in the east wing. No agreement was possible. Yahya ordered the troops into action against the Bengalis on March 25, 1971. Mujib was arrested and taken to West Pakistan, many Bengalis were killed in the initial assaults, and other Bengalis fled to regroup in India to become the government-in-exile and the Mukti Bahini (the national army). The Mukti Bahini fought a tenacious guerrilla war against the larger and far better equipped Pakistani army and by summer appeared to be getting the better of the struggle. India provided a haven and supplies and entered the war directly in late November. On December 16, Dhaka fell to the forces of the Mukti Bahini and the Indians and Bangladesh became independent.

Independent Bangladesh

Bhutto, to whom power in Pakistan had been transferred by Yahya, freed Mujib, who returned to a war-weary and badly damaged, but independent, Bangladesh on January 10, 1972. He became prime minister in an Awami League government. A constitution based on a parliamentary system became effective on December 16, 1972. It also enshrined the four principles of *Mujibbad* (Mujibism): nationalism, secularism, democracy, and socialism.

Mujib's associates in the cabinet had little experience in governing; they had been oppositionists during the thirteen years of Ayub and Yahya. The transposition was not an easy task. Furthermore, the Bengali members of the Civil Service of Pakistan were often viewed almost as enemies during that period. Some had quickly joined the exile government, many had remained at their posts in Dhaka, and some were posted in West Pakistan and were interned. The military saw a similar division, although very few stayed at Pakistani posts in East Pakistan. Yet the work of government required personnel. Many were brought into the administration who had not taken or passed the entrance examinations; many of these were failures. When repatriation of those detained in Pakistan took place in 1973, there was hesitation on the part of the Mujib government about reinstating them in the civil or military services. Bangladesh therefore suffered from poor administration as well as the vast problems of reconstruction and the food shortages which, peaked in 1974.

Opposition to Mujib began to increase as the problems mounted. Rapid nationalization of much industry caused severe setbacks in production. Corruption became a common occurrence. Although the Awami League won widely in the parliamentary election held in 1973 (292 of 300 directly elected seats), this did not confer legitimacy on what was seen by many as a failing and inefficient government.

To meet the criticism, Mujib drew back from one of his pillars, democracy. On January 25, 1975, the constitution was amended to create a presidential system with Mujib as president and almost all power in his hands. On June 6, 1975, Bangladesh became a one-party state with the Mujib-led Bangladesh Krishak Sramik Awami League (BAKSAL) as the sole legal political grouping. The name was intended to combine the heritage of Fazlul Haq's Krishak Sramik Party and Suhrawardy's Awami League.

On August 15, 1975, a group of army officers, mostly majors, assassinated Mujib and much of his family (a daughter, Sheikh Hasina Wajid, was abroad and escaped to lead the Awami League later; see below). The majors chose a member of Mujib's cabinet, Khondakar Mushtaque Ahmad, to be president. Mushtaque promised new elections, abolished BAKSAL, and said he would work to restore democracy and faith in the government. However, he remained very much the tool of the majors.

The three days of November 3-5, 1975, were ones of utter confusion in Dhaka. A rebellion took place under the leadership of Brigadier Khalid Musharaf who pledged to restore Mujibism. This uprising was put down by the main units of the army, many of which supported Major General Ziaur Rahman (Zia). Mushtaque resigned, was asked to return, but refused. Chief Justice A.S.M. Sayem became president and chief martial law administrator (CMLA). The key and rising person was Zia.

Zia became CMLA on November 30, 1976, and Sayem remained president. Sayem resigned the presidency on grounds of ill health and Zia became president on April 21, 1977. On May 30, he held a referendum on his continuance in office, and although he gained overwhelming approval, it did not gain legitimacy for him in that no alternative was presented. Having announced a new program (see below), he held a contested election on June 3, 1978. The major contenders were two who had played key roles in the civil war: Zia had commanded a unit of the Mukti Bahini and had, in fact, declared the independence of Bangladesh on March 28, 1971; his opponent, General M. A. G. Osmany, a retired Pakistani officer (as a colonel) had been the commander of the Mukti Bahini and later minister of defense. Zia was backed by the newly formed Jatiyatabadi Ganotantrik Dal (JAGODAL, the National Democratic Party); Osmany by a coalition among which the Awami League was most prominent. Zia's party was formally led by Justice Abdus Sattar, who was appointed vice president on the day of the election. Zia won with 76.7 percent of the vote to Osmany's 21.7 percent, the balance going to minor candidates.

Zia, looked upon as almost a fish out of water when he first gained power, developed into a charismatic leader. He traveled extensively, preaching his program of self-reliance to get Bangladesh moving in development. The key aspects of his Nineteen-Point Program were increased food production and family planning, goals which were important for President Hussain Muhammad Ershad as well. Zia began to open up the political system and to curtail the socialist program of the Mujib period. A parliamentary election was held in February 1979. Zia's party, expanded and renamed as the Bangladesh Jatiyatibadi Party (Bangladesh Nationalist Party—BNP) won 207 of the 300 seats in a poll generally judged as fair. The larger faction of a then divided Awami League won 39 seats and the revived Muslim League 20. Mashiur Rahman, who had been expected to become prime minister, died suddenly, and the post was given to Shah Azizur Rahman.

There were other accomplishments and some failures of the Zia regime. Among the former was his championing of the concept of cooperation among the countries of South Asia. He visited the other countries in the region, and eventually, after his death, seven countries (the others being India, Pakistan, Sri Lanka, Nepal, Bhutan, and the Maldives) agreed in New Delhi in August 1983 to form what is today called the South Asian Association for Regional Cooperation (SAARC). A summit meeting in Dhaka in December 1985 ratified the formation of SAARC. Annual summits have been held in the other capitals, and a permanent secretariat has been established in Kathmandu, Nepal.

On the other hand, Zia failed to establish his system firmly. It was dependent on him. When he was assassinated on May 30, 1981, he was succeeded by the vice president, Abdus Sattar, temporarily. The constitution required a new election. Infighting in the BNP did not permit the choice of a younger candidate. Sattar ran in the November 15, 1981, election and won, defeating his principal opponent, Kamal Hossain of the Awami League, by a margin of 65.5 percent to 26.0 percent.

Sattar's term turned out to be only an interlude. He was challenged by the army chief of staff, Hussain Muhammad Ershad, who took deserved credit for quelling the insurrection in which Zia was assassinated. Ershad called for the cleaning up of the corruption that undoubtedly existed but, more importantly, demanded a regularized role for the military in the governance of the country. He asked specifically for a national security council, which would be dominated by the military. Sattar did reshuffle his cabinet but refused to accept the council. Ershad overthrew Sattar on March 24, 1982.

Ershad's martial law period was not as successful as Zia's in returning the country to some type of representative government. He did not assume the presidency until December 11, 1983. He also used the referendum pattern to gain support for himself and his program. He won what was reported to be a huge majority in the March 1985 poll, but most observers felt that the voting was rigged. His opposition clustered in three groups. The largest was a coalition led by the Awami League headed by Sheikh Hasina Wajid (a daughter of Sheikh Mujibur Rahman). Another group coalesced around the BNP led by Khaleda Zia, the widow of Ziaur Rahman. Much less important was a cluster around former president Mushtaque Ahmad, and there were leftist and Islamic fundamentalist groupings as well. Ershad made a number of concessions and finally was able to convince the Awami League-led coalition to contest elections in which it and Ershad's party, the Jatiyo Dal, were the major contenders. The May 1986 election resulted in a slim majority of the 300 seats for the Jatiyo Dal, with about 100 seats going to the Awami League and its allies. There were many reports of rigging and some switching of parties by winners so that the final party totals remained in some doubt. The BNP-led group boycotted the election.

Parliament first met briefly to hustle through a bill that would grant immunity to Ershad and his government for any acts taken during martial law. Hasina and her group boycotted that session.

In the fall of 1986, however, she officially became leader of the opposition and began to participate, but the parting of ways between Ershad and Sheikh Hasina was soon to come.

Ershad had revamped the local government system, elevating the former subdivisions to the status of districts in a move intended to gain greater popular participation in development and, not incidentally, support for him and his Jatiya Party, as the Jatiya Dal had been renamed. His proposal to include military personnel in the councils was scuttled in the summer of 1987 by wide-scale demonstrations.

The success of these demonstrations apparently whetted the appetite of the opposition, for major demonstrations began in November 1987. Hasina had withdrawn her party from parliament. On December 6, 1987, Ershad dissolved parliament, having declared a state of emergency about two weeks earlier. New elections were held on March 3, 1988, but both the BNP and the Awami League boycotted them along with the smaller opposition groups. The Jatiya Party of Ershad won about 250 of the 300 seats, and Ershad appointed Moudud Ahmed as prime minister and Kazi Zafar Ahmad as his deputy. An amendment to the constitution was passed declaring that Islam was the state religion of Bangladesh but adding that other religions were free to practice their beliefs. Ershad went no further than this in creating an Islamic state.

Complaints by the opposition continued but reached their peak in the fall of 1990. Some changes were made in the Jatiya Party command structure: Moudud Ahmed was advanced to vice president and Kazi Zafar Ahmad was made prime minister. Ershad decreed that the vice president, previously appointed, would hereafter be elected jointly with the president. In March 1990, elections were held at the *upazilla* (sub-district) level and the Jatiya Party secured control of a bare majority; it was not a good sign for future elections.

By October and November, 1990, demonstrations against Ershad were so widespread that Ershad resigned the presidency on December 4 (to be effective December 8) and appointed Chief Justice Shahabuddin Ahmed as vice president so that he would become acting president when Ershad's resignation became effective. A factor in Ershad's fall was that the army seemed unwilling to support him. Shahabuddin Ahmed had, in effect, one task: to hold "free and fair" elections under a neutral caretaker government led by him. This he did in March 1991. Including the women's seats, the BNP achieved a small majority. Khaleda Zia became prime minister, but in a presidential system.

Ershad, who never approached the charismatic role of either Mujib or Zia, nonetheless accomplished a number of things in his presidency. Food production increased markedly and the effectiveness of family planning improved substantially, as did health delivery. He greatly extended the program of privatization and worked to open the economy of Bangladesh. Unfortunately for him, his aversion to democracy and the corruption of his government (allegedly touching him) were heavy factors on the negative side.

The Awami League had campaigned calling for the restoration of the parliamentary system; the BNP preferred a presidential system. However, after looking carefully at the election results, the BNP saw clearly that winning a presidential election on the basis of a popular vote was anything but a sure thing. The BNP switched its view and supported a constitutional amendment changing to a parliamentary system with a ceremonial president. With the amendment passed, Khaleda became "head of government," and Abdur Rahman Biswas was elected by the parliament (not the people at large) as president and "head of state."

The path for Khaleda and the BNP has not been easy. On May 5, 1994, the opposition began a boycott of parliament as it demanded a constitutional amendment that would require the resignation of the government and the appointment of a neutral caretaker government to conduct the elections. The boycott was followed by the mass resignation from parliament of the opposition on December 28, 1994. As a result of legal maneuvers, the resignations did not become effective until June 20, 1995.

As the opposition said it would not contest by-elections for the vacant seats, Khaleda was forced to ask for the dissolution of parliament on November 24, 1995. A new general election was held on February 15, 1996. As the opposition again refused to contest, the election was a farce in which the BNP won almost all seats. However, the new parliament passed a constitutional amendment that provided for a neutral government to conduct elections in the future. That done, the parliament was dissolved once again and a new election under a neutral government was held on June 12, 1996. The Awami League and others had stated that they did not trust the outgoing government to conduct the elections, as is the rule in most parliamentary systems. Despite this, the BNP government performed quite well in the economic sphere.

In the June 12 election, the Awami League fell just short of a majority of the seats, but will form a government with the support of the Jatiya Party.

The future of democracy and of a market economy is anything but certain in Bangladesh. Perhaps a second "free and fair" election will go a considerable distance to clinch the issue.

THE DICTIONARY

-A-

ABBASUDDIN AHMED (1901-1959). A disciple of Kazi Nazrul Islam (q.v.), he spent about twenty years with him. He was a master of at least two varieties of folk songs: *bhawiya* and *palligeeti*. He influenced the resurgence of Bengali Muslims and with poet Jasimuddin (q.v.), was instrumental in popularizing folksongs. Abbasuddin is credited with having popularized Islamic songs. He is also known for using a two-string musical instrument (*duo tara*). He received Pakistan's Pride of Performance award. Abassuddin's autobiography is entitled *Amer Shilpa Jeban*.

ABDUL GHANI MIAN, NAWAB SIR KHWAJA (d. 1896). A member of the Nawab of Dhaka family, he served as a member of the Bengal Legislative Council in 1866 and as a member of the Legislative Council of the Governor General. He is best remembered for donating the first waterworks in Dhaka. Abdul Ghani was succeeded as nawab by his son Nawab Khwaja Ahsanullah Khan (q.v.).

ABDUL HAI, MIRZA (1919-1984). A civil servant who was also a noted short-story writer and novelist. He contributed to a wide range of magazines.

ABDUL HAMID (1886-1963). Born in Sylhet District (then in Assam), he was a member of the Assam Legislative Council, 1924-1937, and served in various ministerial positions, 1929-1937. He was deputy leader of the Muslim League in the Assam Legislative Assembly from 1937 to partition and strongly supported the Pakistani position in the plebiscite (see Sylhet Referendum) that resulted in the transfer of most of Sylhet District to East Bengal. Abdul Hamid was minister of education in the Muslim League East Bengal government until its fall in the 1954 provincial election.

ABDUL KARIM, MAULVI (1863-1943). A prominent educationist and Muslim League politician, he entered politics after serving in the presidency education department. Abdul Hamid was president of the Bengal Muslim League and a member of the Council of State and the Bengal Legislative Council, 1926-1937.

ABDUL LATIF, NAWAB (1828-1893). A leading Muslim intellectual figure in Calcutta in the nineteenth century, a period when Muslims lagged well behind Hindus in education. He was an educationist, author and later prime minister of the princely state of Bhopal in Central India (1885-1886). Abdul Latif was born in Faridpur District and studied in Calcutta. He taught for some time and then was appointed a deputy magistrate in 1849. He served in a number of positions, including presidency magistrate, before retiring in 1887. Abdul Latif was a member of the Bengal Legislative Council, 1862-1864 and 1870-1874. He was the founder of the Mohammadan Literary and Scientific Society in 1863, the goal of which was the education of Muslims and the dissemination of Western knowledge. Abdul Latif worked with Sir Syed Ahmed Khan in the founding of the Muslim Anglo-Oriental College (now Aligarh Muslim University) and agreed with Sir Syed that Muslims would fare best under British rule in the face of the large Hindu majority in India. He was also a founder of the Central Mohammedan Association (see Amir Ali, Syed).

ABDUR RAHIM, SIR (1867-1947). A prominent Bengali Muslim political and legal figure. He was born in Midnapur where his father was posted as deputy collector. He attended Presidency College and later was called to the bar from the Middle Temple in 1890. Abdul Rahim specialized in Muslim law, and his *Principles of Muhammadan Jurisprudence* (first published in 1911) is considered a classic on the subject. He practiced law and became involved in politics, being one of the founding members of the Muslim League (q.v.) in 1906. Abdur Rahim was also a member of the delegation of Muslim leaders that met with the viceroy, Lord Minto, at Simla earlier in the same year; the delegation proposed the creation of separate electorates (q.v.) for Muslims. In 1908, he was appointed a justice of the Madras High Court, where he served until 1920; during his service there he was twice officiating chief justice. Also during that period, Abdur Rahim was a member of the Royal Commission on Public Service (1912-1915) and achieved recognition for a strong dissenting minute in which he strongly urged the rapid appointment of Indians to the highest levels of the civil service. He was a member of the executive council of the governor of Bengal, 1921-1925, holding the portfolio of justice, and then a member of the legislative council from 1926 to 1930. In 1931, Abdur Rahim was elected as an independent to the Central Legislative Assembly and presided over that body, 1935-1945. He also was a member of the Muslim portion of the Indian delegation to the Round Table Conferences in the early 1930s. He is reported to have been opposed to partition of Bengal, but moved to East Bengal after partition and died soon thereafter. Abdur Rahim's daughter was the first wife of Husain Shahid Suhrawardy (q.v.), who supported the creation of a separate dominion for Bengal and Assam.

ABDUR RASHID, KAZI (d. 1944). A pioneer in Muslim publishing in Bengal, he founded Bengal Moslem Provincial Library and associated publishing firms. He was born in Dhaka district and represented that district in the Bengal Legislative Council, 1937-1944.

ABDUR RASUL, MAULVI (1872-1917). He was born in Tipperah (now Comilla) district and educated at Oxford before being called to the bar from the Middle Temple in 1898. He began a lucrative practice at the Calcutta High Court, but also engaged in politics in the *swadeshi* (q.v.) and antipartition movements. Abdul Rasul became a member of the Muslim League (q.v.) and was part of the group (working under Muhammad Ali Jinnah [q.v.]) that drafted the Congress League accord at Lucknow in 1916 in which the Congress accepted the Muslim League demand for separate electorates (q.v.)

ABU TAHER, COLONEL (1938-1976). Awarded *Bir Uttam* for bravery during the war of liberation, he was executed during the regime of President Ziaur Rahman (q.v.) for his radical leftist beliefs and alleged treason. He joined Jatiya Samajtantrik Dal (q.v.) in 1974 and introduced to the party the concept of a people's army. Abu Taher was a major power broker during the coup and countercoup of August-November 1975 but later lost out to Ziaur Rahman. He joined the Pakistan army in 1960 and served in the Special Services group. He was decorated for his bravery during the Indo-Pakistan war of 1965. After the Pakistan army crackdown on the civilian population in East Pakistan, Abu Taher escaped from West Pakistan to join the war of liberation. He was the first adjutant general of the Bangladesh army.

ABUL FAZAL (1903-1983). Advisor (i.e., minister) of education in the Ziaur Rahman (q.v.) regime, December 1975 to June 1977. Earlier he had taught at a number of institutions and became vice chancellor of Chittagong University in 1973. Abul Fazal was a founder of the Muslim Literary Society in 1923.

ABUL HASHIM (1905-1974). A member of the Bengal Assembly (1937-1947). He joined the Muslim League in 1937 and became general secretary of the provincial Muslim League in 1943. After the independence of Pakistan he remained in India until 1950 and was the leader of the opposition in the West Bengal Assembly. For his role as the president of the organizing committee of the language movement, Abul Hashim was arrested and was jailed for a period of sixteen months. In 1964 he formed the Khilafat-e-Rabbani Party in opposition to Ayub Khan (q.v.) and was its president until 1966. He was the first director of the Islamic Academy.

ABUL HUSAIN (1896-1938). Founder of the Dhaka Muslim Literature Society in 1923, he was one of the main proponents of the "freedom of thought" movement. He was involved with the education of the Muslims of Bengal. A liberal thinker, Abul

Husain wrote a number of books, including *The Helots of Bengal*, *Religion of the Helots of Bengal*, and *The Development of Muslim Law in British India.*

ABYSSINIANS. The name given to African slaves who came to India. In Bengal in 1486, the Abyssinians led a revolt against the Ilyas Shahi dynasty (q.v.). By 1490, an Abyssinian slave usurped the throne and took the name Shamsuddin Muzaffar Shah (q.v.). His rule was despotic, and he was deposed in 1493 and succeeded by Alauddin Husain Shah (q.v.), founder of the Husain Shahi dynasty (q.v.).

ADAMJEE JUTE MILL. Located in Narayanganj in greater Dhaka, it is the largest such mill in the world. It symbolized the domination of East Pakistani industry by West Pakistanis, as the Adamjee family was based in Karachi. In 1954 it was the scene of a major and violent labor dispute resulting from hiring practices that seemed to Bengali-speakers to discriminate against them and in favor of Urdu-speaking Biharis (q.v.). The strike contributed to the fall of the chief minister, Fazlul Haq (q.v.), and some have alleged it was intended to do so.

ADISURA. Bengal literary tradition asserts that a ruler of this name became king of Gaur (q.v.) in the eighth century A.D. and attempted to revive Brahmanism. There are no contemporary records of him and he may not have existed (see Sura dynasty).

AFGHANISTAN. Bangladesh-Afghanistan relations were not close but were friendly prior to the communist takeover in Afghanistan in 1978. After the Soviet invasion of Afghanistan in 1979, the government of Bangladesh took a position similar to that of Pakistan and most other Islamic nations: the complete withdrawal of Soviet troops, the restoration of the nonaligned position of Afghanistan, and the establishment of a government in Afghanistan acceptable to the Afghan people. It thus agreed with and supported the position of Pakistan and opposed the position of India.

AGA KHAN III (Sir Sultan Muhammad Shah, 1877-1957). The spiritual leader of the Nizari Ismaili sect of Shia Muslims. He also played an important role in Indian-Muslim politics as leader of the Simla delegation to Lord Minto (q.v.) in 1906 and the founding of the Muslim League (q.v.) in the same year. The Aga Khan was several times president of the Muslim League. As India's representative, he was president of the League of Nations in 1937.

AGARTALA CONSPIRACY CASE. Lodged against Sheikh Mujibur Rahman (q.v.) and others in 1968. It was alleged that Mujib and the others had plotted (in the Indian city of Agartala, the capital of Tripura state) with India to win the independence of East Pakistan. The trial was never completed, and the charges were dropped by Ayub Khan (q.v.) as a precondition placed by opposition leaders to meetings held between them and Ayub in early 1969.

AGRICULTURE. Agriculture accounts for 34 percent of gross national product (the data here are for 1992), about 60 percent of employment, and one-third of exports. Agricultural production is heavily dependent on the monsoon and is therefore vulnerable to weather fluctuations. Traditional agriculture is primarily rain-fed; modern irrigation facilities serve 25 percent of the cultivated area. Use of chemical fertilizer is both inadequate and unbalanced. Frequent droughts and floods in the 1980s have resulted in a series of crop failures.

The total gross cropped area is 15 million hectares (about 37 million acres). Rice is the most important crop, accounting for approximately 72 percent of the cropped area; jute (q.v.) and wheat account for 4 percent each; the remaining 24 percent is utilized for pulses, oilseeds, sugar cane, vegetables, and tea (q.v.). The average annual growth in value added of the Bangladeshi agricultural sector was only 1.9 percent for the period 1980-1988. Food grain production increased by about 1 million tons between 1979/1980 and 1984/1985 and then leveled off around 16 million tons in subsequent years. Food grain production, however, rose again, reaching about 20 million tons in 1992. Despite such increases in food grain production there is still a negative ratio between food grain production and population growth, resulting in increased food imports. Food security at the household level continues to remain precarious, and agricultural productivity remains low. While increased productivity is pursued through irrigation, high-yield varieties (HYV) of seeds, and fertilizer technology, only 0.83 million hectares (a bit more than 2 million acres) utilize ground-water irrigation against a potential of about 2 million hectares (5 million acres). Surface-water irrigation is used at less that 50 percent of capacity. Fertilizer application has increased from 0.28 million tons in 1960/1961 to 1.5 million tons in 1987/1988 but remains among the lowest of major agricultural nations. Approximately 60 percent of the areas suitable for HYV seed usage continue to use local seed varieties.

Fish, which is the most important source of animal protein, provides substantial employment and export earning. However, inland fish production has declined in recent years. At the same time, cultivated fishing has increased and is contributing to overall agricultural production. Improvement in livestock through genetic means along with an efficient supply of feed and fodder and small business development in poultry has increased the supply of meat. Overexploitation of forest resources for fuel and cultivation has created serious ecological and environmental problems, especially in southern Bangladesh. Reforestation of forest reserves and afforestation with community participation are in progress to arrest further damage and initiate recovery.

AHAD, ABDUL (1918-1994). A noted lyricist and composer, he had been closely associated with Rabindranath Tagore (q.v.). He worked in Shantiniketan but came to Dhaka after the partition of 1947 and was associated with the Dhaka radio station. Abdul Ahad wrote a number of books on Tagore and Bengali music.

AHMED, ABUL MANSUR (1897-1979). A journalist and a politician. He was the editor of the *Daily Ittehad*, 1945-1950. In the 1920s he participated in both the Khilafat (q.v.) and the noncooperation movements. He first joined the Swaraj party, then the Congress Party, and in 1944 he joined the Muslim League (q.v.). In 1954 he became the minister of health in the United Front (q.v.) government. Abul Mansur was the education and commerce minister when the Awami League (q.v.) was in power in 1956. From 1958 to 1962 he was under arrest. After his release in 1962 he did not return to politics but became a well-known columnist, writing for such papers as *Ittefaq* and *Observer*. Abul Mansur wrote a number of books in Bengali. In English, his *End of a Betrayal and Restoration of Lahore Resolution*, published in 1975, is a valuable look at the period between 1940 and 1971.

AHMED, FARRUKH (1918-1974). A poet and journalist, he was born in Jessore and studied in Calcutta. He was on the staff of *Mohammadi* before partition and then worked with Dhaka radio until 1972. In college, he had been influenced by the Radical Humanist movement of M. N. Roy, but then became an ardent Muslim. This is reflected in his poetry.

AHMED, KAZI ZAFAR (b. 1940). A trade unionist and member of the National Awami Party (q.v.), he joined JAGODAL (q.v.) in support of President Ziaur Rahman (q.v.). He served briefly in 1978 as minister of education. He changed parties to join the Jatiya Party (q.v.) of H. M. Ershad (q.v.) and, as a member of the cabinet, held various portfolios including commerce, education, and information and broadcasting. In November, 1978, Kazi Zafar was designated deputy prime minister and in September, 1989, he was appointed prime minister and remained in that position until the fall of the Ershad regime in December 1990. He remains a key member of the Jatiya Party.

AHMED, MOUDUD (b. 1940). Active in the 1971 liberation movement, he later broke with Mujibur Rahman (q.v.) and worked often as a civil rights lawyer. He held ministerial posts under Ziaur Rahman (q.v.), 1977-1980, and was elected to parliament in 1979. Even though he had earlier been jailed by the

Ershad (q.v.) regime, he was appointed to the Ershad cabinet in 1985 and named deputy prime minister in 1986, a post he held until becoming prime minister in March 1988. Moudud was nominated vice president in September 1989 but resigned in December of that year to make way for the appointment of Shahabuddin Ahmed (q.v.) as vice president and then successor to Ershad when the latter resigned. He was elected to parliament from Noakhali in 1986, 1988, and 1991. His wife, Husna, the daughter of poet Jasimuddin (q.v.), was also elected in 1988.

AHMED, MOYEZUDDIN (MODHU MIAN) (1855-1920). A journalist and writer who lived in Jessore. He published several journals that appealed to the Muslim middle class and wrote several books on Islam.

AHMED, MUZAFFAR (d. 1972). The leader of the pro-Soviet faction of the National Awami Party (q.v.). He was one of the first political leaders to ask for elections after the independence of Bangladesh. He argued that the 1970 election through which the Awami League (q.v.) came to power had been held under conditions that pertained prior to independence, and the mandate required reconfirmation.

AHMED, SHAHABUDDIN (b. 1929). A member of the judicial service, he rose to become chief justice of Bangladesh. During the rioting that led to the resignation of President Ershad (q.v.), Shahabuddin was selected by the opposition to become vice president. The then vice president, Moudud Ahmed (q.v.) resigned, and Shahabuddin was appointed to that position by Ershad on December 6, 1990. He became acting president on December 8. His primary task was to hold a "free and fair" election for a new parliament. Shahabuddin accomplished this in February 1991 (see Elections). The new parliament amended the constitution to provide for a parliamentary system to replace the presidential system. Another amendment permitted Shahabuddin to return to his position as chief justice. This he did when Abdur Rahman Biswas (q.v.) was elected president and assumed office on October 8, 1991. Shahabuddin retired as chief justice in 1994.

AHMED, SHAMSUDDIN (1889-1969). He was born in Kushtia and received a law degree from Calcutta. He took an active part in the noncooperation movement and the Khilafat movement (q.v.). He was elected to the Bengal Legislative Council as a member of Congress in 1927 and to the Bengal Legislative Assembly as a member of the Krishak Praja Party (q.v.) in 1937. Shamsuddin joined the Muslim League (q.v.) in 1944, but after independence formed the Socialist Party of Pakistan. He also served as Pakistan's ambassador to Burma.

AHMED, SULTANUDDIN (1902-1977). Governor of East Pakistan in 1958. A lawyer and pre-independence legislator, he also served as ambassador of Pakistan in Burma, China, and Indonesia.

AHMED, TAJUDDIN (1922-1975). Headed the first provisional government of Bangladesh. He was a close confidant of Sheikh Mujibur Rahman (q.v.) during negotiation with both the Ayub (q.v.) and the Yahya (q.v.) regimes. During the Mujib regime, he held the portfolios of defense (1972), finance (1972-1974), forests, fisheries, and livestock (1974), information and broadcasting (1972), jute (1973-1974), and planning (1972-1974), often heading more than one ministry at a time. Preferring closer ties with the Soviet Union, Tajuddin fell into disgrace when Mujib felt that circumstances required a closer relationship with the United States. He was one of the four political leaders who were assassinated following the Khalid Musharif (q.v.) coup of November 1975.

AHSAN-UL-HUQUE (b. 1919). His father, Sir Muhammad Aziz-ul-Huque (q.v.), was a prominent Muslim Bengali political figure before independence, but Ahsan-ul-Huque was engaged principally in commerce and industry. Ahsan-ul-Huque served as a Pakistan ambassador under Ayub Khan (q.v.) and was a member of the cabinet formed by Yahya Khan (q.v.) in 1969 in the latter's unsuccessful effort toward gradual civilianization of the martial law government.

AHSANULLAH (1873-1965). Born in Satkhira in Khulna district, he was the first Indian to be appointed to the Indian Education Service. He ended one aspect of discrimination on the basis of religion in examinations by assigning numbers rather than using names in examinations. Ahsanullah also worked to improve the quality of education in the Muslim madrasas (primary schools) so that graduates of the madrasas could be admitted to secular colleges. He established libraries and publishing houses.

AHSANULLAH KHAN, NAWAB KHWAJA (1846-1901). Son of Nawab Khwaja Abdul Ghani Mian (q.v.), he succeeded his father as Nawab of Dhaka in 1896. He was a member of the Legislative Council of the Governor General in 1890 and 1899. His philanthropic donations included the Dhaka Mitford Hospital and the Dhaka Electric Supply organization. Ahsanullah was succeeded as nawab by his son, Nawab Sir Salimullah (q.v.).

AID AND TRADE. Since its independence in 1971, Bangladesh has received more than $22 billion in grants and loans from multilateral organizations, such as the World Bank, the Asian Development Bank, and the United Nations Development Program, and bilateral assistance from many countries including, among the major donors, the United States, Japan, and Saudi Arabia.

In the late 1980s, Bangladesh ran an annual trade deficit of approximately $1.5 billion. In the early 1990s, Bangladesh's balance of payments position changed and showed a surplus. While both industry (q.v.) and agriculture (q.v.) have traditionally contributed to export receipts, the surplus in the balance of trade resulted from increased exports of garments as well as from a depressed demand for imports. Another factor for the improved balance of payments position is the remittances from Bangladeshi workers in the Middle East (q.v.).

Although the external debt of Bangladesh reached approximately $11 billion in the early 1990s, successive governments have made a serious effort to improve the economic and investment climate through privatization, trade liberalization, and investment incentives. In 1995, the foreign exchange reserve was $3.15 billion, which is an all-time high. Export earnings were $1.69 billion. Debt servicing is now only 13 percent of foreign exchange earnings.

AKRAM KHAN, MAULANA MUHAMMAD (1870-1968). A founding member of the Muslim League (q.v.) in 1906. He founded the newspaper *Daily Azad* in 1936 as a journal to support the Muslim League. He was the president of the provincial Muslim League and vice president of All-India Muslim League and Pakistan Muslim League. Akram Khan was also a social activist and a litterateur and was given the Pride of Performance in Literature award by the government of Pakistan.

ALAOL (c. 1607-1680). An important medieval Bengali poet, he was born in Chittagong district, but did most of his work while a counselor to the king of Arakan (q.v.). A number of his works have been discovered.

ALAUDDIN HUSAIN SHAH. The sultan of Bengal from 1493 to 1519 and the founder of the Husain Shahi dynasty (q.v.)., having overthrown Sultan Shamsuddin Muzaffar Shah (q.v.), an Abyssinian (q.v.) ruler. As Alauddin was a Sayyid of Arab descent, the dynasty is sometimes known as the Sayyid dynasty (not to be confused with the Sayyid dynasty of the Delhi Sultanate). Alauddin proved to be a very successful and popular ruler, beginning with the restoration of order and the expulsion of the Abyssinian mercenaries. He extended the sultanate to the borders of Orissa and retook Bihar from the rulers of Jaunpur (now in Uttar Pradesh). He was a builder and erected many monuments in his capital, Gaur (q.v.).

ALI, MAHMUD (b. 1919). Leader of the Ganotantrik Dal (q.v.), a constituent of the United Front (q.v.) that swept the 1954 election to the East Bengal Legislative Assembly. After Bangladeshi independence, he chose to move to Pakistan and held a variety of posts under both the Bhutto (q.v.) and Zia ul-Haq regimes.

ALI MARDAN KHALJI. Appointed governor of Bengal by Sultan Qutbuddin of the Mamluk series of rulers of the Delhi Sultanate in 1206, he revolted on Qutbuddin's death in 1210 and attempted to set himself up as an independent ruler. He was defeated by Sultan Iltutmish in 1230.

ALI, MUHAMMAD KORBAN (1924-1990). Political figure first associated with the Awami League (q.v.) and later with the Jatiya Party (q.v.). He was elected to the provincial assembly in 1954 and to parliament in 1973, 1986, and 1988. A senior vice president of the Awami League, Korban Ali changed parties in 1984 and joined the cabinet of the regime headed by Hussain Muhammad Ershad (q.v.).

ALI, SYED MURTAZA (1903-1981). Born in Sylhet (then a part of Assam), he studied in Calcutta and entered the Indian Civil Service. After retirement as a divisional commissioner in 1959, he headed the Bangla Academy. Murtaza Ali published a number of books including *History of Chittagong* (1964).

ALINGARH, TREATY OF. A treaty signed between Nawab Sirajuddaulah (q.v.) and the British, represented by Robert Clive (q.v.) on February 9, 1757, following the British recapture of Calcutta. The terms imposed by the British were stiff, although the violations of the treaty that occurred were by the British and not the Nawab. These included entering into a conspiracy against the Nawab with Mir Jafar (q.v.). This led to the Battle of Plassey (q.v.) on June 23, 1757, and the defeat and death of Sirajuddaulah.

ALIVARDI KHAN (c. 1678-1756). His original name was Mirza Muhammad Khan. He was appointed to positions of power by Nawab Shujauddin (nawab, 1725-1739). Shujauddin's son, Sarfraz Khan, succeeded his father. Alivardi Khan had been Shujauddin's deputy for the Bihar region of the Bengal province of the Mughals. Taking advantage of the confusion in Delhi caused by the raid of the Persian Nadir Shah in 1739 and with the help of dubious documents, he claimed that he had been chosen to replace the incumbent governor. He defeated Sarfraz Khan at Giria and became governor. He was assisted by the banker Jagat Seth (q.v.). Alivardi's term in office was relatively peaceful as he successfully met the challenges presented by the British. An exception to this was the constant struggle with the Marathas in Orissa; in 1751 Alivardi made a peace with the Marathas by transferring some of the revenues of Orissa and agreeing to pay an annual tribute. He was succeeded by his daughter's son, Sirajuddaulah (q.v.).

AMIR ALI, SYED (1849-1928). A Bengali Shia, he wrote extensively on Islam. He was born in Cuttack, Orissa, and educated in India before being called to the bar from the Inner Temple in 1873. He was the first Muslim barrister at the Calcutta High Court and was law lecturer at several colleges in Calcutta. He was a judge at the Calcutta High Court, 1890-1904, the first Muslim to sit on the bench. Amir Ali had been active in politics prior to being named to the court and had founded the National (later Central) Mohammedan Association in 1877, a body created to put forward the ideas of the Muslims in Indian politics. Amir Ali was influenced by Sir Syed Ahmad Khan, whom he had met during his stay in England. In 1882, the association presented a memorial to the viceroy, Lord Ripon, demanding greater representation of Muslims in government service. He reentered politics after his retirement from the bench. Amir Ali was a member of the Simla delegation to Lord Minto (q.v.) in 1906 and led a Muslim League delegation to Lord Morley, the Secretary of State for India, in London in 1909. He was a champion of the cause of separate electorates (q.v.). Amir Ali was active in the Muslim League (q.v.), presiding over its third session in Delhi in 1910. After his retirement from the High Court, he lived in London and represented the Muslim League there. Amir Ali was also the first Indian appointed to the Judicial Committee of the Privy Council, serving from 1908 until his death in 1928. Although a Shia, he supported retention of the Caliphate during the Khilafat movement (q.v.). Amir Ali published a number of books on Islam, the most noted being *The Spirit of Islam* (first published in 1922). He also wrote extensively on Islamic law.

ANWARUL HUQUE, KAZI (b. 1909). A member of the Indian Police Service, he became inspector general of police in 1958 and later, in 1961, chief secretary of East Pakistan. Anwarul Huque joined the cabinet of Ayub Khan (q.v.) in 1965 and remained until 1969. After Bangladeshi independence, he was a member of the cabinets of Sayem (q.v.), Ziaur Rahman (q.v.), and Sattar (q.v.).

ARAKAN. The province of Myanmar (Burma) (q.v.) adjacent to Bangladesh on the Bay of Bengal. Rulers of Arakan controlled the Chittagong (q.v.) region from the fifteenth to seventeenth centuries. The area troubled British and Bengali commerce for many centuries as the base of pirates operating in the bay. Arakanese pirates were often associated with or allies of Portuguese adventurers (See Portugeuse in Bengal). It was an independent kingdom until 1784, when it was conquered by the Burmese. Burmese possession of the area was a contributing factor in the outbreak of the First Anglo-Burmese war in 1824. In the treaty of Yandaboo ending the war in 1826, Arakan was among the territories ceded to the British.

There is a sizable Muslim minority in Arakan, known as Rohingyas. They are assumed by some to be descendants of

Muslim soldiers of the Suri dynasty (q.v.) who fled there when the Mughals defeated the Suri usurpers and restored Humayun to the throne of Delhi in 1555. The Rohingyas have felt themselves oppressed by the Burmese (Myanmarese) government and twice have fled to the southern parts of Chittagong district, in the late 1970s and again in the late 1980s. As this is being written, a substantial number of Rohingyas remain in Bangladesh and are being cared for by the government of Bangladesh, the United Nations High Commissioner for Refugees, and international relief agencies.

ARCHITECTURE. The building art of Bangladesh can be classified into four distinct periods. The first period, identified through archaeology and extending from the third century B.C. to the twelfth century A.D., is the ancient period. Buddhist monuments at Paharpur (q.v.) and Mainamati (q.v.), and Buddhist and Hindu temples at Mahastangarh (q.v.) define this period. Although these ancient monuments are not as spectacular as those discovered in other parts of the subcontinent, they provide sufficient clues to the historical importance of Bangladesh as a crossroads of different cultures.

The second period is that of the Delhi Sultanate (q.v.). This period witnessed the development of terra-cotta floral motifs, delicate stone carvings, and the curvature of the cornice. The architectural design was similar to that of the Tughluq architecture of Delhi. Some of the more noted sites include the tombs of Ghiyasuddin Azam Shah at Sonargaon (q.v.) and Khan Jahan Ali at Bagerhat. Mosques that are representative of this period include the Shair Gumbad mosque in Khulna, the Sura mosque in Dinajpur (q.v.), the Chhota Sona mosque in Rajshahi (q.v.), and the Kherua mosque in Bogra (q.v.).

The third period is that of the Mughal empire (q.v.). This period is characterized by the dominant central dome, the tall central entrance, and the straight horizontal skyline. During the early part of the Mughal period, a blending of the Sultanate and Mughal styles was seen in such buildings as the Atia Jami mosque in Tangail and the Shah Muhammad mosque in Mymensingh (q.v.). Distinctive Mughal architecture is concentrated in Dhaka (q.v.) in such monuments as the Bara and Chhota Katras, the Lalbagh Fort, the tomb of Bibi Pari, the Hussaini Dalan, and the river forts of Munshiganj, Hajiganj, and Narayanganj.

The fourth period is that of the British, who brought with them the European Renaissance style seen in the first churches. Public buildings such as the former State Bank building in Dhaka and private structures such as Ahsan Manzil, residence of the Nawabs of Dhaka (q.v.), are noted from the British period. As the Sultanate and Mughal period blended earlier, there was blending between the Mughal and British periods. Examples of this are seen on the campus of the University of Dhaka in Curzon,

Salimullah, and Fazlul Haq Halls. While Muslim architectural design dominates modern Bangladesh, affluent Hindu *zamindars* (landlords) made an important contribution to continuing the ancient art form through their patronage of temples. Examples of these include the Govinda temple in Rajshahi (q.v.), the Mathurapur Deul in Faridpur (q.v.), and the Satararatna temple in Comilla (q.v.). Buddhist architectural design continues in Bangladesh, resulting from the influx of Magh tribals from Myanmar (Burma) (q.v.) into the Cox's Bazaar region. The Khyangs of Cox's Bazaar and the Ramu and Chitmorong temples near Kaptai are excellent examples.

ARMENIANS. Armenians, based in Persia, were an important trading community in South Asia and in Bengal in particular. The East India Company recognized the "Armenian nation" through an agreement in 1688 that granted the "nation" special trading privileges. In Bengal, there were sizable Armenian settlements in Dhaka and Calcutta. In Dhaka, there remains an Armenian church, but most Armenians in South Asia have left.

ASIATIC SOCIETY OF BANGLADESH. An outgrowth of the Asiatic Society of Bengal, an association of learned men interested in oriental studies. It was founded by Sir William Jones (q.v.) in 1784 and supported by Governor-General Warren Hastings (q.v.). Its initial charge was to inquire "into the history, civil and natural, the antiquities, arts, sciences, and literature of Asia." Today, the society in Bangladesh maintains an extensive library of books and manuscripts. In 1951, the Asiatic Society of Pakistan was formed by Dr. Mohammad Shahidullah (q.v.). When Bangladesh became independent in 1971, the organization was renamed the Asiatic Society of Bangladesh. In addition to lectures and seminars, it maintains an excellent program of publications.

ASOKA. The third emperor of the Maurya dynasty (q.v.) who reigned from c. 272 to c. 232 B.C. He ruled Bengal, which had been conquered by the founder of the dynasty, his grandfather, Chandragupta (reigned c. 322 to c. 298 B.C.). The Bengali port of Tamluk (now in West Bengal) served as the major export and import center for the Mauryas.

ASSOCIATION FOR SOCIAL ADVANCEMENT (ASA). Established in 1978, ASA, a non-government organization (NGO), emphasizes socioeconomic selfreliance and sustainability through financing income generating programs for women. Since 1990, ASA has provided more than 250,000 households living below the poverty line with credit. The ASA program covers twenty-three of the sixty-four districts of Bangladesh.

ATAUR RAHMAN KHAN (1907 1991). Became a member of the Awami League at its inception in 1949. He acted as president of the East Bengal Awami League several times when the head of the provincial organization, Maulana Bhashani (q.v.), was in jail. He was elected to the East Bengal Assembly in 1954 and was leader of the Awami League part of the United Front (q.v.). After representative government was restored to the province in 1956, Ataur Rahman served as chief minister of East Pakistan throughout much of the period from 1956 to 1958 (when Ayub Khan's [q.v.] coup displaced him), with the exception of short periods when the Krishak Sramik Party (q.v.) leader Abu Husain Sarkar (q.v.) was able to form a government.

After the death of Awami League founder Husain Shahid Suhrawardy (q.v.) in 1963, his relations with Sheikh Mujibur Rahman (q.v.) became difficult, and in the 1970 election Ataur Rahman Khan formed the Pakistan (later Bangladesh) National League. He was defeated in 1970 but won election to the Bangladesh Parliament in 1973 (and was leader of the opposition in 1975 when Mujibur Rahman imposed one party rule) and led the opposition again in 1979. On March 30, 1984, Ataur Rahman was appointed prime minister by the martial law president, Husain Muhammad Ershad (q.v.), and held that office until January 7, 1985, when Ershad reshuffled the entire cabinet.

ATISH DIPANKAR SRIGYAN (982 1054). One of a number of Bengali Buddhist scholars who transmitted Buddhist ideas to Tibet. He came from Vikrampur (q.v.), a major Buddhist center, and studied also at Nalanda in Bihar. In Tibet, he gathered and copied Sanskrit manuscripts which he sent to Bengal.

AUGUST COUP. The first coup by the Bangladesh army took place on August 15, 1975. This coup led to the assassination of Sheikh Mujibur Rahman (q.v.) and the collapse of the first democratically elected government of Bangladesh, although by this time the regime of Mujib had become autocratic. The coup was led by junior ranking members of the army, including two lieutenant colonels and five majors. The August coup was followed by the November 1975 coup and countercoup in which Khalid Musharif (q.v.) was killed and Ziaur Rahman (q.v.) became the key person in government.

AUROBINDO. See GHOSE, AUROBINDO.

AWAMI LEAGUE. Founded in June 1949 as the Awami ("People's") Muslim League, by Husain Shahid Suhrawardy (q.v.) as a vehicle for his political ambitions and as a party that would be an alternative to the Muslim League (q.v.). Suhrawardy opposed the clause in the Muslim League constitution that prohibited non Muslims from becoming members, stating that this would cause continued divisions in Pakistan; hence, the word Muslim was soon dropped from the new party's name. The party developed little strength in West Pakistan, but emerged as the strongest party in East Pakistan. It joined with the Krishak Sramik Party (q.v.) and some smaller parties in the United Front (q.v.) of 1954, which won the legislative election in East Bengal from the Muslim League.

Among those closely associated with Suhrawardy were Ataur Rahman Khan (q.v.), chief minister for most of the period from 1956 to 1958; Sheikh Mujibur Rahman (q.v.), organizational leader during the same period and after the death of Suhrawardy, de facto leader of the party; and Maulana Abdul Hamid Khan Bhashani (q.v.).

Bhashani differed with Suhrawardy on domestic and international issues and left the party in 1957 to form the National Awami Party (NAP) (q.v.). The program of the party in economic matters was middle-of-the-road, although after Bangladeshi independence Mujibur Rahman, as prime minister and later as president, pursued a strong program of nationalization of industry and trade. Before independence, Mujib supported a high degree of autonomy for the provinces of Pakistan; this was embodied in the Six-Point Program (q.v.) Mujib proclaimed in 1966.

In the 1970 elections the Awami League swept both the East Pakistan segment of the National Assembly and East Pakistan Provincial Assembly polls (See Elections). After Bangladeshi independence, the Awami League held office until mid-1975, when it merged into BAKSAL (q.v.). After the November 1975 coup and after political parties were permitted to return to activity, the party was revived. It supported Muhammad Ataul Ghani Osmany (q.v.) for the presidency in 1978 and participated in the 1979 parliamentary elections, winning about 10 percent of the seats and becoming the official opposition to the Bangladesh Nationalist Party (BNP) (q.v.). In the presidential election in 1981, following the assassination of Ziaur Rahman (q.v.), the Awami League candidate, Kamal Hossain (q.v.), finished second to the BNP's Abdus Sattar (q.v.). Banned again after the coup led by General Hussain Muhammad Ershad (q.v.) in 1982, the party revived once again to finish second in the 1986 parliamentary elections to Ershad's Jatiya Party (q.v.). The party did not contest the 1986 presidential election, which was won by Ershad, or the 1988 parliamentary election. The Awami League favors a Westminster form of parliamentary government, but it has dropped the socialist economy platform and now favors a market economy.

The present leader of the party (and leader of the opposition in parliament until her resignation from parliament in December 1995) is Sheikh Hasina Wajid (q.v.), daughter of Mujibur Rahman. In the February 1991 election the Awami League won the second largest number of seats. In 1994 and 1995, the Awami League pressed for an amendment to the constitution that would provide for elections to be held under a neutral caretaker government (q.v.) as were those held in 1991. The Awami League parliamentarians and those of other opposition parties (see Jatiya Party, Jama'at-i-Islami) resigned from parliament on December 28, 1994.

Parliament was dissolved in November 1995. A new election was called for February 1996. The Awami League and most other opposition parties boycotted this election and the BNP gained an overwhelming majority. The new parliament passed a constitutional amended providing for a neutral caretaker government. Another election was held in June 1996 in which the Awami League gained a plurality (but not a majority of the seats). It formed a new government with the support of the Jatiya Party (q.v.) with Sheikh Hasina Wajid as prime minister.

AYUB KHAN, MUHAMMAD (1907-1974). President of Pakistan, 1958-1969, was a career military officer in the Indian and Pakistani armies, having been commissioned from Sandhurst in 1928. He reached the rank of major general in 1948 while he was in command of the troops stationed in East Bengal. In 1951, having reached the rank of lieutenant general, he was appointed the first Pakistani to be commander in chief of the army (his predecessors since independence in 1947 had been British officers seconded to the Pakistani Army). Ayub was additionally minister of defense in the "cabinet of talents" headed by Muhammad Ali Bogra (q.v.) from October 1954 to August 1955 and during this time was a key person in the negotiation of military assistance from the United States to Pakistan. On October 7, 1958, he became chief martial law administrator (until 1962) following the dismissal of the civilian government by President Iskandar Mirza (q.v.); Ayub then deposed Mirza on October 28 and became president (until March 25, 1969). Rioting in opposition to his rule began in West Pakistan in September 1968 and quickly spread to East Pakistan. Despite Ayub's offer to restore parliamentary rule and his withdrawal of the Agartala Conspiracy Case (q.v.) against Mujibur Rahman (q.v.) and others, he was forced by leaders of the military to resign the presidency to General Agha Muhammad Yahya Khan (q.v.). While Ayub's period of rule displayed considerable economic growth in East Pakistan, the growth in West Pakistan was much more rapid, leading to a marked increase in the economic disparity between the two provinces.

AZAD, MUHAMMAD ABDUS SAMAD (b. 1922). From Sylhet, he has long been associated with the Awami League (q.v.) and is currently deputy leader of the opposition in Parliament. Azad was a member of the cabinet of Mujibur Rahman (q.v.) as minister of foreign affairs (1972-1973) and agriculture (1973-1975).

AZAM, GOLAM (b. 1922). The *amir* (leader) of the Jama'at-i-Islami (q.v.) since 1992. He was born in Dhaka and educated at Dhaka University where he was actively involved in student politics. Golam Azam taught at Carmichael College in Rangpur (q.v.) and joined the Jama'at in 1955. He was elected president of the East Pakistan Jama'at in 1969 and has served several jail terms for his activities. Golam Azam was accused of collaborating with the Pakistan army in 1971 and was stripped of his Bangladeshi citizenship in 1973 as a result. He returned to Bangladesh from exile to assume the leadership of the Jama'at. Golam Azam's citizenship was restored by a Supreme Court decision in 1994. This brought protests from many in Bangladesh and demands for his trial on charges of murder during 1971. One group, of which Jahanara Imam (q.v.) was a prominent member, held a mock trial and "convicted" him.

AZAM KHAN, MUHAMMAD (1908-1994). Appointed the administrator of Martial Law Zone B, which included the whole of West Pakistan except Karachi, when General Muhammad Ayub Khan (q.v.) took over in 1958. He was given high credit for his reorganization of the Ministry of Refugees and Rehabilitation. In 1960, Azam Khan was appointed governor of East Pakistan. He became a very popular governor because of his untiring effort to reach the people. His popularity was seen as a threat to General Ayub, who removed him in 1962. He came to prominence once again when he joined the opposition and supported the presidential candidacy of Fatima Jinnah against Ayub Khan in 1964. Azam Khan continued to oppose Ayub, but became quite inactive after Ayub's ouster.

AZIZ-UL-HUQUE, SIR MUHAMMAD (1892-1947). A lawyer by profession, he served as a member of the Governor-General's Executive Council, 1943-1946. Prior to that he was the Indian High Commissioner to England (1942-1943). His efforts in the field of education are well recognized. As vice chancellor of Calcutta University from 1928 to 1942, he established the first Department of Islamic History and Culture. He was elected to the Bengal Legislative Council in 1929 and was education minister, 1934-1937. Elected to the new Bengal Legislative Assembly in 1937, Aziz-ul-Huque was chosen Speaker and served until his appointment as high commissioner in London in 1942 in succession to Malik Firoz Khan Noon (q.v.). He was an active member of the Muslim League and supported the League's decision to accept the Cabinet Mission Plan (q.v.). He wrote the book *Man Behind the Plough,* published in 1939. His son, Ahsan-ul-Huque (q.v.), served in the Pakistan cabinet and as a Pakistani ambassador.

AZIZUR RAHMAN, SHAH MOHAMMAD (1925-1988). Secretary general of the All-India Muslim Students Federation and All-

Bengal Muslim Students League from 1945 to 1947. He became the joint secretary of the East Pakistan Muslim League in 1947 and became the general secretary from 1952 to 1958. He joined the Awami League (q.v.) in 1964. In 1969, he was the deputy leader of the Pakistan National Assembly. During the war of independence Shah Aziz remained out of politics, but reemerged when the Bangladesh Muslim League was permitted to operate in 1976. In 1979, he was elected a member of the parliament and became the prime minister of the country. Shah Aziz joined the Bangladesh Nationalist Party (BNP) (q.v.). He remained as the prime minister until December 1981. After the assassination of President Ziaur Rahman (q.v.) in May 1991, Shah Aziz remained with the BNP until he was expelled from the party for "disciplinary reasons" in 1985.

- B -

BACKERGANJ. See BARISAL.

BADRUDDUJA, SYED (1900-1974). A Muslim politician from Murshidabad district, he remained in India after partition. He was associated with both the Muslim League (q.v.) and the Krishak Praja Party (KPP) (q.v.), having been elected to the Bengal Legislative Assembly in 1937 on the League ticket and losing in 1946 on the KPP ticket. Badrudduja was mayor of Calcutta, 1943-1944. After independence he served at various times as a member of the West Bengal Legislative Assembly and the Lok Sabha. One of Badrudduja's daughters, Razia Faiz, has been a member of the Pakistan National Assembly and the Bangladesh parliament as a Muslim League member from Khulna.

BADRUNNESSA AHMAD (1929-1974). Served as minister of education in the Sheikh Mujibur Rahman (q.v.) government that was formed after the parliamentary election of 1973. She was a member of the East Bengal Legislative Assembly from 1954 to 1958. Badrunnessa served as the vice president of the Mahila Samity (Women's Organization) of East Pakistan and later Bangladesh from 1959 to 1972. A member of the Awami League, she actively participated in the war of liberation by propagating the Bangladeshi cause. Like many of her contemporaries, Badrunnessa too was arrested during the language movement (q.v.).

BAKSAL. An acronym for Bangladesh Krishak Sramik Awami League, the name chosen by Sheikh Mujibur Rahman (q.v.) (q.v.) for the single party in Bangladesh decreed by him in June, 1975. The name combined the names of two of the parties, Awami League (q.v.) and Krishak Sramik Party (q.v.), that had joined to form the United Front (q.v.) in 1954. Not all Awami Leaguers agreed to join the new party; those who did not were technically out of politics. BAKSAL was dissolved following the assassination of Mujibur Rahman on August 15, 1975, and the installation of a new government under Khondakar Mushtaque Ahmed (q.v.). A small group has continued to use the name and won five seats in parliament in the 1991 election.

BANERJEA, SURENDRANATH (1848-1925). An important Bengali moderate political figure. He entered the Indian Civil Service in 1871, one of the first Indians to do so, but was dismissed for his nationalist views in 1875. Banerjea devoted himself to education and nationalist politics, serving as president of the Indian National Congress in 1895 and 1902. Opposed to what he considered to be extremism in the Congress, Banerjea and others formed the National Liberal Federation in 1918.

BANERJEE, RAKHALDAS (1886-1930). A noted historian and archaeologist, he was born in Murshidabad district, now in West Bengal. He worked first as an archaeologist in the Indus valley, but later studied the Pala dynasty (q.v.) and worked at Paharpur (q.v.). Among Banerjee's works are *Palas of Bengal*, *The Origin of the Bengali Script*, and *Eastern India School of Medieval Sculpture*.

BANG TRIBE. Believed to have been the first Indo-Aryan group to have migrated to the lower Ganges valley and to have given its name to Bengal. (In Sanskrit, the tribe is Vang and the area Vanga [q.v.].)

BANGLADESH ACADEMY OF RURAL DEVELOPMENT. The name now used by the former East Pakistan unit of the Pakistan Academy of Rural Development, which was set up in the early 1960s. The purpose was to apply social science theories to practical problems of administration and to promote rural development. In the beginning, under an agreement with the United States Agency for International Development, the project was aided by Michigan State University. The Comilla *thana* was used as a living laboratory to test projects which could then be applied to other parts of the country. The four major project areas were an improved model for rural administration, a model for reconstruction and expansion of rural infrastructure, a model for utilization of surface and ground water for irrigation, and a new, two-tier cooperative system. Comilla is often used as a model for rural development in the international development community. Akhtar Hameed Khan (from West Pakistan, now working in Karachi) is credited for the success of the program. Much of the research was undertaken in the Matlab *thana* of Comilla district. One of the projects that resulted was the Cholera Research Laboratory in Dhaka (now named the International Centre for Diarrhoeal Disease Research, Bangladesh).

BANGLADESH KRISHAK SRAMIK AWAMI LEAGUE. See BAKSAL.

BANGLADESH MUSLIM LEAGUE. An outgrowth of the Pakistan Muslim League, itself an outgrowth of the All-India Muslim League (see Muslim League), which was established in 1906. The Pakistan Muslim League was the governing party in East Pakistan until the provincial election of 1954 (See Elections), when it lost heavily to the United Front (q.v.). In the 1960s the Pakistan Muslim League broke into two factions: the Pakistan Muslim League (Convention) (q.v.) and the Council Muslim League (q.v.). After the independence of Bangladesh, both factions were banned. These two factions cooperated after the passing of the Political Parties Regulation Ordinance of 1976 and formed the Bangladesh Muslim League. In 1978 this party split into two factions. The more conservative group was led by Abdul Sobur Khan (q.v.) and the more liberal wing by Shah Azizur Rahman (q.v.). Azizur Rahman later joined the Bangladesh Nationalist Party (q.v.), and after Sobur's death the remainder of the party factionalized to the extent that it is all but nonexistent.

BANGLADESH NATIONALIST PARTY (BNP). Originally formed in 1978 as the political vehicle for the associates of the then president, Ziaur Rahman (q.v.). Zia had been elected in June 1978, as the candidate of JAGODAL (q.v.) (an acronym for the Bengali equivalent of "People's Party"). Besides JAGODAL, the party included elements from the leftist National Awami Party (q.v.), the conservative Bangladesh Muslim League (q.v.), and several other smaller parties and groups. The party supported the Nineteen-Point Program (q.v.). The titular leader of the party was Justice Abdus Sattar (q.v.), who succeeded Ziaur Rahman as president when the latter was assassinated in 1981. The BNP won more than two-thirds of the parliamentary seats in the 1979 elections (See Elections).

After Zia's assassination and the coup that ousted Sattar in 1982, the party has been led by Ziaur Rahman's widow, Khaleda Zia (q.v.). It boycotted the 1986 and 1988 parliamentary elections. Before and after the elections it saw many key members defect, usually to support President Hussain Muhammad Ershad (q.v.) and his Jatiya Party (q.v.). However, in November and December 1990, the BNP joined with the Awami League (q.v.) and other smaller groups to lead demonstrations against Ershad, which led to his fall in December and the installation of a caretaker government under Chief Justice Shahabuddin Ahmed (q.v.) that had as its primary charge the holding of elections. The BNP gained a majority in parliament through the February election and Khaleda Zia became prime minister on March 20, 1991. This parliament was dissolved in November 1995 (see Neutral Caretaker Government). In the election held in June 1996, the BNP finished second and will form the principal opposition to the governing Awami League.

BANGLADESH RURAL ADVANCEMENT COMMITTEE (BRAC). BRAC is a private sector development organization that has been operating in Bangladesh since 1972. BRAC implements a number of multisectoral programs to achieve its two major goals of poverty alleviation and empowerment of the poor. BRAC programs cover more than 35,000 villages benefitting more than one million people. BRAC's objectives are: (1) to make the program participants aware of their own problems; (2) to provide them with tools to unite into organized groups; and (3) to increase their capacity to exercise their legal and civic rights.

BARA BHUIYAN. Literally the "twelve landowners," the Bara Bhuiyan were a group of chieftains who resisted Mughal (q.v.) rule in the late sixteenth century. The principal leader was Isa Khan (q.v.), who controlled territory in Comilla, Dhaka, and Mymensingh districts from his base near Sonargaon (q.v.). Another key person among them was Pratapaditya (q.v.), whose lands were in the region of Khulna. In 1584 the Bara Bhuiyan led by Isa Khan inflicted a major naval defeat on the Mughals and followed with almost continuous land combat. In 1594 the Mughal emperor Akbar appointed Raja Man Singh (q.v.) governor of Bengal in the hope of controlling eastern Bengal. Another naval defeat in 1597 tempered that hope, but Isa Khan died in 1598. Man Singh established a military headquarters in Dhaka (q.v.) in 1602. By the time Man Singh retired as governor in 1606, the rebellion had been quelled.

BARISAL. A district and district town. The district was formerly part of Backerganj, which was divided into Barisal and Patuakhali in December 1969. Barisal town was the headquarters of Backerganj district. The area had formed a part of the kingdom of Vanga (q.v.) or Samatata (q.v.) in ancient times. In the sixteenth century, it was under one of the chieftains of the Bara Bhuiyan (q.v.); this chieftain had a marriage alliance with Pratapaditya (q.v.). The area was subject to raids by the Maghs of Arakan (q.v.) in the seventeenth and eighteenth centuries. It then passed into the hands of Agha Bakar, for whom the village of Backerganj is named. The Mughals established a fort, no longer standing, near Barisal to control the region. The British gained the district in 1765 when they obtained the diwani (q.v.) from the Mughal governor of Bengal.

Barisal is a river port, lying on a branch of the Arial Khan river, about 70 miles south of Dhaka and about 100 miles from the Bay of Bengal. Trade is largely in rice, jute, and fish. The city is also home to a curiosity, the "Barisal guns," an unexplained noise similar to cannon firing. It is the home of Fazlul Haq (q.v.). When the Ershad (q.v.) government made subdivisions districts, the former Barisal district was divided into Barisal, Jhalakati, and Pirojpur districts.

BARKATULLAH, MOHAMMAD (1889-1975). A member of the Indian Civil Service, he served in a number of positions but is best known for his role in organizing the Bangla Academy.

BASIC DEMOCRACY. The term used for local government during the Ayub Khan (q.v.) regime. Insofar as local government itself was concerned, it was not a radical change from previous systems. Local (union) councils of seven to fifteen members were elected by direct franchise, each member to represent about 1,000 persons. Parity (q.v.) was applied so that there were 40,000 basic democrats from each wing. Local duties included some powers of taxation, administration, adjudication, and development. Higher levels of government were also covered by the system at the *tehsil* (West Pakistan) and *thana* (East Pakistan) tiers and at the district level. The significant innovation by Ayub was that the 80,000 basic democrats would also serve as an electoral college for the presidency and the members of the national and provincial assemblies. This last aspect was strongly opposed by the Combined Opposition Parties (q.v.) and other opposition groups. These groups favored a system of direct elections at all levels of government (and, generally, also favored a parliamentary system).

BASIC PRINCIPLES REPORT. The working draft that culminated in the 1956 constitution of Pakistan (q.v.). The report was first published in 1950 and was criticized by the United Front (q.v.) because, among other things, of its proposition that Urdu be the national language of Pakistan (see Language Movement).

BAULS. A rustic group of troubadours who travel from one area to another singing devotional songs. They often use a one-string instrument (*ektara*) for their music. They practice a combination of Islam and Hinduism. They are also known for their long, braided hair, which is knotted.

BAYAZID BASTAMI. A Persian who was born in the ninth century and settled in Chittagong (q.v.). He was a preacher, and there are numerous myths and legends about him. He converted a large number of Hindus and Buddhists to Islam. Bayazid's tomb in Chittagong is an important pilgrimage site. The tomb is near a small pond that is known for its numerous large tortoises, suggesting that the site may have an older Hindu connection.

BAYAZID KARRANI. Son of Sulaiman Karrani (see Karrani dynasty), who was sultan of Bengal from 1562 to 1572. He succeeded his father, but soon lost Bengal to the Mughal Emperor Akbar in 1576.

BAYAZID SHAH. Titular ruler of Bengal, 1412-1414, who was overthrown by Raja Ganesh (q.v.).

BENGAL FAMINE (1943). The famine of 1943, at its height from July to December, is estimated to have caused between 1.5 and 3.5 million deaths. It is sometimes described as "man-made," although nature also played a part. There was a decline in food production in India and an increase in population. Imports to Bengal from the usual source, Burma, were unavailable owing to the Japanese conquest, and, at the same time, the British feared a major invasion of India and prepared to deny food to the potential invaders by a scorched- earth policy in eastern Bengal. The governments of Bengal and India had failed to anticipate and prepare for the replacement of the imports and failed in the distribution of what was available.

BENGAL, PARTITION OF (1905). The then viceroy, Lord Curzon (q.v.), determined that the province of Bengal (which then included approximately the present territory of Bangladesh and the Indian states of West Bengal, Bihar, and Orissa) was too large to be administered efficiently. Curzon decreed a partition in 1905. One new province, named Eastern Bengal and Assam, joined roughly what is Bangladesh today with the area north and northeast of it. It had a Muslim majority. The capital was Dhaka. The other province was named Bengal, and included western Bengal, Bihar, and Orissa. It had a Hindu majority, but the Bengalis were no longer the majority group, being outnumbered by the combined Biharis and Oriyas. The capital was Calcutta. Bengali Hindus objected strongly to the partition, and this was expressed through writing, speeches, demonstrations, boycotts of British goods, violence, and terrorism. Bengali Muslims were, expectedly, pleased with the prospect of a province in which they would be a majority, especially as new constitutional reforms (the Government of India Act of 1909 [q.v.] was already under discussion) by the British were expected to include provincial elections. The British finally heeded the Hindu objections, and the partition was annulled in 1911. Bengal was reunited, Assam separated, and Bihar and Orissa joined in a single province (they were separated in 1936). Accompanying the annulment was the British decision to transfer the capital of India from Calcutta to New Delhi.

BENGAL, PARTITION OF (1947). The partition of India in 1947 also required the partition of two provinces: the Punjab and Bengal. A commission headed by a British judge, Sir Cyril (later Lord) Radcliffe, was charged with the task of determining the boundaries. The basic rule was that contiguous areas with Muslim majorities would go to Pakistan. Some leeway was permitted in the decision. In dividing Bengal, the commission decided that Khulna (q.v.) district, despite its Hindu majority, would go to Pakistan, and Murshidabad (q.v.) district, despite its Muslim majority, would go to India. One reason for this decision was that West Bengal would have been split into two parts if a connecting area in Murshidabad were not given to India. Some other districts, e.g., Malda and Dinajpur (q.v.), were divided between the two countries. The Sylhet Referendum (q.v.) was also held to decide the boundary between East Bengal and Assam.

BENGAL TENANCY ACT (1885). The act was intended to provide security to tenants of the landlords in that the right of occupancy and inheritance was given to the tenants. Tenants who held land in the same village could not be evicted. It also limited rent paid by an "occupancy" tenant to one-fifth of the produce. While intended to provide security to the tenants, the act was a complicated one which gave landlords the opportunity to contest matters in the courts, a path that was not available to the almost destitute tenants.

BENGALI. See LANGUAGE.

BERUBARI ENCLAVE. A small piece of territory that was awarded to East Bengal in the partition of 1947 (see Bengal, Partition of [1947]) but is surrounded by Indian territory. Pakistan (and later, Bangladesh) and India have been unable to sort out the question of pieces of territory in north Bengal. The enclaves result primarily from the exclaves of the former princely state of Cooch Behar (q.v.). A portion of the disputed territory, Tin Bigha (literally, three *bighas* or one acre), was transferred by India to Bangladesh in 1992.

BHADRALOK. Literally, means respected people or gentlemen. They are socially privileged, educated members of society who had distinct speech, dress, housing, and eating habits. The bhadralok abstained from manual labor. The term is infrequently used in Bangladesh, as it is linked primarily to the Hindu caste system.

BHASHANI, MAULANA ABDUL HAMID KHAN (1885-1976). A leader of the Muslim League (q.v.) in Assam before independence, although originally from Tangail district of eastern Bengal. He returned to East Bengal after independence and became a founding member of the Awami League (q.v.) in 1949 and president of the East Bengal provincial unit of the party. Although holding the Islamic title "maulana," Bhashani was often viewed as being on the left in politics, espousing the cause of the peasantry against the holders of power in the villages and, in international affairs, opposing the West and favoring closer ties with China, a product, as he saw it, of a peasant revolution. It was principally over international issues that

Bhashani broke with Husain Shahid Suhrawardy (q.v.) in 1956, when Suhrawardy supported Pakistan's growing ties with the United States. Bhashani and his associates from the Awami League formed the National Awami Party (q.v.) in 1957, bringing his East Pakistani group into association with the Pakistan National Party of West Pakistan. In East Pakistan and in national politics Bhashani continued to play a prominent role in opposition (except on Ayub Khan's policy of opening relations with China) until his death. Bhashani opposed Mujibur Rahman (q.v.), most notably when he led protests against the India-Bangladesh treaty (q.v.) in 1972 and against Farraka barrage (q.v.).

BHUTTO, ZULFIQAR ALI (1928-1979). A member of a prominent Sindhi family, began his political career when he was appointed a minister in the first cabinet of Ayub Khan (q.v.) in 1958. He was foreign minister, 1963-1966. Resigning from the cabinet over differences with Ayub Khan on relations with India, he founded the Pakistan People's Party (PPP) in 1967 and remained its chairman until his death. The PPP won the majority of seats from West Pakistan in the National Assembly elected in December 1970, but won none in East Pakistan. In the negotiations following the election, Bhutto maintained that there were two majorities in Pakistan: his in West Pakistan and that of the Awami League (q.v.) led by Mujibur Rahman (q.v.) in East Pakistan. His actions, along with those of President Yahya Khan (q.v.), are credited with bringing about the impasse that led to the breakdown of negotiations and the outbreak of civil war in March 1971. With the defeat of the Pakistani forces in December 1971, Yahya Khan resigned and turned the government over to Bhutto and the PPP. Bhutto was president of Pakistan, 1971-1973, and, after a new constitution was adopted, prime minister, 1973-1977. He was overthrown in a coup led by General Muhammad Zia ul-Haq on July 5, 1977. Charged with complicity in a murder, Bhutto was convicted and hanged on April 4, 1979.

BIHARIS. The term used to describe those Muslim refugees principally from Bihar who fled eastward to East Bengal in 1947. The group is Urdu-speaking and found it difficult to integrate with the Bengali-speakers in whose midst they found themselves. The term may also be derived from *baharis* (Urdu for "outsiders"). Generally, they were and remained strong supporters of the Pakistan idea and many supported the Pakistan army in 1971. There were about 600,000 Biharis at that time. After independence, they were often shunned by Bangladeshis, and their plight made international news. Since then, many have gone to Pakistan, legally or illegally; a large number, perhaps 300,000, remain in camps, and many younger Biharis have integrated into Bangladeshi society.

BISWAS, ABDUL LATIF (1892-1964). A leader of the Krishak Praja Party, was the secretary of the Krishak Sramik Party (q.v.). Between 1926 and 1945 he was a member of the Bengal Legislative Council and the Bengal Legislative Assembly. In 1954, Biswas was the minister of land revenue in the United Front (q.v.) government and became the central minister for food and agriculture in 1955. At his death he was a member of the National Democratic Front in opposition to Ayub Khan (q.v.).

BISWAS, ABDUR RAHMAN (b. 1926). President of Bangladesh since October 8, 1991. He was a member of the cabinet of Ziaur Rahman (q.v.), holding at various times the portfolios of jute, and health and population control. After the February 1991 election, he became Speaker of parliament. Biswas was elected president after the parliament adopted an amendment to the constitution changing the governmental system from a presidential to a parliamentary one.

BLACK HOLE. The name of a small room in old Fort William (q.v.) in Calcutta (q.v.) in which 146 British prisoners were allegedly kept in captivity by Nawab Sirajuddaulah (q.v.) after his capture of Calcutta on June 20, 1756. It is also stated that 123 prisoners died of suffocation. There is some question about the numbers involved. Other accounts have it that there were 64 prisoners of whom 43 died.

BOGRA. District and district town on the banks of the Karatoya river, a branch of the Ganges. The river divides the district into two distinct geological zones: to the east is the alluvial soil typical of deltaic areas; to the west there is the heavier clay of the Barind region (the name is derived from Birendra or Varendra [q.v.]). The river at one time formed the boundary between the Assamese kingdom of Kamarupa and the area of Pundra (q.v.). It then came under the rule of the Palas (q.v.) and later the Senas (q.v.), before being taken by the Delhi Sultanate (q.v.). Nearby Bogra city is the archaeological site of Mahasthangarh (q.v.). The upgrading of sub-divisions in the Ershad (q.v.) regime has resulted in the division of the former Bogra district into Bogra and Sherpur districts. Sherpur town was a Mughal outpost under Raja Man Singh (q.v.).

BOGRA, MUHAMMAD ALI (1901-1963). A member of a leading landowning family in eastern Bengal, he was a grandson of Syed Nawab Ali Choudhury (q.v.). He was elected to the Bengal Legislative Assembly in 1937 and 1946 and was appointed a parliamentary secretary in the Nazimuddin (q.v.) government in 1943 and a minister in the Suhrawardy (q.v.) cabinet in 1946. After independence, he held high diplomatic posts (although retaining his membership of the constituent assembly): ambassador to Burma in 1948; high commissioner to Canada in

1949; and ambassador to the United States in 1952. Bogra was summoned back from the latter post to become prime minister in 1953, following the dismissal of Nazimuddin from that post by Governor-General Ghulam Muhammad (q.v.). His first cabinet was political, but he reorganized the cabinet in 1954 to form a "cabinet of talents," including, among others, General Ayub Khan (q.v.) as minister of defense. Bogra was dismissed in 1955 and returned to the United States as ambassador, 1955-1958. Inactive in the first part of Ayub's regime, Bogra became minister of foreign affairs in 1962, holding the post until his death, when he was succeeded by Zulfiqar Ali Bhutto (q.v.).

BOGRA MUTINY. One of the more significant coup attempts during the regime of President Ziaur Rahman (q.v.). An army tank regiment in Bogra attempted to seize the local air force base in order to negotiate the freedom of Lieutenant Colonel Farook Rahman, who was one of the majors who had led the first army coup in Bangladesh that led to the assassination of Sheikh Mujibur Rahman (q.v.). The Bogra mutiny started on September 30, 1977, and spread to Dhaka on October 2, 1977. The Dhaka phase of the coup attempt coincided with the hijacking of a Japan Airlines aircraft by the Japanese Red Army. The aircraft landed at Dhaka airport. The Dhaka phase of the coup, staged largely by air force personnel against senior air force officers who were at the airport directing Bangladeshi actions against the hijackers, led to eleven air force officers being killed. As a result of the coup attempt a large number of military personnel were executed. Amnesty International protested the summary execution.

BOSE, SIR JAGADISH CHANDRA (1858-1937). Born in Dhaka district, he was educated in Calcutta and at Cambridge. He was noted for his work in both physics and plant physiology, publishing widely in both fields. He taught at Calcutta University and founded the Bose Research Institute in Calcutta. In physics, Bose worked primarily in the field of electrical radiation. In 1994, Bose was honored by Bangladesh by the establishment of a museum in his home village of Rarikhal.

BOSE, SUBHAS CHANDRA (1897-1945). A Bengali political leader who earned from his followers that very title: *Netaji*, which means leader. He passed the examination for the Indian Civil Service, but resigned almost as soon as he had joined in 1921 and became active in the Indian National Congress. He worked with Chittaranjan Das (q.v.) and with Gandhi, but was often to the left of the important leaders of the Congress. Nonetheless, he became president of the Congress in 1938 and was reelected in 1939. Opposition from Gandhi and others forced Bose to resign before completing his second term. He did not agree with Gandhi's concept of the renunciation of violence. Frequently jailed, Bose was able to escape India in January 1941 and made his way to

Afghanistan and eventually to Germany. In 1943, he was transported by a German submarine to Singapore and began to organize a fraction of the Indian prisoners of war held by the Japanese into the Indian National Army to fight alongside the Japanese against Britain, principally in Burma. Bose proclaimed the Provisional Government of India. With Japan's defeat, Bose flew from Singapore to Japan, but the aircraft crashed and he was killed in Taiwan.

BRAHMAPALA. Founder of the Pala dynasty in Kamarupa (Assam) about 1000 A.D. This dynasty is not to be confused with the almost contemporaneous Pala dynasty (q.v.) in Bengal. The Kamarupa Pala dynasty ended in the first half of the twelfth century.

BRAHMAPUTRA. The river of about 1800 miles' length that rises in Tibet (as the Tsangpo), flows through Assam as the Brahmaputra, and enters Bangladesh, where it is known as the Jamuna. Along its way, it picks up a number of tributaries in Tibet, Arunachal Pradesh, and Assam. Among its tributaries in Bangladesh is the Tista (q.v.). It joins the Ganges (q.v.) at Goalundo and these two rivers join the Meghna near Chandpur to flow to the Bay of Bengal. Until the end of the eighteenth century, the Brahmaputra flowed through the center of Mymensingh district (q.v.) to join the Ganges near Bhairab Bazaar. But early in the nineteenth century this route silted up, and the river migrated westward so that it now forms the western boundary of Mymensingh district. The river drains an area of about 360,000 square miles. At high flood its flow is estimated at 500,000 cubic feet per second. During less heavy flow, the river and its tributaries form an essential part of Bangladesh's water transportation system; the river is navigable into Assam.

BUDDHISM. The small Buddhist population in Bangladesh is concentrated in the Chittagong Hill Tracts (q.v.) or is made up of migrants from the hills. The 1981 census enumerated 538,000 Buddhists, of whom 73.2 percent lived in the Hill Tracts and 23.0 percent in the neighboring Chittagong region. These Buddhists are almost invariably members of one of the tribal groups (see Tribes) residing in the area. There are no restrictions on employment, private or public, placed on Buddhists, and their principal holidays are national or regional holidays.

This small remnant, however, obscures the historical impact of Buddhism in Bengal. The religion was presumably brought to Bengal by the Mauryas (q.v.) in the third century B.C. It flourished under the Pala dynasty (q.v.) (about 750-1155 A.D.), as for much of that period it was the equivalent of a state religion. The Sena dynasty (q.v.), which overcame the Palas in the middle of the twelfth century and ruled parts of Bengal until about the middle of the thirteenth century, attempted to reinstate

Brahmanism in Bengal. The importance of noncaste Buddhism is seen as a factor in the rapid conversion of much of eastern Bengal to Islam when the Muslims arrived. The period has left many of the monuments that travelers wish to see (see Architecture).

BULBUL CHOUDHURY (1919-1954). A renowned dancer and writer. His real name was Rashid Ahmad Choudhury. He first achieved prominence because of his work in one of Tagore's (q.v.) dance dramas. In 1937, he founded the Oriental Fine Arts Association in Calcutta and made original contributions to understanding and propounding fine arts. During the period of 1943-1948, Bulbul joined the civil service and worked as a public information officer in the Ministry of Information. In 1948 he resigned from the service and founded his own dance group. In 1950, Bulbul moved to Dhaka from Calcutta. Between 1950 and 1952 he visited a number of European countries, performing with his dance group. In 1955 he established the Bulbul Academy of Fine Arts, which continues to be a major center of fine arts in the country. He also wrote several plays.

BURMA. Now called Myanmar, Burma is the only country other than India (q.v.) to share a border with Bangladesh. The border was undemarcated prior to 1985, when an agreement was reached between the two countries. Relations between them have been at least correct and generally cordial with the exception of an interlude in 1976. At that time a substantial number (estimated variously at 100,000) of Muslims from the Arakan (q.v.) region of Burma known as Rohingyas fled into Bangladesh, apparently as a result of the application of a new citizenship law in Burma that would have left the Arakanese Muslims in a legally subordinate position. Negotiations between the two countries resulted in the return of the refugees to Burma and the restoration of cordial relations. However, in the late 1980s, there was another influx of Rohingyas and a deterioration of relations between Bangladesh and Burma (by then officially Myanmar). Some of the refugees have returned to Myanmar, but many remain in camps in Bangladesh and are unsure of the conditions they would find were they to return to Myanmar.

BUXAR, BATTLE OF. Although the battle took place in Bihar, it had a major impact on British control of Bengal. On October 22, 1764, British forces faced the combined forces of Mughal Emperor Shah Alam II and the Bengalis under Mir Qasim (q.v.) and Nawab of Oudh. The British, although severely outnumbered, won. The victory confirmed that the British were rulers of Bengal and that the Mughal emperor would become a puppet.

-C-

CABINET MISSION PLAN. Proposed by a three-member team of the British cabinet that visited India in 1946. Although not the leader, Sir Stafford Cripps was the most prominent member. The plan called for a three-tier government for a united India in which the powers of the federal (central) government would be limited to foreign affairs, defense, currency, and communications. All other powers would devolve to the provinces. The provinces would be grouped into three zones: (1) Bengal and Assam (Muslim majority); (2) the Punjab, the Northwest Frontier Province, Sindh, and Balochistan (Muslim majority); and (3) the other provinces (Hindu majority). The provinces could delegate upward such powers as they chose to the zonal groupings. A possible example might have been inland waterways in Group One, Assam and Bengal. Minority rights would be guaranteed. The Muslim League (q.v.) accepted the plan. The Congress accepted with such reservations that it was taken by the League to be a rejection. The plan was therefore discarded.

CALCUTTA. Calcutta was founded in 1690 by the British East India Company on the bank of the navigable Hooghly River to serve as a trading station. It became the capital of the Bengal presidency in 1700, being called Fort William (q.v.). It was captured by the nawab (Mughal governor) of Bengal, Sirajuddaulah (q.v.), in 1756, but retaken by the British in 1757 (see Alingarh, Treaty of). In 1773, the British governor of Bengal, Warren Hastings (q.v.), was named governor-general of the company's territories in India, making the governors of Madras and Bombay subordinate to the governor-general in Calcutta. Calcutta remained the capital of British India until 1911, when the seat of the viceroy/governor-general was moved to New Delhi. Calcutta was the capital of Bengal (including other territories at various times and excluding Eastern Bengal and Assam [q.v.] during the period that it was a separate province) until 1947, when India was partitioned and the city became the capital of the Indian state of West Bengal. Long the principal commercial and industrial center of India, it has been eclipsed by Bombay. Nonetheless, it remains a city of highest importance in commerce and industry and in the arts and culture. Its university, founded in 1857, was a magnet for students from all parts of Bengal, even after the founding of Dhaka University in 1921.

CAREY, WILLIAM (1761-1834). A shoemaker by trade originally, he came to Srirampur, in Danish territory near Calcutta, in 1793 as a Baptist missionary. While preaching Christianity, he also studied languages and produced the first translation of the Bible into Bengali. Carey also wrote prose in Bengali of such quality that one writer has called him "the father of Bengali prose." In

1801 he became professor of Sanskrit and Bengali at Fort William College, a post he held until his death. (See also John Marshman and James Keith.)

CASTE. Caste is the hereditary and hierarchical division of society in Hinduism (q.v.). The term is also used loosely in Islam in the subcontinent despite Islam's being an egalitarian religion. Probably a holdover from the pre-Islamic period, caste as used by Muslims is often important in status assignments and in such rites as marriage, especially in rural areas.

CHAITANYA (1486-1533). A Brahmin who popularized Vaishnavism, specifically the Krishna cult, in Bengal. An excellent Sanskrit scholar, he left his family at the age of twenty-four, and took up the life of a *sannyasin* (a wandering mendicant). He emphasized the role of love and devotion *(bhakti)*, that is, a personal relationship between man and god. Chaitanya preached to all castes and religions, and the hymns (*kirtans*) that he wrote remain an important part of the Bengali heritage.

CHANDERNAGORE. See FRENCH EAST INDIA COMPANY.

CHANDRA DYNASTY. Local chieftains in eastern Bengal who assumed control in the area after the decline of the rulers of Harikela (q.v.) during the tenth century. The headquarters of the dynasty appear to have been at Karmanta (q.v.), near Comilla, and at Vikrampur (q.v.), near Dhaka. The dynasty seems to have ended during the latter part of the eleventh century, when there was a period of Pala (q.v.) rule, followed by the establishment of the Varman dynasty (q.v.)

CHATTERJI, BANKIM CHANDRA (1838-1894). Bengali novelist, who was also in government service. His works were viewed as anti-Muslim by Muslims, especially his best known novel *Anandamath*. Chatterji also wrote the nationalist song "Bande Mataram," also seen as opposed to the Muslims. Nonetheless, he is considered the greatest novelist in Bengali of the nineteenth century.

CHINA. Initially, relations between China and Bangladesh did not exist on a formal basis, as China supported the Pakistani position that Bangladesh was an illegal creation. China exercised its veto in the Security Council to exclude Bangladesh from membership in the United Nations. The recognition of Bangladesh by Pakistan through the good offices of members of the Organization of the Islamic Conference (q.v.) rendered the Chinese position null. China and Bangladesh established diplomatic relations in 1976, following the assumption of power by Ziaur Rahman (q.v.). Relationships have grown. There have been a number of high-level visits, China has provided limited military and economic assistance, and, to a degree, trade has been developed. A contributing factor, no doubt, has been the cooling of relations with India (q.v.).

CHINSURA. Established in 1653 by the Dutch East India Company (q.v.) as a trading station. A Dutch challenge to the British East India Company was fought off by the British in 1769. The town remained in Dutch hands until 1825, when in came under British control in return for British cession of territories in Sumatra.

CHITTAGONG. (Also known in history as Chattagram, Chatgaon, and Chatigana.) The leading seaport of Bangladesh at the mouth of the Karnaphuli River and the country's second largest city. It is also the seat of the second oldest university, after Dhaka, in present Bangladesh.

It was known to the West in the early centuries of the Christian era and was used by Arab traders as early as the tenth century. Chittagong had been a part of the Hindu kingdom of Tripura (now reduced to a state in India), which also ruled much of the districts of Comilla (q.v.) and Noakhali (q.v.). It was conquered by the Buddhist king of Arakan (q.v.) in the ninth century and by the Muslims in the thirteenth century, but came again under the control of Arakan (q.v.) in the sixteenth century. The district was ceded to the Mughal empire by the king of Arakan in 1666 after the Mughals defeated the Arakanese. Much involved in the struggle between Arakan and the Mughals were the Portuguese (q.v.), who first arrived in 1538. They were traders, missionaries, and, eventually, pirates who raided along the coast as far west as Barisal and beyond, sometimes in cooperation with and sometimes against the Arakanese (or Maghs). The district was ceded to the British by Mir Qasim (q.v.) in 1760. When Arakan was captured by the Burmese in 1784, many Arakanese fled to Chittagong and comprise the Buddhist Magh community today.

Chittagong city contains a number of shrines, such as that of Bayazid Bastami (q.v.), and of Hazrat Bader Aulia. There are also Buddhist and Hindu temples of architectural note, and there are a number of Muslim shrines in Maizbhandar, about twenty five miles from Chittagong. Nearby is the industrial town of Kalurghat, developed by Abul Kasem Khan (q.v.). Cox's Bazaar in the south of the district, with its excellent beach, has the potential to be developed as a tourist site. With the reorganization of local government (q.v.) under Ershad (q.v.), Cox's Bazaar has become a separate district.

CHITTAGONG HILL TRACTS. Located in the southeast corner of Bangladesh and bordering on both India and Burma, it lies between Chittagong (q.v.) district and the Lushai hills of India. The area was set aside by the British as an area for tribal groups, including such tribes as the Chakmas and Maghs. About 75 percent of the population is Buddhist. Under the British, land ownership in the region was not permitted to nontribals. Since independence there has been some influx of plains people to the Hill Tracts. This has been opposed, often violently, by the tribals, and a low level of guerrilla warfare has been endemic to the region. Some land was lost to the tribals through the building of the Karnaphuli hydroelectric station and the ponding of water behind the dam. The Hill Tracts district has now been divided into three districts: Rangamati, Bandarban, and Khagrachari.

CHOUDHURY, A. K. M. FAZLUL QADER (1919-1973). A lawyer by profession, he served the Muslim League in numerous capacities after joining the party in 1938. He was the general secretary of the All-India Muslim Student Federation. He was an elected member of the East Bengal Legislative Assembly in 1954 and a member of the National Assembly of Pakistan in 1962. A member of the Ayub (q.v.) cabinet in 1962, Fazlul Qader later was Speaker of the National Assembly, 1963-1966. During the movement to oust President Ayub he remained loyal and was the president of Pakistan Muslim League (Convention) (q.v.). Fazlul Qader opposed the liberation of Bangladesh, and for his association with the Razakar Bahini (q.v.) and the Peace Committees (q.v.), he was arrested after the liberation of Bangladesh. He died while he was in jail.

CHOUDHURY, ABDUR RAHMAN (1926-1994). Lawyer and Supreme Court Justice. He was born and educated in Dhaka. He was actively involved in the language movement (q.v.). He was the first Bengali to be elected general secretary of the Pakistan Bar Council. Choudhury was a justice of the Supreme Court of Bangladesh, 1978-1983, and later chairman of the Bangla Academy.

CHOUDHURY, BADRUDDOZA (b. 1932). From Mymensingh, he trained as a physician but has been active in politics in the Bangladesh Nationalist Party (BNP) (q.v.) since it was formed after Ziaur Rahman's (q.v.) assumption of the presidency. He has served in the cabinets of Ziaur Rahman and Abdus Sattar (q.v.) and in 1995 was the deputy leader of the BNP group in Parliament.

CHOUDHURY, HAMIDUL HAQ (1903-1992). A lawyer, political figure, and newspaper owner (of the former *Pakistan Observer*, now *Bangladesh Observer*, published in Dhaka). He was elected to the Bengal Legislative Council in 1937 and to the Legislative Assembly in 1946, serving as a minister in the Nurul Amin (q.v.) cabinet until 1949, when he faced proceedings under the Public and Representative Offices Disqualification Act (PRODA) and was disqualified from holding office. Hamidul Haq was also elected a member of the constituent assembly in 1946 and, despite disqualification, in 1955. He was foreign minister in 1955 in the cabinet of Chaudhury Muhammad Ali and again in the cabinet of Firoz Khan Noon (q.v.) in 1958. He was banned from politics for seven years under Ayub Khan (q.v.), but, his disqualification having ended, Hamidul Haq was a member of the Democratic Action Committee (q.v.) opposing Ayub in 1969. He opposed the separation of East Pakistan and remained for several years in Karachi, but later returned to Dhaka and had his properties, including the newspaper, restored to him.

CHOUDHURY, MOAZZAM HUSSAIN (LAL MIA) (1905-1967). From Faridpur, he studied at Aligarh Muslim University and was central minister for health, labor, and social welfare in 1965. Prior to that he was the chief whip of the Muslim League (q.v.) and member of the National Assembly of Pakistan. Earlier, Lal Mia participated in the noncooperation movement and the Khilafat movement (q.v.) (both in the early 1920s) and was jailed by the British. He joined the Muslim League in 1943. He was also a poet and published two books of poems. He changed his name later to Abdullah Zahiruddin, but was known by the nickname Lal Mia. He was the brother of Yusuf Ali Choudhury (q.v.).

CHOUDHURY, MUNIR (1925-1971). Obtained a master's degree in linguistics from Harvard University. He was fluent in English and Bengali and was a faculty member in both Dhaka and Rajshahi Universities. In 1943 he formed the Writers Association. He joined the Communist Party in Calcutta in 1948. Choudhury actively participated in the language movement (q.v.) to make Bengali one of the national languages of Pakistan and was jailed several times between 1952 and 1955. Some of his major works were written while he was in jail, including the play "Kobor" ("Grave"). He received a number of awards, including the *Sitara-i-Imtiaz* in 1966 which he renounced in 1971. Choudhury also developed the Bengali typewriter. He was one of the intellectuals who was murdered by the Pakistani forces between December 11 and 14, 1971, just prior to the surrender of the Pakistan army.

CHOUDHURY, SHAMSUL HUDA (b. 1920). From Mymensingh he was educated at Calcutta and Aligarh Muslim University. He spent his career in broadcasting, until he was appointed by Ziaur Rahman (q.v.) as minister of information and broadcasting. Shamsul Huda later served as Speaker of the parliament elected in 1988.

CHOUDHURY, SYED NAWAB ALI (1863-1929). A prominent zamindar from Mymensingh, he was part of the delegation that met the viceroy, Lord Minto, at Simla to demand separate electorates (q.v.) for Muslims and one of the founders of the Muslim League (q.v.). Nawab Ali was a nominated member of the East Bengal and Assam Legislative Council, 1906-1911; an elected member of the Bengal Legislative Council, 1912-1916 and again 1920-1929; and a member of the Governor-General's Legislative Council, 1916-1920. Nawab Ali was the first Muslim to be named a minister in Bengal in 1921. His grandson, Muhammad Ali Bogra (q.v.), was prime minister of Pakistan.

CHOUDHURY, YUSUF ALI (MOHAN MIA) (1905-1971). A provincial minister in the United Front (q.v.) government. He started his political life as a member of the Faridpur Municipality and later became the chairman of the Faridpur District Council. He was also a member of the Bengal Legislative Assembly before 1947. Mohan Mia was an active member of the Muslim League (q.v.), serving as the chairman of the Faridpur district Muslim League and in 1952 becoming the president of the East Pakistan Muslim League. He was ousted from the Muslim League in 1953. He then joined the Krishak Sramik Party (q.v.) of A. K. Fazlul Haq (q.v.) and became its general secretary in 1957. In the 1960s, Mohan Mia joined the National Democratic Front and was a member of the National Democratic Movement, which was formed to oust the government of Ayub Khan (q.v.). He became a member of a faction of the Muslim League once again in 1969. Mohan Mia was opposed to the freedom movement of Bangladesh. He started a charity organization called the Khademul Islam (Servants of Islam) and the paper *Daily Millat*. He was the brother of Moazzam Hussain Choudhury (Lal Mia) (q.v.).

CHOUDHURY, ZAHUR AHMED (1916-1974). Joined the Awami League in 1949 and served as its labor secretary in 1957. He was elected to the Bengal Provincial Assembly in 1954, to the East Pakistan Provincial Assembly in 1970, and to the National Assembly of Bangladesh in 1973. According to the Awami League version of the declaration of independence of Bangladesh, Zahur Ahmed Choudhury carried the declaration from Sheikh Mujibur Rahman (q.v.) and gave it to Ziaur Rahman (q.v.) to be announced over Chittagong radio on March 25, 1971. Instead, according to this version, Zia made the announcement but also declared himself acting president of Bangladesh.

CHOWDHURANI, FAIZUNNESSA (1834-1903). Although a woman, she was awarded the title "Nawab" by Queen Victoria for her work in improving the lot of women and the poor. She established the Faizunnessa Girls School in Comilla in 1873, and the Faizunnessa Women's Hospital in 1893.

CHOWDHURY, ABU SAYEED (1921-1987). President of Bangladesh, January 1972-December 1973. Earlier he had been a justice of the Dhaka High Court and a vice-chancellor of Dhaka University. Out of Pakistan, attending a meeting of the UN Commission on Human Rights in March 1971, Abu Sayeed Chowdhury was able to play a key role as a roving ambassador in Europe and the United States on behalf of emerging Bangladesh. He was briefly foreign minister in 1975, but thereafter remained out of politics.

CHOWDHURY, ABUL FAZAL MOHAMMAD AHSANUDDIN (b. 1915). Appointed president of Bangladesh by Hussain Muhammad Ershad (q.v.) in March 1982. He resigned the office in December 1984, when Ershad himself assumed the presidency. Earlier he had been a jurist, retiring from the Supreme Court in 1977.

CHOWDHURY, ANWARA BAHAR (1918-1987). A leading figure in women's education, both before partition in Calcutta and after in Dhaka. She was a cofounder of the Bulbul Academy of Fine Arts (see Bulbul Choudhury) and also began schools in the dance and in music.

CHOWDHURY, MIZANUR RAHMAN (b. 1931). Prime minister of Bangladesh under President Ershad (q.v.), he was a member of the Pakistan National Assembly from 1962 to 1969. He was for a time the acting general secretary of the East Pakistan Awami League. During the movement to oust the regime of President Ayub Khan (q.v.), he was one of the organizers of the Combined Opposition Parties (q.v.). Mizanur Rahman was elected twice to the Bangladesh parliament, in 1970 and 1973, and served in the government of Sheikh Mujibur Rahman (q.v.) as a cabinet minister (1972-1973). After the assassination of Sheikh Mujibur Rahman, Mizanur Rahman split with the main body of the Awami League and headed his own faction of the League in opposition to that of Abdul Malik Ukil (q.v.). He joined President Ershad's (q.v.) party, the Jatiya Dal (q.v.), in 1983 and was named prime minister in 1986. Mizanur Rahman was replaced by Moudud Ahmed (q.v.) in March 1988. He remains a key person in the Jatiya Party and has been acting chairman while Ershad has been in jail.

CHOWDHURY, MUHAMMAD YAKUB ALI (1888-1940). Writer and journalist. He was born in Faridpur and studied in Calcutta, after which he became a schoolteacher. He was jailed for his activities in the Khilafat movement (q.v.). He then took up journalism in Calcutta and was the editor of the monthly literary journal *Kohinoor*.

CHOWDHURY, MUZAFFAR AHMED (1923-1978). Born in Noakhali, he was educated at Dhaka and the London School of Economics. He taught at the University of Dhaka and served as a constitutional adviser to the Government of Pakistan, 1955-1956. During the civil war he served as the head of the planning cell for the government-in-exile in Mujibnagar (Calcutta) and later was the first post-independence vice chancellor of the University of Dhaka. Muzaffar Ahmed later was minister of education in the Mujibur Rahman (q.v.) and Mushtaque Ahmed (q.v.) governments. He was a theorist for the Awami League (q.v.) and the author of a number of works on politics and administration in Pakistan and East Pakistan.

CHRISTIANITY. The Christian community was enumerated in the 1981 census as 275,000, with the largest concentrations in Mymensingh (45,000), Dhaka (44,000), and Khulna (35,000) regions. The Christians in Mymensingh are principally members of tribal groups, such as the Garos, whose main center of population is in the Indian state of Meghalaya to the north of Mymensingh. This group tends to be Protestant, most often Presbyterian. In the metropolitan areas of Dhaka, the Christians belong generally to two groups: Bengali converts and Eurasians (often described as "Anglo-Indians"). In each group Roman Catholicism predominates. Missionaries began to arrive in the seventeenth century and in British territory in the nineteenth century. The missions played and continue to play an important role in education and medical services. There is freedom to propagate religion, but donations from abroad to missions and missionaries are regulated by the government.

CLIMATE. Located on the Tropic of Cancer, Bangladesh has a semitropical climate. The seasons are a hot summer period from March to June; a warm, very humid monsoon period from June to September; a brief, dry, hot period from the end of the monsoon to mid-November; and a cooler, dry winter period from November to February.

There is a wide variation in rainfall, ranging in 1984 from 188 inches at a station in Sylhet region in the northeast to 60 inches at Ishurdi in the northwest. The weather system often includes violent storms, especially the cyclones that arise in the Bay of Bengal. A cyclone in 1970 is believed to have claimed as many as half a million lives and resulted in the postponement of the scheduled general election from October to December of that year and in the affected areas along the coast until January 1971. Damage occurs from the high winds and from the influx of water. For example, as far inland as Khulna the water rose by two feet in the 1970 cyclone. Independent Bangladesh has tried to meet the danger in two ways: the building of more solidly constructed homes, and the use of polders as in the Netherlands.

In 1988 and 1989 the region suffered the worst floods in its history; in 1988 more than 25,000,000 people were made homeless.

CLIVE, ROBERT (Baron Clive of Plassey, 1725-1774). The victor for the British at the Battle of Plassey (1757) and governor of Bengal (1765-1767). He had returned to England during 1760-1765, and was created Baron Clive. Disturbances in India, in which Mir Qasim (q.v.) was a major actor, caused the company to return Clive to Bengal as governor. Before Clive arrived, Mir Qasim and his allies, the Mughal emperor, Shah Alam II, and the nawab of Oudh, had been defeated at the battle of Buxar (1764) (q.v.). Clive's task then was to arrange a settlement, the most important part of which was the acquisition of the *diwani* (q.v.), that is, the right of revenue collection for Bengal, Bihar, and Orissa, which was granted by the Mughal emperor. Clive earlier had earned a reputation as an administrator and a military leader in Madras. Subjected to a parliamentary inquiry on his return to England, Clive eventually committed suicide.

COMBINED OPPOSITION PARTIES (COP). A term that has several meanings, but the one used most often is that for the group that opposed Ayub Khan in the 1960s. The group included the Council Muslim League (q.v.), the Jama'at-i-Islam (q.v.), the Nizam-i-Islam (q.v.), the Pakistan Democratic Party, and other smaller groups. The initial leader of the group was Khwaja Nazimuddin (q.v.). The COP supported the candidacy of Fatima Jinnah, sister of Muhammad Ali Jinnah (q.v.), in the 1965 election for the presidency. She lost to Ayub Khan (q.v.). The COP had ceased to function by 1968 and was superseded by the Pakistan Democratic Movement (q.v.).

COMILLA. A district and district town, about fifty miles southeast of Dhaka, located on the Gumti River. The district was formerly known as Tippera and was for a time ruled by the raja of Tippera (present spelling: Tripura, now a state in India).

The territory of Comilla and neighboring Noakhali (q.v.) are associated with the early region of Samatata (q.v.), which is mentioned in the inscription of Samudragupta (see Gupta dynasty). The region was known as Harikela (q.v.), perhaps a synonym for Vanga (q.v.), in the ninth century. It was ruled by the Chandras (q.v.), the Varmans (q.v.), the Senas (q.v.), and the Devas (q.v.) from the tenth to the thirteenth centuries. After that, the territory was under the rule of the raja of Tippera, who faced frequent Muslim raids until most of the area was incorporated into the Mughal province of Bengal in 1733. The present boundary with "hill" Tippera, the raja's territory, was set by the British. Noakhali was separated from Comilla in 1822.

Comilla city and its environs are important centers of archaeology, most notably nearby Mainamati (q.v.) in the Lalmai hills. A more recent site is that of the Satararatna temple. The city is also the seat of the Bangladesh Academy of Rural Development (q.v.). With the local government (q.v.) changes during the Ershad regime, Brahmanbaria and Chandpur have become districts. Chandpur is a major port on the Meghna River (q.v.).

COMMUNIST PARTY OF BANGLADESH. An outgrowth of the Communist Party of Pakistan, which itself is an outgrowth of the Communist Party of India. The Communist Party of Pakistan was established in 1948 but was banned in 1954. The party existed as an underground party until December 31, 1971, when it was given legal recognition by the new government of Bangladesh. Led by Moni Singh (q.v.), the party was "pro-Moscow" in its orientation and called for political and economic reforms in social institutions that could lead to the establishment of socialism. It cooperated with the Awami League but was banned by Ziaur Rahman (q.v.) during the early part of his regime. The Communist Party of Bangladesh was allowed to resume its legal existence in November 1978. Although sharply factionalized, the party won five seats in the 1991 parliamentary election.

CONSTITUTION OF BANGLADESH, 1972. The Bangladesh constitution adopted a parliamentary system of government with a ceremonial president and a governing prime minister and cabinet. It was modeled very much on the constitution of India (1950), but without the federal concepts, which were obviously not needed in the unitary Bangladeshi system. The constitution also enshrined the four pillars of *Mujibbad* (q.v.): nationalism, secularism, democracy, and socialism. The constitution was modified first in January 1975, when an amendment was passed transforming the system to a presidential one with Mujibur Rahman (q.v.) as president. It was changed again in June 1975, when provisions were made for a one-party state. Military rulers, including Ziaur Rahman (q.v.) and Hussain Muhammad Ershad (q.v.), have also made changes so that the Bangladeshi political system became one in which the president was the focus of power to whom the cabinet and the parliament are subordinate. After the election of 1991, the constitution was again amended to restore a parliamentary system of government with the prime mimister as the head of government and the president as head of state, a primarily ceremonial position.

CONSTITUTION OF PAKISTAN, 1956. Pakistan's first constitution was effective on March 23, 1956. Its adoption followed more than eight years of debate. It provided for a parliamentary system of government with a single house at the center and single-chamber provincial assemblies in East and West Pakistan. The system was said to be federal, but the bulk of the powers were given to the central government. A point of particular concern to the East Pakistanis was that of parity (q.v.). The constitution of 1956 was abrogated by the martial law decree of October 7, 1958. Elections were never held under this constitution.

CONSTITUTION OF PAKISTAN, 1962. The 1962 constitution of Pakistan was the second for the country. It was not passed by a constituent assembly but rather was promulgated by President Ayub Khan (q.v.) as his own "gift" to the nation. It provided for a strong presidential system with an indirectly elected national assembly. The president and the members of the national and provincial assemblies were to be elected by basic democrats (see Basic Democracy). Governors of the two provinces were appointed by the president and served according to his pleasure. The cabinet was also appointed by the president and was not responsible to the assembly. The parity (q.v.) system was continued so that East Pakistani votes counted for less than West Pakistani votes.

CONVENTION MUSLIM LEAGUE. See PAKISTAN MUSLIM LEAGUE (CONVENTION).

COOCH BEHAR. A princely state during British rule and now a district of West Bengal, it lies mainly in the valley of the Tista River (q.v.). The name is apparently derived from the name of a tribal group, the Koches. In the sixteenth century, the ruler, Nara Narayan (r. 1540-1584), extended the territory of the state over much of Assam and south into the present district of Rangpur in Bangladesh. The territory came under the control of the Mughals at the end of the sixteenth century and was recognized as a princely state by the British in 1772, when the British intervened on behalf of Cooch Behar in a conflict with the Bhutanese. After Indian independence, a problem arose between India and first Pakistan and then Bangladesh over exclaves of Cooch Behar (Indian territory) inside Pakistan/Bangladesh. (See Berubari Enclave.)

CORNWALLIS, CHARLES CORNWALLIS, FIRST MARQUESS (1738-1805). For Americans he is remembered as the commander of the British force that surrendered to Washington at Yorktown in 1781. His reputation in Britain was not tarnished and he served twice as governor-general of India, 1786-1793, and again in 1805. During his first term, Cornwallis introduced major reforms in the civil services of the East India Company that separated the governing role of the service from the private commercial activities of the company's officers. He also instituted the "Permanent Settlement" (q.v.) system for the lands in the Bengal presidency (province).

COSSIMBAZAR (KASIMBAZAR). Now an industrial suburb of Berhampur, the district headquarters of Murshidabad (q.v.) district in West Bengal, Cossimbazar was a major trading point in the seventeenth and eighteenth centuries owing to its proximity to Murshidabad. An English factory was established in 1658. The town was captured by Nawab Sirajuddaulah (q.v.) in

1757, but restored to British control after the battle of Plassey (q.v.) the same year. It has never fully recovered, mainly as the result of the westward shifting of the Bhagirathi River.

COUNCIL MUSLIM LEAGUE (CML). The name applied to a Muslim League group opposed to Ayub's Pakistan Muslim League (Convention) (q.v.). When parties were formed after the 1962 election, a group made up of members of the Muslim League (before parties were banned by Ayub in 1958) called a meeting of the council of the League (hence, the name of the new party). They revived the League through the revived council. Conversely, Ayub called a convention of Muslim Leaguers, bypassing the old council, to form his party. The CML became part of the Combined Opposition Parties (COP) (q.v.). Its first leader was Khwaja Nazimuddin (q.v.). After his death, the principal figure was Mian Mumtaz Muhammad Khan Daultana of the Punjab. The CML contested the 1970 election and won nine national assembly seats in West Pakistan but none in East Pakistan. It does not exist as such in either Pakistan or Bangladesh today.

CURZON OF KEDDLESTON, GEORGE NATHANIEL CURZON, FIRST MARQUESS (1859-1925). A British statesman, viceroy and governor-general of India, 1898-1905. Among his goals in India was the improvement, as he saw it, of the administrative system. One act taken in this direction in 1905 was the partitioning of the province (or presidency) of Bengal (see Bengal, Partition of [1905]). He also extended the railway and irrigation systems and established the first national police force. Curzon left India as the loser in a quarrel with Lord Kitchener, then commander-in-chief of the Indian army over control of the army. Curzon also made a major contribution to the preservation of Indian antiquities. His major post after leaving India was British secretary of state for foreign affairs, 1919-1924.

- D -

DACCA. See DHAKA.

DANISH EAST INDIA COMPANY. Founded in 1616, its first and only factory in Bengal was at Srirampur (Serampore), now a suburb of Calcutta, founded in 1755. The town was an operating base for many Christian missionaries, including William Carey (q.v.) and John Marshman (q.v.), when missionary activity was banned in the territory controlled by the British East India Company. The factory never prospered, and it was sold to the British company in 1845.

DAS, CHITTARANJAN (1870-1925). A noted lawyer and politician who went into full-time politics in 1920 to join Gandhi's noncooperation movement. In 1923, he was elected mayor of Calcutta, with Husain Shahid Suhrawardy (q.v.) as deputy mayor and Subhas Chandra Bose (q.v.) as chief executive officer. He became president of the Indian National Congress in 1922, but broke with Gandhi on the issue of boycotting elections. Das and some others, including Motilal Nehru, formed the Swaraj (Independence) Party with the goal of contesting elections and "noncooperating" from within the system created by the Government of India Act of 1919 (q.v.). The Swaraj Party won sufficient seats in the Bengal Legislative Council that it was able to prevent the formation of ministries in Bengal as stipulated in the act. Das attempted to solve the Muslim complaint that Muslims were denied a fair share of government jobs by signing the Das-Haq pact (q.v.) with Fazlul Haq (q.v.) in 1924. He was honored with the title *Deshbandhu* (friend of the country).

DAS, JIBANANDA (1899-1854). Poet. He was born in Barisal and studied in Calcutta. He was a college professor and a journalist. His poetry concentrated on urban themes and the vulnerability of urban life.

DAS-HAQ PACT. An agreement in 1923 between the principal Muslim political figure in Bengal, Fazlul Haq (q.v.), and the leader of the Swarajist faction of the Indian National Congress, Chittaranjan Das (q.v.). They agreed to limited cooperation to permit the system of dyarchy to work in the province and also to informal quotas to permit increased Muslim employment in government posts.

DASTIGAR, PURNENDU (1909-1971). A labor leader with a revolutionary background. He had been arrested by the British in 1930 for involvement in the Chittagong Armory raid. Dastigar organized labor, peasant, and student groups in Chittagong and was arrested again during the martial law of Ayub Khan (q.v.). He was a member of the East Pakistan Provincial Assembly, 1954-1958.

DAUD KHAN (r. 1572-1576). The successor of Sulaiman Karrani of the Afghan Karrani (q.v.) dynasty. He was the last ruler in this dynasty. When he succeeded his father in 1572, he claimed to be the independent ruler of Bengal. The Mughal emperor, Akbar, contested this and his armies began a campaign against Daud Khan in 1574, which ended in 1576 with the death of Daud Khan at the battle of Rajmahal and the full incorporation of Bengal into the Mughal empire (q.v.).

DELHI SULTANATE. The name applied to the Muslim kingdoms based in Delhi from 1206, when Turkish rulers first established a permanent base in India, to 1526, when the last dynasty was defeated in the battle of Panipat by the founder of the Mughal empire (q.v.), Babar. There were five dynasties: Slave (or Mamluk), (1206-1290), Khalji (1290-1320), Tughluq (1320-1413), Sayyid (1414-1451), and Lodhi (1451-1526). Before the setting up of the capital at Delhi, the Sena kingdom based in Nadia in Bengal fell in 1202 to a general of the Afghan sultanate based at Ghor. Bengal remained under at least the nominal control of Delhi until 1336, when Fakhruddin Mubarrak Shah (q.v.) rebelled against the Tughluq dynasty. In 1346, Bengal became independent and remained so for almost two centuries mainly under the Ilyas Shahi (q.v.) and Husain Shahi (q.v.) dynasties. In 1538, forces of the Mughal emperor Humayun conquered Bengal, which became dependent on Delhi once again, but as part of the successor empire to the Delhi sultanate, the Mughal empire (q.v.).

DEMOCRATIC ACTION COMMITTEE. Formed in January 1969, principally composed of the Awami League (q.v.), the National Awami Party (q.v.) of Wali Khan, and the Jama'at-i-Islami (q.v.). The Committee was set up to oppose the rule of President Ayub Khan (q.v.). Its purpose was the full and complete restoration of democracy in Pakistan. It issued an eight-point manifesto that included, among other points, the establishment of a federal parliamentary system of government, direct election by adult franchise, and the release of popular leaders such as Sheikh Mujibur Rahman (q.v.) and Zulfiqar Ali Bhutto (q.v.).

DEMOCRATIC LEAGUE. Organized by defectors from the Awami League in August 1976. This party was established after the enactment of the Political Parties Regulation Act by President Ziaur Rahman (q.v.). The party was headed by Khondakar Mushtaque Ahmed (q.v.) with the support of Mainul Hussain, who was the proprietor and managing editor of the *Ittefaq* newspaper (see Tofazzul Hussain). In mid-1977 the Democratic League split into two factions. Democratic League experienced a resurgence in 1980 after the release from jail of its leader, Mushtaque Ahmed. In 1983 the Democratic League organized a national united front composed of right-wing opposition parties. It has since faded from politics.

DEMOCRATIC PARTY. Formed in December 1980 by the members of National Awami Party (q.v.) led by Maulana Bhashani (q.v.), it was a dissident faction of the United People's Party and two other participants in the 1979 Democratic Front: the Jatiya Gana Makti Union and the Gono Front. The Democratic Party was organized by Mirza Nurul Huda (not the same person as listed in this dictionary), who subsequently joined the Bangladesh Nationalist Party (q.v.).

DEV, GOVINDRA CHANDRA (1907-1971). Educationist. He was born in Sylhet and studied in Calcutta. He remained with Dhaka

University after partition and published a number of works on philosophy. Dev was killed in the initial raid of the Pakistan army on Dhaka University.

DEVA DYNASTY. A dynasty that ruled in southeastern Bengal, probably in the latter part of the eighth century. Information about the dynasty comes from copper plates on which there is no decipherable dating. The dynasty is thought to have been preceded by that of the Khargas (q.v.) and succeeded by that of Harikela (q.v.).

DEVAPALA (r. c. 810-850). The third ruler of the Pala dynasty (q.v.), succeeding Dharmapala (q.v.), he extended the territories controlled by the Palas to their greatest extent during his rule. The domains stretch from Assam in the east to the borders of Kashmir in the west and from the foothills of the Himalaya in the north to the Vindhyas in the south. He was a patron of Buddhism and, particularly, of the university at Nalanda in Bihar.

DHAKA. The capital and largest city of Bangladesh is on the Buriganga River. It first became a capital in 1610 when the Mughals (q.v.) made it the headquarters of the province of Bengal, but it had earlier in 1574 become a military headquarters of the Mughals (q.v.) as a means to suppress the revolt of Isa Khan (q.v.). At that time it became the provincial capital it was renamed Jahangirnagar in honor of the then Mughal emperor. It remained the capital until Murshid Quli Khan (q.v.) moved the headquarters to Murshidabad (q.v.) in 1702. After that time and until the independence of Pakistan and India, it was a district headquarters, except for the period 1905 to 1911, when it was the capital of the short-lived province of Eastern Bengal and Assam (see Partition of Bengal, 1905). With Pakistani independence in 1947, it became the capital of East Bengal (q.v.) and East Pakistan (q.v.). With the independence of Bangladesh, it became the capital of the newly independent state.

The British established a branch factory in Dhaka to trade in the fine muslin and silks manufactured in Dhaka. The city thrived as a trading station and a river port, but the transfer of the capital, a series of famines, and the decreased demand for the hand-woven cloth caused a sharp decline in the city's prosperity in the eighteenth and nineteenth centuries. When it became the capital of East Bengal and Assam, the city began to grow again and became the second city of Bengal after Calcutta. The establishment of the University of Dhaka in 1921 added to its educational stature. Today, with a population of more than 6 million, it is the administrative, economic, and educational center of Bangladesh.

Dhaka preserves much architecture from its past including the Lalbagh Fort begun in 1678 by Azam Shah, a son of the Mughal emperor Aurangzeb. The most interesting building in the fort is the tomb of Bibi Pari, a grandniece of the Mughal Empress Nur Jahan. Other Mughal buildings include the Bara Katra (1664), the Chhota Katra (1663), and the Shia mosque, Hussaini Dalan (1642). Of Hindu temples, the most notable is that devoted to Dhakeshwari, from whom the city may have got its name.

In trade Dhaka was best known for its fine cotton muslin cloth known as *jamdani.* Today the city and its suburb, Narayanganj, is the center of industrial activity in Bangladesh as well as the financial center. Dhaka district has now been divided into Dhaka, Narayanganj, Narsingdi, Gazipur, Manikganj, and Munshiganj districts.

DHAKA JAIL KILLINGS. Resulted in the death of Tajuddin Ahmed (q.v.), Syed Nazrul Islam (q.v.), Mansur Ali (q.v.) and A. H. M. Kamruzzaman (q.v.) on November 3, 1975. Tajuddin Ahmad had been jailed during Mujibur Rahman's (q.v.) regime, and the others following the August coup (q.v.). Responsibility for the orders permitting the murders has not been fixed, although popular belief often assigns it to the majors (q.v.).

DHAKA, NAWAB OF (FAMILY). The family of the Nawab of Dhaka has produced a number of important political leaders in the region now comprising Bangladesh. The title is hereditary, but as a *zamindar* (landlord), not as a ruling prince. Among the members of the family have been Nawab Salimullah (q.v.), a founder of the Muslim League (q.v.); Khwaja Sir Nazimuddin (q.v.), whose last official position was prime minister of Pakistan; and Khwaja Shahabuddin (q.v.), Nazimuddin's younger brother, who served in several Pakistan cabinets. The last nawab in the Pakistan period was Hasan Askari (q.v.). The family was part of the national elite (q.v.; see also vernacular elite) and has not been active in politics in independent Bangladesh, although many collaterals are active in the administration. For example, General Khwaja Wasiuddin, son of Khwaja Shahabuddin, and a former Pakistan army officer, has been a Bangladeshi ambassador. Another collateral, Khwaja Khairuddin, went to Pakistan as the leader of a splinter of the Muslim League.

DHARMAPALA (r. c. 770-810). Considered the greatest king of the Pala dynasty (q.v.), he extended the power of the dynasty beyond the boundaries of Bengal and Bihar. His conquests in northern India were consolidated by his successor, Devapala (q.v). He was an ardent Buddhist and supported a number of Buddhist establishments, including the Somapura Vihara near Paharpur (q.v.) in Rajshahi district.

DINAJPUR. A district and district town in northwestern Bangladesh. The town lies on the Punarbhaba River. The district is dominated by the Barind, a somewhat elevated tract, in what is otherwise a flat plain.

Tradition associates the area of Dinajpur with Matsyadesa of the Hindu epic *Mahabharata*, the place where the Pandhavas of the epic took refuge during their exile and the place of exile of Sita, the wife of Rama of the epic *Ramayana*. It was a part of Varendra (q.v.) and later came under the rule of the Palas (q.v.), who have left Buddhist monuments and the Senas (q.v.). Dinajpur was the home territory of Raja Ganesh (q.v.) who interrupted the rule of the Ilyas Shahi dynasty (q.v.).

Among the architectural sites is the Sura mosque in Dinajpur and the Vishnu temple in Kantanagar. Dinajpur district now comprises Dinajpur and Thakurgaon districts.

DIRECT ACTION DAY. August 16, 1946, was a day set aside by the Muslim League for work stoppages (*hartals*) and demonstrations to emphasize the League's demand for the partition of India. The day had been agreed on at a meeting of Muslim League legislators in New Delhi on July 27, following the Congress rejection of the Cabinet Mission Plan (q.v.). The meeting also endorsed a single state of Pakistan as opposed to the plural "states" used in the Lahore Resolution (q.v.). The day was peaceful except in Calcutta where serious violence between Muslims and Hindus occurred. Suhrawardy (q.v.) was prime minister of Bengal at the time.

DIWANI OF BENGAL. Granted to the British East India Company by the Mughal emperor, Shah Alam II, in 1765. It gave the right to the company to collect taxes in the province of Bengal with portions going to the emperor and the nawab of Murshidabad (successors to Mir Jafar [q.v.]) and the remainder being used by the British. Collection by the British actually began in 1772. As the collection of revenue was inseparable from the governing of the province, the British became rulers of Bengal in fact.

DUDU MIA (1819-1860). His real name was Muhammad Moshini, and he was the son of Haji Shariatullah (q.v.). He furthered the organizational setup of the Faraizi movement (q.v.) by dividing East Bengal into a number of regions and appointing persons to head each of the regions. He was able to keep himself well informed about all forms of suppression and to take countermeasures against them. Dudu Mia propagated the idea that land belongs to Allah and that no one has permanent rights over it. He worked extensively for the equality and welfare of the poor. For his activities, Dudu Mia was arrested a number of times and was tried but never convicted of any crime. He was imprisoned in 1857 and died in 1860.

DUTCH EAST INDIA COMPANY. The company was founded in 1602. Its impact on Asia was mainly in present-day Sri Lanka, Malaysia, and Indonesia, although, like other European trading companies, it also established factories in Bengal (see Chinsura).

DUTT, MICHAEL MADHUSUDAN (1824-1873). Poet and playwright, the first Bengali poet to use the sonnet technique in his poems. In 1843 he converted to Christianity. In 1849 two significant works—*Captive Lady* and *Vision of the Past*—were published. Much of Dutt's early writing was in English, but his best known poem, *Meghanadvadh*, was in Bengali. He was called to the bar from London in 1866 and joined the Calcutta bar. A college bearing his name is located in his birthplace, Jessore (q.v.).

DUTT, ROMESH CHANDRA (1848-1909). He entered the Indian Civil Service in 1871, but added to a distinguished administrative career with the publication of a number of historical works. His most noted work, *Economic History of India*, was published in two volumes in 1902 and 1904. Dutt retired to England in 1897, but returned to India to be president of the Indian National Congress in 1899.

DUTTA, GURUSADAY (1882-1941). Born in Sylhet, he studied in Calcutta and London and passed the examination for the Indian Civil Service. While he was district magistrate in Mymensingh he began a program for the reconstruction of villages. This start led to the founding of the Rural Heritage Preservation Society of Bengal.

DYARCHY. The term used to describe the system of provincial government created by the Government of India Act of 1919 (q.v.) (the Montagu-Chelmsford Act). Elected members became a majority in the legislative councils of the provinces, and they would control, as in a parliamentary system, the ministers heading the "nation-building departments." The control, however, was individual and not collective; the ministers did not form a cabinet. These departments included education, agriculture, public works, and health. The other departments, which represented the "steel frame" of British rule, including home, finance, and revenue, would remain under the control of the governor through executive councilors appointed by and responsible to him. In operation, however, many of the executive councilor posts came to be held by Indians, most of whom had previous experience as ministers. Dyarchy was abolished at the provincial level in 1937 by the Government of India Act of 1935 (q.v.), which created a system of provincial autonomy.

- E -

EAST BENGAL. The official name of the territory that is now Bangladesh from independence in 1947 to the enactment of legislation that consolidated the provinces in the west wing to a single province ("one unit") in 1955, as part of the process of adopting the Constitution of Pakistan of 1956 (q.v.). The Indian portion of the pre-1947 province of Bengal was (and is) designated West Bengal, with its capital at Calcutta.

EASTERN BENGAL AND ASSAM. A province created as the result of the partition of Bengal in 1905. It included the districts in the divisions of Dhaka, Rajshahi, and Chittagong along with Assam. The remainder of the province of Bengal retained that name and included the remaining divisions of Bengal along with Bihar and Orissa. In 1911, the partition of Bengal was revoked. The Bengali districts in East Bengal and Assam were joined with the Bengali districts of the western part of Bengal to form the new province of Bengal. Assam was separated as a chief commissionership, and later elevated to a province. The areas of Bihar and Orissa were joined to form the province of Bihar and Orissa, and later, under the Government of India Act of 1935, divided into two separate provinces.

EAST INDIA COMPANY. The company was founded as a trading company in 1600 and was disbanded in 1858. During that period, the company was transformed from a trading company to an administrative and military organization as it expanded British territory in India and ruled over that territory as if it were a truly colonial regime. The transfer of power from the company to the crown in 1858 barely changed the system of governance as far as the governed in India were concerned. This entry will note briefly the role of the company in Bengal. The reader should consult standard histories of India and the company for more information and an all-India perspective.

The first factory of the company was at Surat, on the west coast of India, established in 1612. The company set up a factory in Calcutta (q.v.) in 1690 and created other trading stations in such cities as Chittagong (q.v.) and Dhaka (q.v.). Calcutta was captired by Sirajuddaulah (q.v.) in 1756, but the city was retaken by a company force led by Robert Clive (q.v.) in 1757. The company then became de facto ruler of Bengal, a situation that was confirmed by the acquisition of the *diwani* of Bengal (q.v.) in 1765. This gave the company the right to collect taxes in Bengal on behalf of the Mughal emperor (then Shah Alam II). As tax collection and general administration were for all practical purposes inseparable, the nawab of Bengal (already a British puppet) became little more than an ornament. The company also recognized the importance of Bengal by designating the governor of Bengal, Warren Hastings (q.v.), as governor-general of all of its Indian territories in 1773. Calcutta then became the capital of the company's possessions.

As the company changed from a trading institution to a governing body, the British parliament increased its interest in the company's activities and began to exercise greater control over its activities. Lord North's Regulating Act in 1773 and William Pitt's India Act of 1784 gave parliament greater control. The company lost its monopoly on trade with India in the early nineteenth century by Charter Acts of 1813 and 1833. Thus by the time of the company's abolition in 1858, it had long ceased to perform its initial objective of trade with the East.

EAST PAKISTAN. The official name for the territory that now comprises Bangladesh from 1955 until Bangladeshi independence in 1971. The territory was often also referred to informally as the "east wing."

EDUCATION. The literacy rate in Bangladesh was reported to be 47 percent of the population aged five or older in 1994. Female literacy is significantly lower than male; data for 1981 show male literacy at 31.0 percent and female at 16.0 percent. Education is not compulsory but is free at the primary level beginning at age five and continuing for five years. In 1991, it was reported that 77 percent of the children aged five to nine were enrolled in primary school. This figure is probably inflated, as it appears to include children who attended for any portion of the school year rather than those who attended the entire school year. At the secondary level, perhaps a more accurate figure, attendance of those aged ten to fourteen was reported to be 19 percent. The state school system operates on the basis of five years of primary school, five years of secondary school, and two years of higher secondary school. The government is concentrating on the extension of primary education, especially in the rural areas.

There are six government universities in Bangladesh: comprehensive universities at Dhaka, Chittagong, Rajshahi, and Jahangirnagar (a suburb of Dhaka); an engineering university in Dhaka; and an agricultural university at Mymensingh. A number of private universities have recently developed. It is reported that 4 percent of those between the ages of fifteen and twenty four attended universities in 1991. Of these students, 83.8 percent were male an 16.2 percent female. Data indicate that females tend to study in the arts faculties; of the students in the Faculty of Arts at Dhaka University, 65.8 percent were male and 39.2 percent female. Education does not receive a large share of the budget; per capita allocations for all levels of education in 1983-84 were Taka 50 (less than $2). Much of the pre-university education takes place in privately operated schools rather than state schools. These private institutions vary widely in quality from the very good schools often run by Christian mission groups to those at the other end of the scale often operated by entrepreneurs for profit. The vocational education system can best be described as very weak. There are also a substantial number of Islamic primary schools (madrasas) of varying quality that are attached to mosques and other religious endowments.

EIGHTEEN POINTS. A program that was announced by President Ershad (q.v.) in March 1983 for the economic and political revival of Bangladesh. Economic self-sufficiency, democra tization of the political system, and decentralization of the administrative system provided the major thrust of the program.

ELECTIONS. There have been a number of elections that are of importance to the history of Bangladesh. This entry provides a comment on each election held since 1945, with the exception of the indirect elections (See Basic Democracy) held during the Ayub (q.v.) period.

Bengal Legislative Assembly Election of 1945-1946

This election was held under the system of separate electorates (q.v.). It was considered by the Muslim League (q.v.) to be a referendum on the question of the partition of India—a strong vote for the League would be interpreted as strong support for partition. In the Muslim seats located in what is now Bangladesh, the Muslim League won 82.04 percent of the vote and its principal rival, the Krishak Praja Party (KPP) (q.v.), only 5.98 percent, with the remainder going to smaller parties and independents. In terms of seats, the Muslim League won ninety-two of the ninety-eight Muslim seats in the future East Pakistan and Bangladesh; the KPP, four; and independents, two. The popular vote for the Muslim League was the highest of any Muslim-majority province (the others being the Punjab, Sindh, and the Northwest Frontier).

East Bengal Legislative Assembly Election of 1954

A legislative assembly election had been due in 1951, but as it seemed clear that the Muslim League was rapidly losing ground over the language issue and other issues it was delayed until 1954. The election showed clearly that the Muslim League had lost its support among Muslim voters. The election was again held on the basis of separate electorates. The United Front (q.v.), comprising the Awami League (q.v.) and the Krishak Sramik Party (KSP) (q.v.), won a major victory in the Muslim seats winning 223 of the 237 seats and reducing the Muslim League to 10 seats. The United Front gained 65.72 percent of the Muslim vote and the Muslim League 19.57 percent.

East Pakistan Vote for the National Assembly of Pakistan of 1970.

The martial law government headed by Yahya Khan (q.v.) held elections for the National Assembly of Pakistan and the Provincial Assembly of East Pakistan in December 1970 and January 1971. The results were overwhelming victories for the Awami League, now led by Sheikh Mujibur Rahman (q.v.). In the National Assembly voting the Awami League won 160 seats of the 162 contested; the others were won by Nurul Amin (q.v.) of the Democratic Party and an independent. The Awami League received 75.22 percent of the popular vote, far ahead of the second place Jama'at-i-Islami (q.v.) with 6.08 percent and no seats.

East Pakistan Provincial Vote of 1970

The results for the Provincial Assembly were similar. The Awami League won 288 of the 300 seats contested with a similar proportion of the popular vote.

Bangladesh Parliamentary Election of 1973

As the Bangladesh Parliament had been formed after independence by a merger of the members of the Provincial Assembly and those Bangladeshi members of the Pakistan National Assembly who remained in Bangladesh, a new election for a parliament was held in 1973. It confirmed overwhelmingly the strength of the Awami League, although there were also reports of substantial rigging of the poll. The Awami League won 291 of 300 seats with 73.18 percent of the popular vote.

Referendum of 1977

President Ziaur Rahman (q.v.) sought to legitimize his assumption of the presidency. A referendum on his continuance in office gave him 98.9 percent of the valid votes. As there was no alternative in the referendum, the goal of legitimacy was not met.

Presidential Election of 1978

President Ziaur Rahman then called for a national election for the presidency. Although there were a number of candidates, the principal opponent was General Muhammad Ataul Ghani Osmany (q.v.), who was supported by a number of parties including the Awami League. Zia polled 76.63 percent; Osmany, 21.70 per-cent. The election was viewed as generally free and fair.

Parliamentary Election of 1979

With the presidency securely in his hands, Zia called a parliamentary election in 1979. His party, the Bangladesh Nationalist Party (BNP) (q.v.), won 207 of the 300 seats contested, with the Awami League faction led by Abdul Malik Ukil (q.v.) winning 39, and the Muslim League-Islamic Democratic League (q.v.) alliance winning 20. The BNP polled 41.16 percent of the popular vote; the Awami League-Malik, 24.52 percent. The vote has been characterized as "free and fair."

Presidential Election of 1981

On the assassination of Zia in May 1991, Vice President Abdus Sattar (q.v.) became acting president pending an election for the presidency to be held within 180 days. The BNP nominated Sattar and the Awami League nominated Kamal Hossain (q.v.); there were other candidates as well. Sattar won the election with 65.5 percent of the vote to Hossain's 26.0 percent.

Referendum of 1985

President Ershad (q.v.) called for a referendum on his continuance in office. It was reported that there was a 72 percent turnout and that 94 percent voted in favor of Ershad. It did not bestow legitimacy on the Ershad regime.

Parliamentary Election of 1986

Ershad called for a parliamentary election in 1986 despite statements by the principal opposition parties, the BNP and the Awami League, that they would not contest. Ershad eventually convinced the Awami League to contest. Despite widespread reports of rigging, Ershad's Jatiya Party (q.v.) barely scraped through to a majority of 152 seats in the 300 seat house. The Awami League won 70 seats and with its allies formed a block of about 100 seats. The BNP did not contest.

Parliamentary Election of 1988

Ershad dissolved Parliament in 1987 after there had been rioting and called a new election. The Awami League, which had resigned from parliament, joined the BNP and other parties in boycotting the election. The result, which was hardly a reflection of political opinion in the country, was a parliament almost entirely composed of members of Ershad's Jatiya Party and a few scattered representatives of small parties prepared to work with Ershad.

Parliamentary Election of 1991

Following the fall of Ershad in December 1990, a general election was held under a neutral caretaker government (q.v.) for a new parliament. The BNP led by Khaleda Zia (q.v.), won 168 seats of the 300 directly elected; the Awami League, 88; the Jatiya Party, 35; and the Jama'at-i-Islami, 20; other parties and independents won the remaining 19. When 30 indirectly elected seats for women were added, the BNP total increased by 28 to 196 and that of the Jama'at to 22. In terms of popular vote, the BNP won 30.6 percent; the Awami League, 30.6 percent; the Jatiya Party, 11.8 percent; and the Jama'at, 12.1 percent. However, if the votes of Awami League allies in seats that were not contested by the Awami League are added to the League's total, the percentage received by the League and its allies is 33.6 percent.

Parliamentary Election of February, 1996

An election was held in February, 1996, following the resignation of opposition members. The opposition, led by the Awami League (q.v.), the Jatiya Party (q.v.), and the Jama'at-i-Islami, boycotted the election, demanding that an election must be held under a neutral caretaker government (q.v.). The result of the election was meaningless as almost all seats were won by the Bangladesh Nationalist Party (BNP) (q.v.). The new parliament passed a constitutional amendment providing for future elections to be held under a neutral caretaker government. It was then dissolved and a new election scheduled for June, 1996.

Parliamentary Election of June, 1996

Following the dissolution of Parliament, a new election was called for on June 12, 1996. The result of the election gave the Awami League (q.v.) a plurality of seats, but not a majority. The Bangladesh Nationalist Party (BNP) (q.v.) won the second largest number of seats. To form a government, the Awami League has gained the support of the Jatiya Party (q.v.), the party that finished a distant third in the polling.

ELECTIVE BODIES (DISQUALIFICATION) ORDER (EBDO). Issued in April 1959 its purpose was to inquire into allegations of misconduct by any person who held any public office or position, including membership in any elective body in the country. Persons appearing before EBDO tribunal were not allowed the assistance of counsel. Proceedings were held under Code of Civil Procedure and not Code of Criminal Procedure. A number of officials were disqualified under the order from participating or holding public office for seven years. The order was repealed in December 1960, but the disqualification of those already disqualified continued until the end of 1967.

ERSHAD, HUSSAIN MUHAMMAD (b. 1930). A regular army officer, rising to the rank of lieutenant colonel in the Pakistan army. During the civil war of 1971, he was posted in Pakistan and detained there, returning to Bangladesh only in 1973. He reached the rank of major general in 1975 and was appointed deputy chief of staff. Ershad succeeded Ziaur Rahman (q.v.) as chief of staff in 1978, when the latter resigned from the army. Ershad was promoted to lieutenant general in 1979.

Ershad led a coup against the elected government of Abdus Sattar (q.v.) in March 1982 and became chief martial law administrator. He assumed the presidency in December 1984. He was elected president in a referendum (see Elections) for a five-year term in October 1986; he ran as a civilian, having resigned from the army, as the candidate of the Jatiya Dal (q.v.), of which he was the chairman. Ershad's title as chief martial law administrator was abolished in November 1986 with the ending of martial law. His government held an election to parliament in 1986 in which his party barely scraped by to a majority. In that election the Awami League (q.v.) contested and became the official opposition, with Sheikh Hasina Wajid (q.v.) as leader. Ershad was challenged in November 1987, when both the Awami League and the Bangladesh Nationalist Party (BNP) (q.v.) demanded free and fair elections. By that time, the Awami League had walked out of the parliament. Ershad dissolved parliament and called new elections in 1988, which were boycotted by both the Awami League and the BNP. The election resulted in a parliament that was overwhelmingly led by the Jatiya Dal.

Demonstrations in November and December 1990, in which the Awami League and the BNP cooperated, led to the resignation of Ershad in December. He has since been in jail facing a number of charges, many of which, in the view of some observers, are frivolous at best. He contested the 1991 election from jail and won all five of the seats he contested, having then to resign four of them, as well as being denied the right to take a seat in parliament.

-F-

FAKHRUDDIN MUBARRAK SHAH (d. 1346). Led a rebellion against the Tughluq dynasty of the Delhi sultanate in 1336. On the death of the governor in 1336, Fakhruddin proclaimed himself the independent ruler of Sonargaon (q.v.). In 1346, he was superseded by the Ilyas Shahi dynasty (q.v.).

FAKIR, LOKMAN HOSSAIN (1934-1991). A lyricist, composer, and vocalist, he established several schools, including the Begum Momtaz Girls School and the Fakir Mainuddin High School. Lokman Hossain was the cultural secretary of the Bangladesh Nationalist Party (BNP) (q.v.) from 1979 to 1984 and again from 1988 until his death in 1991.

FARAIZI MOVEMENT (or Faraidiyyah). A Bengali Muslim movement that had its antecedents in the Wahhabi movement in Arabia. It was founded by Haji Shariatullah (q.v.) of Faridpur in 1818. It preached the oneness of Allah and opposed any deviations from a strict interpretation of the Quran and Sunna, such as the syncretism of the Sufis and Shia and the universalism of some Hindu elites. Shariatullah declared that India under the British was a *dar al-harb* (an abode of war, i.e., not a proper place for Muslims to reside) and said that Friday congregational prayers and the celebration of the two great *eids* (festivals commemorating the end the fasting month of Ramadan and the sacrifice day ending the Hajj) were forbidden so long as the British ruled. Shariatullah was followed by his son, Dudu Mia (1819-1860) (q.v.), whose violent actions in opposition to Hindu landlords and British officials and planters of indigo ended in his arrest in 1841 on charges of murder, but in this trial, as in all others, he was acquitted for lack of evidence, as witnesses would not testify against him. The movement weakened after Dudu Mia's death, although followers remain.

FARID AHMAD (1923-1971). Resigned from the government service because of his support for the language movement (q.v.) of 1952. He was the leader of the Nizam-i-Islam (q.v.) political party. He served as a member of the Pakistan Constituent Assembly in 1955 and was a member of the National Assembly in 1962. In 1964, Farid Ahmad joined the Combined Opposition Parties (q.v.) and was elected as a representative of the party to the National Assembly. He joined the opposition in its movement to oust President Ayub Khan (q.v.) in 1969. Farid Ahmad was opposed to the war of liberation and collaborated with the Pakistani armed forces. He was an adviser to the Razakar Bahini (q.v.) and a leading member of the Peace Committees (q.v.) that were set up to coerce Bengalis to continue the idea of a united Pakistan.

FARIDPUR. A district and district town, it is named for a Muslim saint, Farid Shah, whose shrine is in Faridpur city. The area now comprising Faridpur was a part of Vanga (q.v.) or Samatata (q.v.), and was a base for the rebellion of the Bara Bhuiyan (q.v.) against Man Singh (q.v.). The ruins of the fort of Raja Sita Ram

Rai are at the village of Kilabari. Faridpur is an important rail center lying on the line between Goalundo (where the Ganges [q.v.] and Brahmaputra [q.v.] meet) and Calcutta. The city is also the site of the Hindu structure Mathurapur Deul. With the local government (q.v.) changes during the Ershad period, the former district was divided into Faridpur, Gopalganj, Madaripur, Shariatpur, and Goalundo.

FARRAKA BARRAGE. At the core of the Ganges waters dispute between Bangladesh and India. The idea of a barrage near Farraka was first considered in the early twentieth century. The barrage would divert water from the Ganges River through canals and the Bhagirathi and Hooghly Rivers to reduce salinity in the Hooghly at Calcutta and to augment its flow. This would assure Calcutta a greater supply of drinking water and would lessen the silting of Calcutta harbor. After Indian independence, India revived the idea and built the barrage, which was completed after Bangladesh became independent. Bangladesh claims that it needs the water withdrawn to reduce salinity and improve irrigation in Khulna division.

Significant soil damage is occurring owing to the diversion of the water. The western districts of Bangladesh are experiencing both shortages of water for agriculture and increases in soil salinity. While Bangladesh is dealing with the problem with India in bilateral talks, it is also trying to raise the issue in international forums. India objects to the latter as a place to discuss what it deems to be a bilateral issue.

India has proposed that a link canal be built that would transfer water from the Brahmaputra River to the Ganges above Farraka so that adequate flow would be available both for Calcutta and Khulna division. Bangladesh has countered with a plan that would entail additional storage dams in Nepal to regulate better the flow of the Ganges during the low-flow season (April-June); at other times the flow is usually sufficient for both India and Bangladesh. The two countries reached an interim agreement on sharing the water during the low-flow period in 1978, but a final agreement has not been made. The interim agreement expired in 1988 and has not been renewed, giving India control of the water.

FAZILATUNNESSA (1899-1977). Born in Tangail, she was the first Muslim woman to earn a master of arts degree at the University of Dhaka. She also studied in the United Kingdom and taught in Calcutta. After partition, Fazilatunnessa was principal of Eden Girls College from 1948 to 1957.

FAZLUL HAQ, (MOULVI) ABUL KASEM (1873-1962). The leading Bengali Muslim political figure in the pre-independence period and for many years after independence. He was a member of the Bengal Legislative Council constituted under the

Government of India Act of 1909 (q.v.), 1913-1920, and again under the Dyarchy (q.v.) system established by the Government of India Act of 1919 (q.v.), 1921-1935. He was minister of education in 1924. He was a member of the Muslim League (q.v.), 1913-1942, until his membership was ended in a dispute with Muhammad Ali Jinnah (q.v.). After the elections following the passage of the Government of India Act of 1935 (q.v.), Fazlul Haq served as prime minister of Bengal, 1937-1943, first (1937-1941) in coalition with the Muslim League, whose leader, Khwaja Sir Nazimuddin (q.v.), Fazlul Haq had defeated in the election. During this period he, was for all practical purposes, was a member of both the Krishak Praja Party (q.v.) and the Muslim League and was the mover of the Lahore Resolution (q.v.) in 1940. After the collapse of the coalition with the Muslim League, he formed another coalition with the Hindu Mahasabha and other parties that lasted until 1943.

Fazlul Haq was the founder (in 1927) of the Krishak Praja Party, leading it in the 1937 and 1946 elections. In the latter, the party was badly defeated by the Muslim League, although Fazlul Haq retained his own seat. The party was then dissolved.

After independence, Fazlul Haq was advocate general of East Bengal, 1947-1954, but resigned to revive his party under the altered name Krishak Sramik Party (q.v.) and to enter the United Front (q.v.) with the Awami League (q.v.). The Front swept to victory and Fazlul Haq became chief minister briefly in 1954, but his government was dismissed by the central government of Pakistan, which accused him of wanting to declare an independent Bengali state, drawing on a statement he was alleged to have made while visiting Calcutta just after the election. It was also alleged that the great strike at the Adamjee Jute Mill (q.v.) was "arranged" to embarrass the incoming chief minister. Following a partial settlement with the central government, he became a central minister, 1955-1956, and governor of East Pakistan, 1956-1958. He retired from politics after the coup of Ayub Khan (q.v.) in 1958.

Fazlul Haq was born in Barisal district and educated in the law at Calcutta University. Before his first election to the Legislative Council, he practiced law in Calcutta, taught in Barisal, and edited several Bengali magazines. He became a protégé of Nawab Sir Salimullah of Dhaka (q.v.), a founder of the Muslim League, who assisted him in winning his first election. Fazlul Haq is known as "Sher-e-Bangla," the lion of Bengal.

FAZLUR RAHMAN (1905-1966). A lawyer from Dhaka, was a prominent Muslim League (q.v.) political figure both before and after independence. He was elected in 1937 and 1946 to the Bengal Legislative Assembly and became a minister in 1946. Fazlur Rahman was a member of the cabinet of Pakistan, 1947-1953, but was removed by the governor-general, Ghulam

Muhammad, largely because of his advocacy of Bengali positions on such issues as language and economic parity, despite his remaining in the Muslim League. He was reelected to the constituent assembly in 1955. After martial law was proclaimed by Ayub Khan (q.v.) in 1958, Fazlur Rahman continued to be associated with the Muslim League (the Council Muslim League [q.v.] in his case after 1962) until his death in an automobile accident.

FOREIGN POLICY. Bangladesh is a member of the Non-Aligned Movement and of the Group of Seventy-seven. It is also an active member of the Organization of the Islamic Conference (q.v.). Bangladesh is a member of the (British) Commonwealth of Nations. It became a member of the United Nations (q.v.) in 1974 and was elected to the Security Council in 1978. In 1985, its foreign minister, Humayun Rashid Chowdhury, was elected president of the General Assembly. For relations with specific countries, see separate entries for Afghanistan, Burma, China, India, Middle East, Pakistan, the former Union of Soviet Socialist Republics, Russia, and the United States. See also Islamic Conference.

FORT WILLIAM. The fort built during the period 1696-1715 to protect Calcutta (q.v.). It was captured by Nawab Sirajuddaulah (q.v.) in 1756 but retaken by the British in 1757. The original site, near the present Dalhousie Square, was vacated in 1819 and new buildings built there. The present fort is on a different site.

FRENCH EAST INDIA COMPANY. It was founded as a trading company by the French mercantilist Jean-Baptiste Colbert in 1662. In Bengal, it established a trading station at Chandernagore in 1690. The company was dissolved in 1795, but its possessions in India remained French enclaves. Chandernagore was transferred to India on February 2, 1951.

- G -

GANESH, RAJA. A noble from Dinajpur, he rose to be the most powerful person in the court of the sultan, Ghiyasuddin Azam (r. c. 1393-1410). At the sultan's death a succession struggle took place and Ganesh assumed the rule in 1414. He fought off an invasion from Jaunpur and died in 1418. His elder son, Jalaluddin, who had converted to Islam, ruled until 1431. Jalaluddin's son, Shamsuddin Ahmad, was a tyrant and was murdered in 1442, leading to the restoration of the Ilyas Shahi dynasty.

GANGES RIVER. (Ganga) The river rising in the Himalaya and fed by other rivers rising in the same mountains as well as other streams from the south is worshipped by Hindus as a goddess.

The most sacred city of Hindus, Varanasi (Banares), is located on the river and the confluence of the Ganges, Yamuna (Jumna), and mythical Saraswati at Allahabad is another sacred place. The river itself is 1,557 miles long. Until the latter part of the sixteenth century, the principal distributary of the river was the Bhagirathi-Hooghly route (see Farraka Barrage and below). At that time, the route turned east to the present primary distributary through Bangladesh.

In Bangladesh the river is known as the Padma. Its enormous flow of water during most seasons provides the flooding that enriches the fertile soil of Bangladesh with the silt carried by the river. Flooding, which is often beneficial, can also be extraordinarily destructive, especially in areas where the flow of the Ganges is combined with that of the Brahmaputra (q.v.) at Goalundo and the Meghna (q.v.) at Chandpur.

During the months of April and May the flow of the river is low. The construction by India of the Farraka Barrage (q.v.) to divert Ganges waters to Calcutta has made the flow during that period insufficient for the operation of irrigation works in southwestern Bangladesh and to curtail the salinization of that region resulting from the infusion of sea water. The barrage and its results are the major point of dispute between Bangladesh and India.

GANOTANTRIK DAL. A short-lived political party led by Mahmud Ali (q.v.). It was leftist and attempted to be noncommunal. It gained its only (and very small) electoral success when it was part of the United Front (q.v.) in 1954.

GAUDA or GAUR. (Also known as Lakhnauti, and earlier as Lakshmanavati when the city and its region were under Hindu rule.) Now in ruins, located in Malda district, West Bengal. It was the capital of Sasanka (q.v.) in the seventh century and was the Sena (q.v.) dynasty's capital in the eleventh and twelfth centuries. It was captured by an army of the Delhi sultanate (q.v.) led by Ikhtiyaruddin Muhammad Bakhtiyar Khalji (q.v.) in 1202 and made the capital of the province of Bengal in 1220. The city was destroyed in 1538 by Sher Shah Suri (q.v.) but restored and occupied when the Mughals took Bengal in 1576. It and its neighboring sites of Pandua and Tanda served as capitals during various periods of Muslim control of Bengal from the beginning of the thirteenth century to the latter part of the sixteenth century. A shift in the flow of the Ganges in 1564 caused Gaur to be abandoned as a capital in favor of Tanda, which was closer to the main stream, but there were other times when Gaur was occupied. In the eighteenth century, the city was little more than a place of ruins, and in the 1870s much of the city was plowed for agriculture. Several ruins, however, are of historical and tourist interest. Among these are the Great Golden Mosque, the

Small Golden Mosque, and the Kadam Rasul Mosque, the last of which is in good condition and in use.

GHASITI BEGUM. The eldest daughter of Alivardi Khan (q.v.), she was caught up in the intrigues surrounding the succession of Alivardi's grandson, Sirajuddaulah (q.v.), as nawab. She supported another nephew in the succession, who eventually was killed by Sirajuddaulah in 1756. After the death of her husband, Ghasiti Begum allegedly had an illicit relationship with another relative, who was also killed by Sirajuddaulah. She entrusted her wealth to another courtier, who eventually fled with the funds and joined the British in the conflict between the British and Sirajuddaulah. She died in oblivion, and her residence, Motijheel, is a ruin.

GHAZNAVI, SIR ABDUL HALIM (1876-1953). A politician and social activist, was a *zamindar* (landlord) from Mymensingh (now Tangail) district. He was educated in Calcutta. He actively participated in political, economic, and educational movements in India. In 1929, Sir Abdul Halim was the President of the All-India Muslim Conference, a short-lived rival of the Muslim League (q.v.). He participated in the Round Table Conference in London. He was not associated with the Muslim League and appealed to Lord Wavell in 1945 to add non-League Muslims to the viceroy's council. Sir Abdul Halim served both as chairman of the Calcutta Chamber of Commerce and the sheriff of Calcutta. He was a brother of Sir Abdul Karim Ghaznavi (q.v.).

GHAZNAVI, SIR ABDUL KARIM (1872-1939). Educated outside India, he was a politician and social activist. He was a member of the Imperial Legislative Council, 1909-1916. As a representative of the British raj he went to Syria, Palestine, Egypt, and Saudi Arabia. Sir Abdul Karim was a member of the Bengal Legislative Council, 1926-1929, and a minister in 1924 and 1927. From 1929 to 1934 he was an executive councilor in Bengal. While giving evidence before the Reforms Commission in 1924, Sir Abdul Karim expressed doubt about India's ability to accept democratic institutions. He was the author of *Moslem Education in Bengal*. He was a brother of Sir Abdul Halim Ghaznavi (q.v.).

GHOSE, AUROBINDO (1872-1950). He first gained prominence as a scholar, studying in England as well as Bengal, but on his return he became engaged in politics and is often known as a revolutionary. Aurobindo actively opposed the partition of Bengal in 1905 and spent time in jail. He changed direction in 1910 and founded an ashram (a religious retreat) in French-controlled Pondicherry. From this base, he wrote extensively on Hindu philosophy.

GHOSE, JOGESH CHANDRA (1887-1971). One of the Hindu intellectuals killed by the Pakistan army at the beginning of the civil war. He had been professor of chemistry and also principal of Jagannath College, Dhaka. A scholar of ayurvedic medicine, Ghose founded a company to manufacture ayurvedic medicines in 1914 and wrote extensively on the subject.

GHULAM HUSAIN KHAN TABATABA, SYED (late seventeenth-early eighteenth century). A noted historian who was a cousin of Alivardi Khan (q.v.). He worked at the Mughal court in Delhi and at the court of the nawab of Bengal. He represented Nawab Mir Qasim (q.v.) in Calcutta and later was employed by the East India Company. Tabataba's works on the decline of the Mughal empire and the rise of the British are noted near-contemporary accounts of the events of the seventeenth and eigthteenth centuries.

GHULAM MUHAMMAD (1895-1956). Governor-general of Pakistan, 1951-1955. Although he was born in Lahore, his family home was in East Punjab (now part of India). Before independence, Ghulam Muhammad was a civil servant and later in business. He was finance minister of Pakistan prior to succeeding Khwaja Nazimuddin (q.v.) as governor-general.

GOLAM MUSATAFA (1897-1964). A major Bengali Muslim poet. He began his career by very much imitating the style of Rabindranath Tagore (q.v.) to the extent that he was criticized by Muslim writers as being "Hinduized." His major work was *Rakta Rag* (1924), which received high praise from Tagore.

GOPACHANDRA. The first of three kings who ruled over Vanga (q.v.) in the early sixth century during the period of decline of the Gupta empire. The other two rulers were Dharmaditya and Samacharadeva. The information about them is primarily numismatic.

GOPALA I. The founder of the Pala dynasty (q.v.). He ruled from about 750 to 770. In a period of anarchy in Bengal and Bihar, he appears to have been selected as king by common consent.

GOVERNMENT OF INDIA ACT OF 1909. Also known as the Morley-Minto Act after Lord (John) Morley, secretary of state for India in the British cabinet, and Lord Minto (q.v.), viceroy of India. The act was a major step along the route toward Indian self-government. The act admitted Indians to the executive councils (i.e., cabinets) of the governor-general and the governors of the provinces. It provided for election of Indians to the legislative councils at the central and provincial levels, although a majority of the members (including some Indians) were appointed. The act also introduced the system of separate electorates (q.v.) for Muslims and "others" (i.e., primarily Hindus, but not all in this category were Hindu).

GOVERNMENT OF INDIA ACT OF 1919. Also known as the Montagu-Chelmsford Act after Edwin Montagu, secretary of state for India in the British cabinet, and Lord Chelmsford, the viceroy. At the central level the act created two legislative houses, the (upper) Council of State and the (lower) Central Legislative Assembly. In each house, elected Indians would form a majority. However, the final powers continued to be held by the viceroy, and no concept of parliamentary responsibility was introduced. The viceroy's executive council of seven would have three Indian members. At the provincial level, the legislative councils would also have a majority of elected Indians. A limited admission of the principle of responsibility at the provincial level was the system of dyarchy (q.v.).

GOVERNMENT OF INDIA ACT OF 1935. The last such act passed by the British parliament before independence. At the provincial level, the act provided for autonomy in the sense that responsible governments were introduced in each of the provinces. The prime minister (as he was then designated—the title would become "chief minister" after independence in both India and Pakistan) and his cabinet must enjoy the confidence of the legislative assembly. "Legislative assembly," as a term, replaced "legislative council," although in a few provinces, including Bengal, there was also an upper chamber, which retained the name "legislative council."

In the provinces, in the case of a breakdown of the cabinet government or in a financial emergency (e.g., failure to pass a budget), the governor retained powers to act to permit government to continue. At the center, a federal system was contemplated that would include the princely states. The princes did not agree to this arrangement, so the system of dyarchy (q.v.), which was to have been introduced at the center, was never adopted. Power, therefore, was distributed as under the Government of India Act of 1919 (q.v.). The 1935 act, as amended by the India Independence Act of 1947, served as the "constitution" of both India and Pakistan until each adopted its own constitution.

GRAM SARKAR. A village government (see Local Government) scheme introduced by President Ziaur Rahman (q.v.) in 1980. Each Gram Sarkar was to be responsible for a number of activities, including family disputes, population control, food production, and law and order. A twelve-member committee was to head the unit with two members coming from each of the following groups: landless peasants, women, landed peasants, shopkeepers, fishermen/artisans. The chairman and the secretary were to be chosen by these ten members.

GRAMEEN BANK. The outcome of an experimental project undertaken by Muhammad Yunus in one village, Jobra, it has become one of the most creative models of development banking for the poor. Its five primary purposes were: (1) to extend banking facilities to poor men and women; (2) to eliminate exploitation by moneylenders; (3) to create opportunities for self-employment for underutilized and unutilized manpower; (4) to bring the disadvantaged into an organizational format; and (5) to reverse the age-old cycle of low income, low saving, and low investment. Its success can be measured by the fact that it currently reaches about one million households in Bangladesh in about 28,000 villages. Its success can also be measured by its program's being copied in a number of countries. For his contribution to international development, Professor Yunus was awarded the World Food Prize in 1994.

GUHA, AJITKUMAR (1914-1969). Writer and educationist. He taught in the Bengali department of Dhaka University. In 1952, he was jailed with others during the language movement (q.v.). He wrote extensively on Bengali.

GUPTA DYNASTY. Founded by Chandragupta I in about 320, the dynasty ruled much of northern India until about 510. The dominions of the empire included Bengal. It appears, however, that Gupta control over all of Bengal was not firm. In an inscription from the reign of the second Gupta ruler, Samudragupta, Samatata (q.v.) in southeastern Bengal is referred to as a frontier state.

- H -

HABIBULLAH, ABU MUHAMMAD (1911-1984). A well-known historian and educationist who was the president of the Asiatic Society of Bangladesh and the Bangladesh History Association and served two terms as the curator of the Dhaka Museum. Habibullah wrote a number of books, including *The Foundation of Muslim Rule in India* (1975). For his research in Bengali literature he was awarded the Bangla Academy award in 1980.

HAFIZ, MIRZA GHULAM (b. 1920). A lawyer, he was earlier considered to be on the left, as exemplified by his presidency of the Bangladesh-China Friendship Society. He joined the cabinet of Ziaur Rahman (q.v.) in July 1978 as minister of land administration and land reform. Following the 1979 parliamentary election, Ghulam Hafiz was elected Speaker of parliament. In the Khaleda Zia (q.v.) government he has been minister of law and justice.

HAJI AHMAD. Brother of Alivardi Khan (q.v.), whom he helped in gaining control of Bengal. His youngest daughter was the mother of Nawab Sirajuddaulah (q.v.).

HAJI ILYAS. See ILYAS SHAH, SHAMSUDDIN.

HALHEAD, NATHANIEL BRASSEY (1751-1830). Grammarian. Already fluent in Arabic and Persian, he came to India with the East India Company in 1772. At the request of Warren Hastings (q.v.), Halhead prepared a book in Hindu law entitled *Code of Gentoo Laws*. In 1778 he wrote a grammar of the Bengali language.

HAMOODUR RAHMAN COMMISSION. Appointed by Pakistani president Bhutto (q.v.) in 1972 to look into the political and military causes of the loss of East Pakistan. The head of the commission, himself a Bengali, was a retired chief justice of the Supreme Court. The report has not been released to the public. This has caused speculation that the report was critical of Bhutto as well as other political figures and of the military.

HAQUE, ANWARUL (1918-1981). Artist. He studied in Calcutta and taught at a number of art schools. In 1948, he worked with Zainol Abedin (q.v.) and other artists to establish the East Pakistan Art Institute. Many of his works are on display at the Dhaka Museum.

HAQUE, MAZHARUL (1911-1974). He was born in Noakhali and studied economics at Dhaka University and the London School of Economics. In addition to teaching, Mazharul Haque was an adviser to the government on a number of economic issues including tariffs, small and cottage industries, and agricultural loans.

HAQUE, MUHAMMAD ENAMUL (1902-1982). From Chittagong, he studied in Calcutta. He taught at a number of institutions and was vice chancellor of Jahangirnagar University. Enamul Haque was a senior fellow at the Dhaka Museum and worked with the Bangla Academy. His work was on Bengali language and various aspects of Islam including Sufism.

HARIKELA. The rulers of this place seem to have dominated eastern Bengal during the ninth century, possibly succeeding the Deva dynasty (q.v.). There is some indication from copper plates that the third ruler, the only one given royal titles, may have been the grandson of the last Deva ruler, Bhavadeva. There is speculation that Harikela may be a synonym for Vanga (q.v.) or that it may refer to Sylhet (q.v.). By the beginning of the 10th century the rulers of Harikela were superseded by the Chandra dynasty (q.v.).

HASAN ASKARI, NAWAB KHWAJA (1921-1984). The last Nawab of Dhaka during the Pakistan period. He assisted the Pakistan army during the war of liberation and stayed in Pakistan. A military officer by profession, he joined the Indian armed forces as a commissioned officer and served in the Burma front during World War II. From 1948 to 1961, Hasan Askari was in the Pakistan army. In 1962 he became a member of the Pakistan National Assembly and later communication minister of East Pakistan.

HASINA WAJID. See SHEIKH HASINA WAJID.

HASTINGS, WARREN (1732-1818). Came to India in 1750 as a clerk in the East India Company and rose to become the first governor-general of India in 1773. He had been named the governor of Bengal in 1772. He abolished the *diwani* (q.v.) set up by Clive (q.v.) and began to collect revenue directly. Payments to the Mughal emperor were also discontinued. Hastings had a remarkable knowledge of Indian languages and sponsored many scholarly activities such as the Royal Asiatic Society (q.v.) and the Calcutta Madrasa and supported the work of Sir William Jones (q.v.). He left India in 1780. Hastings was accused by his opponents of financial improprieties, but his impeachment by the British parliament ended in acquittal on all counts.

HEALTH DELIVERY. The health delivery system of Bangladesh can best be classified as weak. The ratio (1991) of population to doctors is 12,500 to 1, and to nurses 20,000 to 1. While these data refer to the country as a whole, there is a strong bias toward urban areas, and the rural areas have much lower medical coverage. Infant mortality was 108 per 1,000 in 1992. Life expectancy at birth was 55.6 years (1992) for both males and females. In 1992, the daily caloric supply per person was 2,019, an increase from 1,899 calories in 1985. The country is subject to a number of the debilitating diseases often associated with tropical areas and with areas in which the availability of safe drinking water and the provision of adequate sewage facilities is rare. Most prevalent are diarrheal diseases, including cholera, that are among the principal causes of the high infant mortality rate. The government is placing a high priority on health delivery and is utilizing foreign assistance as well as its own resources to improve conditions.

HEBER, REGINALD (1783-1826). Anglican Bishop of Calcutta, 1822-1829. He traveled extensively, as his diocese included all of British India. The travels are described in his *Journey Through India* (1828), which has been described as one the best early British accounts of life in India. Heber was a founder of Bishop's College in Calcutta and the writer of many hymns, including the well-known missionary hymn "From Greenland's Icy Mountains."

HINDUISM. Hinduism, as defined most broadly, was presumably the religion of all Bengalis prior to the expansion of Buddhism during the Pala dynasty (q.v.). With the Sena dynasty (q.v.), Brahmanical Hinduism revived briefly before the advent of Islam in the thirteenth century. According to the 1991 census, there were about 11.2 million Hindus in Bangladesh, comprising 10.5 percent of the population. This showed a considerable decrease from the last pre-independence census, that of 1961, when the Hindu population was recorded to be 18.4 percent of the population. The substantial out-migration to India during the 1971 civil war was not offset, by any means, by the return of the Hindu refugees. The regions (former districts) with the highest ratio of Hindus in the 1981 census (comparable data for 1991 are not yet available) were Khulna (27.2 percent), Dinajpur (21.9 percent), Jessore (19.6 percent), Faridpur (18.8 percent), and Sylhet (18.0 percent).

Although caste census data are not reported for 1981, it is widely believed that the majority of the Hindus in Bangladesh belong to the Scheduled Castes (the group once described as "untouchables," or in Gandhi's term, Harijans, i.e., children of God). In the 1961 census, caste (q.v.) Hindus were enumerated separately and represented 53.2 percent of all Hindus. As a basis for comparison, the 1961 census of India indicated that 12.6 percent of Indian Hindus were from the Scheduled Castes. It is clear that the two major out-migrations of Hindus, in the early 1950s and in 1971, were comprised primarily of caste Hindus. In the 1954 election, Hindus voted separately from Muslims under the system of separate electorates (q.v.). In elections since then, the system of joint electorates (see Separate Electorates) has been used. Hindus are under no legal restrictions, and several have served in parliament and in the cabinet. Data appear to show that Hindu voters have favored the Awami League (q.v.).

HOSSAIN, KAMAL (b. 1937). A British-educated barrister who was a close associate of Sheikh Mujibur Rahman (q.v.). He was elected to the National Assembly in a by-election in 1971. After independence he served in the Mujib cabinets as minister of law and then as minister of foreign affairs. In the former post, Kamal Hossain piloted the constitution bill. After Mujib's assassination, he went into self-imposed exile in England, but returned to run for the presidency in 1981 as the candidate of the Awami League (q.v.), being defeated by Abdus Sattar (q.v.). He has since ended his association with the Awami League and has formed a new political group called the Gano Forum (People's Forum).

HOSSAIN, ROKEYA SAKHAWAT (1880-1932). She, and her sister, Karimunnessa Khanam, were early champions for the education of Muslim women. She founded the Sakhawat Memorial School in Calcutta and, in 1916, the Muslim Women's Society to assist distressed Muslim women and girls.

HOSSAIN, SUFI MOTAHAR (1907-1975). A poet, he was born in Faridpur and studied in Dhaka before becoming a government officer and teacher. He was inspired by Kazi Nazrul Islam (q.v.) and wrote a large volume of poetry.

HUDA, MIRZA NURUL (1919-1991). An economist, civil servant, and educator, he was also finance minister of East Pakistan, 1965-1969, and, very briefly, governor, 1969. He was a member of the Pakistan Muslim League (q.v.) delegation to the roundtable conference held by Ayub Khan (q.v.) in 1969, in opposition to the Democratic Action Committee (q.v.). Nurul Huda returned to teaching during the Mujibur Rahman (q.v.) regime, but joined the cabinet of Ziaur Rahman (q.v.) in 1975 as minister of commerce and later as minister of finance and planning until 1980 (he also held temporary charge of other ministries during this period). Nurul Huda was the appointed vice president during all but the last few days of the presidency of Abdus Sattar (q.v.).

HUQ, MUHAMMAD SHAMSUL (b. 1910). A noted educationist who was vice-chancellor of Rajshahi University (1965-1969), served also in the Pakistan cabinet of Yahya Khan (q.v.) (1969-1971) and in the Bangladesh cabinets of Ziaur Rahman (q.v.) (1977-1981) and Abdus Sattar (q.v.) (1981-1982). In the Bangladeshi cabinets, Shamsul Huq was minister of foreign affairs. He was instrumental in bringing to fruition the goal of Zia to form the South Asian Association for Regional Cooperation (SAARC) (q.v.). It is reported that Shamsul Huq was offered the presidency by Hussain Muhammad Ershad (q.v.) in 1982, but refused in opposition to the military coup that ousted the elected civilian government of Sattar. After leaving office, he headed the Bangladesh Institute of International and Strategic Studies, an important and influential "think tank." He is a national professor and the author of a study of Bangladesh foreign policy.

HUSAIN SHAHI DYNASTY. Ruled Bengal from 1494 to 1538. The dynasty was founded by Alauddin Husain Shah (q.v.), from whom it derives its name. The first ruler extended the kingdom to the borders of Orissa and into northern Bihar. He also recaptured Chittagong (q.v.) from the Arakanese (q.v.). The period was one of great building at Gaur (q.v.) as well as the patronizing of literature. The Husain Shahis, for example, sponsored the translation of the Hindu epic *Mahabharata* into Bengali. The dynasty ended in 1538 when the last ruler, Ghiyasuddin Mahmud Shah, was defeated by Sher Shah Suri (q.v.).

HUSSAIN, QAZI MOTAHAR (1897-1981). He was a founder, in 1921 of the Muslim Sahitya Samaj, an organization of educated Muslim youth. He also was instrumental in launching the Free Thinking Movement and was the editor of its journal, *Shikha*.

- I -

IBRAHIM KHAN. Mughal governor in Bengal, 1689-1697, whose weak rule allowed the placement and fortification of European settlements in Bengal. His predecessor, Shaista Khan, had driven the English out of Bengal, but Ibrahim Khan invited them back and permitted the settlement of what became Calcutta (q.v.) in 1690. He also permitted the English, the French, and the Dutch to fortify their settlements. He was dismissed by Aurangzeb in 1697.

IBRAHIM KHAN (1894-1978). An educationist, litterateur, and social activist, participated in the noncooperation movement and the Khilafat movement (q.v.) in the early 1920s. He joined the Congress in 1920 and the Muslim League (q.v.) in 1937. He was a member of the Pakistan National Assembly in 1962. Ibrahim Khan established a number of schools and colleges, of which the Korotia College in Tangail, which he managed after it was founded with the financial assistance of Wajid Ali Khan Panni (q.v.), is the best known.

IBRAHIM, MUHAMMAD (1894-1966). A member of the judicial service and a firm believer in parliamentary democracy, he was appointed a justice of the Dhaka High Court in 1950, vice-chancellor of Dhaka University in 1956, and the Central Law Minister in 1958 during the Ayub Khan (q.v.) government. It was during Ibrahim's leadership of the law ministry that the Muslim Family Law Ordinance was promulgated in 1962.

IHTISHAMUDDIN, MIRZA SHEIKH (Eighteenth century). In 1765, he was the first educated Indian to visit England; he brought a letter from the Mughal emperor, Shah Alam II, to King George II. He also visited France. Although he was asked to remain in Europe to teach Persian, he returned to India. The written account of his journey has not been critically published, although an unauthorized edition was published in 1827. Some think that there may be additional material written by Ihtishamuddin.

ILYAS SHAHI DYNASTY. Ruled Bengal from 1346 to 1490. It was founded by Shamsuddin Ilyas Shah following a period of turmoil during the previous decade as local Bengali chiefs overthrew the rule of the governor of the Tughluq Dynasty of the Delhi sultanate. Shamsuddin was able to repulse an attack by the Tughluqs during the 1350s, and he established his capital at

Pandua (q.v.), near Gaur (q.v.). He captured eastern Bengal in 1352 and repulsed attacks from the Delhi sultan Firuzshah Tughluq. The rule of the dynasty was interrupted by the seizure of power by a Hindu minister, Raja Ganesh (q.v.), in 1417, but the dynasty was restored in 1437. The dynasty was overthrown in 1490 by the Abyssinians (q.v.).

IMAM, JAHANARA (1929-1994). An educationist, she gained acclaim as the author of *Of Blood and Fire*, her diary of the civil war of 1971, during which one son was killed and her husband died. She was born in Murshidabad district (now in West Bengal) and educated in Calcutta and Dhaka and in the United States. Jahanara Imam was an important leader of a group opposing the restoration of the citizenship of Golam Azam (q.v.), the amir of the Jama'at-i-Islami (q.v.), and demanding his trial for collaboration with the Pakistan army in 1971.

INDIA. India contributed greatly to the independence of Bangladesh by providing refuge, sanctuary, supplies, training, and arms to the Mukti Bahini (q.v.), the Bangladeshi personnel in rebellion against Pakistan. In late November 1971 (early December according to Indian sources), India intervened directly in the conflict and, with the Mukti Bahini, defeated the Pakistani forces. The latter surrendered at Dhaka on December 16, 1971, in a ceremony that excluded representatives of the Mukti Bahini and Bangladesh government-in-exile. This began a series of events that cooled relations between the two countries. Others included the commissioning by India of Farraka Barrage (q.v.), the overstaying (by Bangladeshi standards) of Indian troops in the Chittagong Hill Tracts (q.v.), and the taking of Pakistani military equipment by India. Nonetheless, during the period of Sheikh Mujibur Rahman (q.v.) relations were close and culminated in the signing of a twenty-five year treaty of friendship between the two nations (see India-Bangladesh Treaty) in 1972. There is some opposition in Bangladesh to renewing the treaty when it expires in 1997.

India, under Indira Gandhi, took the assassination of Mujib in August 1975 as an event aimed against India. India supported insurgents under an opponent of Ziaur Rahman (q.v.). Although relations improved under Morarji Desai (1977-1979) in India and Hussain Muhammad Ershad (q.v.) in Bangladesh, a number of problems remain. Chief among these is the unresolved Farraka dispute; an interim agreement was made during the Morarji Desai period in 1978, but it was not renewed in 1988. Others include the land (see Berubari Enclave) and maritime boundaries, trade relations in which Bangladesh has a sizable deficit, the migration of Bangladeshis into West Bengal and Assam and other northeastern states of India, and the possible interference of each country in the other's tribal problems. Both countries are members of the South Asian Association for

Regional Cooperation (q.v.). The four principal Bangladeshi leaders (Mujib, Zia, Ershad, and Khaleda Zia) have made official visits to India.

INDIA-BANGLADESH TREATY. A twenty-five year agreement between the two countries contracted in March 1972. It is formally termed a treaty of friendship, cooperation, and peace. It was signed as India completed its withdrawal from Bangladesh, and is seen by some as a quid pro quo for the removal of Indian troops from the Chittagong Hill Tracts (q.v.). The treaty, which in itself is not exceptional from the general class of treaties between neighbors, was seen by some Bangladeshis as substituting Indian dominance for that of Pakistan. In the June 1996 election, the major parties pledged that the treaty would not be renewed when it expires in 1997.

INDIAN COUNCILS ACTS. Three Indian Councils Acts of 1861 and 1892 were passed by the British Parliament prior to the first major constitutional reform, the Government of India Act, 1909 (q.v.) Each of these was intended to permit and increase Indian representation in the executive and legislative parts of the British Indian government. The Indians who were associated were appointed and not elected.

INDIGO. A plant native to South Asia (hence, its name) producing a blue dye. Known in ancient times as a product of India, it was grown extensively on a commercial basis for export by the East India Company during the nineteenth century. Exploitation of farmers resulted in conflict between planters and farmers in midcentury. The development of a synthetic dye at the end of the century ended the plant's commercial cultivation.

INDO-PAKISTAN WAR OF 1965. A conflict over Kashmir. Pakistani forces attacked Indian troops in Kashmir; India responded by attacking along the Punjab border and farther south. The war on the Punjab boundary began on September 6, and a cease-fire on all fronts came in three weeks. Although, there was no conflict involving territory in East Pakistan East Pakistanis were nonetheless concerned that the concentration of Pakistani troops in the west wing left them vulnerable to an Indian attack. This formed a basis for the last of the Six Points (q.v.) announced by Sheikh Mujibur Rahman (q.v.) in January 1966, that of separate militias for each of the provinces of Pakistan.

INDO-PAKISTAN WAR OF 1971. An outgrowth of the civil war in East Pakistan that began on March 26. India provided, early on, a sanctuary and training areas for the Mukti Bahini (q.v.) and a home for the Bangladesh government-in-exile. It also served as a home for a large number of refugees (some estimates are as high as ten million) and as a provider of arms for the Mukti Bahini. In late November, Indian forces began to operate with the Mukti Bahini against Pakistani troops. Indian troops captured Dhaka on December 16, ending the conflict in the east. There were also actions in December in the west between Pakistan and India, but a unilateral cease-fire declaration by India was accepted de facto by Pakistan on December 18.

INDUSTRY. The industrial sector produces a small portion of the gross domestic product: 17 percent in 1992, with the manufacturing subsector at 9 percent in the same year. The industrial sector grew at an annual rate of 5.1 percent from 1980 to 1992. Large-scale manufacturing enterprises provide jobs for only 20 percent of the industrial labor force, although they contribute 58 percent of the value added. The bulk of employment is provided by small and cottage industries. Sustained industrial growth is constrained by the small size of the domestic market and especially by the small size of what might be called the middle class with disposable income.

Jute (q.v.) processing and cotton textiles are the largest industries. However, the declining demand for jute has left the industry with excess capacity. Since the early 1980s, the garment industry has been a growth industry with high demand externally. Bangladesh is the fifth largest supplier of cotton apparel to the United States. Breaking up ships supplies most of Bangladesh's steel requirements; the scrap is processed in Chittagong. Other industries include sugar refining, tea processing, leather, newsprint, pharmaceuticals, and fertilizers.

The nationalization of industries during the Mujib (q.v.) period was a hindrance to industrial growth. The policy of privatization instituted by the Ershad (q.v.) regime and continued by the Khaleda Zia (q.v.) government has improved both efficiency and investment to some degree, but lack of demand and of investment funds still inhibit rapid growth. Banking has been partially freed up from government ownership. There are no limits on foreign investment other than the lack of demand, raw materials, and trained labor and a concern about political stability.

INTERNATIONAL TRADE AND AID. See AID AND TRADE.

ISA KHAN (d. 1598). The chief member of the bara bhuiyan (twelve landlords) (q.v.) who resisted Mughal (q.v.) rule in the late sixteenth century. Isa Khan was based at Katrabo near Sonargaon (q.v.) and controlled much of Comilla, Dhaka, and Mymensingh districts. He inflicted a number of defeats on the Mughals, including naval defeats in 1584 and 1597. His exploits against the Mughals have made Isa Khan a symbol of the eastern Bengalis' resisting power imposed upon them by the Mughals, which at the present time can be transmuted into "Pakistanis." He was succeeded by his son, Daud Khan, but the Mughals consolidated their hold under Man Singh (q.v.), who established a Mughal military headquarters at Dhaka (q.v.) not far from Sonargaon. Isa Khan's descendants were major landlords in Mymensingh.

ISLAM. Islam is professed by 86.7 percent of the population of Bangladesh, according to the 1981 census. Almost all Bengali Muslims are Sunni with a small number of Ithna Ashari Shia and of Ismaili Shia. Most who adhere to the latter two sects are descendants of non-Bengalis who migrated to Bengal during the period of Muslim rule from Delhi or later. With about 100 million Muslims (1994), Bangladesh ranks after Indonesia and with India and Pakistan as a state with the largest number of Muslims. This has given Bangladesh an important position in the Organization of the Islamic Conference (q.v.).

Leadership among Muslims includes the local mullah or imam; the maulana, who is presumed to be learned in Islam (a member of the ulema); and the pirs, who preside over shrines usually dedicated to deceased Sufi saints. There is among Sunnis no designated hierarchy. The Islamic leadership is generally confined to religious matters, and political activity is limited; there is no significant fundamentalism in Bangladesh. Rather, Islam is generally considered to be a personal matter, and there is no state enforcement of Islamic law or custom. Nonetheless, Islam in the personal sense is deeply rooted in the country.

Bengali Muslims, as do all subcontinental Muslims, formally eschew caste (q.v.), but in practice, hereditary groupings are recognized and in rural Bangladesh are important in such rites as marriage. Within the Muslim society certain distinctions are admitted: the *ashraf*, the upper class and often members of the national elite (q.v.); the *ajlaf*, a middle urban and rural class that has included many of the leaders of the vernacular elite (q.v.); and the *arzal*, the lower classes.

ISLAMIC CONFERENCE, ORGANIZATION OF THE . The Islamic Conference was established in 1971. The secretariat of the Organization of the Islamic Conference (OIC) is located in Jiddah, Saudi Arabia. The second summit of the OIC was held in Lahore, Pakistan, in February 1974. Bangladesh was not invited to the meeting. Through the efforts of several Muslim heads of state, Pakistani Prime Minister Zulfiqar Ali Bhutto (q.v.) was prevailed upon to invite Mujibur Rahman (q.v.) to attend. Pakistani recognition of Bangladesh as well as that of most Arab nations dates from this meeting, although formal diplomatic relations were not established in most cases (including Pakistan) until after the death of Mujib. Bangladesh has been active in the OIC and presented an unsuccessful candidate for the secretary generalship in 1985.

ISLAMIC DEMOCRATIC LEAGUE. Formerly an ultraconservative political party composed of members of the Nizam-i-Islam (q.v.), the Jama'at-i-Islami (q.v.), and two smaller parties, the People's Democratic Party and the Islamic Ganotantrik Dal. It was established in 1976. Its leader, Maulana Abdur Rahim, contested the 1981 presidential election. The party stood against Westernization and secularism and aims to make Bangladesh an Islamic republic. One of its demands was that the national anthem of Bangladesh be changed because it was written by Rabindranath Tagore (q.v.), who was a Hindu. The party has since broken up.

ISMAIL, KHAN BAHADUR MUHAMMAD (1871-1945). Received the title of Khan Bahadur by the British. He was a contemporary of Nawab Sir Salimullah (q.v.). He organized the Krishak Praja Party (q.v.) in Mymensingh district of Bangladesh. Ismail was actively involved with the Mymensingh district council, serving as its vice chairman from 1906 to 1920 and as itschairman from 1920 to 1929. He was a lawyer by profession.

ISPAHANI FAMILY. A Shia Muslim business family that originated in Iran, as the name indicates. They moved to India in the eighteenth century. Based first in Madras, the family achieved prominence in Bengal before 1947. After Pakistani independence, the group maintained headquarters in Karachi and Dhaka. Activities included tea processing, jute manufacture, insurance, and banking. The group also established Orient Airlines, the predecessor of the nationalized Pakistan International Airlines. In the 1960s, the group was ranked eight among Pakistani business houses in assets. Mirza Abol Hasan Ispahani (q.v.) was a prominent political figure as well as a part of the managing group of the family. Since 1971 the family has maintained holdings in both Bangladesh and Pakistan.

ISPAHANI, MIRZA ABOL HASAN (1902-1981). A member of the important business house of the Ispahani family (q.v.), he was a close associate and later a biographer of Muhammad Ali Jinnah (q.v.). He was a member of the Bengal legislature before independence (1937-1947) and the constituent assembly of Pakistan (1947-1955) afterward. Ispahani was the first Pakistani ambassador to the United States (1947-1952) and later high commissioner to the United Kingdom (1952-1954) and a central minister (1954-1955). In politics, he represented the small Muslim commercial and industrial community in Bengal, having been president of the Muslim Chamber of Commerce, Calcutta, 1945-1947, and would oppose the Awami League (q.v.) and Husain Shahid Suhrawardy (q.v.) in their regionalist goals. Ispahani was therefore a member of the "national elite" (q.v.).

- J -

JAGAT SETH. Title, meaning "banker of the world," conferred on Fatehchand by the Mughal emperor Muhammad Shah in 1723. The banking house, whose members originally came from Marwar in Rajasthan, had its headquarters in Murshidabad (q.v.) and branches in Dhaka (q.v.) and Patna. It functioned almost as a central bank for the Mughal province of Bengal. At Fatehchand's death in 1744, the title passed to his grandson, Mahatabchand. He and his cousin and partner, Maharaja Swarupchand, had great influence during the governorship of Alivardi Khan (q.v.), but were alienated by Alivardi Khan's grandson and successor, Sirajuddaulah (q.v.). They joined a conspiracy with the British to overthrow Sirajuddaulah, providing much financial assistance, both before and following the battle of Plassey (1757) (q.v.). Jagat Seth's (Mahatabchand's) influence was restored during the rule of Mir Jafar (q.v.), but fell again when Mir Qasim (q.v.) became governor. Mir Qasim caused the cousins to be killed in 1763. Successors to the title Jagat Seth continued to use the title until the early twentieth century, but were persons of little influence.

JAGODAL (acronym for Jatiyatabadi Ganotantrik Dal). A political party formed largely by nonpolitical figures, to support President Ziaur Rahman (q.v.). In 1978, it merged into the broader Bangladesh Nationalist Party (BNP) (q.v.), although a small group remains, retaining the name JAGODAL.

JAHAN ALI, KHAN (d. 1459). A military officer under Sultan Nuruddin Mahmud Shah of the Ilyas Shahi dynasty (q.v.) who fought rebellious non-Muslim landlords in the region of Jessore (q.v.) and Khulna (q.v.) districts. Local legend adds that he tried unsuccessfully to cultivate the Sunderbans (q.v.). In his old age Jahan Ali renounced the world and became an ascetic. He died at Bagerhat, where his tomb attracts pilgrims. He is also honored at Bidyanandakati, where a tank reportedly excavated by Jahan Ali is the site of an annual fair. (See Jessore for Bidyanandakati and Khulna for Bagerhat.)

JAIDEV. A poet at the Sena (q.v.) court in the late twelfth century. He was the author of the still popular *Gita Govinda.*

JALALUDDIN AHMAD, MOLLAH (1926-1979). A close friend of Sheikh Mujibur Rahman (q.v.), he was a lawyer by profession. A member of the Muslim League (q.v.) student organization during the movement for Pakistan, he was a very active participant and worked extensively during the Sylhet Referendum (q.v.). He left the Muslim League to join the Awami League (q.v.) in 1949. Jalaluddin Ahmad was, for nearly twenty-nine years, a member of the Working Committee of the Awami League. He actively supported the war of liberation and after the independence of Bangladesh held a number of ministerial positions. Jalaluddin Ahmad was among the few members of the Awami League who was elected to the National Assembly of Bangladesh in 1979.

JALIL, M. A. (d. 1989). He was a freedom fighter in 1971 and later a political figure. In politics, he was at first associated with the Jatiya Samajtantrik Dal (q.v.) but changed groups as that party factionalized. At his death, Jalil was the president of the newly formed Jatio Mukti Andolan, which then dissolved.

JAMA'AT-I-ISLAMI. A political party generally described as Islamic fundamentalist. It was founded in India in 1941 by Maulana Syed Abu Ala Maududi. It supports the return of the political system to that of the period of the first four caliphs (A.D. 632-661) and opposed the creation of Pakistan, as it believed the Europeanized leaders of the Muslim League (q.v.) such as Jinnah (q.v.) would create a secular state that would be a homeland for the Muslims of India but would not be an Islamic state. For similar reasons, the Jama'at opposed the breakaway of Bangladesh, as it feared the Awami League (q.v.), led by Sheikh Mujibur Rahman (q.v.), would do the same thing. Members of the Jama'at in East Pakistan supported the military action taken by the Pakistan army in 1971.

While Maududi's writings and his emphasis on religious purity have had an impact throughout the Islamic world (for example, on the Muslim Brotherhood in Egypt), the party has had but little success in Pakistani elections. Its principal base was in West Pakistan. In Bangladesh it is among the lesser political groups in electoral terms but has some influence through the network of Islamic organizations. The Jama'at won twenty seats in the 1991 parliamentary election and added two more in the separate election for thirty seats for women (see Elections). It supported the Bangladesh Nationalist Party (BNP) (q.v.) in the women's election and thereby permitted the BNP to win the remaining twenty-eight and gain an absolute majority in Parliament. In 1994, however, it joined with the Awami League (q.v.) and the Jatiya Party (q.v.) in the opposition's demand that a Neutral Caretaker Government (q.v.) be installed prior to the next general election. In the June 1996 election for parliament the party saw a marked decline in the number of seats won, dropping to three. The party's leader is Golam Azam (q.v.).

JAMIL, GOUHAR (d. 1980). He was the founder of the Jago Art Centre, an institute of the dance, in 1959. He was an expert in Bharatya Natyam and Kathak dance. Originally a Hindu named Ganesh, he converted to Islam.

JASIMUDDIN (1903-1976). A noted Bangladeshi author. He is principally known for his collection of traditional stories about village life, turning them into ballads depicting the joys and sorrows of the Bangladeshi countryside. Jasimuddin's daughter, Husna, is married to Moudud Ahmed (q.v.).

JATIYA DAL, JATIYA PARTY. Originally called the Jatiya Dal, the Jatiya Party was formed to support President Hussain Muhammad Ershad (q.v.). The party drew members primarily from the Bangladesh Nationalist Party (BNP) (q.v.), which had been formed to support Ziaur Rahman (q.v.). It also drew some members from the Awami League (q.v.). It is a centrist party and favors denationalization of many industries that were nationalized during the period of Mujibur Rahman (q.v.). As is the case with most parties formed around an individual, it is weak in organization. The Jatiya Party won a slight majority in the parliamentary election of 1986 and an overwhelming majority in the 1988 election, which was largely uncontested by the principal opposition parties (see Elections). Its parliamentary leader, Mizanur Rahman Chowdhury (q.v.), became prime minister and was later succeeded by Moudud Ahmed (q.v.) and Kazi Zafar Ahmed (q.v.). After the fall of Ershad in December 1990, many of the leaders, including Ershad, were arrested or, at least, sought by the police. Nonetheless the party contested the 1991 election and won thirty-five seats in parliament, making it the third largest party, after the BNP and the Awami League. Mizanur Rahman Chowdhury (q.v.) is acting leader of the party while Ershad remains in jail and Moudud Ahmed (q.v.) led the party group in parliament that was dissolved in November 1955. In the June 1996 election, the Jatiya Party finished a distant third, but will support the newly formed Awami League government.

JATIYA SAMAJTANTRIK DAL (JSD). Established in October 1972 the JSD was organized by Abdur Rab and Shajahan Siraj, who were student leaders at Dhaka University and also members of the Awami League (q.v.). Two distinguished members of the Bangladesh army, Colonel Abu Taher (q.v.) and Major M. A. Jalil (q.v.), also provided leadership to the party. It opposed Awami League's Mujibbad (q.v.). The JSD is a socialist and left-leaning political party intent on introducing scientific socialism in Bangladesh, and it has comparatively young leaders. It came into prominence as a result of its influence in the army through such units as the Biplobi Sainik Sangsthan (Revolutionary Soldiers Organization) and Biplobi Gana Sena (Revolutionary People's Army). Abu Taher assisted Ziaur Rahman (q.v.) in his rise to power. Ziaur Rahman later disassociated himself from Abu Taher and reduced the influence of the JSD within the army. Abu Taher was later executed for alleged treason.

After 1977, the party was banned, but it reemerged in 1978 favoring the parliamentary system. It has been characterized as an anti-Indian, anti-Soviet and pro-Chinese political party, but this is simplistic. Like many other political parties of Bangladesh, the JSD split into two factions in 1980. One splinter group was called Bangladesh Samajtantrik Dal (BSD), with the other retaining the original name. It has since divided further. One of the factions won a single seat in the 1991 election.

JATIYO RAKKHI BAHINI (also known as Rakkhi Bahini). Established by Sheikh Mujibur Rahman (q.v.) in mid-1972 as a village paramilitary security force. However, it soon came to be known as the personal security force and political enforcement body of the Awami League (q.v.). It functioned out of the presidential secretariat and reported directly to Sheikh Mujibur Rahman. Deemed by the Supreme Court of Bangladesh to be an organization that functioned without any rules of procedure or code of conduct, it was disbanded after the first military coup, which took place in August 1975 (q.v.).

JESSORE. A district town in western Bangladesh located on the Bhairab River. An earlier village, Kasba, was renamed Jessore when it became a district town about 1790. There are some older buildings, including the Rajbari of Chanchra and the shrines of pirs Bahram Shah and Gharib Shah. A local college is named Michael Madhusudan Dutt (q.v.) College, as the writer was born in Jessore. Bidyanandakati has a tank that is a festival site for Jahan Khan (q.v.). Bara Bazaar was once a center for Buddhist studies. At Muhammadpur (originally Mahmudpur) are the remains of buildings, including a temple to Krishna, erected by Sitaram Roy, one of the Bara Bhuiyan (q.v.). With the reorganization of local government (q.v.) during the Ershad regime, Jessore district was divided into Jessore, Narail, Magura, and Jhenidah districts.

JINNAH, MUHAMMAD ALI (1876-1948). Known also as Qaid-i-Azam (great leader) by his admirers in Pakistan and in the Muslim League (q.v.), he was the leader of the League in its struggle for the partition of India and the formation of a separate Pakistan. A London-trained barrister, he entered politics as a member of the Congress but joined the Muslim League as well in 1913. He was a key figure in the negotiation of an agreement between the Congress and the League in 1916 on the question of separate electorates (q.v.) for Muslims, which, through the agreement, the Congress then accepted. Jinnah left the Congress in 1920 and, except for some time in the early 1930s, continued to work for a special status for the Muslims whom he saw as a nation in India separate from the Hindus. With independence in 1947, Jinnah became governor-general of Pakistan, a post he held until his death on September 11, 1948. Jinnah visited East Bengal only once as governor-general (in March 1948) and he angered many East Bengalis by stating, among other things, that

Urdu would be the only official language of Pakistan. The statement touched off the language movement (q.v.).

JONES, SIR WILLIAM (1746-1794). In his official role, Sir William was a jurist and later a member of the Calcutta court, for which he was given a knighthood. To those who study India he is known as "Oriental Jones," whose study of Sanskrit and Persian earned him the distinction of being the founder of comparative philology. Jones had studied Persian and Arabic at Oxford before going to India. He was the founder of the Asiatic Society (q.v.) in 1784 and the translator of major works from Sanskrit to English, such as Kalidasa's *Shakuntala*.

JUTE. A fibrous plant grown extensively in Bengal yielding a fiber that is used for cordage and sacking. The East India Company encouraged its production and export by the end of the eighteenth century. Prior to the partition of 1947, the bulk of the production was in eastern Bengal, and the processing factories were in the Calcutta region or abroad in such cities as Dundee in Scotland. After 1947, East Bengal erected processing factories such as the Adamjee Jute Mill (q.v.), the world's largest. More recent uses for the fiber have been found in carpet backing. Nonetheless, with the development of plastic sacking the demand for jute as a container has slackened. Jute and its processed products remain the largest single export of Bangladesh.

- K -

KABIR, ALAMGIR (1938-1989). During the civil war, he was the English newscaster on Swadhin Bangla Beter (Independent Bangladesh Radio). He was also the writer and narrator of the film *Stop Genocide,* directed by Zahir Raihan (q.v.), and was the first president of the Film Institute, which he founded in 1969.

KABIR, HUMAYUN (1906-1969). From Faridpur district, he was a member of the Bengal Legislative Council, 1937-1947, and was deputy leader of the Krishak Praja Party (KPP) (q.v.) under Fazlul Haq (q.v.). He was educated in Calcutta and at Oxford. Kabir was closely associated with Maulana Abul Kalam Azad , the Congress Party president, whose secretary he was during the Simla conference in 1946. He chose to remain in India, where he became educational adviser to the government (1952-1956) and minister of education in the central government (1958-1965) after Azad's death. Kabir wrote extensively on literature and history. Perhaps his most noted volume was *Muslim Politics, 1906-42*, first published in 1944. He was also involved in the preparation of Azad's *India Wins Freedom* and followed Azad's instructions to withhold parts of the book until after Jawaharlal Nehru's death; the withheld portions have since been published. His daughter, Leila, is married to the Indian socialist leader,

George Fernandes. Kabir's brothers took different directions at independence: Jahangir remained in India and became a member of the Bengal Legislative Assembly; Alamgir and Akbar held official positions in East Pakistan and Bangladesh.

KAIKOBAD (1857-1951). Given the title of great poet for his work entitled *Mohashoshan* (or Great Funeral Pyre). His actual name was Muhammad Kazem Al-Quarashi. He received numerous awards and was the president of the Bengal Muslim Literature Society.

KAISAR, SHAHIDULLAH (1927-1971). Journalist and novelist. He was born in Feni district and educated at Presidency College, Calcutta. After partition in 1947, he worked for the *Weekly Ittefaq*, edited by Maulana Bhashani (q.v.), and later with *Sangbad* until his death at the hands of the pro-Pakistani group Al-Badr. Kaisar's novels earned him an award from the Bangla Academy.

KAISER, KHAWAJA MUHAMMAD (1918-1985). A member of the Indian Police Service, he joined the Pakistan Foreign Service in 1950. He served as Pakistani ambassador to Switzerland, Denmark, and Norway and was high commissioner to Australia and New Zealand. As ambassador to China in 1971, Kaiser switched his allegiance from Pakistan to Bangladesh. From 1976 to 1982 he was the permanent representative of Bangladesh to the United Nations. He resigned from service in 1982 but was later called on by Bangladesh to be its ambassador to China. Kaiser was instrumental in improving the relationship between China and Bangladesh. He was offered the presidency of Bangladesh by General Ershad (q.v.) but refused.

KAMRUZZAMAN, A. H. M. (1926-1975). Assassinated in what is known as the Dhaka jail killings (q.v.), he was president of the Awami League (q.v.) in 1974. A member of the first provisional government of Bangladesh, he also served as the Bangladesh commerce minister. Kamruzzaman was elected to the National Assembly of Pakistan in 1962.

KARIM, ENAYET (1927-1974). A member of the Pakistan Foreign Service, he was deputy chief of mission and the highest ranking Bengali officer in the Pakistan embassy in Washington in 1971. Although ill with heart disease, he led the Bengali officers who defected from the embassy. Karim was foreign secretary of Bangladesh at the time of his death.

KARIM, NAZMUL (1922-1982). Educationist. He studied at Dhaka, Columbia, and the London School of Economics. His work as a sociologist and political scientist was well received in academic circles. Karim's major work was *The Dynamics of Bangladesh Society.*

KARMANTA. In present-day Comilla district. A capital of the Chandra dynasty (q.v.).

KARRANI DYNASTY. Established in 1564 by the leader, Taj Khan Karrani, of north Indian Afghans who fled to Bengal after the recapture of Humayun, the Mughal (q.v.) emperor in 1564. Taj Khan defeated the remnants of the Suri dynasty (see Sher Shah Suri) that had maintained control in Bengal. Mughal armies uring the reign of Akbar defeated the Karranis in 1575. Daud Khan (q.v.), the last Karrani sultan, however, made one more attempt against the Mughals and was defeated and killed in the battle of Rajmahal in 1576.

KAZEM ALI MIAN (1852-1926). An educationist, he was responsible for the founding of several schools in Chittagong, including a middle school and a high school using English as the medium. Kazem Ali also was a member of the Central Legislative Assembly in the 1920s.

KEITH, JAMES (1784-1822). Grammarian and missionary. He came to Calcutta in 1816 as a member of the London Missionary Society. His Bengali work *A Grammar of the Bengalee Language Adapted to the Young in Easy Questions and Answers* (1820) was the first grammar in Bengali. It was used widely in the schools.

KHAFILUDDIN AHMAD (1899-1972). Joined the Muslim League in 1926 but resigned from the party in 1939 because of the domination of the Nawab of Dhaka family (q.v.). He was law minister in the 1954 United Front (q.v.) cabinet. In 1956, Khafiluddin joined the Awami League (q.v.) and was arrested by the martial law authorities in 1958. He reemerged in politics in 1970 when he was elected as a member of the National Assembly of Pakistan. During the liberation movement, Khafiluddin was a member of the Bangladesh provisional government-in-exile.

KHAIRAT HUSAIN (1911-1972). A founding member of the Awami League (q.v.). He participated as a member of the Muslim League (q.v.) in the Lahore session of the Muslim League in 1940, which called for a separate state for the Muslims of India. For his support of the language movement (q.v.), he was jailed by the government of Pakistan for a period of eighteen months. During the first martial law period in Pakistan he was placed in custody. In 1962 Khairat Husain established the National Democratic Front. In 1970 he served as the secretary of the Pakistan National League, which was founded by Ataur Rahman Khan (q.v.).

KHALEDA ZIA (b. 1945). Prime minister of Bangladesh from March, 1991 to March 1996, she was born August 29, 1945, in Jalpaiguri (now in West Bengal), although her family is from Feni district in Bangladesh. She attended school in Dinajpur. She married Ziaur Rahman (q.v.), an officer in the Pakistan army in 1960. She was kept under house arrest during the 1971 civil war, in which her husband played a leading role in the Mukti Bahini (q.v.). She entered politics after Ziaur Rahman's assassination, joining the Bangladesh Nationalist Party (BNP) (q.v.) on January 3, 1982. In March 1983 Khaleda Zia was named senior vice chairperson, and on May 10, 1984, chairperson of the party. Khaleda Zia was consistent in her opposition to the regime of Hussain Muhammad Ershad (q.v.), and the BNP did not contest the elections held in 1986 (as the Awami League [q.v.] did) and 1988 during Ershad's rule (see Elections). She was arrested seven times. Following the fall of Ershad in December 1990, a general election was held in February 1991. The BNP won a majority of seats in parliament and she became prime minister on March 20, 1991. She resigned the office on November 24, 1995, in the face of the opposition demand for new elections to be held under a neutral caretaker government (q.v.). In the June 1996 election the BNP finished second to the Awami League, which formed the new government with the support of the Jatiya Party (q.v.). Khaleda became the leader of the opposition.

KHALIQUZZAMAN, CHAUDHURY (1889-1973). A Muslim League (q.v.) politician from the United Provinces (now Uttar Pradesh) where he gained prominence. He migrated to Pakistan in 1948 and succeeded Muhammad Ali Jinnah (q.v.) as president of the Muslim League later that year. He was governor of East Bengal, 1953-1954.

KHALJI, IKHTIYARUDDIN MUHAMMAD BAKHTIYAR (d. 1206). A leader in the army of the Slave dynasty of the Delhi sultanate (q.v.). He defeated the last Sena (q.v.) king in 1202 at Nadia and brought Bengal under the control of the sultanate. His later excursion through Assam toward Tibet ended in failure in 1205.

KHAN, ABUL KASEM (1905-1991). Headed the largest Bangladeshi industrial establishment. The A. K. Khan group was the only indigenous East Pakistani group ranked in the thirtieth largest Pakistani industrial, commercial, and financial houses in the 1960s. After Bangladeshi independence, many holdings were nationalized during the regime of Sheikh Mujibur Rahman (q.v.), but the group has remained important and some properties were returned during the regime of Hussain Muhammad Ershad (q.v.). A. K. Khan himself was a minister from 1958 to 1962 in the Ayub Khan (q.v.) regime.

KHAN FAMILY OF BRAHMANBARIA. A lineage of musicians starting with Aftabuddin Khan (1862-1933) who earned the title *faqir* (in this case, saint). He had the ability to bridge between classical and folk music. He was joined by two brothers: Ustad Alauddin Khan (d. 1972) and Ustad Ayat Ali Khan (1884-1967). The two brothers modernized musical instruments such as the *chandra sorong*, the *mantranad*, and the *monohara*. The brothers also introduced several new *ragas* and were pioneers in introducing the classical music of the subcontinent to the West. They established the Alauddin Music College in Comilla and Brahmanbaria. Other members of the family include Bahadur Hossain Khan (1931-1991), the son of Ayat Ali, and Khadem Hossain Khan (1922-1990).

KHAN, FAZLUR RAHMAN (1929-1982). Architect and structural engineer, he is best known for his design of the Sears Tower in Chicago. He studied at what is now the Bangladesh University of Engineering and Technology and in the United States. Khan developed the "tube in tube" design that is used in most modern skyscrapers.

KHANDAKAR, MUKARRAM HUSSAIN (1922-1972). Educationist. Born in Dhaka, he was educated in Dhaka and Durham, England. A chemist, he did major research in plastics, food, and road and building materials.

KHARGA DYNASTY. Ruled in the Vanga (q.v.) and Samatata (q.v.) regions of southern and eastern Bengal in the latter part of the seventh century. Badkamta in Comilla district appears to have been the royal seat.

KHILAFAT MOVEMENT (1919-1925). A Muslim movement after World War I in which many Indian Muslims demanded that the status of the Caliph, who was also the sultan of Turkey, be unchanged as the result of the defeat of the Ottoman empire in the war. The principal leader of the movement was Muhammad Ali Jauhar. Gandhi brought the Indian National Congress into the movement as well in an effort to strengthen Hindu-Muslim unity. Differences between the two communities, however, were so great that the net result may have been an increase in communal differences. Although a Shia, Syed Amir Ali (q.v.) supported the Khilafat movement. The question became moot when the Turks, led by Kemal Ataturk, settled the question by ending both the caliphate and the sultanate.

KHULNA. A city and district headquarters, Khulna is the third largest city in Bangladesh. Khulna lies on the Bhairab River. Nearby is the port of Mangla, a man-made anchorage that serves as the second port of Bangladesh after Chittagong. The anchorage was originally situated at Chalna, about twenty-six miles from

Khulna, and opened in 1950. In 1954, the anchorage was shifted to Mangla, about twelve miles from Chalna. In practice the two names are used interchangeably. Khulna itself is an important river port and is connected with Barisal (q.v.), Madaripur, and Narayanganj (see Dhaka).

In ancient times, Khulna was a part of Vanga (q.v.) or Samatata (q.v.). Local traditions associate Khulna with Khanja Ali, who obtained a *zamindari* in the area in the mid-fifteenth century from the rulers of Gaur (q.v.). Khulna is the home district of Pratapaditya (q.v.), one of the Bara Bhuiyan (q.v.) who rebelled against Mughal (q.v.) rule in the latter part of the sixteenth century. Architectural monuments in Bagerhat (formerly a subdivisional headquarters and now a district headquarters include the Sathgumbad mosque and the tomb of Khan Jahan Ali (q.v.).

With the local government (q.v.) reorganization during the Ershad regime, the former Khulna district was divided into Khulna, Bagerhat, and Satkhira districts.

KRISHAK PRAJA PARTY (KPP) (Peasants' and People's Party). The political vehicle of Fazlul Haq (q.v.) before Indian independence. It was founded in 1927 and formally structured prior to the 1937 elections. Intended to be noncommunal, the KPP, in fact, received little non-Muslim support. The KPP found its base among the peasants, principally in eastern Bengal, and it opposed the landlord system. The difficulty of the time was that the restrictive franchise rules, made most of the peasants, many of them tenants, ineligible to vote. The KPP also opposed the landlord-dominated Muslim League (q.v.). The party won about one-third of the seats in the Bengal legislative assembly but was able to form a coalition with the Muslim League and govern Bengal until 1941. The Muslim League withdrew in that year, but the KPP joined with non-Congress Hindus and others and continued in office until 1943. At that time, a Muslim League-led ministry replaced it. In the 1945 election the party did poorly, although Fazlul Haq retained his seat. The party disappeared at the time of independence in 1947. Haq, however, formed the Krishak Sramik Party (KSP) (q.v.) after independence.

KRISHAK SRAMIK PARTY (KSP) (Peasants' and Workers' Party). A revival by Fazlul Haq (q.v.) of the Krishak Praja Party (KPP) (q.v.). Fazlul Haq became advocate general of East Bengal briefly after independence, and had temporarily dropped out of party politics. With the approach of the election to the provincial assembly in 1954, he returned to active politics and formed the KSP. The party continued to champion the cause of the peasant who had, in many cases, gained ownership of his land through, *zamindari* abolition. Also, this election, unlike pre-independence elections, would be held under universal adult franchise. The KSP joined with the Awami League (q.v.) in the United Front (q.v.), which trounced the Muslim League (q.v.) in the election. The KSP leader was chosen as the first chief minister under the United Front, but Fazlul Haq was soon ousted from office by the central government. With the revival of the assembly in 1956, Abu Hussain Sarkar (q.v.) of the KSP became chief minister, but the United Front had divided, and Sarkar and Ataur Rahman Khan (q.v.) of the Awami League alternated chief ministerships until martial law was imposed in October 1958. Fazlul Haq died in 1962, about the same time that party activity was again permitted. A KSP continued to exist after his death, but it has been a small, unimportant group.

KUSHTIA. Kushtia district was a part of Nadia district (now a district in West Bengal) prior to the partition of 1947. With the reorganization of local government (q.v.) during the Ershad government, it has been divided into three districts: Kushtia, Chuadanga, and Meherpur. It is the home district of Titu Mir of the Faraizi movement (q.v.), and of Lalan Shah (q.v.), whose tomb is at Sevria, near Kushtia town.

The Kushtia area, along with Jessore, is the base of the Ganges-Kobadak pump irrigation project under which water is pumped from the Ganges just inside the Bangladesh border with India to water fields. The project is threatened by the shortage of water during the dry season by the Farraka barrage (q.v.) erected by India.

- L -

LAHORE RESOLUTION. Passed March 23, 1940, by the Muslim League. It is often called the Pakistan resolution, although the word Pakistan does not appear in the document. The resolution stated that, if conditions for the Muslims of India did not improve, the League would have no alternative but to call for the creation of independent *states* in the eastern and northwestern Indian areas that had a Muslim majority in the population. The plural "states" was used in 1940, with the implication that there would not be a single Muslim state. At a meeting of Muslim League (q.v.) legislators, this was modified in 1946, using, the singular "state" and a single state was created by the partition of India in 1947. Fazlul Haq (q.v.) was among the movers of the resolution; Suhrawardy (q.v.) supported the alteration in 1946.

LAILI, QAMRUNNAHAR (1937-1984). One of the earliest female lawyers, she entered the Dhaka bar in 1963 and in 1973 was the first women member of the council of the Bangladesh bar. Laili was also one of the founders of the National Awami Party (q.v.).

LAKNAUTI, LAKSHMANAVATI. See GAUR.

LAKSHMANA SENA. The last member of the Sena dynasty (q.v.) to rule from Nadia. He ascended the throne in about 1184 and shortly afterward subdued Kamarupa (Assam). He was a patron of the arts; the poet Jaidev (q.v.) wrote the *Gita Govinda* at his court. He and his governance, however, declined, and his capital was taken by an army of the Delhi sultanate (q.v.) led by Ikhtiyaruddin Muhammad Bakhtiyar Khalji (q.v.) in 1202. Lakshmana Sena fled to eastern Bengal, where his successors reigned for about fifty years until all of Bengal came under Muslim rule.

LALAN SHAH (d. 1890). A syncretistic folk poet and composer. His poetry and songs are considered treasures of Bengali literature. A district gazetteer stated that he "combined in himself all that was best in Hinduism and Islam." At his tomb at Sevria, near Kushtia (q.v.), his disciples assemble for an annual festival of music and poetry.

LALMAI. See MAINAMATI.

LAND FRAGMENTATION. This phenomenon results primarily from Islamic inheritance rules. In the usual pattern, on the death of a landholder the land is divided among his children, with sons receiving a full share and daughters a half share. As the land inherited is not of uniform quality, an effort is made to share the land so that each inheritor will receive shares of the best, the middling, and the poorest land. The outcome is that an heir may receive three or four or more small parcels of land as an inheritance. The result over several generations is evident. Government data (1977 agricultural census) indicate that most holdings contain six to nine fragments, and about 10 percent contain twenty or more. In 1983-84 the average holding (of those who owned land) was 2.2 acres; if the landless are included in the calculation, the average holding would be much less.

LAND REFORM. The Permanent Settlement (q.v.) of 1793 converted tax-farmers into landowners (*zamindars*). Most land in Bengal was owned by zamindars (often absentee), and most tillers were either sharecropping tenants or landless laborers. After Pakistani independence, in 1951, an East Bengal Land Reform Act was passed that limited holdings of a cultivating family to 100 *bighas* (33 acres). In September 1984 the Ershad regime decreed a new land reform ordinance under which the maximum permissible holding was reduced generally to 60 bighas (20 acres). Surplus land would be distributed to the landless and to very small holders, but the amount of surplus land was estimated at less than half a million acres. In the 1983-84 agricultural census, it was reported that only 4.7 percent of farmers who owned land held more than 7.5 acres (see also land fragmentation).

LANGUAGE. Bangladesh is, for all practical purposes, a unilingual nation and is therefore unique among the nations of South Asia. All primary and much secondary and higher education is in Bengali. Other languages used in Bangladesh include English, Urdu, and several tribal languages.

Bengali belongs to the easternmost branch of the Indo-European family of languages known as Indo-Iranian. Its direct ancestor is a form of Prakrit, which descended from Sanskrit. While Sanskrit remained the language of culture and literature for centuries, the spoken language varied considerably from region to region in northern India. By no later than the middle of the tenth century a distinctive Bengali language had developed. Little literature remains from this period.

At present, Bengali has two literary styles: *Sudhobhasa* ("elegant language") and *Chaltibhasa* ("daily language"). The former continues the literary style of Middle Bengali of the sixteenth century. The latter is largely a creation of the twentieth century and is based on the cultivated dialect spoken by residents of Calcutta and its region. The difference between the two as literary styles is not sharp. The vocabulary is largely the same; the difference lies mainly in the forms of the pronoun and the verb. Sudhobhasa has the older forms, while Chaltibhasa uses lighter and more modern forms. Sudhobhasa shows a partiality for lexical words and for compound words similar to Sanskrit. Chaltibhasa was first seriously taken up at the urging of Rabindranath Tagore (q.v.) during the early years of the twentieth century. Soon after, Tagore all but discarded Sudhubhasa, and Chaltibhasa is now generally favored by writers.

The script is based on that of early Sanskrit (*devanagiri*) although the variation is significant. The present form can be dated from the first casting of type by Charles Wilkins in 1778, although since then there have been some changes.

LANGUAGE MOVEMENT. One of the defining moments in the political development of Bangladesh, the language movement of 1952 was intended to establish Bengali as one of the national languages of Pakistan. The movement had its origins as far back as 1948 when Jinnah (q.v.) announced in Dhaka that Urdu, and only Urdu, would be the national language. At that time the Student Action Committee of the University of Dhaka demanded that Bengali be declared the official language of East Pakistan. The central government in 1952 attempted to introduce the Urdu script (modified Arabic) for Bengali, leading to violent reactions by students. During the language movement in 1952 a number of people, including university students, were killed. A monument, the Shahid Minar, has been erected on the spot of police firing on March 21, 1952 (see Martyrs' Day). The language controversy ended in 1954 when the Pakistan parliament declared both Urdu and Bengali to be official languages, but the hard feelings on this and other issues would eventually lead to the independence movement, culminating in civil war and independence in 1971.

LEGAL FRAMEWORK ORDER. Issued by Pakistani President Yahya Khan (q.v.) in 1970 to set parameters for the operation of the constituent assembly to be elected in October of that year (later postponed to December because of a major cyclonic storm that struck East Pakistan). The principal points were: (1) a federal state; (2) Islamic principles would be paramount; (3) direct and regular elections; (4) fundamental rights guaranteed; (5) independent judiciary; (6) maximum provincial autonomy, "but the federal government shall also have adequate powers, including legislative, administrative and financial powers, to discharge its responsibilities;" and (7) disparities between the provinces will be removed. The order was in major part a response to the Six Points (q.v.) of Mujibur Rahman (q.v.). The major conflict in the two documents is between Yahya's sixth and Mujib's fourth, in which the latter stated that all power of taxation would be at the provincial level and the provinces would grant sums to the federal government to carry out its duties.

LIAQUAT ALI KHAN (1895-1951). Although from a prominent east Punjab family, he gained his political experience in the United Provinces (now Uttar Pradesh, India). He served in the provincial legislative bodies, 1926-1940, and in the Central Legislative Assembly, from 1940 until its dissolution in 1947, and was leader of the Muslim League (q.v.) group in that body. He was also a member for finance in the interim cabinet, 1946-1947. Liaquat was Jinnah's (q.v.) principal lieutenant as general secretary of the League from 1936 until independence, when he became prime minister. Liaquat was assassinated in Rawalpindi on October 16, 1951.

LOCAL GOVERNMENT. The basic form of governance in the subcontinent until the sixth century B.C., when large kingdoms came into existence, is generally assumed to have been local government (the idealized "village republics" of Mahatma Gandhi). While not much is known about local governance in ancient Bengal, the first census conducted by the British in the Bengal presidency in 1872 suggests strong village organizations in eastern Bengal (present Bangladesh). Local governance in Bengal was affected by such legislation as the Permanent Settlement (q.v.) Act of 1793, the Chowkidari (village watchmen) Act of 1870, and the Local Self-Government Act of 1885. The last established a three-tier system that included a district board, a local board at the sub-district level, and a union committee at the village level. Local government in Bangladesh conforms to this basic structure.

Since 1971, three major attempts have been made by three successive governments to supply public services to the people through strengthening local government. In the first experiment, during the regime of Mujibur Rahman (q.v.), Bangladesh was divided into sixty-one districts, each of which would be headed by a governor. The purpose was to bring about political control over district administration, a critical issue in the Bangladeshi administrative system, political economy, and local government system. The first experiment did not affect the local government system because the Mujib regime ended shortly after the announcement of the plan.

The second experiment, linked to the democratization of the Ziaur Rahman (q.v.) regime, set up rural local government consisting of *zilla* (district), *thana* (sub-district), and union *parishads* (councils), and *pourashavas* (municipal corporations) in the urban areas. The system was dominated by the bureaucracy as the elections to the local bodies that were integral to the system were never held. The concepts of Gram Sarkar (q.v.) (village rule) and *swarnirvar* (q.v.) (self-reliance) were introduced as major building blocks for local government strengthening and autonomy. The purpose was to mobilize people at the village level for development work. Decision-making was to be based on consensus, and all groups were to be represented at the village level. Gram Sarkars were to be organized around increasing food production, expanding mass literacy programs, promoting family planning activities, and the maintenance of law and order. Mobilization, participation, and involvement are other critical issues that were to be addressed in strengthening the local government system.

The third experiment, also linked to a process of democratization of a military government, took place during the regime of Hussain Muhammad Ershad (q.v.). It upgraded the 464 thanas to *upazillas* (sub-districts) and the 64 former subdivisions to districts. The upazillas became the center of all development activities, policy planning, and implementation. Each upazilla had a council that was partly elected and partly appointed. All central administrative units that had offices at the upazilla level came under the upazilla council. A separate staff functioned as the secretariat for the upazilla council. This plan for strengthening local government brought together for the first time two conflicting elements—popular participation and merit-based administrative units—in the implementation of development plans. The purpose was to pull together the cooperative and relative strength of two key forces in the economic development of Bangladesh. Local government units at the union level were retained but with reduced powers. Pourashavas in the urban areas were also retained.

This experiment continued until the upazilla parishads were abolished in 1992 by the Khaleda Zia government (q.v.). Before this government could reassess the nature and structure of local government the government of Sheikh Hasina (q.v.) came to power and in accordance with its 1996 election manifesto will make another attempt to provide services at the local level.

LOHANI BROTHERS. Fateh (1923-1975) and Fazle (1929-1985) were involved in the film and television industries. Fateh Lohani was one of the first Bengali Muslim filmmakers, and Fazle Lohani was a television performer. A younger brother, Kamal Lohani, is now working in films and television.

- M -

MACAULAY, THOMAS BABINGTON, FIRST BARON (1800-1859). The great British historian, essayist, and political figure spent a part of his career in Calcutta as law member of the governor-general's executive council. He had earlier been a member of the Board of Control of the East India Company (q.v.). Macaulay arrived in India in 1834. He is perhaps best known in Indian history for his "Minute on Education" of 1835. Macaulay argued for a Western (i.e., British) system of education in English in opposition to the "orientalists" who espoused teaching in local languages. Although Macaulay has been criticized for this (for example, as creating a group of "brown sahibs"), his view was that Indians educated under his proposal would eventually demand representative institutions. In the interim, Britain would rule by the sword. Macaulay, as law member, changed the legal system so that British and Indians would be tried under a single court system.

MAHASTHANGARH. An archeological site in the district of Bogra, it is identified with the Pundranagara mentioned in the records of the Maurya empire and the Gupta, Pala, and Sena dynasties. This old ruined city is situated near the Karatuya River. The city is surrounded by eleven-foot-thick defense walls 500 feet long on two sides and 450 feet on the other two sides. Limited excavation has revealed thickly packed dwellings and temples of Hindu and Buddhist origin. Excavations have also resulted in the discoveries of copper, bronze, and gold jewelry, pendants, badges, and coins. This area was later conquered by Muslim generals. It is the site of the Mazar (grave) of Saint Shah Sultan Baki Mahisawar.

MAHIPALA I. A ruler of the Pala dynasty (q.v.) who reigned about 978-1030, under whom the disintegration of the dynasty took place. Southwestern Bengal came under the rule of the Sena dynasty (q.v.) and eastern Bengal under the Chandras (q.v.). He also fought losing battles with the Cholas, a south Indian dynasty that penetrated to the Ganges in 1023, and the Kalachuris, who ruled in central India. Mahipala is remembered, however, for public works at such places as Nalanda, the Buddhist university in Bihar, and for irrigation works in north and west Bengal.

MAHMUD, ALTAF (1930-1971). One of the many intellectuals killed by the Pakistan army. He was a singer and composer whose best-known song was one paying tribute to those killed during the language movement (q.v.) in 1952.

MAINAMATI. Five miles west of Comilla town, contains the archaeological sites of Mainamati and Lalmai. These two sites are thought to be the remains of the one-time political and cultural center of this region. Excavations show that the structures spread along the Lalmai ridge for a distance of eleven miles. The structures are Buddhist monasteries and stupas often inset with characteristic terra-cotta plaques. They date from as early as the seventh century. Archaeological finds here have increased knowledge of southeastern Bengal dynasties such as the Khargas (q.v.), Devas (q.v.), Chandras (q.v.), and Varmans (q.v.), but much of their histories remains speculation.

MAJORS. Refers to the leaders of the August Coup (q.v.) of 1977. They were Lieutenant Colonel Syed Farook Rahman and Majors Shariful Huq Dalim, Abdul Nur Chowdhury, Abdul Hafiz, Badrul Rashid, and Muhammad Huda. After they were ousted in November 1977, they, along with a number of other officers, were forced to leave the country. Some of them were later permitted to join the Bangladesh foreign service. All have been permitted to return to Bangladesh. Two other coup attempts are linked to this group, including the Bogra Mutiny (q.v.). Lieutenant Colonel Syed Farook Rahman returned to Bangladesh and in 1986 he contested the presidential election won by Lieutenant General Hussain Muhammad Ershad (q.v.). Farook has organized a political party, the Freedom Party, which won no seats in the 1991 election.

MAJUMDAR, CHARU (1915-1972). Born in Rajshahi, he turned to socialism while studying in Pabna and worked to organize farmers. He joined the Communist Party. In 1969, he formed the Communist Party of India—Marxist-Leninist. Some of Majumdar's followers were known as Naxalites (from Naxalbari where they operated), a rural terrorist group in West Bengal that has lent its name to similar groups in South Asia. Majumdar was arrested in 1972 and died in jail twelve days later.

MAJUMDAR, PHANI BHUSHAN (1901-1981). A follower of Subash Chandra Bose, he was a member of the Revolutionary Communist Party from 1930 to 1938. He spent a considerable amount of time in jail during the British era in India. He was elected a member of the East Bengal Legislative Assembly in 1954. From 1954 until 1962, Majumdar was under arrest by the Pakistani government. In 1970, as an Awami League (q.v.) nominee, he was elected a member of the Pakistan National Assembly. During the liberation war he was a member of the advisory board of the provisional Bangladesh government-in-exile. Majumdar was a member of the cabinets of Mujibur Rahman (q.v.) and Mushtaque Ahmed (q.v.), 1972-1975.

MAJUMDAR, ROMESH CHANDRA (1888-1980). Historian. Born in Faridpur, he studied at Calcutta and taught in Calcutta and Dhaka. With Sir Jadunath Sarkar (q.v.), he edited the monumental *History of Bengal*. Majumdar also edited the multivolume *History and Culture of the Indian People*, published by the Bharatiya Vidya Bhavan; later volumes were edited by his son, Ashok.

MALIK, ABDUL MUTTALIB (1905-1977). Appointed governor of East Pakistan by Yahya Khan (q.v.) in November 1971, during the civil war, in an attempt to civilianize the embattled Pakistani regime. He had earlier been appointed a minister in the central government by Yahya in 1969. An ophthalmologist by training, Malik entered politics as a member of the Bengal legislature (1937-1947). After Pakistan's independence he served as a cabinet minister and as ambassador to a number of countries. He played no role in independent Bangladesh.

MAMUN MAHMUD (1929-1971). Entered the Police Service in 1947. He served as superintendent of police in Chittagong and Khulna. He was also the deputy inspector general, Rajshahi. He raised the black flag of protest on March 4, 1971, against the military rule of President Yahya Khan (q.v.). On March 26, 1971, a day after the beginning of the civilian massacre by the Pakistan army, Mamun was summoned by a Brigadier Abdullah and was never heard from again.

MAN SINGH, RAJA. A Rajput from Amber (Jaipur) who entered the service of the Mughal emperor Akbar in 1562. He was among the principal Hindu supporters of the Mughals and served the empire until his death in 1614. Among the positions he held was governor of Bengal, 1594-1606, during which period he extended Mughal control eastward in Bengal from his capital of Rajmahal (q.v.).

MANSUR ALI (1919-1975). Assassinated during the Dhaka jail killings (q.v.), he was the last prime minister of Bangladesh during the presidency of Sheikh Mujibur Rahman (q.v.). He was also the general secretary of BAKSAL (q.v.). A lawyer by profession, he was elected three times as the president of the Pabna Lawyers Association. Mansur Ali was a vice president of the Pabna District Muslim League from 1946 to 1950. He joined the Awami League (q.v.) in 1951 and had his first ministerial appointment in 1956 in Ataur Rahman Khan's (q.v.) cabinet. In 1969 he became the vice president of the Awami League. Mansur

Ali served as finance minister in the provisional Bangladesh government-in-exile. After the independence of Bangladesh and before he became prime minister in 1975, Mansur Ali served in a number of ministries, including commerce, finance, and industries.

MANSUR ALI KHAN (1829-1884). He had the dubious distinction of being the last person to hold the title Nawab Nazim of Bengal. The Nawab Nazim title resided in Murshidabad (q.v.). When the ceremonial status of the title was reduced, and following an unsuccessful appeal in London, Mansur Ali resigned the title in 1880.

MANZUR, MUHAMMAD ABUL, Major General (1940-1981). Awarded *Bir Uttam* for bravery during the war of liberation. He was one of the leaders of the coup attempt that led to the assassination of President Ziaur Rahman (q.v.) in May 1981. Following the failure of the coup he was arrested and killed. In 1957 he joined the Pakistan Army and by 1971 was a brigade commander. During the war of liberation, Manzur escaped from Pakistan and actively participated in the war as a sector commander. In 1973, he became the military attaché of Bangladesh in New Delhi. He later was appointed the chief of the general staff of the Bangladesh army. In 1977 he was transferred as the General Officer, Commander of the Twenty-fourth Division based in Chittagong. Manzur was the commander of the Twenth-fourth Division when he became involved in the coup attempt. He was first a friend and later a foe of President Ziaur Rahman. The Manzur case was reopened in 1995 as part of a general review of the assassination of Ziaur Rahman.

MARSHMAN, JOHN. A Christian missionary associated with William Carey (q.v.) in Srirampur (Serampore) and later in Calcutta. He started the journal *The Friend of India,* which advocated reform of such institutions as *sati* (widow burning) and child marriage. The publication was later merged with the *Statesman.*

MARTIAL RACES. A term introduced by the British following the mutiny of the Bengal Army in 1857. The Bengal Army was comprised mainly of soldiers (*sepoys*) recruited from the lower Ganges basin. The British were aided in quelling the rebellion by Sikh and Muslim Punjabi troops and some other groups from northern India. After the mutiny the British determined to recruit only from those areas that had supported them; these peoples were designated "martial races" and included the Punjabis. The peoples of the former recruiting grounds in the lower Ganges basin were described as "nonmartial races" and were not recruited. The designations continued to operate in practice to a large degree even after Pakistani independence and resulted in an army in which the Bengalis were very much underrepresented.

MARTYRS' DAY. Celebrated annually on February 21, it honors those who lost their lives during the language movement (q.v.) to make Bengali a national language of Pakistan. The incident occurred on February 21, 1952, when police fired upon students demon-strating against the plan to make Urdu the national language of Pakistan. A number of students were killed as a result. The shooting took place near the Dhaka Medical College and a monument, called the Shahid Minar, has been erected near the place where the students were killed.

MASHIUR RAHMAN (1928-1979). A prominent parliamentarian, he started his political career as a member of the Muslim League (q.v.). In 1957 he joined the National Awami Party (q.v.) and became a leading member of the organization. He was a member of the Pakistan National Assembly in 1962 and deputy leader of the opposition. He was again elected to the National Assembly in 1965 but resigned in 1969 when the movement to oust President Ayub started. Mashiur Rahman became the general secretary of the East Pakistan National Awami Party. During the war of liberation he first left for India but later surrendered to the Pakistani armed forces and opposed the liberation forces. After the liberation of Bangladesh, he was arrested as a traitor but was later released. After the death of Maulana Bhashani (q.v.), Mashiur Rahman became the leader of the National Awami Party in 1977. During the presidency of Ziaur Rahman (q.v.), his faction of the National Awami Party joined the Bangladesh Nationalist Party (q.v.), and he became the "senior minister" of Ziaur Rahman's cabinet and minister of railways. In the 1979 election he was elected as a member of the parliament once again. It was believed that Mashiur Rahman would be the prime minister, but he died suddenly just before the cabinet was announced. Shah Azizur Rahman (q.v.) became the prime minister in his stead.

MAURYA DYNASTY. Founded by Chandragupta Maurya in about 322 B.C., the dynasty quickly controlled all of northern India, including Bengal. The most noted ruler of the dynasty was Chandragupta's grandson, Asoka (q.v.).

MEDIA. Bangladesh has more than 1,000 national, regional, and local newspapers and periodicals, including 142 daily newspapers. Some of the more prominent daily national-language newspapers are *Ittefaq*, *Inquilab*, *Sangbad*, *Dainik Bangla*, *Ajker Kagoz*, and *Bhorer Kagoz*. Among the English-language dailies are the *Bangladesh Observer*, *Bangladesh Times*, *Morning Sun*, and *Daily Star*.

Radio Bangladesh has nine stations and an external service that is broadcast in seven languages. Radio Bangladesh can be heard throughout South Asia and in the Middle East. Television was introduced in 1964 and operates two channels. Bangladesh TV also permits transmission of Cable News Network (CNN) and the British Broadcasting Corporation (BBC).

The Bangladesh Film Development Corporation, a public-sector enterprise, produces approximately seventy films a year.

The media in Bangladesh have been relatively free although the country has been under military rule for much of its existence. Press freedom has expanded since 1990, after the fall of the Ershad (q.v.) regime.

MEGHNA. A river that becomes a great stream when it is joined by the already combined Ganges (q.v.) and Brahmaputra (q.v.) at Chandpur, about eighty miles from the Bay of Bengal. The Meghna drains the exceptionally rainy areas of Sylhet and some areas of India. It is joined by the Surma River. Some of its channels comprised sections of the "old" Brahmaputra before that river changed course.

MIDDLE EAST. Relations between Bangladesh and most nations in the Middle East did not exist prior to the Lahore meeting of the Islamic Conference (q.v.) in 1974 when several of the Arab delegates persuaded Pakistan (q.v.) to invite Bangladesh to the meeting. Thereafter, during the early part of the Zia regime, most Middle Eastern countries recognized Bangladesh and established formal diplomatic relations. Several countries, especially Kuwait and Saudi Arabia, have provided economic assistance to Bangladesh. Many countries also serve as hosts to Bangladeshi migrant labor. This has generated as much as $500 million per year in remittances to Bangladesh. There have also been objections by some Middle Eastern countries, notably Saudi Arabia, to the principle of secularism contained in the Bangladeshi constitution (see Mujibbad). This provision was modified by Zia to provide that Muslims in Bangladesh would be enabled to order their lives in accordance with the Sunna while retaining provisions allowing freedom of religion. Ershad (q.v.) declared Islam to be the state religion, but this again did not diminish the rights of non-Muslims.

MINTO, GILBERT JOHN ELLIOT-MURRAY-KYNYNMOUND, FOURTH EARL OF (1845-1914). The viceroy of India, 1905-1910. (He was great-grandson of the first earl, who was governor-general, 1806-1813.) Minto was governor-general of Canada, 1898-1904. Minto was required to restore the authority of the office of governor-general, which had been lowered in the dispute between his predecessor, Lord Curzon (q.v.), and the commander in chief, Lord Kitchener. He was successful in doing this. Minto came to office at a time when changes in the constitutional arrangements for India were imminent. He worked with Lord Morley, the secretary of state for India, in framing the Government of India Act of 1909 (q.v.). A key aspect of this was the question of separate electorates (q.v.) for Muslims. Minto received a Muslim delegation headed by the Aga Khan (q.v.) at Simla in 1906. The delegation pressed for separate electorates. They were incorporated into the 1909 act.

MIR JAFAR (d. 1765). Remains a symbol for treachery in Bengal. He was a brother-in-law of Alivardi Khan (q.v.) and played his treachery on Alivardi's grandson and successor, Sirajuddaulah (q.v.). In this he was associated with the banker, Jagat Seth (q.v.). At the battle of Plassey (q.v.) in 1757 between Sirajuddaulah and the British under Clive (q.v.), Mir Jafar deserted Sirajuddaulah, contributing to the latter's defeat. Mir Jafar was rewarded with the governorship of Bengal but was soon displaced (in 1760) by his son-in-law, Mir Qasim (q.v.), at the instance of the British. Mir Jafar returned to the governor's post in 1763 and held it until his death.

MIR QASIM (d. c. 1777). A son-in-law and successor as governor of Bengal to Mir Jafar (q.v.) and was in turn succeeded by Mir Jafar. He was installed as governor in 1760 at the instance of the British, at the same time ceding the districts of Chittagong, Midnapur, and Burdwan to the East India Company. His actions to curb the private trade of British Company officers led to a worsening of relations between Mir Qasim and the Company. He is said to have perpetrated a massacre of British at Patna. In 1764, the British attacked Mir Qasim, defeating him at the battle of Buxar (q.v.) on October 22, 1764. Mir Qasim fled and died in poverty in Delhi about 1777.

MIRZA, ISKANDAR (1899-1969). A collateral of the family of the nawabs of Murshidabad (q.v.), he was in 1919 the first Indian cadet to graduate from Sandhurst, but he served his career primarily in the Indian Political Service. After independence he was defense secretary (1947-1954), governor of East Bengal (1954), a central minister (1954-1955), and governor-general (1955-1956). Mirza then became the first president of Pakistan in 1956. On October 7, 1958, he ended parliamentary government and proclaimed martial law but was dismissed on October 28 by the chief martial law administrator, Ayub Khan (q.v.); Mirza left Pakistan on November 2 for London. He died in exile in London and was buried in Tehran.

MITRA, DINBONDHU (1830-1873). Playwright. Born in Nadia, his most famous play, *Neel Dorpon*, depicts the exploitation of poor farmers by the British indigo (q.v.) planters.

MOHAMMADULLAH (b. 1921). President of Bangladesh from January 1974 to January 1975, when Mujibur Rahman (q.v.) assumed the presidency. After Mohammadullah stepped down from the presidency, he was minister of land administration and land reform until August 1975, when the regime of Mujibur Rahman (q.v.) was overthrown. Mohammadullah was named vice president by Abdus Sattar (q.v.) in March 1982 just prior to the coup by Ershad (q.v.).

MOHSIN, HAJI MOHAMMAD (1732-1812). A philanthropist and social activist, he was a lifelong bachelor who withdrew from an active life at age thirty-two to become a *fakir,* in which capacity he visited Egypt, Turkey, Iran, and Saudi Arabia. In 1906 he donated all of his property for the education of Muslims in India. Mohsin was the founder of the Hooghly College in Calcutta and established madrasas (religious schools) in Dhaka, Rajshahi and Chittagong. He also established the Moshin Scholarship Fund for Higher Education of meritorious students. Today, when someone donates a large sum, that person is called Haji Mohsin in honor of Haji Mohammad Mohsin.

MONEM KHAN, ABDUL (1899-1971). A member of the Muslim League since 1935, he was the founder-secretary of the Mymensingh district Muslim League. He was a member of the Constituent Assembly of Pakistan until 1954. A protégé of Nurul Amin (q.v.), Monem Khan was a midlevel political leader of East Pakistan who did not have the stature or the personality of leaders such as Abul Kasem Fazlul Haq (q.v.) or Hussain Shahid Suhrawardy (q.v.). Nonetheless, he was a shrewd politician who spoke the language of the people. Elected as a member of the National Assembly of Pakistan in 1962, he was brought into the national limelight by President Ayub Khan (q.v.), first as central minister of health, labor, and social welfare, and then as Governor of East Pakistan, 1962-1969. Monem Khan was assassinated in 1971, during the Bangladesh civil war.

MONI SINGH (1901-1994). Chairman of the Communist Party of Bangladesh (q.v.). His participation in anti-British movements and his leadership in organizing the peasant movement brought him to the forefront of politics. For these activities, Moni Singh was arrested a number of times by the British. During the Pakistani period he was also frequently under arrest. He was associated with the freedom movement of Bangladesh and was a member of the Consultative Committee of the Bangladesh provisional government-in-exile. After independence, Moni Singh cooperated with the Sheikh Mujibur Rahman (q.v.)government.

MONTAGU-CHELMSFORD ACT. See GOVERNMENT OF INDIA ACT OF 1919.

MORLEY-MINTO ACT. See GOVERNMENT OF INDIA ACT OF 1909.

MOTHAR HUSAIN, KAZI (1897-1981). Granted the title of National Professor in 1975 for his contribution to science. In 1926 he organized the Muslim Literature Society and became the President of the Pakistan Literature Society in 1952.

MOUNTBATTEN OF BURMA, LOUIS MOUNTBATTEN, FIRST EARL (1900-1979). The son of Prince Louis of Battenberg (later Mountbatten) and Princess Victoria of Hesse (a granddaughter of Queen Victoria), was viceroy of India in 1947 and governor-general of India, 1947-1948. Mountbatten's task was the withdrawal of British power from India and (reluctantly) arranging for the partition of the British dominions between India and Pakistan.

MUGHAL EMPIRE. The Mughal Empire (1526-1857) was the successor ruler in Delhi to the Delhi Sultanate (q.v.). Babar, the founder of the dynasty, defeated the last Lodhi sultan at the battle of Panipat in 1526. The dominions of the Mughals soon spread from Afghanistan to Bengal and as far south as the Deccan. The principal rulers were the first six: Babar (1526-1530), Humayun (1530-1540 and 1555-1556), Akbar (1556-1605), Jahangir (1605-1627), Shahjahan (1627-1658), and Aurangzeb (1658-1707). Thereafter, the dynasty declined and was, in effect, under British control from the early nineteenth century until the final collapse in 1857 following the sepoy mutiny (see Martial Races).

With respect to Bengal, control was taken by the Mughals under Humayun in 1538, but was lost a year later to Sher Shah Suri (q.v.) whose descendants ruled Bengal until 1564. A short non-Mughal period (see Karrani dynasty) followed until 1576 when the Mughals regained control under Akbar. Mughal governors (nawabs) ruled from Dhaka (q.v.) and Murshidabad (q.v.), and in 1765 the emperor Shah Alam II granted the *diwani* (q.v.) to the British.

MUJIBBAD (Mujibism). The term used for the four pillars espoused by Sheikh Mujibur Rahman (q.v.) as the key principles on which the government of independent Bangladesh would be based: nationalism, secularism, socialism, and democracy. They are part of the 1972 constitution. Mujibbad follows closely the four principles attributed to Jawaharlal Nehru of India: democracy, socialism, secularism, and nonalignment.

MUJIBUR RAHMAN (d. 1940). A prominent Bengali Muslim journalist who also involved himself in politics. He was an editorial writer for the *Mussalman*, an important weekly that began its publication in 1906 as a reaction to the partition of Bengal (q.v.). Mujibur Rahman also was a member of the Muslim League (q.v.), and as such his major impact was his strong opposition to Muslim League association with the Simon Commission (1928), a British parliamentary commission sent to survey the operation of the Government of India Act of 1919 (q.v.). Many Indians, including the Congress Party, objected to the exclusion of Indians from the commission.

MUJIBUR RAHMAN, SHEIKH (1921-1975). Prime minister (1972-1975) and president (1975) of Bangladesh. He began his political career as a student in Calcutta in 1940 with the Muslim Students' Federation, an arm of the Muslim League (q.v.). He was a founding member with Husain Shahid Suhrawardy (q.v.), of the Awami League (q.v.) in 1949. Mujib was the principal organizer of the party in East Bengal, later East Pakistan. He was minister of commerce in East Pakistan, 1956-1957, but was best respected for his party organizational abilities rather than for his administrative skills, a factor that would make his management of Bangladesh difficult.

After Suhrawardy's death in 1963, Mujib became de facto national leader of the Awami League, although his official position pertained only to East Pakistan. In this role, he proclaimed the Six-Point Program (q.v.) in 1966. Mujib led the Awami League to an overwhelming victory in the 1970 elections (see Elections) in East Pakistan, but his party was unable to win any seats in West Pakistan. Following the negotiations among Mujib, Bhutto, (q.v.) and Yahya Khan (q.v.) in early 1971, Mujib came under increasing pressure to declare independence, rather than autonomy within Pakistan, as the goal of the Awami League. When the army took action in March 1971, Mujibur Rahman was arrested and held in West Pakistan until after the surrender of the Pakistan army in East Pakistan. Much of this time was spent under the threat of death, but Bhutto, who replaced Yahya Khan after the defeat, released Mujib and permitted him to return to Bangladesh. He arrived on January 10, 1972, and assumed the prime ministership. Under his leadership the parliament enacted a constitution that called for a parliamentary system and embraced what came to be called Mujibbad (q.v.). However, the administration was very poorly run, and, under increasing opposition, Mujib obtained parliamentary approval for a presidential system with himself as president in January, 1975. In June 1975 he dissolved the Awami League into BAKSAL (q.v.), which became the only legal party in Bangladesh.

Mujib was assassinated along with many members of his family by disgruntled army officers on August 15, 1975. His daughter, Sheikh Hasina Wajid (q.v.), was not in Bangladesh at the time and has since become leader of the Awami League and leader of the opposition in parliament following the 1986 and 1991 elections. She became prime minister in 1996.

MUKTI BAHINI. Literally means freedom force. It was initially an ad hoc fighting force formed after the beginning, in March 1971, of military operations against the civilian population of Bangladesh by units of the Pakistani army. It was mainly composed of Bengali personnel serving in the Pakistan army, the East Bengal Regiment, the East Pakistan Police, and civilians who took arms against the Pakistani army. The Mukti Bahini received Indian assistance in small arms and training. Some members of the Mukti Bahini were incorporated into the Jatiyo Rakkhi Bahini (q.v.) after independence.

MURSHED, SYED MAHBUB (1911-1979). A nephew of Abul Kasem Fazlul Haq (q.v.), he was a barrister who became a judge in 1955 and chief justice in 1964 of the Dhaka High Court. He resigned in 1968 to enter politics and was a member of the Democratic Action Committee (q.v.) that negotiated with Ayub Khan (q.v.) in 1969. Murshed announced himself a candidate for the presidency for the election in 1969, a poll that was not held.

MURSHID QULI JAFAR KHAN (d. 1726). A Persian who was a Mughal government official and who had risen to the post of *diwan* (collector of revenue) of the Deccan under Aurangzeb. He was appointed *diwan* of Bengal in 1701. He performed so well that he was made independent of the governor and moved the revenue offices from Dhaka to the town that would bear his name, Murshidabad, in 1704. He became governor of Bengal, Bihar, and Orissa in 1707 and held the post until his death.

MURSHIDABAD. A city on the Bhagirathi River in West Bengal. It was already a substantial commercial town when Murshid Quli Jafar Khan (q.v.) moved the headquarters of the *diwan* to it from Dhaka in 1704. As Murshid rose from *diwan* to Nawab of Bengal, Murshidabad became the capital of Bengal until 1773. Administratively, the city was superseded by Calcutta (q.v.), but many important monuments remain. Murshidabad is separated from Bangladesh by the river Padma. A number of prominent Bengali Muslim families come from Murshidabad (see, e.g., Iskandar Mirza).

MUSHARAF HUSAIN, NAWAB (1871-1966). A businessman, politician, and philanthropist, he was given the title of Nawab in 1926. In 1918 he was a member of the Bengal Legislative Council and became education minister of Bengal in 1927. He was responsible for passing the first education bill calling for free primary education in Bengal. Musharaf Husain was law minister in the Fazlul Haq (q.v.) cabinet, 1937. He established a number of schools and madrasas or religious schools.

MUSHARRAF HUSAIN, MIR (1847-1912). Proclaimed as the "father of Bengali Muslim literature," he was an advocate of Hindu-Muslim unity. His book *Go-Jivan* (The Life of Cattle), in which he opposed cow slaughter, was, to say the least, controversial and led to some Muslim opposition to him.

MUSHARIF, KHALID (d. 1975). A Bengali major in the Pakistan army in 1971, he came to prominence as a hero during the war of independence. He was an ambitious officer who was promoted to brigadier by Sheikh Mujibur Rahman (q.v.). Pro-Indian in his outlook, Khalid Musharif masterminded the countercoup of November 3, 1977, that resulted in the ouster of majors who were responsible for the August Coup (q.v.). He himself was overthrown and killed by a popular uprising in the army on November 7, 1977.

MUSHTAQUE AHMED, KHONDAKAR (1918-1996). President of Bangladesh from August 1975 to November 1975. Active in the language movement, he was also a founding member of the Awami League (q.v.). In 1954 he served as the chief whip of the United Front (q.v.) government. During the 1969 political movement to oust President Ayub Khan (q.v.) he was the convenor of the East Pakistan Democratic Action Committee (q.v.) and participated in the roundtable conference held at that time. Mushtaque was elected to the national assembly in 1970. During the liberation war he was the foreign minister and minister for law and parliamentary affairs in the Bangladesh government-in-exile. He was a member of the cabinet of Mujibur Rahman (q.v.), 1972-1975. Mushtaque became president of the country after Mujibur Rahman was assassinated but gave up the presidency when a countercoup led by Khalid Musharif (q.v.) took place in November 1975. He was arrested in 1976 and released in 1980. He is characterized as a conservative, Western-oriented politician. Mushtaque has headed the all-but-defunct Democratic League (q.v.).

MUSLIM LEAGUE. A political party formed in Dhaka in December 1906. Its initial goals were to support the Crown and to further the cause of the Muslims of India without opposing the other groups in India. Its founding followed the Simla meeting of Muslims with Lord Minto (q.v.). The Muslims demanded separate electorates (q.v.) for Muslims. This demand was met in the Government of India Act of 1909 (q.v.) and accepted by the Indian National Congress in an agreement with the Muslim League signed in 1916 at Lucknow. The League gained its most important member when Muhammad Ali Jinnah (q.v.) joined in 1913. He led the Muslim League negotiations with the Congress at Lucknow. The Congress soon repented of its acceptance of separate electorates and worked to end the system beginning in the 1920s up to partition in 1947. Jinnah agreed in 1928 to yield on the issue if other safeguards for the Muslim minority were given; this was not done by the Congress or the British.

The League contested elections as a single body first in 1937. It did well in the Muslimminority provinces but poorly in the Muslim-majority provinces. It was seen by many Bengali Muslims as the party of Calcutta Muslims and of those Muslims who belonged to the national elite (q.v.). At a session of the League in Lucknow later in 1937, four of the Muslim prime ministers (including Fazlul Haq [q.v.]) agreed to support the League in national matters in return for a free hand in their own provincial affairs. This greatly strengthened Jinnah's position and that of the League.

On March 23, 1940, the Lahore Resolution (q.v.) was passed in which the possibility of a demand for partition was expressed. In the 1946 election the League won handsome majorities in the Muslim seats in all the Muslim-majority provinces except the Northwest Frontier Province. Jinnah took this as a mandate to press for partition. The demand was accepted, and Pakistan was created on August 14, 1947. After independence and the death of Jinnah (1948), the League began to weaken. It was defeated badly in the election to the East Bengal provincial assembly in 1954 (see Elections) and shortly thereafter split in West Pakistan.

All parties were banned by Ayub Khan (q.v.) when martial law was declared in October 1958. In 1962, Ayub resurrected the Pakistan Muslim League (Convention) (q.v.); some of his opponents formed the Council Muslim League (q.v.). Both parties did poorly in the 1970 election; neither won a seat in East Pakistan. In Bangladesh, since independence, the party was banned during the period of Mujibur Rahman (q.v.) but permitted to return during the period of Ziaur Rahman (q.v.). The party, led by Abdul Sobur Khan (q.v.) won twenty seats in the 1979 parliamentary election but has since splintered and is of small consequence. (See Bangladesh Muslim League.)

MUZAFFAR AHMED (1889-1973). Born in Chittagong, he was one of the early members of the Communist Party of India (CPI). As such, he was involved in a number of conspiracy cases brought by the British colonial government. With others, including Kazi Nazrul Islam (q.v.), he organized the Bengal Peasants and Workers Party in 1925, which was merged with the CPI. Muzaffar Ahmed wrote extensively on the communist movement and the party, and his publications are important primary sources for the study of Indian communism. He remained in India after partition.

MUZAMMEL HAQ, MUHAMMAD (1860-1933). A poet and writer of prose who was important in the Muslim revival in Bengal early in the twentieth century. He also edited a number of literary journals. In addition to poetry and novels, his writing includes history and biographies, all in Bengali.

MYANMAR. See BURMA.

MYMENSINGH. A district and district town, the city lies on the banks of the old channel of the Brahmaputra (q.v.), the river having diverted its main channel westward in the early nineteenth century so that it now forms the boundary between Mymensingh and Pabna (q.v.), Bogra (q.v.) and Rangpur (q.v.). Mymensingh town was formerly known as Nasirabad.

The area was under the control of Kamarupa (Assam) in ancient times and a series of rulers after that including, the Senas (q.v.) just prior to Muslim control. In 1351 Mymensingh was taken by Shamsuddin Ilyas Shah (q.v.) as he united Bengal. The region was subject to rebellions, most notably in the latter part of the sixteenth century when Isa Khan (q.v.) and the Bara Bhuiyan (q.v.) led a revolt against Man Singh (q.v.) and Mughal (q.v.) rule.

Mymensingh city is the seat of the Bangladesh Agricultural University. The Ershad period local government (q.v.) reorganization resulted in the creation of three districts: Mymensingh, Netrakona, and Kishorganj. Earlier, two other subdivisions, Jamalpur and Tangail, had been elevated to district status. Most of the Madhupur jungle reserve lies within the present Mymensingh district. Bhairab Bazaar, in Kishorganj district at the junction of the Old Brahmaputra and the Meghna (q.v.), is a major river port.

- N -

NAJIBUR RAHMAN (1878-1923). A teacher and novelist, whose writings emphasized Hindu-Muslim unity, therefore earning him criticism from conservative Muslims. His writings are in Bengali.

NASIRUDDIN, MOHAMMAD (1889-1994). A journalist, he was born in Chandpur district and had his first employment in life insurance. He moved to journalism, concentrating on topics relating to women and children.

NASRIN, TASLIMA (b. 1962). A physician and author, she attracted international attention when her novel *Lajja* (Shame) was banned by the government in 1993 as being offensive to the religious sensibilities of many Bangladeshi Muslims. The work condemned Muslim religious leaders for their persecution of Hindus in Bangladesh. An ardent feminist who had been accused earlier for similar writings, Taslima was sentenced to death by fundamentalist religious leaders and charged by the government for offending religious sensibilities. She at first hid from arrest but then reported to the court. She fled to Sweden in August 1994, where she remains.

NATIONAL AWAMI PARTY (NAP). Formed in East Pakistan by Maulana Abdul Hamid Khan Bhashani (q.v.) when he withdrew in 1957 from the Awami League (q.v.). Bhashani objected to the program of Suhrawardy (q.v.), which he saw as too pro-Western and too market-economy oriented. Bhashani coalesced with several West Pakistani leaders of small parties that were either regional or leftist or both. In the 1960s the party split, with one branch remaining with Bhashani (called the NAP[B]) and often incorrectly referred to as "pro-China." The other splinter was headed nationally by Khan Abdul Wali Khan (the NAP[W]) and in East Pakistan by Muzaffar Ahmad.

Both factions in East Pakistan failed to attract appreciable support in the 1970 election. Since independence and especially since the death of Bhashani in 1976, the NAP(B) splintered many times and has ceased to exist. Some members even joined the Bangladesh Nationalist Party (q.v.), including Mashiur Rahman (q.v.), the presumptive prime minister in 1979 (he died as the election results were coming in). The Muzaffar Ahmad group, reinitialed NAP(M) after 1971, has also been of little consequence since independence although winning an occasional seat. Muzaffar strongly supported BAKSAL (q.v.) in 1975 as a means toward political survival. A party bearing the initials NAP(M) won one seat in the 1991 election.

NATIONAL ELITE. A term applied to those in Muslim Bengali leadership who tended to use Urdu as a family language (hence they are also known as the Urdu elite) rather than Bengali. This distinguished them from the Hindu elite of Bengal but also had several other consequences. The members were often descendants of Mughal empire (q.v.) or Delhi sultanate (q.v.) officers who had been sent to Bengal to govern and whose families remained in the region. Often, they were also Muslim *zamindars*, e.g., the nawab of Dhaka (q.v.). In the Muslim League (q.v.) they tended to support national issues rather than Bengali issues. Among these were such leaders as Khwaja Nazimuddin (q.v.). Their use of Urdu detached them from the mass of Bengalis and permitted such vernacular elite (q.v.) leaders as Fazlul Haq (q.v.) to achieve prominence. After Pakistan's independence, this group continued to support the Muslim League even to the extent of supporting Urdu as the Pakistani national language. Their power was destroyed in the East Bengal election of 1954, in which the Muslim League was trounced by the United Front (q.v.). To a limited degree, the national elite also supported the Pakistan Muslim League (Convention) (q.v.) formed by Ayub Khan (q.v.).

NATIONAL SOCIALIST PARTY. See JATIYA SAMAJTANTRIK DAL.

NAUSHER ALI, SYED (1891-1972). Born in Jessore district, he was educated in Calcutta and became an advocate. Before independence, he was associated with the Krishak Praja Party (q.v.), but after independence, remaining in India, he had close connections with the Communist Party of India (CPI). Nausher Ali served in the Bengal Legislative Council, 1929-1936, and in the Bengal Legislative Assembly, 1937-1946, in both cases being elected from Jessore. From 1943 to 1945, he was Speaker. After independence, he was a member of the Rajya Sabha, 1952-1956 and 1962-1968, associated as an independent with the CPI.

NAZIMUDDIN, KHWAJA (SIR) (1894-1964). A member of the Nawab of Dhaka family (q.v.). He was educated at Aligarh Muslim University and Cambridge University. He was a member of the Bengal Legislative Council, 1923-1934, and the Bengal Legislative Assembly, 1937-1945, until the assembly was dissolved by the governor. During the 1934-1937 period, Nazimuddin was a member of the governor's executive council. Earlier, he was minister of education, 1929-1934. As a member of the legislative assembly of Bengal, he served as home minister, 1937-1941, under the premiership of Abul Kasem Fazlul Haq (q.v.) during a coalition between the Krishak Praja Party (q.v.) and the Muslim League (q.v.). With the breakup of the coalition, Nazimuddin became leader of the opposition, 1941-1943, but became prime minister in 1943, serving until the ministry was terminated by the governor in 1945. After the 1946 elections, Nazimuddin was denied a return to the premiership, as he was defeated by a rival Muslim Leaguer, Hussain Shahid Suhrawardy (q.v.). However, after independence in 1947, he became chief minister of East Bengal, serving until he was appointed in 1948 to succeed Muhammad Ali Jinnah (q.v.) as governor-general.

When Liaquat Ali Khan (q.v.) was assassinated in 1951, Nazimuddin stepped down from the governor-generalship to become prime minister, remaining in office until he was dismissed in 1953 by Governor-General Ghulam Muhammad (q.v.) although it was not demonstrated that Nazimuddin had lost the confidence of the constituent assembly. Nazimuddin remained a member, though less active, of the constituent assembly and parliament until the imposition of martial law in 1958. When political parties were again permitted to function in 1962, Nazimuddin became president of the Council Muslim League (q.v.) and was a leader of the Combined Opposition Parties (q.v.) in opposition to Ayub Khan (q.v.) until he died in 1964.

Nazimuddin's brother, Khwaja Shahabuddin (q.v.), was also prominent in politics. Although they were often rivals, Nazimuddin, Fazlul Haq, and Suhrawardy are buried in adjacent graves in a Dhaka park.

NAZRUL ISLAM, KAZI (1899-1976). A Muslim poet, born in Burdwan district, whose principal writings were done between 1919 and 1941. He served in the British Indian army, 1917-1919, and wished to use that training in his opposition to British rule in India. During the British period his writing was frequently proscribed, and he was arrested several times. Nazrul Islam's political views were much to the left. He was associated with Muzaffar Ahmed (q.v.) in the founding of the Bengal Workers and Peasants Party, which later was absorbed into the Communist Party of India. He wrote love songs, drawing often on the legends and myths of Bengal, but he also composed revolutionary poetry, which drew the negative attention of the British. Nazrul Islam suffered neurological disease in 1942, which ended his literary career and left him incapacitated. Although he lived most of his life in Calcutta, he moved to Bangladesh at the invitation of Sheikh Mujibur Rahman (q.v.). He was buried on the campus of the University of Dhaka.

NAZRUL ISLAM, SYED (1925-1975). Assassinated in the Dhaka jail killings (q.v.). He was a close confidant of Sheikh Mujibur Rahman (q.v.) and headed the Bangladesh government-in-exile in 1971 when Mujib was in jail in Pakistan. It was during his tenure as minister of industry that a large number of industries and banks were nationalized. In 1975 Nazrul Islam became vice president of Bangladesh. As a student leader in his youth, he actively participated in the language movement. He joined the Awami League in 1953 and rose through the ranks to be the senior vice president of the Awami League.

NEUTRAL CARETAKER GOVERNMENT. A demand raised by the opposition led by the Awami League (q.v.) and the Jatiya Party (q.v.), who were joined by the Jama'at-i-Islam (q.v.) and smaller opposition parties in 1994. The demand was raised in response to allegations that the ruling Bangladesh Nationalist Party (BNP) (q.v.) had acted improperly in a by-election in which the BNP was declared to have won a seat long held by the Awami League. The demand is that a constitutional amendment be passed that would require the ruling party to resign prior to a general election and turn the reins of government over to a neutral government whose primary task would be the conduct of the election. The precedent for this is in the election held in 1991 (see Elections) following the resignation of Ershad (q.v.). The BNP refused to accept the demand. The opposition resigned en masse from parliament on December 28, 1994. The opposition has taken the demand to the streets, using demonstrations and *hartals* (general strikes).

The resignation of the opposition forced the dissolution of parliament in November 1995. A new election in February 1996 resulted in a walkover by the BNP as the opposition boycotted the poll. The unrepresentative parliament however passed a constitutional amendment providing for future elections to be held under neutral caretaker governments. The parliament was then dissolved and a new election held in June 1996 in which the opposition participated (see Elections).

NINETEEN POINTS. A program outlined by Ziaur Rahman (q.v.) in 1979. Zia provided, through the nineteen points, his ideas of the direction that Bangladesh would be taking in economic, political, and social sectors. Affirming such fundamental constitutional principles as faith and reliance upon Allah, democracy, nationalism, and socialism, he wanted to set up a self-reliant Bangladesh. Participation, food self-sufficiency, enhanced provision of services including health and shelter, privatization, and decentralization were some of the other program goals.

NIZAM-I-ISLAM. A small conservative Muslim political party led by Farid Ahmad (q.v.) established in 1953. It was said to have been influenced by Abul Kasem Fazlul Haq (q.v.). Nizam-i-Islam wanted a government based on Islam and wanted separate electorates. This party joined the United Front (q.v.) government in East Pakistan. It opposed the martial law regime of President Ayub Khan (q.v.). During the 1970s it did not support the Bangladesh freedom movement led by the Awami League (q.v.). After the independence of Bangladesh it was banned. Nizam-i-Islam reemerged after the passing of the Political Parties Regulation in 1976. It later merged with the Islamic Democratic League (q.v.).

NIZAMUDDIN AHMED (1929-1971). A journalist who was killed by collaborators with the Pakistan army four days before the surrender of the army. He was born in Munshiganj and educated in Dhaka. As general manager of the Dhaka office of Pakistan Press International, Nizamuddin avoided censorship and sent many pictures and documents out of Bangladesh during the civil war.

NOA MIA (1852-1883). Second son of Dudu Mia (q.v.), was named Abdul Ghafar Noa Mia. In 1864 he became the leader of the Faraizi movement (q.v.). Like his father, he stressed religion rather than politics or economics.

NOAKHALI. A district (now region) in southeastern Bangladesh that became well known in 1946 when Mahatma Gandhi traveled there to help relieve the communal violence that was occurring. Gandhi achieved some success and then moved to other areas, including Calcutta (see Husain Shahid Suhrawardy) and Bihar to attempt to accomplish the same results.

The history of Noakhali is closely entwined with that of Comilla (q.v.). Noakhali was created as a district separate from Comilla (then Tippera) in 1822. The reorganization of local government (q.v.) during the Ershad government resulted in the detaching of Feni as a separate district.

NOON, MALIK FIROZ KHAN (SIR) (1893-1970). A prominent Punjabi political figure who held many positions in the Punjab government before independence, he was Indian High Commissioner to London (1936-1941) and a member of the Viceroy's council (1941-1945). After independence, in addition to being a member of the constituent assembly, Noon was governor of East Bengal, 1950-1953, serving during some of the more difficult periods of the Bengali language agitation. Noon, nonetheless, was popular personally, and a school bearing his wife's name still operates in Dhaka. He later was chief minister of the Punjab (1953-1955), foreign minister under Suhrawardy (q.v.) (1956-1957), and prime minister (1958) until the imposition of martial law in October 1958.

NURUL AMIN (1897-1974). He was born in Mymensingh, where he practiced law after completing studies in Calcutta. He first entered the legislature as a member of the Bengal Legislative Council in 1942, was elected to the Bengal Legislative Assembly in 1946, and was chosen Speaker. At independence, Nurul Amin became a member of the Nazimuddin (q.v.) cabinet in East Bengal and succeeded Nazimuddin as chief minister when the latter became governor-general in 1948. Both he and the Muslim League (q.v.) as a party were defeated in the United Front (q.v.) sweep in the 1954 elections. Nurul Amin remained leader of the Muslim League in East Pakistan until parties were banned after the coup of Ayub Khan (q.v.) in 1958. In 1965 he was elected to the National Assembly as a member of the National Democratic Front. In 1969 Nurul Amin played a prominent role in the negotiations that ended with the resignation of Ayub Khan. In 1970, as a candidate of the Pakistan Democratic Party, Nurul Amin was one of only two non-Awami Leaguers elected to the National Assembly from East Pakistan. He strongly opposed the separatist position taken by the Awami League in 1971 that led to the breakup of Pakistan. He remained in Pakistan and became vice president in 1971 under Zulfiqar Ali Bhutto (q.v.), who was president. Nurul Amin held the office until the parliamentary constitution of Pakistan took effect in 1973.

- O -

OSMANY, MUHAMMAD ATAUL GHANI (1918-1984). Commanded the Mukti Bahini (q.v.) during the Bangladesh war of independence in 1971. He had joined the British Indian army in 1939 and retired from the Pakistan army in 1967 with the rank of colonel. He became active in politics, associating with the Awami League (q.v.), and was elected to the National Assembly in the 1970 poll. After the independence of Bangladesh, Osmany was promoted to general and made commander in chief of the Bangladesh army, a post he held until April 1972. He then retired and returned to politics, and he was a member of the cabinet of Mujibur Rahman (q.v.). In January 1975 he resigned his parliamentary seat in protest of Mujibur Rahman's creation of BAKSAL (q.v.) as the sole party in the country. Osmany formed a separate party in 1977 and in 1978 he was the candidate of most of the opposition in the presidential election, standing against Ziaur Rahman (q.v.). Osmany was soundly defeated. He also ran for president in 1981, but not as a consensus opposition candidate, and again lost.

- P -

PABNA. A district and district town. There is speculation that the name may have been derived from Pandua (q.v.). The present district was separated from Rajshahi (q.v.) in 1832, and its early history is closely connected with that of Rajshahi. The other subdivision (now a district, as is Pabna), Serajganj, was added to Pabna from Mymensingh (q.v.) in 1855 as a result of the shift in course of the Brahmaputra (q.v.). At Shahzadpur there is the tomb of an important seventeenth century Sufi-leader, Makhdum Shah Daulat Shahid, as well as tombs of a number of his followers.

PAHARPUR. A Buddhist archaeological site located near Rajshahi. This site, with its massive central *vihara* (monastery) measuring about 350 yards in diameter, is one of the largest such monasteries south of the Himalaya. It was erected by the Pala dynasty (q.v.).

PAKISTAN. Relations between Pakistan and Bangladesh were, to say the least, strained after Bangladesh attained independence from Pakistan in December 1971. Pakistan proclaimed a doctrine under which it would break diplomatic relations with any state recognizing Bangladesh, a policy that became impractical when the major nations did so. Pakistan, with the aid of the veto of China (q.v.), kept Bangladesh from membership in the United Nations (q.v.). The Lahore summit of the Islamic Conference (q.v.) in 1974 began a reversal of this policy, as Pakistan was persuaded by other Islamic countries to accept the fait accompli of Bangladeshi separation from Pakistan. Pakistan recognized Bangladesh and withdrew its opposition to Bangladeshi membership in the United Nations and other bodies, although the formal exchange of ambassadors did not occur until 1976.

Bangladesh and Pakistan as separate entities retain the fear of Hindu (now Indian) hegemony in South Asia that led Bengali Muslims to support so strongly the Pakistan concept in the 1946 election. The two countries cooperate in the Islamic Conference and in the South Asian Association for Regional Cooperation (q.v.) and often take almost identical positions on international issues (e.g., on Afghanistan and Cambodia in opposition to India, and on Palestine). One outstanding issue, the division of the assets and liabilities of united Pakistan, is unlikely ever to be resolved and has recently been ignored. Another issue is the continued presence of Biharis (q.v.) in Bangladesh who demand to be sent to Pakistan.

PAKISTAN DEMOCRATIC MOVEMENT. The term applied to a group of opposition parties that challenged the continued rule of Ayub Khan (q.v.). Most, but not all, opposition parties were formal members of the movement. However, other parties were also represented at the roundtable discussions in early 1969. These included the Pakistan People's Party of Zulfiqar Ali Bhutto (q.v.) and the Awami League (q.v.), led by Mujibur Rahman (q.v.).

PAKISTAN MUSLIM LEAGUE (CONVENTION). The name generally given to the political party formed to support Ayub Khan (q.v.). The name derived from a convention of Muslim Leaguers called by Ayub following the 1962 elections to the national and provincial assemblies. Among the East Pakistanis who supported the Ayub League were Abdul Sobur Khan (q.v.) and Khwaja Shahabuddin (q.v.). Shahabuddin's brother, Nazimuddin (q.v.), supported the rival Council Muslim League (q.v.). Neither party won a seat in East Pakistan in the 1970 election.

PAKISTAN RESOLUTION. See LAHORE RESOLUTION.

PALA DYNASTY. Ruled Bengal from about 750 to about 1155. The dynasty received its name from all the rulers' names, which ended in "-pala." (See Appendix 1 for the rulers and their approximate dates.) At its peak, the kingdom extended well into present-day Uttar Pradesh in India. Pala rule in Bihar lasted until the Muslim conquest in 1199. The capital of the dynasty was Pataliputra (Patna), but was transferred to Monghyr by Devapala (q.v.). Decline in the empire set in during the reign of Mahipala I (q.v.) with pressure from the Chola rulers from south India and the Kalachuris from central India. Control of the "home" of the Palas, Bengal, was lost to the Sena dynasty (q.v.) in the twelfth century.

The rulers were Buddhists and patronized the scholars of that religion. Much was expended on the Buddhist universities at Nalanda (near present Rajgir, Bihar) and Vikramasila (Bhagalpur district of Bihar). They patronized art and architecture, though little remains of this patronage. Irrigation works in Dinajpur district are credited to the Palas.

PANDUA. Located in the present Malda district of West Bengal, Pandua lies on the banks of the Mahananda River near its confluence with the Kalindri River, a main stream of the Ganges (q.v.). The port of Pandua had a large trade with Europeans in the eighteenth century in silk and cotton fabrics. English Bazaar is the headquarters of the district, signifying the importance of British trade. Gaur (q.v.) is about ten miles from English Bazaar and Pandua about twenty miles. Pandua succeeded Gaur as the capital of Bengal about 1340, but in 1455 Gaur became the capital again and Pandua declined. The fourteenth-century Adina and Sona mosques survive.

PANNI, WAJID ALI KHAN (1869-1936). An educationist, philanthropist, and social activist belonged to the national elite (q.v.). He was a *zamindar* who was credited with establishing a number of educational institutions, small hospitals, and dispensaries, and with building roads and canals. He participated in the noncooperation movement against British rule and was jailed for fifteenth months. Panni's family has remained active in politics and administration. His sons Khurram Khan Panni and Humayun Khan Panni were legislators and ambassadors.

PARITY. A term associated with the Constitution of Pakistan, 1956 (q.v.). East Pakistanis agreed to accept the equality (or parity) of membership in the national parliament, 150 members each from the east and west wings. This diluted the value of a vote from East Pakistan. The quid pro quo for this was that the government of Pakistan would commit itself to working for parity also in the administrative services and in the economy. Although steps were taken to try to redress the imbalance in the services, it was not possible to convince investors or to divert government investment funds to lessen the economic imbalance. Although the East Pakistani economy grew between 1956 and 1971, it grew at a slower rate than that of West Pakistan so that the disparity increased rather than decreased. The legislative parity was continued in Ayub Khan's (q.v.) Constitution of Pakistan, 1962 (q.v.), but was discarded by Yahya Khan (q.v.) when he called for elections in 1970. At that time elections were held on a population basis: East Pakistan had 162 directly elected seats in the national assembly and West Pakistan had 138.

PATUAKHALI. A district formed in 1969 by the division of Backerganj into Barisal (q.v.) and Patuakhali. The history of Patuakhali is covered in the entry for Barisal. The district has since been divided into Patuakhali and Barguna districts.

PEACE COMMITTEES. Set up in 1971 in various cities of Bangladesh and in localities within each city. The purpose of the committees was to persuade the Bangladeshis to accept the idea of maintaining a united Pakistan.

PERMANENT SETTLEMENT. Promulgated by Lord Cornwallis (q.v.) in 1793. Cornwallis designated the tax collectors (*zamindars*) as owners of the land from which they raised revenue. Previously these persons were, in effect, tax farmers who collected revenue from the farmers (*ryots*). With Permanent Settlement, the ryots became tenants of the zamindars. As it turned out, most, but not all, of the zamindars in eastern Bengal were Hindus. This led to challenges from such leaders as Fazlul Haq (q.v.) and his Krishak Praja Party (q.v.) in the 1930s. The system, however, was not changed until after the independence of Pakistan by land reform acts passed by the provincial assembly.

PLASSEY (Pilasi), BATTLE OF. The battle between the British, led by Robert Clive (q.v.), and the Bengal forces, under Nawab Sirajuddaulah (q.v.) occurred on June 23, 1757. The British had lost Calcutta (q.v.) to the nawab in 1756 and, although the city was regained earlier in 1757, wished to replace him with a more pliable governor of Bengal. Sirajuddalulah's forces numbered about 50,000; Clive's about 3,000. Aided by the treachery of Mir Jafar (q.v.), the British routed the Bengali force. Sirajuddaulah was killed and replaced as governor by Mir Jafar.

POPULATION PLANNING. The high density of population (2,184 per square mile) and the rapid rate of population growth (2.3 percent, 1980-1992) has made population planning a key aspect of government policy. At the current projected rate of growth (1.9 percent) the population of Bangladesh is expected to reach 132 million in 2000 from the 1992 population of 114 million. Population policy is designed to influence demographic behavior through education, information, and motivation and through the delivery of family planning services. The policy recognizes that long-term success will depend on socioeconomic factors such as employment, education, health delivery reduction in infant and maternal mortality, and, most of all, the participation of women in development. Efforts by government and nongovernment organizations raised the use of contraceptives from 18 percent in 1980 to 32 percent in 1988. Efforts by Bangladesh were recognized the United Nations, which awarded a prize to Ershad (q.v.).

PORTUGUESE IN BENGAL. The main thrust of Portuguese power in India was on the west coast. Goa, Daman, and Diu remained Portuguese colonies until 1961 when they were forcibly incorporated into India. In Bengal, the Portuguese were the first European traders to arrive, visiting Chittagong (q.v.) and Satgaon (on the Hooghly River) beginning in about 1530. By the end of the sixteenth century they were well established at Hooghly, which the Portuguese had founded in 1537 to replace Satgaon, whose estuary has silted up. In the early seventeenth century, some Portuguese were active as pirates, operating from Arakan (q.v.), Chittagong, and islands near the mouth of the Meghna (q.v.). In retaliation for the piracy, Hooghly was attacked by Mughal troops in 1632 and many Portuguese were killed or captured. The Portuguese were permitted to return to Hooghly in 1633, but the city was granted to the British East India Company in 1651, thereby ending Portuguese use of territory in Bengal.

PRATAPADITYA. A local hero of the Jessore area, he refused to pay taxes to the government of the Emperor Akbar after the conquest of Bengal by Akbar's forces in 1576. He defeated a Mughal army, but was eventually captured and sent to Delhi for trial. He died en route to Delhi (see Bara Bhuiyan).

PUNDRA, PUNDRANAGARA. See MAHASTHANGARH.

- Q -

QUADRAT-E-KHUDA, MUHAMMAD TOFAZZIL (1900-1977). A prominent scientist who received eighteen patents. Most of his patents are in the area of agricultural products. He served in a number of different capacities, including the first directorship of the Pakistan Scientific and Industrial Research Center. Soon after the independence of Bangladesh he was called to chair the first Educational Reform Committee.

QUAZI, DOWLAT (c. 1600-1638). Poet. Born in Chittagong, he worked at the court of the kings of Arakan (q.v.). His *Shati Maina* and *Lore Chandrani* are considered a fine examples of middle Bengali poetry.

- R -

RAHMAN, A.S.M. MOSTAFIZUR (b. 1934). He served in the Pakistan and Bangladesh armies, retiring in 1973. He joined the cabinet of Ziaur Rahman (q.v.) as minister of home affairs in April 1978 and served under Zia and Abdus Sattar until December 1991. In the Khaleda Zia (q.v.) government, Mostafiz has been minister of foreign affairs.

RAHMAN, HABIBUR (b. 1908). President of the Dhaka Muslim League and member of the Working Committee of the East Pakistan Muslim League between 1948 and 1950. He served as Pakistan's ambassador to a number of countries including Australia, New Zealand, Switzerland, Belgium, and Yugoslavia. During the Ayub (q.v.) regime (1958-1962), Habibur Rahman served as minister of education, information and broadcasting, and minority affairs. He became a member of the National Assembly of Pakistan in 1962.

RAHMAN, HABIBUR (1922-1976). Journalist. He was assistant director of the National Book Centre from 1974 to 1976. Earlier he had worked for several newspapers and wrote a number of books addressed to children.

RAHMAN, HABIBUR (1928-1988). An architect, he designed the Shahid Minar, the monument to those killed in the language movement (q.v.) in 1952. He was also a well-known painter.

RAHMAN, SHEIKH MUJIBUR. See MUJIBUR RAHMAN, SHEIKH.

RAHMAN, ZIAUR. See ZIAUR RAHMAN.

RAIHAN, ZAHIR (1933-1971) Writer and film director. He studied photography in Calcutta and began a career in film, his first being released in 1961. An English-language film, *Let There Be Light*, was not completed owing to the civil war. He turned away from that project to create a documentary on the war: *Stop Genocide*. Raihan was killed by opponents of independence in 1971.

RAJMAHAL. Although it is located in the present Santal Parganas district of the Indian state of Bihar, it twice served as the capital of the Bengal province under the Mughals. Raja Man Singh (q.v.), who was a governor under Emperor Akbar, chose the city as capital in 1595 primarily because of its command of the Ganges (q.v.). In 1610, the capital was transferred to Dhaka (q.v.). The capital was moved back to Rajmahal in 1639, but returned to Dhaka in 1659.

RAJSHAHI. A district and district town in northern Bangladesh, it was once known as Rampur Boalia. The present name is said to mean the "royal territory," as it combines the words *raj* and *shah*. It lies on the Ganges (q.v.) (called the Padma in the area) about 120 miles northwest of Dhaka. It is the site of a university and of the Varendra (q.v.) Research Society, founded in 1910, which is devoted to the study of the ancient history of the area. The district was part of the kingdom of Pundra whose capital was Mahasthangarh (q.v.). During the Sena (q.v.) period, the area was known as Barendra Bhumi (the land of Varendra). During the eighteenth century, the extent of Rajshahi district was much greater that at present. During the nineteenth century various parts were detached to form Murshidabad (q.v.), Nadia, Jessore (q.v.), Malda, Bogra (q.v.), and Pabna (q.v.) districts. The larger territory was under the control of the raja of Natore.

Muslim period monuments in Rajshahi city include the Chhota Sona mosque and from the Hindu period the Govinda temple. The region also contains the sites of Paharpur (q.v.),

Gaur (q.v.), and a number of other archaeological and historical locations.

The reorganization of local government (q.v.) during the Ershad period divided the former Rajshahi district into Rajshahi, Natore, Naogaon, and Nawabganj districts.

RAMAKRISHNA MISSION. Founded in 1897 by Swami Vivekananda (q.v.) as a means for a group of devotees of Ramakrishna Paramahamsa (q.v.) to preach the latter's doctrines and serve humanity. The mission runs schools, colleges, and hospitals and teaches useful crafts to those who seek its assistance. Its branches in Bangladesh have remained open.

RAMAKRISHNA PARAMAHAMSA (1834-1886). An important Hindu spiritual leader in Bengal. He preached the concept that as various languages have different words for the same idea (e.g., water) so different religions have different names for God: Allah, Hari, Christ, Krishna, and so on. He preached compassion to all, and with this idea his successors established the Ramakrishna Mission (q.v.).

RANGPUR. A district and district town, the city lies on the Little Ghaghat River. It and its neighboring city of Saidpur (about twenty miles west) are major railway centers. The district's eastern boundary is the Brahmaputra (q.v.). Several other rivers, including the Tista (q.v.), cross the district. Were a link canal to be built between the Brahmaputra and the Ganges (q.v.) at Farraka (see Farraka barrage) most of the canal would run through the district.

In ancient times, Rangpur was a part of the kingdom of Kamarupa (Assam), being described in the *Mahabharata*, the Hindu epic, as the most western part of Kamarupa. Assamese rule apparently continued until 1498 when the region was taken by the Afghan kings of Gaur (q.v.), but it was again lost to the Koch rulers (see Cooch Behar). Rangpur was formally annexed by the Mughals (q.v.) in 1584 but not completely subdued until 1661.

The former district has now been divided into four districts: Rangpur, Nilphamari, Kurigaon, and Gaibandha.

RAZA, HASAN (1854-1922). He was a member of the *zamindar* family of Sunamganj in Sylhet district. He founded an English language high school, but he is best known for the devotional songs he wrote. These songs focus on love, mysticism, and spiritual consciousness. They are still used by both the Muslim and Hindu communities.

RAZAKAR BAHINI. A force set up by the Pakistan army to counter the Mukti Bahini (q.v.), mainly composed of pro-Pakistani Bengalis and Biharis (q.v.). The purpose of the force was to maintain order. Members of the force gained a poor reputation because they worked toward the suppression of the demands of the Bangladeshis.

ROHINGYAS. See ARAKAN.

ROY, NIHARRANJAN (1903-1981). Art Historian. Born in Mymensingh, he was educated at Calcutta and Leiden. Among his works was *Metal Sculptures of Bengal.*

ROY, RAJA RAM MOHAN (1772-1833). A reformer, he was born in Hooghly district to a Brahmin family. He recognized that the British were to remain in control of Bengal and beyond and that the best course for Indians was to work with the British. He traveled several times to England and was in the employ of the East India Company from 1804 to 1814. His reforming religious views — opposition to idolatry and superstitions — led Roy to form a new religious body, the Brahmo Samaj, which, though drawn from Hindus, followed in many ways the congregational system of Christianity. The Brahmo Samaj would be in the forefront of the Bengal renaissance in the nineteenth century, including, among many other leaders, Rabindranath Tagore (q.v.) as a member. Ram Mohan Roy was opposed to what he saw as social evils, including *sati*, child marriage, polygamy, and caste distinctions. Although members of the Brahmo Samaj were generally drawn from upper castes, caste distinctions were not permitted within the organization. Raja Ram Mohan Roy is remembered as the first major Indian modernist reformer.

ROY, SIR PRAFULLA CHANDRA (1861-1944). Scientist. Born in Khulna, he studied in Calcutta, London, and Edinburgh. After teaching chemistry in Calcutta, he founded the Bengal Chemical and Pharmaceutical Works in 1901, the first such company in India. Roy continued his research. His *History of Hindu Chemistry* was the major publication of its kind at the time.

RUSSIA. Since the collapse of the Union of Soviet Socialist Republics (q.v.), the interests of Bangladesh with Russia have been almost exclusively in the area of trade. Bangladesh seeks Russian markets for its exports, principally garments, jute, and tea. Data are not yet available on the extent of Russo-Bangladesh trade.

-S-

SAIFUR RAHMAN, MUHAMMAD (b. 1932). A chartered accountant, he has served in the cabinets of Ziaur Rahman (q.v.) and Khaleda Zia (q.v.). In the Ziaur Rahman cabinet he was minister of commerce (1977-1980) and minister of finance (1980-1982), continuing into the Sattar (q.v.) cabinet. Saifur Rahman has been minister of finance since the Khaleda Zia government assumed office. He is a spokesman for a market economy as the route for Bangladeshi development.

SALAAM, ABDUS (1910-1976). Journalist. He joined *The Pakistan Observer*, owned by Hamidul Haq Choudhury (q.v.), in 1949 and became editor in 1950. A bitter critic of the Pakistan government's Urdu language program, he was jailed in 1952 for his support of the language movement (q.v.). Salaam was elected to the provincial assembly in 1954, but he did not remain in politics and continued to publish the *Observer*. The paper came under the control of the government after 1971. Salaam left the now *Bangladesh Observer* in 1972, but worked for *The Bangladesh Times*, also government controlled, until his death.

SALIMULLAH KHAN, NAWAB SIR (1866-1915). Nawab of Dhaka, son of Ahsanullah Khan (q.v.). A social activist and a politician, he was known for his efforts to elevate the status of the Muslims of India. He was the founder of both the Dhaka University and the Ahsanullah Engineering College, which is now the Bangladesh Engineering University. Salimullah was one of the founders of the All-India Muslim League (see Muslim League); the founding meeting was held in his palace, Ahsan Manzil in Dhaka. He supported Curzon (q.v.) in the latter's decision to partition Bengal in 1905. A number of organizations such as the Dhaka Orphanage, a medical school, and a Dhaka University dormitory are named in his honor. Salimullah served briefly as a nominated member of the East Bengal and Assam Legislative Council while that province existed.

SAMAD, LAILA (1928-1989). She was a trailblazer among women in journalism. She was assistant editor of the women's magazine *Begum* and was in charge of the women's section of the national daily *Sangbad*.

SAMATATA. Mentioned in inscriptions of the second Gupta emperor, Samudragupta (reigned c. A.D. 330-380), as a frontier state and as a kingdom in eastern Bengal captured by him. Its capital is believed to have been Badkamta, in the vicinity of present-day Comilla.

SARFRAZ KHAN. The nawab of Bengal (1739-1740). He was a grandson of Nawab Murshid Quli Jafar Khan (q.v.) and was defeated and killed by a lieutenant, Alivardi Khan (q.v.), who then became the nawab.

SARKAR, ABU HUSSAIN (1894-1969). Served as chief minister of East Pakistan from 1955 to 1956 and again briefly in 1958. He was a lawyer by profession. Arrested a number of times by the British, he took part in the *Swadeshi* movement and in the national movement for the independence of India. In 1935,

Sarkar joined the Krishak Praja Party (q.v.) of Abul Kasem Fazlul Haq (q.v.) and as representative of KPP was elected to the Bengal Legislative Assembly in 1937. As a nominee of the United Front (q.v.), he was elected to the East Pakistan Legislative Assembly in 1954. He also served as a central minister in 1955.

SARKAR, SIR JADUNATH (1870-1958). Historian. He was born in Rajshahi and educated at Calcutta. He was vice-chancellor of Calcutta University, 1926-1928. Sarkar's books on Indian history were among the standard works of his time. He and Romesh Chandra Majumdar (q.v.) edited the two-volume *History of Bengal.*

SASANKA. The first ruler of Bengal, so far as we know, who was able to extend his rule outside Bengal. About the beginning of the seventh century, he became king of Gaur (q.v.), with his seat at Karnasuvarna, which has been identified with Rangamati in present Murshidabad district. He extended his rule over the Magadha region of Bihar and south to Chilka Lake in Orissa. He met opposition from rulers in north India in alliance with the ruler of Kamarupa (Assam), but retained the heart of his kingdom until his death, perhaps about 625. His coins indicate that he was a Shaivite; there are reports from Chinese pilgrims that he persecuted Buddhists.

SATTAR, ABDUS (1906-1985). President of Bangladesh, 1981-1982, had a career both in law and in politics. Associated with the United Front (q.v.), he was appointed a minister in the Pakistan government in 1956, a judge of the East Pakistan High Court in 1957, and a justice of the Pakistan Supreme Court in 1968. He was also chief election commissioner and conducted the elections of 1970 to the national and provincial assemblies. Sattar was able to flee Pakistan via Afghanistan in 1972 and held a number of posts in Bangladesh. He became a special assistant to President A. S. M. Sayem (q.v.) in 1975 and law minister in 1977, a post he retained after he was appointed vice president the same year by President Ziaur Rahman (q.v.). Sattar succeeded Zia as acting president when the latter was assassinated on May 30, 1981, and was elected to the office on November 15, 1981. He was removed from the presidency by the coup led by Hussain Muhammad Ershad (q.v.) on March 24, 1982. Sattar headed JAGODAL (q.v.), founded in 1978 as a party to support Zia and his program, and its successor, the Bangladesh Nationalist Party (BNP) (q.v.), until 1979 when, with a parliament in office, Zia assumed the chairmanship himself.

SATYA PIR. Satya Pir is a mythological mendicant who is worshipped by Hindus as an incarnation of Vishnu and honored by Muslims as a powerful saint. Still popular today, his tales were especially prominent along the frontiers of Bengal in the seventeenth to the nineteenth centuries. He is lauded for his ability to reduce penury and produce general weal for those who offer a mixture of rice, sugar, milk, and spices.

SAYEM, ABU SADAT MUHAMMAD (b. 1916). Became the president of Bangladesh in November 1975, when a compromise took place between Khalid Musharif (q.v.) and Khondakar Mushtaque Ahmed (q.v.) over who should lead Bangladesh. Sayem, who was the chief justice at that time, was chosen. He was a lawyer by profession who spent a considerable amount of time at the bar. While president, he held a number of important ministries, including defense and foreign affairs. He was also Chief Martial Law Administrator until November 1976. Sayem relinquished his presidency in April 1977 to Ziaur Rahman (q.v.).

SEN, DINESH CHANDRA (1866-1939). A folklorist, he collected folklore material from rural eastern Bengal. His publications include *Folk Literature of Bengal* and two massive works, *Purbabanga Gitika* (Songs of Eastern Bengal) and *Mymensingh Gitika* (Songs of Mymensingh).

SEN, HIRALAL (1866-1917). Born in Manikganj, he was the first person to introduce moving pictures in Bengal. His entry into the film industry came with his organizing of the Royal Bioscope Company in 1900. He imported still film equipment, from which developed his early entry into moving pictures.

SEN, SURJA (1893-1934). A revolutionary who was hanged by the British because of his anti-British activities, he is noted for his organization of the Chittagong Armory raid of 1930. He formed his revolutionary group toward the end of World War I and for a time joined in the noncooperation movement of Mahatma Gandhi. By 1923, Sen was disenchanted with nonviolence and began his radical movement, which included the attempt to murder a British judge. He was in prison from 1926 to 1928 and in 1930 served as the secretary of the Chittagong District Congress. He was betrayed in 1933, arrested by the British and hanged in 1934.

SENA DYNASTY. Ruled Bengal from about 1095 to 1245, succeeding after consolidating the domains of the Pala dynasty (q. v.). The dynasty apparently traces its ancestry to one Samantasena, who came to Bengal from Karnataka. His grandson, Vijayasena, was the first to assume the royal title. Vijayasena's grandson, Lakshmana Sena (q.v.), extended the territories of the kingdom to Bihar and Orissa. In 1202, Lakshmana Sena was attacked at his capital, Nadia, by troops under the command of Ikhtiyaruddin Muhammad Bhakhtiyar

Khalji (q.v.), the son of the ruler of the Delhi Sultanate, Bhakhtiyar Khalji, and forced to flee. The Senas continued to rule in eastern Bengal until 1245, when that part of Bengal also came under Muslim rule. Unlike the Palas, the Senas were Brahmanical Hindus who perhaps set the stage for the rapid conversion of many in eastern Bengal to Islam, a casteless religion as is the Buddhism the people once espoused. (See Appendix 1 for the Sena dynasty rulers and their approximate dates.)

SEPARATE ELECTORATES. A system of voting under which members of each (religious) community would vote separately for representatives from their own community in legislative bodies. The Muslims demanded this system in a meeting at Simla with Lord Minto (q.v.) in 1906. The concept was included in the Government of India Act of 1909 (q. v.) and was accepted in an agreement between the Muslim League (q.v.) and the Congress at Lucknow in 1916. It remained an item high on the League agenda throughout the pre-independence period. After independence, India abolished separate electorates. Pakistan continued to use the system until the indirect elections of the Ayub Khan (q.v.) period were held. Independent Bangladesh has not used separate electorates, but they revived in Pakistan under Zia ul-Haq. In changes after 1909, several other groups gained separate representation, including Sikhs and Indian Christians. The opposite of separate electorates is described as joint electorates.

SERNIABAT, ABDUR RAB (d. 1975). A lawyer and a politician, he was a member of the National Awami Party (q.v.) of Maulana Bhashani (q.v.). He joined the Awami League in 1969 and became a minister in the Bangladesh provisional government-in-exile. After independence, Serniabat became minister for land reform and irrigation. A brother-in-law of Sheikh Mujibur Rahman (q.v.), he was assassinated at the same time that Mujib was.

SHAH JALAL MUJARRAD, HAZRAT (1271-1346). A religious preacher and soldier, he probably was born in Turkestan in 1271 and educated in Mecca. Reference to his death in 1346 was made by Ibn Batuta. In 1303, Shah Jalal conquered Sylhet after having fought Gaur Govind and established his *khanqah* (Sufi hospice) there. He preached in Sylhet for thirty years and built a mosque that is in use today. A number of legends are associated with Shah Jalal, including the story that he crossed a river on his prayer rug in order to defeat Gaur Govind. His burial place in Sylhet is a pilgrimage site.

SHAH, PANJU (1851-1914). A noted Sufi "saint" from Chittagong. He composed a number of spiritual songs that are sung today by his devotees.

SHAHA, RONANDA PRASAD (1896-1971). A well-known social activist and philanthropist. He was a successful businessman who was initially involved in the supply of coal. He later expanded his business to include shipping, insurance, and jute. In 1938 he set up a twenty-bed hospital and a residential girls' school. Both these enterprises are well known throughout Bangladesh. During the great famine in Bengal in the early 1940s, Shaha donated generously to the Red Cross and maintained 250 free kitchens. After 1947, he chose to remain in Pakistan and was a leading member of the Hindu community. He and his only son were killed by the Pakistani army sometime in 1971. The now much larger hospital at Mirzapur in the Tangail region remains a monument to the Shaha family.

SHAHABUDDIN, JUSTICE (1895-1969). Governor of East Bengal, 1954-1955. A south Indian Muslim from Mysore state, he entered the civil service in 1921 and rose to the position of chief justice of East Bengal. After serving as governor, Shahabuddin became a justice of the Supreme Court and chief justice for a brief period in 1960.

SHAHABUDDIN, KHWAJA (1898-1977). A member of the Nawab of Dhaka family (q.v.) and younger brother of Khwaja Sir Nazimuddin (q.v.), he had a long career of government service, often in the shadow of his elder brother. He was a member of the Bengal Legislative Assembly, 1937-1946, and a member of the Nazimuddin cabinet, 1943-1945. Shahabuddin served as governor of the Northwest Frontier Province, 1951-1954, and a member of the central cabinet, 1954-1955, and then undertook a number of diplomatic assignments. He returned to the central cabinet as minister of information under Ayub Khan, 1965-1969, thereby supporting a regime that was opposed by Nazimuddin. During this term of office he angered East Pakistanis by banning the works of Sir Rabindranath Tagore (q.v.) from Pakistan radio and television. After Bangladeshi independence, Shahabuddin stayed in Pakistan until his death.

SHAHIDULLAH, DR. MOHAMMAD (1885-1969). Considered the foremost educationist of his time. He served in a number of educational institutions, including Calcutta, Dhaka, and Rajshahi Universities. Shahidullah is credited with writing more than twenty-five books, including *Essays on Islam*, *Traditional Culture in East Pakistan*, and *Hundred Sayings of the Holy Prophet*.

SHAMSUDDIN, ABUL KALAM (1897-1978). Journalist and politician. As a college student he was active in the non-cooperation movement and the Khilafat movement (q.v.). In 1923, he became an associate editor of the *Daily Mohammadi*, but was best known as editor of the important Muslim newspaper the *Daily Azad*, then published in Calcutta and now in Dhaka (see Maulana Muhammad Akram Khan). Shamsuddin was elected to the Bengal Legislative Assembly in 1946. In 1952, he played a prominent role in the language movement (q.v.) and resigned his assembly seat.

SHAMSUDDIN MUZAFFAR SHAH. An Abyssinian (q.v.) originally named Sidi Badr, he rose to prominence during the rule of Nasiruddin Mahmud II of the Ilyas Shahi dynasty (q.v.). In 1490, Sidi Badr murdered the ruler, usurped the throne, and assumed his royal title. He was a thoroughly cruel ruler, and the nobles under the leadership of Alauddin Husain Shah (q.v.) besieged the capital, Gaur (q.v.), in 1493, in the course of which Shamsuddin Muzaffar Shah died. Alauddin Husain Shah assumed the throne as the first ruler of the Husain Shahi dynasty (q.v.).

SHAMSUL HUDA, NAWAB SYED SIR (1862-1922). A jurist, educator, and political figure, he was born in Comilla district and educated at Calcutta University in law and in Persian. He attended the founding session of the Muslim League (q.v.) in 1906, but withdrew from active politics when he became the first Muslim to serve on the Executive Council of the governor of Bengal in 1912, serving until 1917. Shamsul Huda earlier had been elected to the Imperial Legislative Council from Eastern Bengal and Assam (q.v.) in 1910. In 1917, he was appointed the first Muslim judge on the Calcutta High Court. Shamsul Huda left this position when he was elected to the Bengal Legislative Council in 1921, where he served as the first president of the council. He was one of the founders of Dhaka University.

SHAMSUZZOHA, MUHAMMAD (1934-1969). An educationist, he was born in Bankura district, now in West Bengal. He studied in Dhaka and was active in the language movement (q.v.). He taught at Rajshahi University. In 1969, while students were protesting the government of Ayub Khan (q.v.), Shamsuzzoha, who was provost of one of the residence halls, tried to stop the army from shooting at the students. The soldiers killed him.

SHARIATULLAH, HAJI (1779-1840). The founder of the Faraizi movement (q.v.), he studied in Mecca and returned to Bengal after twenty years. While there he studied Wahhabi principles and practices. Upon his return, he began the movement based on his Islamic beliefs. The essential principles of the movement were: (1) political and economic freedom for peasants and workers, (2) protection of peasants and workers from the suppression of the *zamindars* (proprietors), and those who were involved in the cultivation of indigo (q.v.), (3) redirection of people from forms of worship to exclude such "un-Islamic practices as veneration of saints;" and (4) avoidance of performing such important Islamic practices as the Friday prayers or the Eid prayers in India until India became a Muslim society.

SHEIKH HASINA WAJID (b. 1947). The daughter of Sheikh Mujibur Rahman (q.v.), Sheikh Hasina was born September 28, 1947, in Tungipara, Gopalganj district. She graduated from Dhaka University in 1973. Hasina was absent from Bangladesh on August 15, 1975, when the coup took place that took the lives of her father and many other members of the family. After being kept out of Bangladesh for some time, she returned on May 17, 1981, to a wide welcome from members of the Awami League (q.v.) and became the leader of the League. After the takeover of the government by Hussain Muhammad Ershad (q.v.), Hasina was arrested several times, but in 1986 she was elected to parliament and became the leader of the opposition (see Elections). She and her party left parliament in November 1987, and the League did not contest the 1988 election held by Ershad. Hasina was a leader of the demonstrations that caused Ershad to resign and led to the election of February 1991. In that election, the Awami League finished second, and she became the leader of the opposition in March,1991. She led the movement for a neutral caretaker government (q.v.). In the June 1996 election, the Awami League won a plurality (but not a majority) of the parliamentary seats. The Awami League gained the support of the Jatiya Party (q.v.) and formed a government with Sheikh Hasina as prime minister.

SHELLEY, MIZANUR RAHMAN (b. 1943). A former member of the Pakistan and Bangladesh civil services, he was minister of information and broadcasting in the Ershad (q.v.) regime as a nonpolitical member of the cabinet. Before and since his cabinet service, Shelley has been the head of an important "think tank," the Centre for Development Research Bangladesh.

SHER SHAH SURI (1472-1545). Rebelled against the Mughal emperor Humayun in 1539 and established himself as emperor of India until his death in 1545. His successors continued to rule north India until 1555, when Humayun reclaimed the throne. His descendants then continued to rule independently in Bengal until 1564, when they were overthrowm by the Karrani dynasty (q.v.).

SIKDAR, SIRAJ (1944-1975). A civil engineer by profession, he became involved with the labor movement in 1968. He was a member of the Communist Party and was a student leader. In June 1971 he formed the East Bengal Sarvohara (Proletariat)

Party, which espoused a radical philosophy. Sikdar argued that East Pakistan was a colony of West Pakistan and similarly that Bangladesh was a colony of India. He called for the overthrow of the Sheikh Mujibur Rahman (q.v.) regime by force. Sikdar went underground in 1974 but was arrested and killed by the Jatiyo Rakkhi Bahini (q.v.) in 1975.

SIKDER, DEBEN (1917-1994). A Communist party leader, he was involved in the Chittagong Armory raid of 1930 and was jailed by the British. Sikder left terrorist organizations in 1937 and joined the Communist Party of India. He was a member of one of the factions of the Bangladesh Communist Party at his death.

SIRAJI, ISMAIL HUSSAIN (1880-1931). Born in Sirajganj, he was active in the noncooperation and Khilafat (q.v.) movements, but made his career as a poet and novelist.

SIRAJUDDAULAH (1733-1757). Governor (nawab) of Bengal from April 1756 to June 1757. He succeeded his maternal grandfather, Alivardi Khan (q.v.), although the succession was contested by another grandson, Shaukat Jang, whom Sirajuddaulah defeated and killed. On June 20, 1756, he attacked Calcutta (q.v.) and was held responsible for the incident of the Black Hole (q.v.). The British recaptured Calcutta on January 2, 1757, but sought to replace Sirajuddaulah with a more pliable governor. Subverting officers on Sirajuddaulah's side, including Mir Jafar (q.v.), the British under Clive (q.v.) defeated Sirajuddaulah at the Battle of Plassey (q.v.) on June 23, 1757. Sirajuddaulah was captured and executed. His immediate successor was Mir Jafar.

SIX POINTS. A plan for the accommodation of the grievances of East Pakistan put forward by Sheikh Mujibur Rahman (q.v.) in 1966. It became the platform of the Awami League (q.v.) in the 1970 elections. The six points were: (1) federal parliamentary government, with free and regular elections; (2) federal government to control only foreign affairs and defense; (3) a separate currency or separate fiscal accounts for each province, to control movement of capital from east to west; (4) all power of taxation at the provincial level, with the federal government subsisting on grants from the provinces; (5) each federating unit could enter into foreign trade agreements on its own and control the foreign exchange earned; and (6) each unit could raise its own militia. These points are based on the twenty-one point (q.v.) program of the United Front (q.v.) in 1954. Yahya Khan (q.v.) issued a legal framework order (q.v.) prior to the 1970 elections, which was a response and a challenge to several of the points (see Legal Framework Order for a discussion of this).

SOBUR KHAN, ABDUL (1910-1982). A political leader associated with the Muslim League (q.v.), he was a minister in the Ayub

Khan (q.v.) government, 1962-1969. After Bangladeshi independence in 1971, the Muslim League was banned, but the party was permitted to return to political activity in 1976. As the leader of the Bangladesh Muslim League (q.v.), Sobur was elected to parliament in 1979.

SONARGAON. In this archaeological site located near Dhaka (q.v.), there have been found a number of seals that date from the Deva dynasty (q.v.). It was a provincial center during the period of Delhi sultanate (q.v.) and Ilyas Shahi rule and a number of monuments remain. In the latter part of the sixteenth century, a neighboring town, Katrabo, was the seat of Isa Khan (q.v.), the principal member of the Bara Bhuiyan (q.v.), who resisted Mughal (q.v.) rule. It was a center of the cotton textile industry and an export center for the textiles. In the early seventeenth century it was overtaken by Dhaka, which had become the capital of the Mughal province of Bengal, and its importance greatly diminished. The city is the site of the Museum of Folk Art and Culture.

SOUTH ASIAN ASSOCIATION FOR REGIONAL COOPERATION (SAARC). A regional group initiated by President Ziaur Rahman (q.v.). Member countries are Bangladesh, Bhutan, India, the Maldives, Nepal, Pakistan, and Sri Lanka. Formally inaugurated at the first summit of the leaders of the seven nations at Dhaka in December 1985, the purpose is to have a forum for discussing regional but not bilateral issues. All decisions are to be on the basis of consensus rather than on majority principle.

SUHRAWARDY FAMILY. A family of great prominence in government and intellectual circles in Calcutta. Husain Shahid Suhrawardy (q.v.) was the son of Sir Zahid Suhrawardy, a judge of the Calcutta High Court. Another branch of the family, that of Maulana Obaidullah Suhrawardy (a great-uncle of Husain Shahid), included this important religious figure and his sons Mahmud, a member of the Council of State, and Sir Hasan (q.v.), one-time vice-chancellor of Calcutta University. Sir Hasan's daughter, Shaista Suhrawardy Ikramullah, was a member of Parliament (her book *From Purdah to Parliament* describes the change in her life; she has also written a biography of Husain Shahid Suhrawardy). Her husband, Ikramullah, was a foreign secretary of Pakistan (and his brother, Hidayatullah, a vice president of India). Their daughter, Sarwath, is married to Crown Prince Hasan of Jordan. Through other connections, Husain Shahid Suhrawardy was related to Abul Hashim (q.v.), Sir Abdur Rahim (q.v.) (his daughter was Husain Shahid's first wife), and Fazlul Haq (q.v.).

SUHRAWARDY, DR. SIR ABDULLAH AL-M'AMUN (d. 1935). A politician and educator, he received a doctorate from Edinburgh

University and was called to the bar in London. He taught in Lahore and Calcutta after returning from Britain, but devoted much of his career to politics. He was a member of the Bengal Legislative Council, 1910-1920 and 1921-1926. In 1926 Sir Abdullah was elected to the Central Legislative Assembly, where he remained a member until his death.

SUHRAWARDY, DR. LT. COL. SIR HASAN (1884-1946). He was born in Dhaka, the son of Maulana Obaidullah Suhrawardy, and educated at the Calcutta Medical School and in Great Britain. He was a member of the medical service and a professor of medicine at Calcutta University. Sir Hasan was a member of the Bengal Legislative Council, 1921-1924, and of the Central Legislative Assembly, 1946-1947.

SUHRAWARDY, HUSAIN SHAHID (1893-1963). Founder of the Awami League (q.v.) in 1949, he had previously been a key member of the Muslim League (q.v.). He was a member of a prominent Bengali Muslim family (see Suhrawardy family) and was educated at Oxford and the Inns of Court in London. Suhrawardy was elected to the Bengal Legislative Council in 1921 and remained a member until 1936. He was also deputy mayor of Calcutta, 1923-1925, during the period that Chittaranjan Das (q.v.) was mayor. He entered the Bengal Legislative Assembly in 1937 and served in the Fazlul Haq (q.v.) coalition cabinet (1937-1941) and in the Nazimuddin (q.v.) cabinet (1943-1945).

After the 1946 election, Suhrawardy successfully challenged Nazimuddin for the leadership of the Muslim League group in the assembly and became prime minister of Bengal, 1946-1947. The period was distinguished by the Great Calcutta Killing in August 1946, and then by Suhrawardy's working with Mahatma Gandhi to attempt (rather successfully) to tamp down the communal rioting. The period also saw Suhrawardy's floating of the concept of a third dominion to include Bengal and Assam as an eastern balance to Pakistan and "Hindustan." He had the support of some Congress party members (including Sarat Chandra Bose, brother of Subhas Chandra Bose [q.v.]), but incurred the wrath of Muhammad Ali Jinnah (q.v.). Jinnah effectively barred Suhrawardy from continuing in office as chief minister of East Bengal, a post to which Nazimuddin was elected.

In 1949, after a period of residence in India, Suhrawardy floated his concept of a party that would include non-Muslims as well as Muslims and founded the Awami League. This party, which never gained significant strength in the western wing of Pakistan, joined with the Krishak Sramik Party (q.v.) in the United Front (q.v.) to defeat the Muslim League in the 1954 East Bengal legislature elections (see Elections). Suhrawardy left the legislative leadership in East Bengal to Ataur Rahman Khan (q.v.) to concentrate his attention on national politics. He was a minister in the cabinet of Muhammad Ali Bogra (q.v.), 1954-1955, and was prime minister of Pakistan, 1956-1957. After martial law was instituted he opposed Ayub Khan (q.v.) and worked for the restoration of the parliamentary system. Suhrawardy died in Beirut on December 5, 1963.

SULTAN, MUHAMMAD (1928-1983). Founder-president of the East Pakistan Student Union, one of the most active student unions in the country. He joined the National Awami Party of Bhashani and was the secretary general of the party from 1966 to 1968. In 1970 Sultan retired from politics and returned to his earlier profession in the book printing and publishing world. He always fought for Bengali nationalism and for that reason his books were banned. For his contribution to Bengali nationalism he was awarded the 21 February (see Martyrs' Day) award.

SULTAN, SYED MAHMUD (1917-1991). He was a member of the constituent assembly of Pakistan. After 1971, Sultan was sent to the United Nations (q.v.) when Bangladesh was trying to gain admission to the world body. He was the first Bangladeshi High Commissioner to the United Kingdom. After the assassination of Mujibur Rahman (q.v.), he resumed his law practice.

SUNDERBANS. A tract of mangrove swamp that lies along the coast of Bangladesh and West Bengal between the mouth of the Meghna (q.v.) and that of the Hooghly. It contains a vast number of streams that are tidal rivers and an uncountable number of islands. Except for a portion of the north of the region, the area is not cultivated. It is the home of the Bengal tiger and of crocodiles.

SURA DYNASTY. Tradition represents Adisura (q.v.) as the founder of the dynasty, but there is no contemporary evidence to support this. Literary tradition is the only support for the presumption that about A.D. 700 he attempted the revival of Brahmanism in Bengal, which was dominated then by Buddhism. His supposed seat was Gaur (q.v.) or Lakshmanavati. He is said to have imported the Brahmins who are the ancestors of the Varendra (north Bengal) and Radhiya (west Bengal) Brahmins in Bengal. Whatever the historical basis, there is some evidence that the Sura family was powerful as late as the eleventh century, as it is recorded that King Vijayasena of the Sena dynasty (q.v.) married a Sura princess. Southern Bengal (Radha) was ruled by a king named Ranasura when the Cholas invaded Bengal in 1023. (See Mahipala I.)

SURI DYNASTY. See SHER SHAH SURI.

SWADESHI. Literally, "self country," the term was used during the opposition by Hindus to the partition of Bengal of 1905 (see Bengal, Partition of, 1905) for the boycott of British-made goods in favor of goods made in India. Gandhi also used the term during the struggle for the independence if India.

SWARNIRVAR. A district-level effort to boost agricultural production begun in 1974. Swarnirvar means "self-reliance." It was initially organized around a village committee on which all segments of the village would be represented. Some of the slogans of the swarnirvar movement were "Let the hands of beggars turn into the hands of workers" and "We will beg no more, we will not allow the nation to beg."

SYLHET. Also known earlier as Srihatta, it is a district and district town in the northeast of Bangladesh. Before the partition of 1947, the district was included in the province of Assam. (See Sylhet referendum for the transfer of four of the five subdivisions to East Pakistan.) The city is on the Surma River which flows into the Meghna (q.v.).

Sylhet has been a center of Islamic activity and many Muslim saints have shrines there, including Hazrat Shah Jalal Mujarrad (q.v.) and several of his followers. The Muslim occupation of Sylhet in 1303 was led by Shah Jalal. In its earlier history, Sylhet was divided into several small states that at times were under the control of the raja of Tippera. Shah Jalal defeated (or, perhaps, outwitted, if the legends about him are to be believed) the ruler of Gor, or Sylhet proper. The British at first included Sylhet in Bengal, but in 1874 it was added to the newly created chief commissionership of Assam.

The district produces tea (q.v.) in the higher elevations. Rainfall is very heavy, averaging about 160 inches a year. The district is also a major center of natural gas production.

The former district of Sylhet has been divided into Sylhet, Sunamganj, Habiganj, and Moulvi Bazaar districts.

SYLHET REFERENDUM. Held in 1947 in Sylhet district of Assam to determine whether that district would go to India or Pakistan in the partition. It was agreed that if the district voted for Pakistan the boundary commission would delimit the contiguous areas of Muslim majority. The district did vote to go to Pakistan. The subdivisions of Sylhet, Moulvi Bazaar, Sunamganj, and Habiganj were awarded to Pakistan, with the subdivision of Karimganj going to India.

- T -

TAGORE FAMILY. A distinguished Brahmin family that contributed greatly to the intellectual development of Bengal ("The Bengal Renaissance"). Most famed of the family was the Nobel laureate

Rabindranath Tagore (q.v.). The founder of the family in the period of note was Dwarkanath (1794-1846). He was a successful businessman who supported liberal movements of the day and was an early member of the Brahmo Samaj, founded by Raja Ram Mohan Roy (q.v.). His son, Debendranath (1817-1905), continued the successful business and succeeded his father as leader of the Brahmo Samaj. Debendranath's son, Satyendranath (1842-1923) was the first Indian to pass the entry examination into the Indian Civil Service. The youngest son of Debendranath, Rabindranath (q.v.), was the poet. Another member of the family, Abanindranath (1871-1951), was a noted artist and the founder of the Indian Society of Oriental Arts.

TAGORE, RABINDRANATH (SIR) (1861-1941). The most noted of modern Indian poets, winning the Nobel prize for literature in 1913. His works are as well accepted by the Muslims of Bengal as they are by the Hindus. The banning of Tagore's works from Pakistan radio in 1965 by Khawja Shahabuddin (q.v.) was one of the straws that eventually broke the camel's back of Pakistan's unity. One of Tagore's poems, "Sonar Bangla" (Golden Bengal), serves as the national anthem of Bangladesh, and another of his poems is the national anthem of India. His work was not limited to poetry, as he wrote novels and plays and even took up painting in his last years. Tagore was active politically, especially when he urged moderate opposition to the 1905 partition of Bengal. He founded the Vishwa Bharati University at Shantiniketan ("the abode of peace") in rural Bengal in 1901. One of the principal characteristics of Tagore's writing was his ability to understand rural Bengal despite his urban upbringing.

TAMIZUDDIN KHAN (1889-1963). He was born in Faridpur district and educated in the law at Calcutta University. He was active in the Congress, the Khilafat movement (q.v.), and the Muslim League (q.v.), achieving his official positions as a member of the League. Tamizuddin was a member of the legislature in Bengal, 1926-1945, and was elected to the Central Legislative Assembly in 1946. He was a member of both the Fazlul Haq (q.v.) and Nazimuddin (q.v.) cabinets. After independence Tamizuddin became a member of the Pakistan Constituent Assembly and succeeded Jinnah (q.v.) as president of the assembly in 1948 on Jinnah's death and held the office until the assembly was dissolved by Governor-General Ghulam Muhammad (q.v.) in 1954.

Tamizuddin challenged the dissolution in a notable case in which, in effect, the judicial system stated that Tamizuddin was correct in maintaining that the governor-general had no right to dissolve the assembly, but that the governor- general had caused a new assembly to be elected and, therefore, representative government had been restored. Tamizuddin returned to public office as the Speaker of the National Assembly elected in 1962, retaining that position until his death.

TARKABAGISH, MAULANA ABDUL RASHID (d. 1986). A prominent member of the Muslim League (q.v.), he left the League because of its policies in East Pakistan and joined the Awami League (q.v.). He became the president of the East Pakistan Awami League in 1957. Tarkabagish relinquished his position when Sheikh Mujibur Rahman (q.v.) took over as the new leader. In 1976 he formed a new political party and named it the Gana Azad League (People's Freedom League).

TEA. Tea was imported to India from China in the 1820s. In 1834 the governor-general, Lord William Bentinck, had tea seeds and skilled labor obtained and set up a government plantation in Assam. This was sold to the Assam Tea Company in 1839, and the industry expanded rapidly. In the northeast, the principal tea-growing areas are in Darjeeling district of West Bengal, Assam, and Sylhet district of Bangladesh. Tea is the second largest agricultural export of Bangladesh after jute (q.v.).

TIKKA KHAN (b. 1915). A military officer, he was martial law administrator and governor of East Pakistan in 1971. In the latter office, he succeeded Admiral S. M. Ahsan and was replaced later in the year by Abdul Muttalib Malik (q.v.). Described by Bangladeshis as the "butcher of Bangladesh," Tikka Khan administered the province during the worst period of the civil war. After retirement, he entered politics in Pakistan as a member of the People's Party of Pakistan, the group founded by Zulfiqar Ali Bhutto (q.v.).

TISTA. A river that flows through northwestern Bangladesh. It rises in Sikkim, flows rapidly through gorges, crosses the Jalpaiguri district of West Bengal and, in season, rushes violently through Rangpur (q.v.) district in Bangladesh to its confluence with the Brahmaputra (q.v.). Formerly, the Tista flowed into the Ganges, but about 1787 it diverted to the Brahmaputra.

TOAHA, MOHAMMAD (b. 1922). Associated with the communist movement in Bengal since the early 1950s. He was a member of the Awami League (q.v.) and a close political associate of Sheikh Mujibur Rahman (q.v.). He left the position of joint secretary of the Awami League in 1957 and joined the National Awami Party (q.v.) with Maulana Bhashani (q.v.). He was imprisoned in 1958 and released in 1967. Toaha formed the Communist Party of East Bengal in 1969 and went underground in 1972. Returning to open politics in the late 1970s, he was elected to parliament in 1979 as a member of the Samyabadi Dal-(Marxbadi, Leninbadi) (Communist Party). He was the only communist member to be elected.

TOFAZZUL HUSSAIN (MOHAN MIA) (1911-1969). Editor and proprietor of the newspaper *Daily Ittefaq*. He started his career as a civil servant but resigned from the service in the late 1930s. His association with Husain Shahid Suhrawardy (q.v.) led him to be associated with the Muslim League (q.v.). In 1951 he established *Ittefaq*. He was a renowned columnist and used his paper to express the desires and expectations of the Bengali Muslims. His paper evolved into the mouthpiece of the Awami League (q.v.), which brought together leaders of Bengali nationalism. The newspaper was banned and Tofazzul arrested during the Ayub (q.v.) regime. After his death the *Ittefaq* group has been managed by his sons. The paper did not support Mujibur Rahman's (q.v.) authoritarian steps and was again proscribed. *Ittefaq* now has the largest circulation of any daily in Bangladesh.

TRADE. See AID AND TRADE.

TRANSPORTATION. While there are 2,818 kilometers (about 1750 miles) of railroad and more than 10,000 kilometers (about 6,200 miles) of paved roads, the main means of transportation for the people of Bangladesh is the waterways. Chittagong (q.v.) and Mongla (see Khulna) are the only two seaports. There are also major river ports, such as Dhaka (q.v.), Narayanganj, Chandpur, Barisal (q.v.), and Khulna (q.v.). Most of the river and road transportation is provided by private-sector organizations, although the state-owned Bangladesh Inland Waterways Corporation provides some service. Domestic air service is provided by the state-owned Bangladesh Biman, which also is the national flag carrier. Biman connects to twenty-six international destinations. Fifteen foreign carriers fly to Bangladesh.

TRIBES. There are three distinct groups of tribals in Bangladesh. One of these groups is composed of tribes that are actually southern extensions of tribes whose main bodies are in the states of northeastern India. These include the Garos, Khasis, and others, residing principally in Mymensingh region. The second group is located primarily in the Chittagong Hill Tracts (q.v.) and the adjacent Chittagong region and is related to the peoples of Myanmar (Burma) and of areas of India such as the state of Tripura. The largest of these tribes are the Chakmas (48.1 percent of the tribal population of the Chittagong Hill Tracts), the Marmas (27.8 percent), and the Tripuras (12.3 percent); none of the other nine groups identified in the census comprises more than 4 percent of the tribal population of the Chittagong Hill Tracts. It is from these tribes that insurgency against the central government arises. (See also Christianity and Buddhism.) One other tribal group, the Santhals, originates from West Bengal, Bihar, and Orissa in India. They are predominantly Hindu and are often employed in tea estates.

TWENTY-ONE POINTS. The election manifesto of the United Front (q.v.) used during the East Pakistan provincial election of 1954. Among the twenty-one points were: the recognition of Bengali as an official language of Pakistan; complete autonomy for East Bengal in all matters except defense, foreign affairs, and currency; the headquarters of the navy to be located in East Bengal; land reform to be instituted and surplus land be given to the landless; irrigation to be improved; agricultural cooperatives to be set up; agricultural production to be increased; jute trade to be nationalized; discrimination against Bengalis in the armed forces to cease; the repeal of laws that allowed imprisonment without trial; and labor conventions of the International Labor Organization to be practiced.

- U -

UKIL, ABDUL MALIK (1924-1987). A long- time stalwart of the Awami League (q.v.), he had been active in the language movement (q.v.) and in the Democratic Action Committee (q.v.) against Ayub Khan (q.v.). Ukil was elected a member of the East Pakistan Provincial Assembly in 1954 and the National Assembly of Pakistan in 1962. He served as a minister in the cabinet of Mujibur Rahman (q.v.). When the Awami League split prior to the 1979 parliamentary election, Ukil was the leader of the larger faction, although he lost his own election. After the 1986 election, he was named deputy leader of the opposition by the Awami League leader, Sheikh Hasina Wajed (q.v.).

UNION OF SOVIET SOCIALIST REPUBLICS. Initially, relations between Bangladesh and the Soviet Union were cordial, in recognition of Soviet support for Bangladeshi independence. Some members of the cabinet of Mujibur Rahman (q.v.), such as Tajuddin Ahmed (q.v.), were reported to have favored a treaty of friendship with the Soviet Union along the lines of the Indo-Soviet treaty of 1971.

The Soviets gave assistance to the rehabilitation of Bangladesh, especially the clearing of Chittagong Harbor. However, after the death of Mujib, the large Soviet presence became suspect in the eyes of the new leadership. Bangladesh strongly opposed the 1979 Soviet invasion of Afghanistan and Soviet support to Vietnam's actions in Cambodia. In the 1983-1984 period, the Ershad regime ousted a number of Soviet diplomats and officials on the grounds that they were acting against Bangladesh. Relations afterward were correct if not cordial. The Soviet Union supplied limited military assistance during the Mujib period and continued to give limited economic aid. It also sponsored a substantial number of scholarships for study in the Soviet Union.

Since the breakup of the Soviet Union, relations between Bangladesh and Russia (q.v.) have been correct, as Bangladesh wishes to continue and expand such markets as exist there. Generally, Bangladesh is too remote from the newly independent Central Asian republics to have a direct relationship with them, but there is some affinity resulting from Islam and from prospective trade relationships.

UNITED EAST INDIA COMPANY OF THE NETHERLANDS. See DUTCH EAST INDIA COMPANY.

UNITED FRONT (UF). An umbrella political grouping consisting of the Awami League (q.v.), the Krishak Sramik Party (KSP) (q.v.), the Nizam-i-Islam (q.v.), Ganotantrik Dal (q.v.), and some smaller political parties. It was formed to oppose the Pakistan Muslim League in the East Pakistan provincial election of 1954. A twenty-one point (q.v.) manifesto, which included the importance of the Bengali language, regional autonomy, limitations of the powers of the central government, and rejection of the Basic Principles Committee (q.v.) report, won for the UF strong public support. The UF won an overwhelming victory and formed the first non-Muslim League government in April 1954 (see Elections). The East Pakistan Legislative Assembly had a total of 309 seats, of which the UF won 237 and the Muslim League won only 10. In May 1954 the UF government, led by Fazlul Haq (q.v.) as chief minister, was dismissed by the central government because of the purportedly anti-Pakistani statements of the UF leaders. By the time representative government was restored in 1955, under a KSP government led by Abu Hussain Sarkar (q.v.), rivalries between the KSP and the Awami League had ended the UF.

UNITED NATIONS. Bangladesh became a member of the United Nations in 1974, following the withdrawal of the veto by China (q.v.) that had been exercised at the request of Pakistan (q.v.). Bangladesh was elected to the Security Council in 1978, winning election against Japan for the "Asian seat." In 1986, Bangladeshi Foreign Minister Humayun Rashid Chowdhury was elected president of the General Assembly. Bangladesh is also a member of the affiliated agencies of the United Nations. It chaired the Group of Seventy-seven in 1982 and 1983 (see Foreign policy). Bangladesh has participated in a number of peacekeeping operations by sending troops and/or civil officers to such places as Cambodia, Somalia, Bosnia, and Haiti.

UNITED STATES. Relations with the United States were difficult, initially, because of the American "tilt" toward Pakistan in the civil war. The United States delayed formal recognition of the new state until February 1972. However, American assistance for rehabilitation had already begun to flow from the United States government and from a wide range of private organizations. Bangladeshis also remembered the nearly unanimous support for their country from American academics and social organizations and from much of the press and many in Congress during the civil war. Despite opposition from some members of his cabinet (see Tajuddin Ahmed), Mujibur Rahman (q.v.) saw the United States as the major source of the assistance he badly needed. He also visited the United States. Relations from the latter part of the Mujib period through the regimes of his successors have developed a high degree of cordiality and cooperation.

The United States is the largest overall donor of economic assistance in the period since 1971, although in some recent years the commitments of Japan have exceeded those of the United States among national donors (in some years commitments by international financial organizations, such as the International Development Association, have been higher than bilateral arrangements). The United States has refused to give military assistance to Bangladesh other than a modest grant for training. American activity in educational programs has been much less than that of the Soviet Union (see Union of Soviet Socialist Republics). It is not yet certain to what extent Russia will continue the exchange programs of the Soviet Union.

-V-

VANGA. The name used in ancient Hindu literature for central and southern Bengal. It provided the name for all of Bengal. The Sanskritic "v" is changed in Bengali to a "b."

VARENDRA. Ancient name applied to the northern region of present-day Bangladesh, centered on Rajshahi.

VARMAN DYNASTY. Rulers of southeastern Bengal from about 1045 to about 1150. Some historians believe that the Varmans arrived in Bengal, possibly from Orissa, in the train of the Kalachuris, invaders from central India. The Varmans were under the suzerainty of the Palas to about 1080, when they became independent. They were overthrown by the Sena dynasty (q.v.) in about 1150.

VERNACULAR ELITE. A term applied to the Bengali Muslim leadership that used Bengali as a family and political language, as opposed to the national elite (q.v.), which used Urdu. Most prominent of this group both before and after Pakistani independence was Fazlul Haq (q.v.). He used Bengali to appeal to the masses and formed the Krishak Praja Party (q.v.) to represent their interests. He and others in the group were concerned with the matters of Bengal first and of Muslims elsewhere in India second. After independence, Fazlul Haq was joined by Suhrawardy (q.v.), whose Awami League (q.v.) was almost entirely an East Bengal party. Mujibur Rahman (q.v.) represented the group most prominently in the later years of the rule of Ayub Khan (q.v.) and in the first period of Bangladeshi independence.

VIDYASAGAR, ISVARCHANDRA (1820-1891). A Sanskritist and Bengali scholar who had a major impact on education in Bengal. He studied at Sanskrit College in Calcutta and rose to become a professor and later principal of the college. Vidyasagar worked for widespread education in Bengali and supported the more liberal causes of his time: widow remarriage, monogamy, and, especially, women's education.

VIKRAMPUR. A site near Dhaka that was ruled by several Hindu dynasties, including the Chandra (q.v.), Varman (q.v.), Sena (q.v.), and Deva (q.v.). It is thought to have served as the capital of the Chandra dynasty. It was the capital of the Sena dynasty after that dynasty's expulsion from Nadia in 1202 (see Sena dynasty and Lakshmana Sena).

VIVEKANANDA, SWAMI (1863-1902). A noted Hindu religious person who founded the Ramakrishna Mission (q.v.). His original name was Narendranath Dutta. While he was studying law in Calcutta, he became a disciple of Ramakrishna Paramahamsa (q.v.). Vivekananda traveled extensively, including to the United States in 1893, where he represented Hinduism at the Parliament of Religions held in connection with the Chicago World's Fair. He held that the West had declined spiritually and that the East held a religious message for the world. The Vedanta groups are another legacy of Vivekananda.

- W -

WAHIDUZZAMAN (1912-1976). A successful businessman, he entered politics as an associate of Abul Kaseem Fazlul Haq (q.v.) and was elected to the Bengal Legislative Assembly in 1942. After Pakistani independence, however, Wahiduzzaman joined the Muslim League and was a member of the constituent assembly, 1951-1955. During the rule of Ayub Khan (q.v.) he was minister of commerce, 1962-1965. Wahiduzzaman left the Muslim League in 1969 and supported the movement against Ayub for the restoration of democracy.

WAJID, SHEIKH HASINA. See SHEIKH HASINA WAJID.

WALIULLAH, SYED (1922-1971). Novelist and journalist. He was born in Chittagong, studied in Calcutta, and began his work with *The Statesman*. After partition in 1947, he was with Radio Pakistan and served as press attaché at several embassies. Waliullah's novel *Tree Without Roots* was widely acclaimed, was translated into English and French, and earned an award from the Bangla Academy.

WOMEN. The constitution of Bangladesh grants equal rights to women and men in all spheres of public life. Other laws, such as the Family Law Ordinance of 1961, the Family Courts Ordinance of 1985, the Dowry Prohibition Act of 1980, and the Cruelty to Women (Deterrent Protection) Act of 1983, provide special protection for women's rights. In the industrial sector, the rapid entry of women is the most significant recent change in Bangladesh. Approximately 90 percent of the laborers in the garment industry are women. Women are also employed in the pharmaceutical, electronic, and fish processing industries in large numbers.

With the assistance of nongovernmental organizations such as the Grameen Bank (q.v.), women in Bangladesh have had a strong impact on small business development. In addition, women in rural areas have established more than 500 organizations with more than 2 million members to empower themselves for personal, social, economic, and political development. These organizations are significantly different from women's groups in urban areas, which are primarily social welfare units.

In the political area, there is increasing participation of women in the electorate and as members of political parties, as can be demonstrated by Prime Minister Khaleda Zia (q.v.) and the leader of the opposition, Sheikh Hasina Wajid (q.v.)

Despite such advances, women bear a disproportionately large share of the country's poverty. In most, if not all, development indicators, such as education, nutrition, and employment, women are invariably poorer than men. Even in social, economic, and political areas in which women have significant presence, the wage and status differential continues to be a major barrier. In Bangladesh, a patriarchal society, women are still viewed mainly in their reproductive roles and are given subsidiary status as economically dependent liabilities and the cause of nonproductive expenditures.

- Y -

YAHYA KHAN, AGHA MUHAMMAD (1917-1980). A career military officer, he was president of Pakistan, 1969-1971, succeeding Ayub Khan (q.v.). He entered the British Indian army in 1938. He was commander in East Pakistan from 1962 until 1966, when he became deputy commander in chief of the army.

From that position, Yahya replaced Ayub as president in March 1969, in a palace coup. With the Pakistan army's loss to the Mukti Bahini (q.v.) and their Indian allies in December 1971, Yahya resigned the presidency and turned the government over to Zulfiqar Ali Bhutto (q.v.).

YUNUS, MUHAMMAD. See GRAMEEN BANK.

- Z -

ZAFAR AHMED, KAZI (b. 1940). A trade union leader who has been associated with Maulana Bhashani (q.v.), Kazi Zafar joined the Bangladesh Nationalist Party (BNP) (q.v.) and was added to the Ziaur Rahman (q.v.) cabinet in 1978 as minister of education. After the coup led by Husain Muhammad Ershad (q.v.), he joined the Jatiya Party (q.v.) and served as a minister, deputy prime minister, and prime minister (1990-1991). He remains a leader of the Jatiya Party.

ZAHURUL HUQUE (1935-1969). One of the co-accused in the Agartala conspiracy case (q.v.) against Sheikh Mujibur Rahman (q.v.). In what was described as an attempt to escape, he was shot dead by the Pakistan army.

ZAINUL ABEDIN (1914-1976). A National Professor of the Arts, a title bestowed on him by Sheikh Mujibur Rahman (q.v.). He became principal of the Art Institute, later the Art College, in 1949, and retired in 1967. He was instrumental in the founding of the Bangladesh Shilpakala Academy. Zainul Abedin is most famous for his more than 100 black-and-white sketches of the Calcutta famine of 1943. He is also well known for his abstract painting. Many of his works are on display in the Zainul Abedin Gallery of the Dhaka Museum.

ZIA, KHALEDA. See KHALEDA ZIA.

ZIAUR RAHMAN (1936-1981). The effective leader of Bangladesh from 1975 to 1981. An army officer commissioned in 1953, he rose to the rank of major in 1971. In the civil war, he led his unit (the "Z force") against the Pakistan army and had proclaimed Bangladeshi independence from Chittagong on March 27, 1971, with himself as provisional president. This act apparently earned him the displeasure of Mujibur Rahman (q.v.), under whose regime Zia's career did not prosper to the extent that other Mukti Bahini (q.v.) leaders' careers did. Following the assassination of Mujib, Zia was appointed chief of staff of the army in August 1975. Although displaced briefly during the coup attempt by Khalid Musharif (q.v.), Zia emerged from the November 1975 coups as the dominant leader of the country. He was designated deputy chief martial law administrator then and replaced

President A. S. M. Sayem (q.v.) as chief martial law administrator in 1976.

With Sayem's retirement from the presidency for purported health reasons, Zia became president in 1977. He had this confirmed through a referendum, but then won the post in a contested election in 1978, defeating M. A. G. Osmany (q.v.) and others (see Elections). With his election as president, Zia resigned his army commission and was replaced as chief of staff by Hussain Muhammad Ershad (q.v.). His favoring of Ershad, who was not a freedom fighter, earned him some opposition from passed over freedom fighters. Zia remained president until his assassination on May 30, 1981, at the hands of a disgruntled freedom fighter, Muhammad Abul Manzur (q.v.).

Not considered a likely candidate for a charismatic role, Zia nonetheless created one for himself and provided capable and pragmatic leadership emphasizing such points as rural development, food self-sufficiency, and family planning, as shown in his program of the Nineteen Points (q.v.). The Bangladesh Nationalist Party (BNP) (q.v.) was founded as his political vehicle, although the actual leader of the party was Abdus Sattar (q.v.). The BNP succeeded the earlier JAGODAL (q.v.). Zia is also regarded as the "father" of the South Asian Association for Regional Cooperation (q.v.). His widow, Khaleda Zia (q.v.), was called to be the leader of the BNP and became prime minister of Bangladesh in March 1991.

APPENDIX 1

RULERS OF SELECTED PRE-MUSLIM DYNASTIES IN BENGAL

Pala Dynasty (c. 750-c. 1159)

(Dates are approximate)

750-770	Gopala
770-810	Dharmapala
810-850	Devapala
850-854	Vigrahapala (or Surapala)
854-908	Narayanapala
908-940	Rajyapala
940-960	Gopala II
960-988	Vigrahapala II
988-1038	Mahipala I
1038-1055	Nayapala
1055-1070	Vigrahapala III
1070-1075	Mahipala II
1075-1077	Surapala II
1077-1120	Ramapala
1120-1125	Kumarapala
1125-1140	Gopala III
1140-1155	Madanapala (Loss of Bengal to the Senas)
1155-1159	Govindapala (Loss of Bihar to Delhi Sultanate)

Sena Dynasty (c. 1095-1245)

(Dates are approximate)

1095-1158	Vijayasena
1159-1178	Vallalasena
1178-1206	Laksmanasena (Loss of Nadia in 1202)
1206-1220	Visvarupasena
1220-1223	Kesavasena

APPENDIX 2

MUSLIM RULERS OF BENGAL

Ilyas Shahi Dynasty (1342-1415)

1342-1357	Shamsuddin Ilyas Shah
1357-1389	Sikandar Shah
1389-1410	Ghiyasuddin Azam Shah
1410-1411	Saif Hamza Shah
1411-1414	Shihabuddin Bayazid Shah
1414	Alauddin Firoz Shah

Raja Ganesh Dynasty (1415-1433)

1415-1432	Jalaluddin Muhammad Shah
1432-1433	Shamsuddin Ahmad Shah

Ilyas Shahi Dynasty Restored (1433-1486)

1433-1459	Nasiruddin Mahmud
1459-1474	Ruknuddin Barbak Shah
1474-1481	Shamsuddin Yusuf Shah
1481	Sikandar
1481-1486	Jalaluddin Fath Shah

Abyssinians (1486-1493)

1486	Barbak Shahzada
1486-1490	Saifuddin Firoz Shah
1490-1493	Shamsuddin Muzaffar Shah

Husain Shahi Dynasty (1493-1538)

1493-1519	Alauddin Husain Shah
1519-1532	Nasiruddin Nusrat Shah
1532	Alauddin Firoz Shah
1532-1538	Ghiyasuddin Mahmud Shah

Suri Dynasty (1538-1564)

1538-1545	Sher Shah Suri
1545-1553	Islam Shah
1553-1555	Shamsuddin Muhammad Shah
1556-1560	Ghiyasuddin Bahadur Shah
1560-1563	Ghiyasuddin II
1563-1564	Ghiyasuddin III

Karrani Dynasty (1564-1575)

1564-1565	Taj Khan Karrani
1565-1572	Sulaiman Karrani
1572	Bayazid Karrani
1572-1575	Daud Karrani

APPENDIX 3

LIEUTENANT GOVERNORS AND GOVERNORS OF BENGAL DURING THE BRITISH PERIOD

Lieutenant Governors

1898-1903	J. Woodburn
1903-1908	A. H. L. Fraser
1908-1912	E. N. Baker

Governors

1912-1917	Lord Carmichael
1917-1922	The Earl of Ronaldshay (later the Marquess of Zetland)
1922-1927	The Earl of Lytton
1927-1930	F. S. Jackson
1930-1932	H. L. Stephenson
1932-1937	Sir John Anderson
1937-1939	Lord Brabourne
1939-1944	Sir John Herbert
1944-1946	Lord Casey
1946-1947	F. J. Burrows

Lieutenant Governors of Eastern Bengal and Assam

1905-1906	J. B. Fuller
1906-1911	Sir Lancelot Hare
1911-1912	C. S. Bayley

APPENDIX 4

GOVERNORS AND CHIEF MINISTERS OF EAST BENGAL/EAST PAKISTAN

(Asterisk indicates individual is included in the Dictionary.)

Governors

1947-1950	Sir Frederick Bourne
1950-1953	Malik Sir Firoz Khan Noon*
1953-1954	Chaudhury Khaliquzzaman*
1954	Iskandar Mirza*
1954	Sir Thomas Ellis (acting)
1954-1955	Justice Shahabuddin*
1955-1956	Justice Amiruddin Ahmad
1956-1958	Moulvi Abul Kasem Fazlul Haq*
1958	Hamid Ali (acting)
1958	Sultannuddin Ahmed (acting)*
1958-1960	Zakir Husain
1960-1962	Muhammad Azam Khan*
1962	Ghulam Faruque
1962-1969	Abdul Monem Khan*
1969	Mirza Nurul Huda*
1969-1971	Syed Muhammad Ahsan
1971	Abdul Muttalib Malik*

Chief Ministers

1947-1948	Khwaja Sir Nazimuddin*
1948-1954	Nurul Amin*
1954	Moulvi A.K. Fazlul Haq*
1954-1955	(under central government rule)
1955-1956	Abu Hussain Sarkar*
1956-1958	Ataur Rahman Khan*
1958	Abu Hussain Sarkar*
1958	Ataur Rahman Khan*
1958-1971	(parliamentary system abolished)

APPENDIX 5

PRINCIPAL OFFICERS OF THE GOVERNMENT OF BANGLADESH 1971-1995

Source: The serial publication *Chiefs of State and Cabinet Members of Foreign Governments* produced by the Directorate of Intelligence, Central Intelligence Agency. The serial is either monthly or bimonthly. Dates entered in the list are those of the issue in which the name first appeared. It may not be the actual date on which the office was assumed by the individual.

In early phase of the Ershad period many portfolios were not held separately but were grouped with other portfolios. There were also frequent vacancies during which Ershad or another of the military officers held charge of the ministries.

MUJIB PERIOD (1971-1975)

President

Dec. 1971-Jan. 1972 Sheikh Mujibur Rahman* (Syed Nazrul Islam*, acting)
Jan. 1972-Dec. 1973 Abu Sayeed Chowdhury*
Jan. 1974-Jan. 1975 Mohammadullah*
Jan. 1975-Aug. 1975 Sheikh Mujibur Rahman*

Vice President

Jan. 1975-Aug. 1975 Syed Nazrul Islam*

Prime Minister

Dec. 1971-Jan. 1972 Tajuddin Ahmad*
Jan. 1972-Jan. 1975 Sheikh Mujibur Rahman*
Jan. 1975-Aug. 1975 Mansur Ali*

Minister of Agriculture

Jan. 1972-Feb. 1972 Phani Bhushan Majumdar*
Apr. 1973-Aug. 1975 Muhammad Abdus Samad Azad*

Minister of Commerce

Jan. 1972-Feb. 1972 Mansur Ali*
Feb. 1972-Mar. 1972 Syed Nazrul Islam*
Mar. 1972-Aug. 1975 Khondakar Mushtaque Ahmed*

Minister of Communications

Jan. 1972-Feb. 1972	Sheikh Abdul Aziz
Feb. 1972-Aug. 1975	Mansur Ali*

Minister of Defense

Dec. 1971-Jan. 1972	Muhammad Ataul Ghani Osmani*
Jan. 1972-Feb. 1972	Tajuddin Ahmad*
Feb. 1972-Aug. 1975	Sheikh Mujibur Rahman*

Minister of Education

Mar. 1973-Feb. 1975	Yusuf Ali
Feb. 1975-Aug. 1975	Muzaffar Ahmed Chowdhury*

Minister of Finance

Dec. 1971-Feb. 1972	Mansur Ali*
Feb. 1972-Nov. 1974	Tajuddin Ahmad*
Dec. 1974-Jan. 1975	(vacant)
Jan. 1975-Aug. 1975	Azizur Rahman Mallick

Minister of Food and Civil Supplies

Jan. 1972-June 1974	Phani Bhushan Majumdar*
July 1974-Aug. 1975	Abdul Monim

Minister of Foreign Affairs

Jan. 1972-Apr. 1973	Muhammad Abdus Samad Azad*
Apr. 1973-Aug. 1975	Kamal Hossain*

Minister of Foreign Trade
(Included with Minister of Commerce except below)

Apr. 1973-Feb. 1974	A. H. M. Kamruzzaman*

Minister of Forests, Fisheries, and Livestock

Apr. 1972-Mar. 1973	Muhammad Sohrab Hossain
Apr. 1973-Jan. 1974	Abdur Rab Serniabat*
Feb. 1974-Feb. 1974	Mollah Jalaluddin Ahmad*
Mar. 1974-June 1974	Sheikh Mujibur Rahman*
July 1974-Nov. 1974	Tajuddin Ahmad*
Dec. 1974	(vacant)
Jan. 1975-Aug. 1975	Abdur Rab Serniabat*

Minister of Health and Family Planning

Jan. 1972-Mar. 1972	Zahur Ahmad Chowdhury
Apr. 1972-Mar. 1973	Abdul Malik Ukil*
Apr. 1973-Aug. 1975	Abdul Mannan

Minister of Home Affairs

Dec. 1971-Feb. 1972	A. H. M. Kamruzzaman*
Feb. 1972-Mar. 1972	Sheikh Mujibur Rahman*
Apr. 1972-Mar. 1973	Abdul Mannan
Apr. 1973-June 1974	Abdul Malik Ukil*
July 1974-Aug. 1975	Mansur Ali*

Minister of Industries

Dec. 1972-Feb. 1972	Mansur Ali*
Feb. 1972-Mar. 1972	Syed Nazrul Islam*
Apr. 1972-Mar. 1973	Mustifizur Rahman Siddiqui
Apr. 1973-Feb. 1974	A. H. M. Kamruzzaman*
Mar. 1974-Aug. 1975	Syed Nazrul Islam*

Minister of Information and Broadcasting

Jan. 1972-Feb. 1972	Tajuddin Ahmad*
Feb. 1972-Mar. 1972	Sheikh Mujibur Rahman*
Apr. 1972-Mar. 1973	Mizanur Rahman Chowdhury*
Apr. 1973-Sep. 1973	Sheikh Abdul Aziz
Oct. 1973-Jan. 1975	Sheikh Mujibur Rahman*
Jan. 1975-Aug. 1975	Muhammad Korban Ali*

Minister of Jute

Apr. 1973-June 1974	Tajuddin Ahmad*
July 1974-Jan. 1975	Sheikh Mujibur Rahman*
Jan. 1975-Aug. 1975	Asaduzzaman Khan

Minister of Labor and Social Welfare

Jan. 1972-June 1974	Zahur Ahmad Chowdhury
July 1974-Jan. 1975	Abdul Mannan
Jan. 1975-Aug. 1975	Muhammad Yusuf Ali

Minister of Land Revenue
(After Mar. 1974, titled Minister of Land Administration and Land Reform)

Jan. 1972-Mar. 1972	Khondakar Mushtaque Ahmed*
Apr. 1972-Feb. 1974	Abdur Rab Serniabat*
Mar. 1974-June 1974	Mollah Jalaluddin Ahmad*

July 1974-Jan. 1975	Phani Bhushan Majumdar*
Jan. 1975-Aug. 1975	Mohammadullah*

Minister of Law and Parliamentary Affairs

Jan. 1972-Feb. 1972	Khondakar Mushtaque Ahmed*
Feb. 1972-Mar. 1973	Kamal Hossain*
Apr. 1973-Aug. 1975	Manoranjan Dhar

Minister of Local Government, Rural Development, and Cooperatives

Jan. 1972-Feb. 1972	Phani Bhushan Majumdar*
Feb. 1972-Mar. 1972	Sheikh Abdul Aziz
Apr. 1972-Mar. 1973	Shamsul Haq
Apr. 1973-June 1974	Matiur Rahman
July 1974-Jan. 1975	Muhammad Abdus Samad Azad*
Jan. 1975-Aug. 1975	Phani Bhushan Majumdar*

Minister of Planning

Jan. 1972-Nov. 1974	Tajuddin Ahmad*
Dec. 1974-Jan. 1975	(vacant)
Jan. 1975-Aug. 1975	Syed Nazrul Islam*

Minister of Posts, Telephones, and Telegraph

Apr. 1972-Mar. 1973	Mollah Jalaluddin Ahmad*
Apr. 1973-Sep. 1973	Mohammad Ataul Ghani Osmany*
Oct. 1973-June 1974	Sheikh Abdul Aziz
July 1974-Aug. 1975	Mansur Ali*

Minister of Power, Natural Resources, Scientific and Technological Research, and Atomic Energy
(Title varied; "Power" dropped in Mar. 1974)

Apr. 1972-June 1974	Hafiz Ahmad Choudhury
July 1974-Jan. 1975	Kamal Hossain*
Jan. 1975-Aug. 1975	(Remaining divisions included with Education)

Minister of Power, Flood Control and Irrigation
(Title varied)

Feb. 1972-Feb. 1974	Khondakar Mushtaque Ahmad*
Mar. 1974-Aug. 1975	Abdur Rab Serniabat*

Minister of Public Works and Housing

Jan. 1972-Feb. 1972	Muhammad Yusuf Ali
Feb. 1972-Mar. 1972	Kamal Hossain*

Apr. 1972-Mar. 1973	Matiur Rahman
Apr. 1973-Aug. 1975	Mohammad Sohrab Hossain

Minister of Relief and Rehabilitation

Dec. 1971-Mar. 1973	A. H. M. Kamruzzaman*
Apr. 1973-May 1973	Mizanur Rahman Chowdhury*
June 1973-June 1974	Sheikh Mujibur Rahman*
July 1974-Aug. 1975	Abdul Monim

Minister of Shipping, Inland Waterways, and Water Transport

Apr. 1972-June 1974	Mohammad Ataul Ghani Osmany*
July 1974-Jan. 1975	Sheikh Mujibur Rahman*
Jan. 1975-Aug. 1975	Mansur Ali*
Aug. 1975	Abu Sayeed Choudhury*

MUSHTAQUE INTERREGNUM
(August-November 1975)

President: Khondakar Mushtaque Ahmed*

Vice President: Mohammadullah*

Ministers

Agriculture: Abdul Monim
Defense: Khondakar Mushtaque Ahmad*
Education, Scientific and Technological Research and Atomic Energy:
Muzaffar Ahmad Choudhury
Finance: Azizur Rahman Mallick
Food: Abdul Monim
Foreign Affairs: Abu Sayeed Chowdhury*
Health and Family Planning:
Abdul Mannan
Home Affairs: Khondakar Mushtaque Ahmed*
Law, Parliamentary Affairs and Justice:
Manoranjan Dhar
Local Government, Rural Development and Cooperatives:
Phani Bhushan Majumdar*
Planning: Muhammad Yusuf Ali
Ports, Shipping and Inland Water Transport:
Asaduzzaman Khan
Public Works and Urban Development:
Mohammad Sohrab Hossain
Relief and Rehabilitation:
Khitish Chandra Mondal

ZIA PERIOD
(1975-1982, including the period of Abdus Sattar)

President

Nov. 1975-Apr. 1977	Abu Sadat Muhammad Sayem*
Apr. 1977-May 1981	Ziaur Rahman*
May 1981-Mar. 1982	Abdus Sattar*

Vice President

June 1977-May 1981	Abdus Sattar*
Nov. 1981-Mar. 1982	Mirza Nurul Huda*
Mar. 1982	Mohammadullah*

Chief Martial Law Administrator

Nov. 1975-Nov. 1976	Abu Sadat Muhammad Sayem*
Nov. 1976-Mar. 1979	Ziaur Rahman*

Deputy Chief Martial Law Administrators

Nov. 1975-Nov. 1976	Ziaur Rahman*
Nov. 1975-Nov. 1977	Mosharraf Hossain Khan
Nov. 1975-Apr. 1976	Muhammad Ghulam Tawab
May 1976-Sep. 1976	Mohammad Khademul Bashar
Sep. 1976-Nov. 1977	Abdul Ghaffar Mahmud

Prime Minister

Mar. 1979-Mar. 1982	Shah Mohammad Azizur Rahman*

Deputy Prime Ministers

Apr. 1979-Aug. 1979	A. Q. M. Badruddoza Choudhury*
Apr. 1979-Dec. 1979	Moudud Ahmed*
Sep. 1979-Jan. 1982	Jamaluddin Ahmad
Sep. 1979-Dec. 1981	S. A. Bari A. T.

Minister of Agriculture
(Includes Forests except where separate entry is given)

Nov. 1975-Nov. 1975	Muhammad Ghulam Tawab
Dec. 1975-Jan. 1976	Abu Sadat Muhammad Sayem*
Feb. 1976-June 1976	Mirza Nurul Huda*
July 1976-Mar. 1979	Azizul Haq
Apr. 1979-Dec. 1981	Nurul Islam
Jan. 1982	Fasihuddin Mahtab
Feb. 1982	Abdul Kalim Chowdhury
Mar. 1982	Riazuddin Ahmad

Minister of Civil Aviation and Tourism

Nov. 1975-Jan. 1976	Muhammad Ghulam Tawab
Feb. 1976-Dec. 1976	(Included with Communications)
Jan. 1977-June 1978	Abdul Ghaffar Mahmud
July 1978-Mar. 1979	Kazi Anwarul Huque*
Apr. 1979-Aug. 1979	M. A. Matin
Sep. 1979-Apr. 1980	Kazi Anwarul Huque*
May 1980-Dec. 1981	K. M. Obaidur Rahman
Jan. 1982-Mar. 1982	A. K. M. Moidul Islam

Minister of Commerce
(Included Foreign Trade until Feb. 1978)

Nov. 1975-Nov. 1975	Ziaur Rahman*
Dec. 1975-Dec. 1976	Mirza Nurul Huda*
Jan. 1977-Apr. 1980	Mohammad Saifur Rahman*
May 1980-Dec. 1981	(vacant)
Jan. 1982	A. S. M. Mostafizur Rahman*
Feb. 1982-Mar. 1982	Mirza Nurul Huda*

Minister of Communications

Nov. 1975-Nov. 1975	Musharraf Hossain Khan
Dec. 1975-Jan. 1976	Kazi Anwarul Huque*
Feb. 1976-Nov. 1977	Musharraf Hossain Khan

(After Nov. 1977 divided into several ministries)

Minister of Defense

Nov. 1975-Apr. 1977	Abu Sadat Muhammad Sayem*
May 1977- May 1981	Ziaur Rahman*
May 1981-Mar. 1982	Abdus Sattar*

Minister of Education

Nov. 1975-Nov. 1975	Ziaur Rahman*
Dec. 1975-June 1977	Abul Fazal
July 1977-June 1978	Syed Ali Ahsan
July 1978-Oct. 1978	Kazi Zafar Ahmed*
Nov. 1978-Mar. 1979	Abdul Baten
Apr. 1979-Jan. 1982	Shah Mohammad Azizur Rahman*
Feb. 1982-Mar. 1982	Tofazzul Husain Khan

Minister in charge of the Establishment Division

Nov. 1977-June 1978	Ziaur Rahman*
July 1978-Jan. 1982	Mohammad Majidul Huq
Feb. 1982-Mar. 1982	Abdus Sattar*

Minister of Finance

Nov. 1975-Nov. 1978	Ziaur Rahman*
Dec. 1978-Apr. 1980	Mirza Nurul Huda*
May 1980-Jan. 1982	Muhammad Saifur Rahman*
Feb. 1982-Mar. 1982	Fasihuddin Mahtab

Minister of Fisheries and Livestock

Nov. 1975-Jan. 1976	Mosharraf Hossain Khan (included Forests)
Feb. 1976-Nov. 1977	(included in Agriculture)
Dec. 1977-June 1978	M. R. Khan
July 1978-Apr. 1980	K. M. Obaidur Rahman
May 1980-Jan. 1982	S. A. Bari A. T.
Feb. 1982-Mar. 1982	(at minister of state level)

Minister of Food

Nov. 1975-Apr. 1976	Muhammad Ghulam Tawab
May 1976-Aug. 1976	Mohammad Khademul Bashar
Aug. 1976-June 1977	Abdul Ghaffar Mahmud
July 1977-Jan. 1982	Abdul Momen Khan
Feb. 1982-Mar. 1982	Abdul Halim Chowdhury

Minister of Foreign Affairs

Nov. 1975-Mar. 1977	Abu Sadat Muhammad Sayem*
Apr. 1977-Mar. 1982	Muhammad Shamsul Huq*

Minister of Health and Population Control

Nov. 1975-Nov. 1975	Muhammad Ghulam Tawab
Dec. 1975-Nov. 1977	Mohammad Ibrahim (from July 1977 to Aug. 1977, Ibrahim held only Population Control; Mohammad Masudul Haque held Health, Labor and Social Welfare)
Dec. 1977-Aug. 1979	A. Q. M. Badruddoza Choudhury*
Sep. 1979-Mar. 1981	M. A. Matin
May. 1981-June 1981	(vacant)
July 1981-Dec. 1981	M. A. Matin
Jan. 1982	Abdur Rahman Biswas*
Feb. 1982-Mar. 1982	Khondker Abdul Hamid

Minister of Home Affairs

Nov. 1975-June 1978	Ziaur Rahman*
July 1978-Dec. 1981	A. S. M. Mustafizur Rahman*
Jan. 1982-Mar. 1982	M. A. Matin

Minister of Industries

Nov. 1975-Nov. 1975	Ziaur Rahman*
Dec. 1975-Jan. 1976	Mirza Nurul Huda*
Feb. 1976-June 1977	A. K. M. Hafizuddin
July 1977-Jan. 1982	Jamaluddin Ahmad
Feb. 1982	Mirza Nurul Huda*
Mar. 1982	Muhammad Yusuf Ali

Minister of Information and Broadcasting

Nov. 1975-Sep. 1976	Ziaur Rahman*
Oct. 1976-Oct. 1977	Akbar Kabir
Nov. 1977-June 1978	Shamsul Huda Choudhury*
July 1978-Apr. 1980	Habibullah Khan
May 1990-Jan. 1992	Shamsul Huda Choudhury*
Feb. 1982	Tofazzul Husain Khan
Mar. 1982	Shamsul Huda Choudhury*

Minister of Jute

Nov. 1975-Nov. 1975	Ziaur Rahman*
Dec. 1975-July 1977	Kazi Anwarul Huque*
Aug. 1977-Mar. 1979	A. M. Shafiul Azam
Apr. 1979-Apr. 1980	Abdur Rahman Biswas*
May 1980-Dec. 1981	Habibullah Khan
Jan. 1982-Mar. 1982	Muhammad Yusuf Ali

Minister of Labor

(At times included Social Welfare)

Nov. 1975-Nov. 1975	Mosharraf Hossain Khan
Dec. 1975-Jan. 1976	Abul Fazal
Feb. 1976-June 1976	Mohammad Ibrahim
July 1976-Jan. 1977	Mohammad Masudul Haque
Feb. 1977-Aug. 1977	(included with Health)
Sep. 1977-June 1978	(included with Manpower Development)
July 1978-Apr. 1979	Shah Mohammad Azizur Rahman*
May 1979-Aug. 1979	(vacant)
Sep. 1979-Jan. 1982	Riazuddin Ahmad
Feb. 1982-Mar. 1982	Khondker Abdul Hamid

Minister of Land Administration and Land Reforms

Nov. 1975-Nov. 1975	Mosharraf Hossain Khan
Dec. 1975-Jan. 1976	Mrs. Benita Roy
Feb. 1976-Nov. 1977	Kazi Anwarul Huque*
Dec. 1977-June 1978	Enayetullah Khan
July 1978-Mar. 1979	Mirza Ghulam Hafiz*

Apr. 1979-Mar. 1979	Mohammad Abdul Haque
Feb. 1982	Abdus Sattar*
Mar. 1982	Tofazzul Husain Khan

Minister of Law, Parliamentary Affairs, and Justice

Nov. 1975-Jan. 1977	Abu Sadat Mohammad Sayem*
Feb. 1977-Dec. 1981	Abdus Sattar*
Jan. 1982	Tofazzul Husain Khan
Feb. 1982-Mar. 1982	Shah Mohammad Azizur Rahman*

Minister of Local Government, Rural Development, and Cooperatives

Nov. 1975-Nov. 1975	Muhammad Ghulam Tawab
Dec. 1975-Jan. 1976	Mohammad Abdur Rashid
Feb. 1976-June 1978	Kazi Anwarul Huque*
July 1978-Jan. 1982	Abdul Halim Chaudhury
Feb. 1982-Mar. 1982	Shah Mohammad Azizur Rahman*

Minister of Manpower Development and Social Welfare

Nov. 1975-Aug. 1977	(under other ministries)
Sep. 1977-Nov. 1977	Mohammad Majidul Haque
Dec. 1977-June 1978	Zakaria Chowdhury
July 1978-Jan. 1982	S. A. Bari A. T.
Feb. 1982-Mar. 1982	(to ministry of Labor)

Minister of Petroleum and Natural Resources

Nov. 1975-Apr. 1976	Mohammad Ghulam Tawab
May 1976-Aug. 1976	Mohammad Khademul Bashar
Aug. 1976-June 1977	Abdul Ghaffar Mahmud
July 1977-June 1978	Ashfaque Hussain Khan
July 1978-Oct. 1978	Enayetullah Khan
Nov. 1978-June 1981	Akbar Hussain
July 1981-Jan. 1982	Kazi Anwarul Huque*
Feb. 1982-Mar. 1982	(vacant)

Minister of Planning

Nov. 1975-Nov. 1975	Abu Sadat Muhammad Sayem*
Dec. 1975-Apr. 1979	Mirza Nurul Huda*
May 1979 -Dec. 1981	Fasihuddin Mahtab
Jan. 1982-Mar. 1982	Abdus Sattar*

Minister of Ports, Shipping, and Inland Water Transport

Nov. 1975-Jan. 1976	Mosharraf Hossain Khan
Feb. 1976-Nov. 1977	(included in Communications)
Dec. 1977-Dec. 1981	Nurul Huq

Jan. 1982	(vacant)
Feb. 1982	Shamsul Huda Choudhury*
Mar. 1982	Sultan Ahmad Choudhury

Minister of Posts, Telegraph, and Telephones

Nov. 1975-Jan. 1976	Muhammad Ghulam Tawab
Feb. 1976-Nov. 1977	(included in Communications)
Dec. 1977-Mar. 1979	Moudud Ahmed*
Apr. 1979-Feb. 1982	A. K. M. Moidul Islam
Mar. 1982	Sultan Ahmad Choudhury

Minister of Power, Flood Control, and Water Resources

Nov. 1975-Nov. 1977	Mosharraf Hossain Khan
Dec- 1977-Mar. 1979	B. M. Abbas A.T.
Apr. 1979-Dec. 1979	Moudud Ahmed*
Jan. 1980-Dec. 1981	Kazi Anwarul Huque*
Jan. 1982	I. K. Siddiqui
Feb. 1982	(vacant)
Mar. 1982	Abdus Sattar*

Minister of Public Works and Urban Development

Nov. 1975-Nov. 1975	Muhammad Ghulam Tawab
Dec. 1975-June 1978	Mohammad Abdur Rashid
July 1978-Apr. 1980	Abdur Rahman
May 1980 -May 1981	(vacant)
June 1981-Jan. 1982	Abul Hasnat
Feb. 1982-Mar. 1982	(vacant)

Minister of Railways, Roads, Highways, and Road Transport

Dec. 1975-Dec. 1975	Kazi Anwarul Huque*
Jan. 1976-Nov. 1977	(included with Communications)
Dec. 1977-June 1978	Mohammad Majidul Huq
July 1978-Feb. 1979	Mashiur Rahman*
Mar. 1979-Apr. 1979	(vacant)
May 1979-Jan. 1982	Abdul Alim
Feb. 1982-Mar. 1982	Shamsul Huda Choudhury*

Minister of Relief and Rehabilitation

Nov. 1975-Nov. 1975	Mohammad Ghulam Tawab
Dec. 1975-Jan. 1976	Muhammad Abdur Rashid
Feb. 1976-June 1978	Mrs. Benita Roy
July 1978-Mar. 1979	Rasa Raj Mondal
Apr. 1979-Jan. 1982	Imran Ali Sarkar
Feb. 1982-Mar. 1982	(vacant)

Minister of Science and Technology

Nov. 1975-Nov. 1975	Ziaur Rahman*
Dec. 1975-Jan. 1976	Abul Fazal
Feb. 1976-May 1981	Ziaur Rahman*
May 1981-Mar. 1982	Abdus Sattar*

Minister of Sports, Cultural Affairs, and Religion

(title varies; Religion added in May 1979)

July 1978-Jan. 1982	Shamsul Huda Choudhury*
Feb. 1982	Tofazzul Husain Khan
Mar. 1982	Shamsul Huda Choudhury*

Minister of Textiles

Nov. 1975-June 1977	(included with Industry)
July 1977-June 1978	Muzaffar Ahmad
July 1978-Mar. 1979	Abdul Alim
Apr. 1979-Mar. 1981	Mansur Ali
Apr. 1981-Mar. 1982	Muhammad Yusuf Ali

Minister of Women's Affairs

July 1978-Apr. 1980	Mrs. Amina Rahman
May 1980-Mar. 1982	(vacant)

Minister of Youth Development

July 1978-Mar. 1979	Kazi Anwarul Huque*
Apr. 1979-Apr. 1980	Khondakar Abdul Hamid
May 1980-Mar. 1981	Abdus Sattar*
Apr. 1981-Dec. 1981	M. A. Matin
Jan. 1982	Abul Qasim
Feb. 1982-Mar. 1982	(vacant)

ERSHAD PERIOD
(March 1982-December 1990)

President

Mar. 1982-May 1984	A. F. M. Ahsanuddin Chowdhury*
June 1984-Dec. 1990	Hussain Muhammad Ershad*

Vice President

Jan. 1987-Sep. 1989	A. K. M. Nurul Islam
Sep. 1989-Dec. 1990	Moudud Ahmed*

Chief Martial Law Administrator

Mar. 1982-Jan. 1987	Hussain Muhammad Ershad*

Prime Minister

Mar. 1984-Jan. 1985	Ataur Rahman Khan*
July 1986-Jan. 1988	Mizanur Rahman Chowdhury*
Jan. 1988-Sep. 1989	Moudud Ahmed*
Sep. 1989-Dec. 1990	Kazi Zafar Ahmed*

Deputy Prime Minister

Nov. 1988-Sep. 1989	Kazi Zafar Ahmed*
Nov. 1988-Jan. 1988	Moudud Ahmed*
Nov. 1988-Sep. 1989	M. A. Matin
Jan. 1988-Dec. 1990	Shah Moazzem Hussain

Minister of Agriculture

July 1982-June 1984	A. Z. M. Obaidullah Khan
Feb. 1984-Jan. 1985	Mahboob Ali Khan
Feb. 1985-Mar. 1987	Muhammad Abdul Munim
Mar. 1987-Sep. 1987	Mirza Ruhul Amin
Sep. 1987-Jan. 1988	M. Mahbubuzzaman
Jan. 1988-May 1989	Mahmudul Hasan
May 1989-May 1990	Muhammad Abdul Munim
May 1990-Dec. 1990	Sardar Amzad Hussain

Minister of Civil Aviation and Tourism

Aug. 1982-Jan. 1985	Hussain Muhammad Ershad*
Feb. 1985-Oct. 1985	A. R. Yusuf
July 1986-Mar. 1987	Shafiqul Ghani Swapan
Mar. 1987-Sep. 1987	M. A. Sattar
Sep. 1987-May 1989	(at minister of state level)
May 1989-Sep. 1989	Ziauddin Ahmed

Sep. 1989-Dec. 1990 H. M.A. Gaffar

Minister of Commerce

May 1982-Apr. 1984 Shafiul Azam
May 1984-Jan. 1985 M. A. Matin
Feb. 1985-May 1985 Sultan Mahmud
June 1985-Apr. 1986 Kazi Zafar Ahmed*
May 1986-June 1986 Sultan Mahmud
July 1986-Mar. 1987 Kazi Zafar Ahmed*
Mar. 1987-Jan. 1988 Mohammad Abdul Munim
Jan. 1988-May 1988 Abdus Sattar
May 1988-Jan. 1989 (at minister of state level)
Jan. 1989-May 1990 Abdus Sattar
May 1990-Dec. 1990 Shamsul Haq

Minister of Communications

Mar. 1982-June 1984 Mahboob Ali Khan
July 1984-Jan. 1985 A. Z. M. Obaidullah Khan
Feb. 1985-Oct. 1985 Sultan Ahmad
Nov. 1985-Apr. 1986 Moudud Ahmed*
May 1986-June 1986 Sultan Ahmad
July 1986-Mar. 1987 M. A. Matin
Mar. 1987-Jan. 1988 M. Motiur Rahman
Jan. 1988-Dec. 1990 Anwar Hussain Manju

Minister of Culture

Jan. 1988-Nov. 1989 Nur Mohammad Khan
Nov. 1989-Nov. 1989 Zafar Imam
Nov. 1989-Dec. 1990 (at minister of state level)

Minister of Defense

Apr. 1982-Dec. 1990 Hussain Muhammad Ershad*

Minister of Education

June 1982-June 1984 Abdul Majeed Khan
July 1984-Jan. 1985 Shamsul Huda Choudhury*
Feb. 1985-Oct. 1985 Hussain Muhammad Ershad*
Nov. 1985-Feb. 1986 Shamsul Huda Choudhury*
Mar. 1986-Apr. 1986 M. A. Matin
May 1986-June 1986 Nurul Islam
July 1986-Mar. 1987 Mominuddin Ahmad
Mar. 1987-Jan. 1988 Mahbubur Rahman
Jan. 1988-May 1988 Sheikh Shahidul Islam
May 1988-Jan. 1989 Anisul Islam Mahmud
Jan. 1989-May 1990 Sheikh Shahidul Islam

May 1990-Dec. 1990	Kazi Zafar Ahmed*

Minister of Energy and Mineral Resources

Mar. 1982-Apr. 1982	Abdul Gaffar Mahmud
May 1982-July 1984	Sultan Mahmud
Feb. 1985-May 1985	Hussain Muhammad Ershad*
June 1985-Apr. 1986	Anwar Hossain Manju
May 1986-June 1986	Muhammad Abdul Munim
July 1986-Jan. 1988	Anwar Hossain Manju
Jan. 1988-Sep. 1989	A.B.M. Ghulam Mustafa
Sep. 1989-Dec. 1990	Ziauddin Ahmed Bablu

Minister of Establishment and Reorganization

Oct. 1983-Jan. 1985	Mohabbat Jan Chowdhury
Feb. 1985-Dec. 1990	Hussain Muhammad Ershad*

Minister of Finance

Mar. 1982-Jan. 1984	Abul Maal Abdul Muhith
Feb. 1984-Mar. 1987	Hussain Muhammad Ershad*
Mar. 1987-Jan. 1988	M. Syeduzzaman
Jan. 1988-May 1988	Wahidul Haq
May 1988-Sep. 1988	Mohammad Abdul Munim
Sep. 1988-May 1990	Wahidul Haq
May 1990-Dec. 1990	Mohammad Abdul Munim

Minister of Fisheries and Animal Husbandry

Nov. 1985-Apr. 1986	Sirajul Hussain Khan
May 1986-June 1986	Abdul Mannan Siddiqui
July 1986-Sep. 1987	Sirajul Hussain Khan
Sep. 1987-Jan. 1988	Mirza Rahul Amin
Jan. 1988-May 1988	Sardar Amzad Hussain
May 1988-Sep. 1988	Hussain Muhammad Ershad*
Sep. 1988-Jan. 1989	Sirajul Hussain Khan
Jan. 1989-Nov. 1989	Sardar Amzad Hussain
Nov. 1989-May 1990	Sunil Kumar Gupta
May 1990-Nov. 1990	M.A. Sattar
Nov. 1990-Dec. 1990	Mustafa Jamal Haider

Minister of Food

Apr. 1982-Jan. 1985	Abdul Gaffar Mahmud
Feb. 1985-Apr. 1986	Mohabbat Jan Chowdhury
May 1986 -June 1986	Abdul Mannan Siddiqui
July 1986-Mar. 1987	Mohabbat Jan Chowdhury
Mar. 1987-Jan. 1988	Sardar Amzad Hussain
Jan. 1988-May 1988	Iqbal Hussain Chowdhury

May 1988-Jan. 1989	Sardar Amzad Hussain
Jan. 1989-Jan. 1990	Iqbal Hussain Chowdhury
Jan. 1990-Dec. 1990	Shah Moazzem Hussain

Minister of Foreign Affairs

May 1992-June 1994	A. R. S. Doha
July 1984-May 1985	Hussain Muhammad Ershad*
June 1985-Jan. 1988	Humayun Rashid Choudhury
Jan. 1988-Dec. 1990	Anisul Islam Mahmud

Minister of Forests and Environment

Sep. 1988-Jan. 1990	A. K. M. Moyeedul Islam
Jan. 1990-Dec. 1990	Zafar Imam

Minister of Health and Family Planning

Mar. 1982-Apr. 1986	Shamsul Huq
July 1986-Jan. 1988	Salahuddin Qadir Chowdhury
Jan. 1988-May 1988	Mohammad Abdul Munim
May 1988-Sep. 1988	M. A. Matin
Sep. 1988-May 1989	Mohammad Abdul Munim
May 1989-Sep. 1989	M. A. Matin
Sep. 1989-Dec. 1990	Azizur Rahman

Minister of Home Affairs

Sep. 1982-Sep. 1983	Mohabbat Jan Chowdhury
Oct. 1983-Feb. 1986	Abdul Mannan Siddiqui
Mar. 1986-Mar. 1987	Mahmudul Hasan
Mar. 1987-May 1989	M. A. Matin
May 1989-Dec. 1990	Mahmudul Hasan

Minister of Industries

Mar. 1982-June 1984	Shafiul Azam
July 1984-June 1986	Sultan Mahmud
July 1986-Sep. 1990	Moudud Ahmed*
Sep. 1990-Dec. 1990	M. A. Sattar

Minister of Information and Broadcasting

Mar. 1982-May 1982	A. R. S. Doha
July 1982-Mar. 1984	Syed Najmuddin Hashim
Apr. 1984-Jan. 1985	Shamsul Huq
Feb. 1985-June 1985	A. R. Yusuf
July 1985-Oct. 1985	Serajul Hussain Khan
Nov. 1985-June 1986	Moazzem Hussain
July 1986-Nov. 1987	Anwar Zahid

Nov. 1987-Jan. 1988	Hussain Muhammad Ershad*
Jan. 1988-May 1988	Kazi Zafar Ahmed*
May 1988-Jan. 1989	Mahbubur Rahman
Jan. 1989-May 1990	Kazi Zafar Ahmed*
May 1990-Dec. 1990	Mizanur Rahman Shelley*

Minister of Irrigation, Water Development, and Flood Control

Mar. 1982-Apr. 1982	Abdul Gaffar Mahmud
May 1982-June 1983	Sultan Mahmud
July 1983-June 1984	A. Z. M. Obaidullah Khan
July 1984	A. R. S. Doha
Aug. 1984-Jan. 1985	Muhammad Aminul Islam Khan
Feb. 1985-June 1985	Sultan Ahmad
July 1985-Oct. 1985	Muhammad Aminul Islam Khan
Nov. 1985-Apr. 1986	Anisul Islam Mahmud
May 1986 -June 1986	Sultan Ahmad
July 1986-Jan. 1988	Anisul Islam Mahmud
Jan. 1988-May 1988	Mahbubur Rahman
May 1988-Nov. 1988	(to minister of state level)
Nov. 1988-Jan. 1989	Anisul Islam Mahmud
Jan. 1989-Sep. 1989	Mahbubur Rahman
Sep. 1989-Nov. 1990	A. B. M. Ghulam Mustafa
Nov. 1990-Dec. 1990	Mizanur Rahman Shelley*

Minister of Jute and Textiles
(Jute only after September, 1986; see Minister of Textiles)

July 1984	Muhammad Aminul Islam Khan
Aug. 1984-Jan. 1985	Muhammad Korban Ali*
Feb. 1985-June 1985	Sultan Ahmad
July 1985-Apr. 1986	Muhammad Abdus Sattar
May 1986-June 1986	Sultan Mahmud
July 1986-Mar. 1987	Hashimuddin Ahmad
Mar. 1987-Jan. 1988	Zafar Imam
Jan. 1988-May 1988	A. K. M. Moyeedul Islam
May 1988-Sep. 1988	Muhammad Korban Ali*
Sep. 1988-Sep. 1989	A. K. M. Moyeedul Islam
Sep. 1989-May 1990	Mahbubur Rahman
May 1990-Dec. 1990	Shahidul Islam

Minister of Labor and Manpower

Mar. 1982-June 1984	Muhammad Aminul Islam Khan
July 1984-Jan. 1985	Shah Moazzem Hossain
Feb. 1985-Oct. 1985	Anisul Islam Mahmud
Nov. 1985-June 1986	Muhammad Korban Ali*
July 1986-Mar. 1987	Muhammad Abdus Sattar
Mar. 1987-Sep. 1987	Abdur Rashid
Sep. 1987-Jan. 1988	Anwar Zahid

Jan. 1988-May 1988	Shah Moazzem Hussain
May 1988-Dec. 1990	Sirajul Hussain Khan

Minister of Land Administration and Land Reforms

(Name of ministry changed at various times)

Mar. 1982-Mar. 1984	Khondakar Abu Bakr
Apr. 1984-Jan. 1985	M. A. Haq
Feb. 1985-June 1985	T. I. M. Fazle Rabbi Chowdhury
July 1985-Oct. 1985	Muhammad Korban Ali*
Nov. 1985-Apr. 1986	A. K. M. Mayeedul Islam
May 1986-June 1986	Zakir Khan Chowdhury
July 1986-Mar. 1987	Mirza Rahul Amin
Mar. 1987-Sep. 1987	A.K.M. Moyeedul Islam
Sep. 1987-Jan. 1988	Sirajul Hussain Khan
Jan. 1988-May 1988	Sunil Kumar Gupta
May 1988-Jan. 1989	Mostafa Jamal Haider
Jan. 1989-Nov. 1989	Sunil Kumar Gupta
Nov. 1989-May 1990	Sardar Amzad Hussain
May 1990-Dec. 1990	Tajul Islam Chowdhury

Minister of Law and Justice

Mar. 1982-Mar. 1984	Khondakar Abu Bakr
July 1984-Jan. 1985	Ataur Rahman Khan*
Feb. 1985-Feb. 1986	A. K. M. Nurul Islam
Mar. 1986-Apr. 1986	A. K. M. Aminul Islam
May 1986-Nov. 1989	A. K. M. Nurul Islam
Nov. 1989-May 1990	Moudud Ahmed*
May 1990-Dec. 1990	Habibul Islam Bhuiyan

Minister of Local Government, Rural Development, and Cooperatives

Mar. 1982-Jan. 1985	Mahbubur Rahman
Feb. 1985-Feb. 1986	Mahmudul Hasan
Mar. 1986-Apr. 1986	Amanul Islam
May 1986-June 1986	Mahmudul Hasan
July 1986-Sep. 1988	Shah Moazzem Hossain
Sep. 1988-Sep. 1989	(to minister of state level)
Sep. 1989-Dec. 1990	Mohammad Naziur Rahman Manzur

Minister of Planning

Mar. 1982-Jan. 1984	Abul Maal Abdul Muhith
Apr. 1984-June 1984	Shamsul Huda Chowdhury
July 1984-Oct. 1985	Abdul Majeed Khan
Nov. 1985-Apr. 1986	Sultan Ahmad Chowdhury

July 1986-Mar. 1987	Muhammad Shamsul Haq
Mar. 1987-July 1990	Abdul Karim Khondaker
July 1990-Dec. 1990	Moudud Ahmed*

Minister of Ports, Shipping, and Water Transport

Aug. 1984-Jan. 1985	Reazuddin Ahmad
Feb. 1985-Oct. 1985	Sultan Ahmad
Nov. 1985-Apr. 1986	Moudud Ahmed*
May 1986-June 1986	Sultan Ahmad
July 1986-Mar. 1987	A. K. M. Moyeedul Islam
Mar. 1987-Sep. 1987	Kazi Zafar Ahmed*
Sep. 1987-Nov. 1987	A. K. M. Moyeedul Islam
Nov. 1987-Jan. 1990	(see Minister of Shipping)
Jan. 1990-Mar. 1990	Mohammad Korban Ali*
Mar. 1990-Sep. 1990	(see Ministry of Shipping)
Sep. 1990-Dec. 1990	Mohdudur Rahman Chowdhury

Minister of Posts and Telecommunications

Nov. 1985-Feb. 1986	Mizanur Rahman Chowdhury*
May 1986-June 1986	Sultan Ahmad
July 1986-Mar. 1988	Mizanur Rahman Chowdhury*
Mar. 1988-Sep. 1989	(at minister of state level)
Sep. 1989-Dec. 1990	Qazi Firoz Rashid

Minister of Relief and Rehabilitation

Apr. 1982-July 1984	Abdul Gaffar Mahmud
Aug. 1984-Jan. 1985	Muhammad Yusuf Ali
Feb. 1985-June 1985	Hussain Muhammad Ershad*
July 1985-Oct. 1985	T. I. M. Fazle Rabbi Chowdhury
Nov. 1985-Feb. 1986	Salahuddin Qadir Chowdhury
Mar. 1986-June 1986	Abdul Mannan Siddiqui
July 1986-Sep. 1987	Muhammad Shamsul Haq
Sep. 1987-Jan. 1988	Maulana M. A. Mannan
Jan. 1988-Jan. 1988	Sirajul Hussain Khan
Jan. 1988-Jan. 1989	(at minister of state level)
Jan. 1989-Jan. 1990	Sirajul Hussain Khan
Jan. 1990-Sep. 1990	Mahdudur Rahman Chowdhury
Sep. 1990-Dec. 1990	Manzur Quader

Minister of Religious Affairs and Endowments

June 1982-May 1983	Abdul Majeed Khan
June 1983-June 1984	Mahbubur Rahman
July 1984-Jan. 1985	Khondakar Abu Bakr
Feb. 1985-June 1985	Hussain Muhammad Ershad*
July 1985-Oct. 1985	A. K. M. Nurul Islam

Nov. 1985-Feb. 1986	Muhammad Aminul Islam Khan
Mar. 1986-Apr. 1986	Shamsul Huda Choudhury*
May 1986-June 1986	A. K. M. Nurul Islam
July 1986-Jan. 1988	Maulana M.A. Mannan
Jan. 1988-May 1988	(at minister of state level)
May 1988-July 1988	Maulana M.A. Mannan
July 1988-Jan. 1989	Mufti Maulana Mohammad Wakkas
Jan. 1989-Jan. 1990	(at minister of state level)
Jan. 1990-May 1990	Nazimuddin al-Azad
May 1990-Dec. 1990	(vacant)

Minister of Social Welfare and Women's Affairs

(Women's Affairs separated in January, 1990)

Apr. 1982-Jan. 1985	Shafia Khatun
Feb. 1985-June 1985	Hussain Muhammad Ershad*
July 1985-Sep. 1987	Rabia Bhuiyan
Sep. 1987-Jan. 1988	M. Shamsul Haq
Jan. 1988-Dec. 1990	Rezwanul Haq Chowdhury

Minister of Textiles

(see Minister of Jute and Textiles)

July 1986-Mar. 1987	Hashimuddin Ahmed
Mar. 1987-Jan. 1988	Sunil Kumar Gupta
Jan. 1988-Nov. 1989	Zafar Imam
Nov. 1989-Jan. 1990	M. Abdul Malek
Jan. 1990-Dec. 1990	A. B. M. Ruhul Amin Havaldar

Minister of Women's Affairs

Jan. 1990-Dec. 1990	Syeda Razia Faiz

Minister of Works

Mar. 1982-Sep. 1983	Abdul Mannan Siddiqui
Oct. 1983-Jan. 1985	Mohammad Abdul Munim
Feb. 1985-June 1985	Mahmudul Hasan
July 1985-Feb. 1986	M. A. Matin
Mar. 1986-Apr. 1986	Salahuddin Qadir Chowdhury
May 1986-June 1986	Mohammad Abdul Munim
July 1986-Mar. 1987	A. K. M. Aminul Islam
Mar. 1987-Nov. 1987	Shafiqul Ghani Swapan
Nov. 1987-Jan. 1988	Hussain Muhammad Ershad*
Jan. 1988-May 1988	Mustafa Jamal Haider
May 1988-May 1989	Sheikh Shahidul Islam
May 1989-Nov. 1990	Mustafa Jamal Haider
Nov. 1990-Dec. 1990	Abul Hasnat

Minister of Youth and Sports

July 1985-June 1986	Zakir Khan Chowdhury
July 1986-Mar. 1987	Sunil Kumar Gupta
Mar. 1987-Sep. 1987	Sheikh Shahidul Islam
Sep. 1987-Jan. 1988	(at minister of state level)
Jan. 1988-May 1988	Iqbal Hossain
May 1988-Jan. 1989	Sunil Kumar Gupta
Jan. 1989-Sep. 1989	Iqbal Hossain
Sep. 1989-Jan. 1990	A. B. M. Havaldar
Jan. 1990-Dec. 1990	(vacant)

Ministers without portfolio

Apr. 1984	Syed Najmuddin Hashim
Nov. 1984-Jan. 1985	Mizanur Rahman Chowdhury*

INTERIM GOVERNMENT
(December 1990-March 1991)

Acting President: Chief Justice Shahabuddin Ahmed*

Advisers:

Agriculture and Land: A. M. Anisuzzaman
Civil Aviation, Tourism, and Shipping: Mohammad Rafiqul Islam
Commerce: Imamuddin Ahmed
Communications, Posts, and Telecommunications: A. B. M. G. Kibria
Cultural Affairs and Food: Reazuddin Ahmed
Education: Zillur Rahman Siddique
Energy, Mineral Resources, and Works: Wahiduddin Ahmed
Finance: Kafiluddin Ahmed
Foreign Affairs: Fakhruddin Ahmed
Forest and Environment, Livestock and Fisheries: Qazi Fazlur Rahman
Health and Family Welfare: M. A. Majed
Industries, Jute, and Textiles: A. K. M. Musa
Irrigation, Water Development, and Flood Control: Qazi Fazlur Rahman
Labor and Manpower: A. K. M. Aminul Haq
Law and Justice: Mohammad Abdul Khaleque
Planning: Rahman Sobhan
Relief : B. K. Das
Social Welfare, Women's Affairs, Youth, and Sports: Alamgir M. A. Kabir

KHALEDA ZIA MINISTRY
(Through November, 1995)

Acting President

Mar. 1991-Nov. 1991 Shahabuddin Ahmed

President

Nov. 1991- Abdur Rahman Biswas*

Prime Minister

Mar. 1991-Nov. 1995 Khaleda Zia*

Minister of Agriculture, Irrigation, Flood Control, and Water Resources

Mar. 1991-Nov. 1995 Najudul Haq

Minister of Commerce

Mar. 1991-Nov. 1991 M. Keramat Ali
Nov. 1991-Oct. 1993 M. K. Anwar
Oct. 1993-Nov. 1995 Mohammad Shamsul Haq Khan

Minister of Communications, Railways, Roads, and Highways

Mar. 1991-Nov. 1995 Oli Ahmed

Minister of Defense

Mar. 1991-Nov. 1991 Shahabuddin Ahmed*
Nov. 1991-Nov. 1995 Khaleda Zia*

Minister of Education

Mar. 1991-Nov. 1991 A. Q. M. Badruddoza Chowdhury
Nov. 1991-Nov. 1995 Zamiruddin Sirkar

Minister of Energy and Mineral Resources

Mar. 1991-Nov. 1991 Khaleda Zia*
Nov. 1991-Nov. 1995 Khondakar Mosharraf Hossain

Minister of Environment, Forests, Fisheries, and Livestock

Nov. 1991-Oct. 1993 Abdullah al-Noman
Divided October 1993.

Minister of Environment and Forests

Oct. 1993-Nov. 1995 Abdullah al-Noman

Minister of Establishment

Mar. 1991-Nov. 1995 Khaleda Zia*

Minister of Finance

Mar. 1991-Nov. 1995 Muhammad Saifur Rahman*

Minister of Fisheries and Livestock

Oct. 1993-Nov. 1995 Akbar Hussain

Minister of Food

Nov. 1991-Oct. 1993 Mohammad Shamsul Islam Khan
Oct. 1993-Nov. 1995 Mir Shawkat Ali

Minister of Foreign Affairs

Mar. 1991-Nov. 1995 A. S. M. Mustafizur Rahman

Minister of Health and Family Planning

Mar. 1991-Nov. 1995 Chaudhury Kamal Ibne Yusuf

Minister of Home Affairs

Mar. 1991-Nov. 1991 Khaleda Zia*
Nov. 1991-Nov. 1995 Abdul Matin Chowdhury

Minister of Industry

Mar. 1991-Oct. 1993 Mohammad Shamsul Islam Khan
Oct. 1993-Nov. 1995 Zahiruddin Khan

Minister of Information

Mar. 1991-Nov. 1991 Khaleda Zia*
Nov. 1991-Mar. 1995 Najmul Huda

Minister of Jute

Nov. 1991-Nov. 1995 Hannan Shah

Minister of Labor and Manpower

Nov. 1991-Nov. 1995 Abdul Mannan Bhuiyan

Minister of Law and Justice

Mar. 1991-Nov. 1995 Mirza Ghulam Hafiz*

Minister of Local Government, Rural Development, and Cooperatives

Mar. 1991-Nov. 1995 Abdus Salam Talukdar

Minister of Planning

Mar. 1991-Nov. 1991 Saifur Rahman*
Nov. 1991-Nov. 1993 A. M. Zahiruddin Khan
Nov. 1993-Nov. 1995 Khaleda Zia*

Minister of Posts and Telecommunications

Nov. 1991-Sep. 1993 M. Keramat Ali
Sep. 1993-Nov. 1995 Tariqul Islam

Minister of Religious Affairs

Sep. 1993-Nov. 1995 M. Keramat Ali

Minister of Science and Technologgy

Sep. 1993-Nov. 1995 Abdul Mannan

Minister of Shipping

Mar. 1991-Nov. 1991 M.K. Anwar
Nov. 1991-Oct. 1993 At minister of state level
Oct. 1993-Nov. 1995 M.K. Anwar

Minister of Social Welfare and Women's Affairs

Nov. 1991-Sep. 1993 Tariqul Islam
Ministry divided September, 1993

Minister of Social Welfare

Sep. 1993-Nov. 1995 Fazlur Rahman Patel

Minister of Women's Affairs

Sep. 1993-Nov. 1995 Sarwari Rahman

Minister of Works

Nov. 1991-Nov. 1995 Rafiqul Islam Mian

Minister of Youth Development and Sports

Nov. 1991-Nov. 1995 Sadiq Hussain Khan

BIBLIOGRAPHY

This bibliography is arranged generally in accordance with the topics used by the *Bibliography of Asian Studies*, published annually by the Association for Asian Studies. The following is an index to the topics:

- General and Miscellaneous
- Anthropology and Sociology
  - Folklore
  - Population
  - Overseas Communities
  - Rural Conditions
  - Social Conditions
  - Social Work
  - Women
- Arts
  - Architecture
  - Painting
  - Sculpture
  - Theater
- Communications and Media
- Economics
  - Agriculture
  - Irrigation
    - Ganges Flood Plain
    - Ganges Water Dispute
  - Economic Conditions
  - Economic History
  - Economic Planning
  - Economic Theory
  - Finance
  - Industry
  - International Economics
  - Labor
  - Land Development and Settlement
  - Rural Development
  - Transportation
  - Urban Development
- Education
- Geography
- History
  - General History
  - Ancient, Buddhist and Hindu Periods
  - Muslim Period
  - British Period
  - Pakistan Period and War of Independence
  - Local History
  - Archaeology
- Language
- Literature
  - Fiction
  - Poetry
- Politics and Government
  - Armed Forces
  - Defense
  - Elections
  - International Relations
  - Law
  - Local Government
  - Political Parties
  - Public Administration
  - Regional Associations
- Science and Technology
  - Environmental Science
  - Public Health

General and Miscellaneous

Afsaruddin, Mohammad. *Society and Culture in Bangladesh*. Dhaka: Book House, 1990.

Ahmed, A. F. Salahuddin. *Bangladesh Tradition and Transformation*. Dhaka: University Press, 1987.

Ahmed, Rafiuddin, ed., *Bangladesh: Society, Religion, and Politics*. Chittagong: South Asia Studies Group, 1985.

Ali, Kauser. *Bangladesh, A New Nation*. Dacca: Ali Publications, 1982.

Baumer, Rachel Van M., ed. *Aspects of Bengal History and Society*. Honolulu: University Press of Hawaii, 1975.

Baxter, Craig. *Bangladesh: A New Nation in an Old Setting*. Boulder, CO: Westview Press, 1984.

Chakravarty, S. B., and Virendra Narain, eds. *Bangladesh*, 3 volumes. New Delhi: South Asian Publishers, 1986.

Davis, Martin, ed. *Conference on Bengal Studies, 1975, University of Iowa*. East Lansing, MI: Asian Studies Center, Michigan State University, 1976.

Fishwick, Marshall W., ed. *Bangladesh: Inter-Cultural Studies*. Dhaka: Ananda, 1983.

Gunderson, Warren M., ed. *Bengal Studies Conference, 1971, University of Minnesota*. East Lansing, MI: Asian Studies Center, Michigan State University, 1975.

Haque, Chowdhury E., ed. *Bangladesh: Politics, Economy, and Society*. Winnipeg: Bangladesh Studies Assemblage, University of Manitoba, 1987.

Heitzman, James, and Robert L. Worden, eds. *Bangladesh, A Country Study*. Washington, DC: Superintendent of Documents, 1989.

Husain, Syed Sajjad, ed. *East Pakistan: A Profile*. Dacca: Orient Longmans, 1962.

Johnson, Basil L. C. *Bangladesh*. Totowa, NJ: Barnes and Noble, 1982.

Khan, Mohammad Mohabbat, and John P. Thorp, eds. *Bangladesh: Society, Politics, and Bureaucracy*, Dhaka: Centre for Administrative Studies, 1984.

Langsten, Ray, ed. *Research on Bengal*. East Lansing, MI: Asian Studies Center, Michigan State University, 1983.

Lipski, Alexander, ed. *Bengal: East and West*. East Lansing, MI: Asian Studies Center, Michigan State University, 1970.

Mahmud, Abu Zafar Shahabuddin. *Introducing East Pakistan: Geography, Everyday Life, Places of Interest*. Dacca: Roushan Akhter Begum, 1969.

McLane, John R., ed. *Conference on Bengal Studies, 1973, Columbia University: Bengal in the Nineteenth and Twentieth Centuries*. East Lansing, MI: Asian Studies Center, Michigan State University, 1975.

Novak, James J. *Bangladesh: Reflections on the Water*. Bloomington, IN: Indiana University Press, 1993.

O'Donnell, Charles Peter. *Bangladesh: Biography of a Muslim Nation*. Boulder, CO: Westview Press, 1984.

Paul, Robert, and Mary Jane Beech, eds. *Conference on Bengal Studies (1969: University of Illinois)* East Lansing, MI: Asian Studies Center, Michigan State University, 1971.

Roy, Samaren. *The Roots of Bengali Culture*. Calcutta: Firma KLM, 1981.

Seely, Clinton B. *Bengal Studies Conference, 1990*. East Lansing, MI: Asian Studies Center, Michigan State University, 1991.

Stewart, Tony K., ed. *Shaping Bengali Worlds, Public and Private*. East Lansing, MI: Asian Studies Center, Michigan State University, 1989.

Tagore, Rabindranath, Sir. *Glimpses of Bengal, Selected from the Letters of Sir Rabindranath Tagore*. London: Macmillan, 1921.

Tepper, Elliot L., and Glen A. Hayes, eds. *Bengal and Bangladesh: Politics and Culture of the Golden Delta*. East Lansing, MI: Asian Studies Center, Michigan State University, 1990.

Bibliography

Bertocci, Peter J. *Bangladesh History, Society, and Culture: An Introductory Bibliography of Secondary Materials.* East Lansing, MI: Asian Studies Center, Michigan State University, 1973.

Gustafson, W. Eric, ed. *Pakistan and Bangladesh: Bibliographic Essays in Social Science*. Islamabad: University of Islamabad Press, 1976.

Kayastha, Ved P. *The Crisis on the Indian Sub-Continent and the Birth of Bangladesh: A Selected Reading List.* Ithaca, NY: South Asian Program, Cornell University, 1972.

Khan, Mohammad Abdul Aziz. *Devindex Bangladesh: Documents on and about Bangladesh Published Abroad.* Dacca: Bangladesh Institute of Development Studies, 1982.

Kozicki, Richard J. *International Relations of South Asia, 1947-1908: A Guide to Information Sources.* Detroit: Gale Research Co., 1981. Mamoon, Muntassir. *Index to Articles in the Dhaka University Studies, Part A, Volumes 1-40.* Dhaka: Dhaka University Library, 1986.

Meyer, Milton Walter. *South Asia: An Introductory Bibliography.* Los Angeles: Department of History, California State University, 1972.

Nelson, David N. *Bibliography of South Asia.* Metuchen, NJ: Scarecrow Press, 1994.

Noyce, John L. *Bangladesh: A Select Bibliography.* Brighton: Noyce, 1977.

Rahim, Joyce, and Enayetur Rahim. *Bangladesh: A Select Bibliography of English Language Periodical Literature, 1971-1986.* Dhaka: Asiatic Society of Bangladesh, 1986.

Razzak, Mohammad Abdur. *Bangladesh: A Select General Bibliography.* Rajshahi: Razzaque, 1987.

Satyaprakash. *Bangladesh: A Select Bibliography.* Gurgaon: Indian Documentation Service, 1976.

Shamsuddoulah, A. B. M. *Introducing Bangladesh through Books: A Select Bibliography with Introductions and Annotations, 1855-1976*. Dacca: Great Eastern Books, 1976.

Sukhwal, B. L. *South Asia: A Systematic Geographic Bibliography*. Metuchen, NJ: Scarecrow Press, 1974.

Talukder, Alauddin. *Bangladesh Studies: A Select List of Basic Books and Background. Documents* Dacca: Bangladesh Institute of Development Studies, 1975.

Anthropology and Sociology

Bibliography

Qadir, S. A. *Social Science Research in Bangladesh*. Dhaka: National Institute of Local Government, 1987.

Folklore

Abbasi, Mustafa Zaman. *Folkloric Bangladesh*. Dacca: Bangladesh Folklore Parishad, 1979.

Bradley-Birt, Francis Breadley. *Bengal Fairy Tales*. London: John Lane, 1920.

Chowdhury, Kabir. *Folktales of Bangladesh*. Dacca: Bangla Academy, 1972.

Chowdhury, Kabir, Serajul Islam Chowdhury, and Khondakar Ashraf, translators. *Folk Poems from Bangladesh*. Dhaka: Bangla Academy, 1985.

Damant, Gaborn Henry. *Tales from Bangladesh*. Dacca: Bangladesh Books International, 1976.

Hafiz, Abdul. *Folktales of Bangladesh*. Dhaka: Bangla Academy, 1985.

Karima, Anoyarula. *The Myths of Bangladesh*. Kushtia: Folklore Research Institute, 1988.

Khan, Shamsuzzaman, ed. *Folklore of Bangladesh*. Dhaka: Bangla Academy, 1987-1992.

Roy Choudhury, Pranab Chandra. *Folk Tales of Bangladesh.* New Delhi: Sterling, 1982.

Sen, Dineshchandra. *The Folk Literature of Bengal.* New Delhi: D.K. Publishers, 1985. (Lectures delivered at Calcutta University in 1917.)

Siddiqui, Ashraf. *Our Folklore, Our Heritage* Dacca: Bangladesh Books International, 1977.

———, *Folkloric Bangladesh.* Dacca: Bangla Academy, 1976.

———, *Our Folk-Literature: Ballad Stories.* Dacca: Bureau of National Reconstruction, 1968.

Population

Ahmad, Alia. *Women and Fertility in Bangladesh.* Newbury Park, CA: Sage Publications, 1991.

Akbar, Mohammad Ali. *Socio-Economic Factors Affecting Family Size and Fertility Pattern in Bangladesh.* Rajshahi: Popular Press, 1978.

Akhter, Farida. *Depopulating Bangladesh: Essays on the Politics of Fertility.* Dhaka: Narigrantha Prabartana, 1992.

Banerjee, Sumanta. *Bangladesh.* New York: United Nations Fund for Population Activities, 1982.

Bangladesh Fertility Survey, 1989. Dhaka: National Institute of Population Research and Training, 1990.

Blanchet, Therese. *Meanings and Rituals of Birth in Rural Bangladesh: Women, Pollution, and Marginality,* Dhaka: University Press, 1984.

Cain, Mead. *Development Policy and the Prospects for Fertility Decline in Bangladesh.* New York: Population Council, 1982.

Cleland, John, et al. *The Determinants of Reproductive Change in Bangladesh: Success in a Challenging Environment.* Washington, DC : The World Bank, 1994.

Estimation of Recent Trends in Fertility and Mortality in Bangladesh. Washington, DC: National Academy Press, 1981.

Ghulam Rabbani, A. K. M. *Bangladesh Population Census, 1981: Analytical Findings and National Tables.* Dhaka: Bangladesh Bureau of Statistics, 1984.

———. *Bangladesh Population Census in Retrospect: Sub-National and Inter-District Comparisons of 1961 and 1974 Census.* Dacca: Bangladesh Bureau of Statistics, 1979.

Green, Lawrence W., et al. *The Dacca Family Planning Experiment: A Comparative Evaluation of Programs Directed at Males and at Females.* Berkeley, CA: School of Public Health, University of California, 1972.

Haider, Muhiuddin. *Village Level Integrated Population Education: A Case Study of Bangladesh.* Lanham, MD: University Press of America, 1982.

Haq, Muhammad Nazmul. *Study of Compensation Payments and Family Planning in Bangladesh: A Synthesis.* Dhaka: National Institute of Population Research and Training, 1989.

Hossain, Monowar, M. Aminur Rahman Khan, and Lincoln C. Chen, eds. *Seminar on Fertility in Bangladesh (1976: Cox's Bazaar) Fertility in Bangladesh: Which Way is it Going?* Dacca: National Institute of Population Training and Research, 1979.

Hussain, Zahid. *Correlates of Effectiveness of Field Supervision in Family Planning Programme.* Dhaka: Centre for Population Management and Research, 1983.

Hye, Hasnat Abdul. *Community Participation: Case Studies of Population Health Programmes in Bangladesh.* Comilla: Bangladesh Academy for Rural Development, 1989.

Maloney, Clarence. *Beliefs and Fertility in Bangladesh.* Dacca: International Centre for Diarrohoeal Disease Research, 1981.

Miranda, Armindo. *The Demography of Bangladesh: Data and Issues.* Fantoft, Bergen, Norway: Chr. Michelson Institute, 1982.

Miyan, Mohammad Alimaulya. *Assessment of Management Assistance to Population Programme in Bangladesh.* Kuala Lumpur:

International Committee on the Management of Population Programmes, 1982.

———. *Marketing of Social Products: Family Planning in Bangladesh*. Dacca: Centre for Population Management and Research, 1981.

———. *The Management of Population Assistance Programmes: Examples of Public Management of Population Projects in Bangladesh and Indonesia*. Paris: Development Centre of the Organization for Economic Co-operation and Development, 1984.

Noman, Ayesha. *Status of Women and Fertility in Bangladesh*. Dhaka: University Press, 1983.

Recent Trends in Fertility and Mortality in Bangladesh. Dhaka: Population and Development Planning Unit, Planning Commission, 1984.

Spitler, James F. *Bangladesh*. Washington, DC: U.S. Department of Commerce, Bureau of Census, 1983.

Stoeckel, John E., and Moqbul A. Choudhury, *Fertility, Infant Mortality, and Family Planning in Rural Bangladesh*. Dacca: Oxford University Press, 1973.

Sudan, Falendra K. *Demographic Transition in South Asia*. New Delhi: Anmol Publications, 1992.

Bibliography

Alauddin, Mohammad. *Population and Family Planning in Bangladesh: A Survey of the Research*. Washington, DC: World Bank, 1983.

Haque, Serajul. *Bangladesh Demography: A Select Bibliography*. Dacca: Bangladesh Institute of Development Studies, 1976.

Overseas Communities

Ali, Syed Ashraf. *Labor Migration from Bangladesh to the Middle East*. Washington, DC: World Bank, 1981.

Eade, John. *The Politics of Community: The Bangladeshi Community in East London*. Aldershot, Hants.: Avebury, 1990.

Islam, Muinul, et al., eds. *Overseas Migration from Rural Bangladesh: A Micro Study*. Chittagong: University of Chittagong, 1987.

Tinker, Hugh. *The Banyan Tree: Overseas Emigrants from India, Pakistan, and Bangladesh*. New York: Oxford University Press, 1977.

Rural Conditions

Afsaruddin, Mohammad. *Rural Life in Bangladesh: A Study of Five Selected Villages*. Dacca: Nawrose Kitabistan, 1979.

Ahmed, Raisuddin. *Developmental Impact of Rural Infrastructure in Bangladesh*. Washington, DC: International Food Policy Research Institute, 1990.

Anisuzzamam, Mohammad. *Planning for Local Development: An Evaluation of Three Training Courses on Local Level Planning and Management*. Comilla: Bangladesh Academy for Rural Development, 1989.

Barman, Dalem Ch. *Emerging Leadership Patterns in Rural Bangladesh: A Study*. Dhaka: Centre for Social Studies, 1988.

Bose, Sugata. *Peasant Labour and Colonial Capital: Rural Bengal Since 1770*. New York: Cambridge University Press, 1993.

———. *Agrarian Bengal: Economy, Social Structure, and Politics, 1919-1947*. New York: Cambridge University Press, 1986.

Chowdhury, Anwarullah. *Agrarian Social Relations and Development in Bangladesh*. New Delhi: Oxford, 1982.

———. *A Bangladesh Village: A Study in Social Stratification*. Dacca: Centre for Social Studies, 1978.

Dutt, Romesh Chunder. *The Peasantry of Bengal*. Calcutta: Thacker,Spink, 1874; Reprint, Calcutta: Manisha, 1980.

Hartmann, Betsy, and James K. Boyce. *A Quiet Violence: View from a Bangladesh Village*. London: Zed Press, 1983.

Huq, M. Ameerul, ed. *Exploitation and the Rural Poor*. Comilla: Bangladesh Academy for Rural Development, 1976.

Hye, Hasnat Abdul. *Dateline, Gram Bangla: Notes from Rural Bangladesh*. Comilla: Bangladesh Academy for Rural Development, 1986.

Islam, A. K. M. Aminul. *A Bangladesh Village, Conflict and Cohesion: An Anthropological Study of Politics*. Cambridge, MA: Schenkman Publishing Company, 1974.

———. *Victorious Victims: A Political Transformation in the Transitional Society of Bangladesh*. Cambridge, MA: Schenkman Publishing Company, 1978.

Islam, M. Rafiqul. *Human Resource Development in Rural Bangladesh*. Dhaka: National Institute of Local Government, 1990.

Jahangir, Burhanuddin Khan. *Differentiation, Polarisation, and Confrontation in Rural Bangladesh*. Dacca: Centre for Social Studies, 1979.

———. *Violence and Consent in a Peasant Society and Other Essays*. Dhaka: Centre for Social Studies, 1990.

Sadeque, Mohammed. *Survival Pattern of the Rural Poor: A Case Study of Meherchandi, a Village in Bangladesh*. New Delhi: Northern Book Centre, 1990.

Sarker, Profulla Chandra. *Ideas and Trends in Rural Society of Bangladesh*. Dhaka: International Union for Child Welfare, 1983.

Schendel, Willem van. *Three Deltas: Accumulation and Poverty in Rural Burma, Bengal, and South India*. Newbury Park, CA: Sage Publications, 1991.

Seraj, Toufiq M. *The Role of Small Towns in Rural Development: A Case Study of Bangladesh*. Dhaka: National Institute of Local Government, 1989.

Thorp, John P. *Power among the Farmers of Daripalla: A Bangladesh Village Study*. Dacca: Caritas Bangladesh, 1978.

Zaman, Wasim Alimuz. *Public Participation in Development and Health Programs: Lessons from Rural Bangladesh*. Lanham, MD: University Press of America, 1984.

Bibliography

Saqui, Q. M. Afsar Hossain. *Village Studies in Bangladesh: An Annotated Bibliography*. Dhaka: National Institute of Local Government, 1987.

Schendel, Willem van. *Bangladesh: A Bibliography with Special Reference to the Peasantry*. Amsterdam: Antropologisch-Sociologisch Centrum, Universiteit van Amsterdam, 1976.

Social Conditions

Bhattacharya, Ranjit Kumar. *Moslems of Rural Bengal: A Study in Social Stratification and Socio-cultural Boundary Maintenance*. Calcutta: Subarnarekha, 1991.

Bhowmick, P. K. *Socio-Cultural Profile of Frontier Bengal*. Calcutta: Punthi Pushtak, 1976.

Cumming, David. *The Ganges Delta and Its People*. New York: Thompson Learning, 1994.

Karim, A. K. Nazmul. *The Dynamics of Bangladesh Society*. New Delhi: Vikas, 1980.

Rahman, A. T. R. *Volunteerism and Nation-Building for Bangladesh*. Dhaka: Academic Publishers, 1993.

Shahidullah, Muhammad. *Traditional Culture in East Pakistan*. Dacca: Department of Bengali, University of Dacca, 1963.

Zehadul Karim, A. H. M. *The Pattern of Rural Leadership in an Agrarian Society: A Case Study of the Changing Power Structure in Bangladesh*. New Delhi: Northern Book Centre, 1990.

Social Structure

Ahmed, Rahnuma. *Brides and the Demand System in Bangladesh: A Study*. Dhaka: Centre for Social Studies, Dhaka University, 1987.

Ali, A. F. Imam. *Changing Social Stratification in Rural Bangladesh: A Case Study of Two Selected Villages*. Chittagong: University of Chittagong, 1990.

An Analysis of the Situation of Children in Bangladesh. Dhaka: UNICEF, 1987.

Aziz, K. M. Ashraful. *Kinship in Bangladesh*. Dacca: International Centre for Diarrhoeal Disease Research, 1979.

Barkat-e-Khuda. *Power Structure in Rural Bangladesh*. Canberra: ANU Press, 1981.

Barua, Tushar Kanti. *Political Elite in Bangladesh: A Socio-Anthropological and Historical Analysis of the Processes of their Formation*. Bern: Las Vegas P. Lang, 1978.

Brauns, Claus-Dieter. *Mru: A Hill People on the Border of Bangladesh*. Basel: Birkhauser Verlag, 1989.

Choudhury, Anwarullah, Qamrul Ahsan Chowdhury, and Kibriaul Khaleque, ed. *Sociology of Bangladesh: Problems and Prospects*. Dhaka: Bangladesh Sociology Association, 1987.

Chowdhury, Bazlul Mobin, and Syed Zahur Sadeque, eds. *Bangladesh Social Structure and Development*. Dhaka: Bangladesh Sociological Association, 1989.

Chowdhury, Rafiqul Islam, ed. *Tribal Leadership and Political Integration: A Case Study of the Chakma and Mong Tribes of Chittagong Hill Tracts*. Chittagong: Faculty of Social Science, University of Chittagong, 1979.

Disadvantaged Children in Bangladesh. Dacca: Women for Women, 1981.

Gomes, Stephen G. *The Paharias: A Glimpse of Tribal Life in Northwestern Bangladesh*. Dhaka: Caritas Bangladesh, 1988.

Gupta, Dipankar, ed. *Social Stratification*. New York: Oxford University Press, 1992.

Inden, Ronald B. *Marriage and Rank in Bengali Culture: A History of Caste and Clan in Middle Period Bengal*. Berkeley: University of California Press, 1976.

Jahangir, Burhanuddin Khan. *Rural Society, Power Structure, and Class Practice*, Dacca: Centre for Social Studies, 1982.

Karim, M. Bazlul. *Participation, Development, and Social Structure*. Lanham, MD: University Press of America, 1993.

Laure, Jason; and Ettagale Laure, *Joi Bangla! The Children of Bangladesh*. New York: Farrar, Straus and Giroux, 1974.

Rahman, Alimur. *Social Development in a Tribal Society: A Socio-Economic Profile of the Northern Valleys in the Chittagong Hill Tracts*. Dacca: United Nations Children's Fund and Institute of Business Administration, University of Dacca, 1982.

Risley, Herbert Hope. *The Tribes and Castes of Bengal: Ethnographic Glossary*. Calcutta: Firma KLM, 1981.

Sattar, Abdus. *Tribal Culture in Bangladesh*. Dacca: Muktadhara, 1975.

Timm, Richard W. *The Adivasis of Bangladesh*. London: Minority Rights Group, 1991.

The Situation of Children in Bangladesh. Dacca: Foundation for Research on Educational Planning and Development, 1977.

The Study on the Situation of Children in Bangladesh. Foundation for Research on Educational Planning and Development, 1981.

White, Sarah C. *Arguing with the Crocodile: Gender and Class in Bangladesh*. London: Zed Books, 1992.

Zehadul Karim, A. H. M. *The Pattern of Rural Leadership in an Agrarian Society: A Case Study of the Changing Power Structure in Bangladesh*. New Delhi: Northern Book Centre, 1990.

Social Work

Reference

A Directory of NGO Networks in Bangladesh and an Introduction to Networks. Dhaka: PACT Bangladesh/PRIP, 1992.

Women

Abdullah, Tahrunnessa Ahmed. *Village Women of Bangladesh: Prospects for Change, a Study*. New York: Pergamon Press, 1982.

Ahmad, Perveen. *Income Earning as Related to the Changing Status of Village Women in Bangladesh*. Dacca: Women for Women Study and Research Group, 1980.

Akanda, Latifa, and Roushan Jahan, eds. *Women for Women: Collected Articles*. Dhaka: Women for Women, 1983.

Bangladesh: Strategies for Enhancing the Role of Women in Economic Development. Washington, DC: World Bank, 1990.

Begum, Hamida A., et al., eds. *Women and National Planning in Bangladesh*, Dhaka: Women for Women, 1990.

Borthwick, Meredith. *The Changing Role of Women in Bengal, 1849-1905*. Princeton: Princeton University Press, 1984.

Chen, Martha Alter. *A Quiet Revolution: Women in Transition in Rural Bangladesh*. Cambridge, MA: Schenkman, 1983.

Chowdhury, Rafiqul Huda. *Married Women in Urban Occupations of Bangladesh: Some Problems and Issues*. Dacca: Bangladesh Institute of Development Studies, 1976.

———. *Female Status in Bangladesh*. Dacca: Bangladesh Institute of Development Studies, 1980.

Dixon-Mueller, Ruth. *Jobs for Women in Rural Industry and Services*. Dacca: Ford Foundation, 1980.

Farouk, A. *Time Use of Rural Women: A Six-Village Survey in Bangladesh*. Dacca: Bureau of Economic Research, Dacca University, 1979.

Ghulam Murshid. *Reluctant Debutante: Response of Bengali Women to Modernization, 1849-1905*. Rajshahi: Sahitya Samsad, Rajshahi University, 1983.

Hossain, Hameeda, Roushan Jahan, and Salma Sobhan. *No Better Option?: Industrial Women Workers in Bangladesh*. Dhaka: University Press, 1990.

Hussain, Muhammad Sahadad. *Women's Contribution to Homestead Agricultural Production Systems in Bangladesh.* Comilla: Bangladesh Academy for Rural Development, 1988.

Integration of Women in Development. Dhaka: United Nations Information Centre, 1985.

Islam, Mahmuda. *Training Course on Research Methodology and Women's Issues.* Dhaka: Women for Women, 1985.

———. *Women, Health, and Culture: A Study of Beliefs and Practices Connected with Female Diseases in a Bangladesh Village.* Dhaka: Women for Women, 1985.

———. *Folk Medicine and Rural Women in Bangladesh.* Dacca: Women for Women, 1980.

Islam, Shamima, ed. *Exploring the Other Half: Field Research with Rural Women in Bangladesh.* Dacca: Women for Women, 1982.

Jorgensen, Vibeke. *Poor Women and Health in Bangladesh: Pregnancy and Health.* Stockholm: Swedish International Development Authority, 1983.

Kabeer, Naila. *The Quest for National Identity: Women, Islam, and the State in Bangladesh.* Brighton, England: Institute of Development Studies, University of Sussex, 1989.

Kafi, Sharif Abdullahel. *Disaster and Destitute Women: Twelve Case Studies.* Dhaka: Bangladesh Development Partnership Centre, 1992.

Khan, Salma. *The Fifty Percent: Women in Development and Policy in Bangladesh.* Dhaka: University Press, 1988.

Khan, Zarina Rahman. *Women, Work, and Values: Contradictions in the Prevailing Notions and the Realities of Women's Lives in Rural Bangladesh.* Dhaka: Dana Publishers, 1992.

Kotalova, Jitka. *Belonging to Others: Cultural Construction of Womanhood Among Muslims in a Village in Bangladesh.* Stockholm: Almqvist and Wiksell International, 1993.

Nilufar Banu. *Some Socio-Economic Problems of the Educated Working Women of Dhaka City: Socio-Economic Survey, 1983-84*. Dhaka: Bureau of Economic Research, University of Dhaka, 1988.

Quddus, Mohammad Abdul. *Rural Women in Households in Bangladesh: with a Case Study of Three Villages in Comilla.* Comilla: Bangladesh Academy for Rural Development, 1985.

Rozario, Santi. *Purity and Communal Boundaries: Women and Social Change in a Bangladeshi Village*. North Sydney, NSW, Australia: Allen and Unwin, 1992.

Sarkar, Shikha Rani. *Open and Hidden Cash-Economy of Village Women in Bangladesh: A Case Study of a Village in the Bogra District*. Bogra: Rural Development Academy, 1987.

Scott, Gloria L. *The Impact of Technology Choice on Rural Women in Bangladesh: Problems and Opportunities.* Washington, DC: World Bank, 1985.

Selected Statistics and Indicators on Demographic and Socio-Economic Situation of Women in Bangladesh. Dhaka: Statistics Division, Ministry of Planning, 1989.

The Situation of Women in Bangladesh. Dacca: Women for Women, 1979.

Talukder, Manjusree. *Women: Right and Development*. Dhaka: Community Development Library, 1991.

Wallace, Ben, et al. *The Invisible Resource: Women and Work in Rural Bangladesh*. Boulder, CO: Westview Press, 1987.

Westergaard, Kirsten. *Pauperization and Rural Women in Bangladesh: A Case Study*. Comilla: Bangladesh Academy for Rural Development, 1983.

Bibliography

McCarthy, Florence E. *Bibliography and Selected References Regarding Rural Women in Bangladesh*. Dacca: Women's Section, Planning and Development Division, Ministry of Agriculture, 1978.

Arts

Biswas, S. S. *Terracotta Art of Bengal*. Delhi: Agam, 1981.

Contemporary Art of Bangladesh. Dacca: Shilpakala Academy, 1978.

Ghuznavi, Sayyada R. *Naksha: A Collection of Designs of Bangladesh*. Dacca: Design Centre, Bangladesh Small and Cottage Industries Corp., 1981.

Haque, Enamul, ed. *An Anthology of Crafts in Bangladesh*. Dhaka: National Crafts Council of Bangladesh, 1987.

———. *Islamic Art Heritage of Bangladesh*. Dhaka: Bangladesh National Museum, 1983.

Haque, Zulekha. *Gahana, Jewellery of Bangladesh*. Dhaka: Bangladesh Small and Cottage Industries Corp., 1984.

———. *Terracotta Decorations of Late Mediaeval Bengal: Portrayal of a Society*. Dacca: Asiatic Society of Bangladesh, 1980.

Huntington, Susan L., and John C. Huntington. *Leaves from the Bodhi Tree: The Art of Pala India (8th-12th Centuries) and Its International Legacy*. Dayton, OH: Dayton Art Institute in association with the University of Washington Press, 1990.

Mahmud, Firoz. *The Museums in Bangladesh*. Dhaka: Bangla Academy, 1987.

Michell, George, ed. *The Islamic Heritage of Bengal*. Paris: UNESCO, 1984.

———. *Brick Temples of Bengal: From the Archives of David McCutchion*. Princeton, NJ: Princeton University Press, 1983.

Morshed, Abul Kalam Manzur. *Relativization in Bangladesh*. Dhaka: University of Dhaka, 1986.

Sirajuddin, Muhammad. *Living Crafts in Bangladesh*. Dhaka: Markup International, 1992.

Skelton, Robert, and Mark Francis, eds. *Arts of Bengal: The Heritage of Bangladesh and Eastern India: An Exhibition*. London: Whitechapel Art Gallery, 1979.

Tofayell, Z. A. *Bangladesh: Antiquities and Museums*. Dacca: Atikullah, 1972.

Zaman, Niaz. *The Art of Kantha Embroidery*. Dacca: Bangladesh Shilpakala Academy, 1981.

Architecture

Ahmed, Nazimuddin. *The Buildings of Khan Jahan in and around Bagerhat*. Dhaka: University Press, 1989.

Basu, Dwijendra Nath. *Functional Analysis of Old Bengali Structures*. Calcutta: Basudha, 1976.

Hasan, Sayed Mahmudul. *Gaud and Hazrat Pandua: Romance in Brick and Stone*. Dhaka: Islamic Foundation Bangladesh, 1987.

———. *The Adina Masjid, the Largest Mosque ever Built in Indo-Pak Sub-continent at Hazrat Pandua, A.H.776/A.D.1374/1375: A Monograph*. Dacca: Society for Pakistan Studies, 1970.

———. *Muslim Monuments of Bangladesh*. Dhaka: Islamic Foundation Bangladesh, 1987.

———. *Glimpses of Muslim Art and Architecture*. Dhaka: Islamic Foundation Bangladesh, 1983.

———. *Mosque Architecture of Pre-Mughal Bengal*. Dacca: University Press, 1979.

———. *A Guide to the Ancient Monuments of East Pakistan*. Dacca: Society for Pakistan Studies, 1970.

Khan, Muhammad Hafizullah. *Terracotta Ornamentation in Muslim Architecture of Bengal*. Dhaka: Asiatic Society of Bangladesh, 1988.

Nazimuddin Ahmad, and John Sanday. *Buildings of the British Raj in Bangladesh*. Dhaka: University Press, 1986.

Zahiruddin, Shah Alam, Abu H.Imamuddin, and M. Mohiuddin Khan, eds. *Contemporary Architecture, Bangladesh*. Dhaka: University Press, 1990.

Painting

Abedin, Zainul. *Zainul Abedin.* Dacca: Bangladesh Shilpakala Academy, 1977.

Chowdhury, Qayyum. *Qayyum Chowdhury.* Dacca: Bangladesh Shilpakala Academy, 1977.

Jehangir, Burhanuddin Khan. *Contemporary Painters, Bangladesh,* Dacca: Bangla Academy, 1974.

Life in Bangladesh. Dacca: Bangladesh Shilpakala Academy, 1976.

Nandi, Sudhirakumara. *Art and Aesthetics of Abanindranath Tagore.* Calcutta: Rabindra Bharati University, 1983.

Roy, Kshitis. *Rabindranath Tagore.* New Delhi: National Gallery of Modern Art, 1988.

Sultan, S. M. *S M. Sultan.* Dacca: Bangladesh Shilpakala Academy, 1976.

Sculpture

Shamsul Alam, A. K. M. *Sculptural Art of Bangladesh: Pre-Muslim Period.* Dhaka: Department of Archaeology and Museums: 1985.

Theatre

Banerjee, Brajendra Nath. *Bengali Stage, 1795-1873.* Calcutta: Ranjan Publishing House, 1943.

Bharucha, Rustom. *Rehearsals of Revolution: The Political Theatre of Bengal.* Honolulu: University of Hawaii Press, 1983.

Das Gupta, Hemendra Nath. *The Indian Stage.* Calcutta: Metropolitan Printing and Publishing, 1934.

Guha-Thakurta, Prabhucharan. *The Bengali Drama.* London: K. Paul, Trench, Trubner, 1930.

——— *The Bengali Drama: Its Origin and Development.* Westport, CT: Greenwood Press, 1974.

Raha, Kironmoy. *Bengali Theatre*. New Delhi: National Book Trust, 1978.

Communications and Media

Kabir, Alamgir. *This Was Radio Bangladesh, 1971*. Dhaka: Bangla Academy, 1984.

Kibriya, Golam. *The Press in Bangladesh and Issues of Mass Media*. Dhaka: Sunday Publications, 1985.

Rahman, Farhana Haque. *Stalking Serendipity and Other Pasquinades*. Dhaka: University Press, 1990.

Tofayell, Z. A. *The Journalist and Bangladesh*. Dacca: Nauroz, 1972.

Economics

Bibliography

Talukder, Alauddin. *Bangladesh Economy: A Select Bibliography*. Dacca: Bangladesh Institute of Development Studies, 1976.

Zahurul Huq, A. T. M. *Sources of Statistics on Bangladesh: A Guide to Researchers*. Dacca: Bureau of Economic Research, University of Dacca, 1978.

Agriculture

Abul Kassem, A. B. M. *Jute and Its Diversification*. Ashar Kota, Comilla District: Hosene Ara Kassem, 1992.

Agricultural Research in Bangladesh: Contributing to National Development. Dhaka: Bangladesh Agricultural Research Council, 1983.

Ahmad, Alia. *Agricultural Stagnation under Population Pressure: The Case of Bangladesh*. New Delhi: Vikas, 1984.

Ahmed, Jasimuddin. *Agriculture Development Strategies, Bangladesh: A Comparative Analysis of Effects on Production and Distribution*. Gottingen: Edition Herodot, 1984.

Ahmed, Mushtaq. *Modern Rice Production Technology: Employment and Income Generation in Bangladesh*. Dhaka: Bangladesh-German Seed Development Project, 1984.

———. *Bangladesh Agriculture: Towards Self Sufficiency*. Dhaka: Ministry of Information, 1988.

Ahmed, Noazesh. *Development Agriculture of Bangladesh*. Dacca: Bangladesh Books International, 1976.

Ahmed, Raisuddin. *Rice Price Fluctuation and an Approach to Price Stabilization in Bangladesh*. Washington, DC: International Food Policy Research Institute, 1989.

Alam, Shamsul, ed. *Action Research Project on Small Farmers and Landless Labourers*. Mymensingh: Bureau of Socio-Economic Research and Training, Bangladesh Agricultural University, 1979.

Alamgir, Mohiuddin. *Famine in South Asia: Political Economy of Mass Starvation*. Cambridge, MA: Oelgeschleger, Gunn and Hain, 1980.

Alauddin, Mohammad, and T. A. Tisdell, *The "Green Revolution" and Economic Development: The Process and its Impact on Bangladesh*. New York: St. Martin's Press, 1991.

Ali, Altaf. *Bangladesh Agriculture: Its Potential and Development*. Tokyo: Association for International Cooperation of Agriculture and Forestry, 1984.

Alim, Abdul. *A Handbook of Bangladesh Jute*. Dacca: Effat Begum, 1978.

Ameen, Mahmud-ul. *Fisheries Resources and Opportunities in Freshwater Fish Culture in Bangladesh*. Dhaka: Dhanshish, 1987.

Ashrafi, Siddiqur Rahman, ed. *Guide to Bangladesh Agriculture*. Dhaka: Banglar Mukh Publications, 1982.

A Study Report on Fruits and Vegetables Processing and Preservation in Bangladesh. Dacca: Bangladesh Sugar and Food Industries Corp., 1977.

Bakht, Zaid, ed. *Sericulture Industry in Bangladesh: Analysis of Production, Performance, Constraints, and Growth Potentials.* Dhaka: Bangladesh Unnayan Gobeshona Protishtan, 1988.

Boyce, James K. *Agrarian Impasse in Bengal: Institutional Constraints to Technological Change.* New York: Oxford University Press, 1987.

Chowdhury, Nuimuddin. *Tea Industry of Bangladesh: Problems and Prospects.* Dacca: Bangladesh Institute of Development Studies, 1974.

Douglas, James J. *A Re-appraisal of Forest Development in Developing Countries.* The Hague: M. Nijhoff, 1983.

Farm Management Research in Retrospect. Dacca: Ministry of Agriculture, 1973.

Food Strategies for Bangladesh: Medium and Long Term Perspectives. Dhaka: University Press, 1989.

Goletti, Francesco. *The Changing Public Role in a Rice Economy Approaching Self-Sufficiency: The Case of Bangladesh.* Washington, DC: International Food Policy Research Institute, 1994.

Ghosh, Tushar Kanti. *The Bengal Tragedy.* Lahore: Hero Publications, 1944.

Greeley, Martin. *Postharvest Losses, Technology, and Employment: The Case of Rice in Bangladesh.* Boulder, CO: Westview Press, 1987.

Hossain, Mahabub. *Nature and Impact of the Green Revolution in Bangladesh.* Washington, DC: International Food Policy Research Institute, 1988.

Hossain, Mosharaff. *Agriculture in Bangladesh: Performance, Problems, and Prospects.* Dhaka: University Press, 1991.

Huque, Azizul (Sir). *The Man Behind the Plow.* Dacca: Bangladesh Books International, 1980.

Hussain, Mohammad Sultan. *Soil Classification with Special Reference to the Soils of Bangladesh.* Dhaka: University of Dhaka, 1992.

Jabbar, Mohammad Abdul. *Farm Structure and Resource Productivity in Selected Areas of Bangladesh*. Dacca: Bangladesh Agricultural Research Council, 1977.

Jannuzi, F. Thomasson and James T. Peach. *The Agrarian Structure of Bangladesh: An Impediment to Development*. Boulder, CO: Westview Press, 1980.

Johnson, Alec (pseud.). *Another's Harvest*. Calcutta: Bookman, 1947.

Khalil, Mohammad Ibrahim. *The Agricultural Sector in Bangladesh: A Database*. Dhaka: USAID/Bangladesh, 1991.

Khan, Shakeeb Adnan. *The State and Village Society: The Political Economy of Agricultural Development in Bangladesh*. Dhaka: University Press, 1989.

Mahmud, Wahiduddin, ed. *Development Issues in an Agrarian Economy, Bangladesh*. Dacca: Centre for Administrative Studies, 1981.

Mahmudur Rahman, Khandker. *Development of Agricultural Marketing in Bangladesh*. Comilla: Bangladesh Academy of Rural Development, 1973.

Masum, Muhammad. *Unemployment and Underemployment in Agriculture: A Case Study of Bangladesh*. Delhi: B. R. Publishing Corp., 1982.

Motiur Rahman, Pk. Md. *An Econometric Analysis of Production and Consumption of Sugar in Bangladesh: A Thesis*. Dacca: Institute of Research and Training, University of Dacca, 1977.

Negi, Sharad Singh. *Forests and Forestry in SAARC Countries*. Delhi: Periodical Experts Book Agency, 1992.

Nuruzzaman, A. K. M. *Aquaculture in Bangladesh: Challenges and Opportunity*. Dhaka: Bangladesh Agricultural Research Council, 1991.

Parikh, Ashok K. *The Economics of Fertilizer Use in Developing Countries: A Case Study of Bangladesh*. Aldershot, Hants.: Avebury Gower, 1990.

Population in Forestry Communities Practicing Shifting Cultivation: A Case Study of Bangladesh. Dacca: Bangladesh Institute of Development Studies, 1979.

Rahman, Alimur. *Production Procurement and Agricultural Price Policy in Bangladesh*. Dhaka: Institute of Business Administration, University of Dhaka, 1984.

Rahman, Atiur. *Peasants and Classes: A Study in Differentiation in Bangladesh*. Dhaka: University Press, 1986.

Rahman, Mohibur. *A Preliminary Report on Two Experimental Bamboo Wells in Comilla Kotwali Thana*. Comilla: Bangladesh Academy for Rural Development, 1976.

Rahman, Sultan Hafeez. *Evolution of Jute Policies and a Jute Policy Model for Bangladesh*. Dhaka: Bangladesh Institute of Development Studies, 1984.

Seminar on Agricultural Marketing. Dacca: Agriculture Information Service, 1968.

Shahabuddin, Quazi. *Peasant Behaviour under Uncertainty: Decision-Making among Low-Income Farmers in Bangladesh*. Dhaka: Q. Shahabuddin, 1989.

Shamsul Huda, A. T. M. *The Small Farmer and the Problem of Access*. Dhaka: Bangladesh Agricultural Research Council, 1983.

Shibli, M. Abdullah. *Investment Opportunities, Household Savings, and Rates of Return on Investment: A Case Study of the Green Revolution in Bangladesh*. Lanham, MD: University Press of America, 1991.

Sikdar, Mohammad Firoze Shah. *Jute Cultivation in India and Bangladesh: A Comparative Study*. New Delhi: Mittal Publications, 1990.

Wennergren, E. Boyd. *Agricultural Development in Bangladesh*. Boulder, CO: Westview Press, 1984.

Yunus, Muhammad. *Story of a Deep Tubewell with a Difference: A Report on Osmania School Purba Beel Tubewell, Raozan, Chittagong*. Chittagong: Department of Economics, Chittagong University, 1977.

Irrigation

Hamid, Muhammad Abdul, ed. *Irrigation Technologies in Bangladesh: A Study in some Selected Areas.* Rajshahi: Department of Economics, Rajshahi University, 1978.

Howes, Michael. *Whose Water?* Dhaka: Bangladesh Institute of Development Studies, 1985.

Khan, A. Aziz. *Tube-well Irrigation in Comilla Thana.* Comilla: Pakistan Academy for Rural Development, 1965 (reprinted 1972).

Ganges Flood Plain

Abbas, B. M. *Utilization and Development of the Deltaic Area of East Pakistan* N.p., (1963?).

Adnan, Shapan. *Floods, People, and the Environment: Institutional Aspects of Flood Protection Programmes in Bangladesh, 1990.* Dhaka: Research and Advisory Services, 1990.

Ahmad, Mohiuddin, ed. *Flood in Bangladesh.* Dhaka: Community Development Library, 1989.

Berkoff, D. J. W. *Irrigation Management in the Indo-Gangetic Plain.* Washington, DC: World Bank, 1990.

Biswas, M. R., and M. A. S. Mandal, eds. *Irrigation Management for Crop Diversification in Bangladesh.* Dhaka: University Press, 1993.

Farouk, A. *Irrigation in a Monsoon Land: Economics of Farming in the Ganges-Kobadak.* Dacca: Bureau of Economic Research, Dacca University, 1968.

Flood Action Plan Conference (Proccedings). Dhaka: n. p., 1992.

Flood Control in Bangladesh, An Action Plan. Washington, DC: World Bank, 1990.

Hossain, Mosharaff. *Floods in Bangladesh: Recurrent Disasters and People's Survival.* Dhaka: Universities Research Centre, 1987.

Improved Distribution Systems for Minor Irrigation in Bangladesh: Proceedings of a Workshop Held at BARC on 8-9 July 1984. Dhaka: Bangladesh Agricultural Research Council, 1984.

Institutional Aspects of Flood Protection Programmes: A Progress Report, Dhaka: Research and Advisory Services, 1990-1992.

Khan, Hamidur Rahman. *Study of Water Sector in Bangladesh.* Dacca: United Nations Development Programme, 1982.

———. *Some Issues of Water Resource Management in Bangladesh,* Dacca: Ford Foundation, 1978.

Miah, M. Maniruzzaman. *Flood in Bangladesh: A Hydromorphological Study of the 1987 Flood.* Dhaka: Academic Publishers, 1988.

Sadeque, Abdus. *A Comprehensive Scheme for the Regulation of Floods and Super-Floods in East Pakistan.* Dacca: East Pakistan Government Press, 1960.

Water Resources Development in Bangladesh. Dhaka: Bangladesh Water Development Board, 1979.

Ganges Water Dispute

Abbas, B. M. *The Ganges Water Dispute*, New Delhi: Vikas, 1982.

Basic Documents on Farakka Conspiracy from 1951 to 1976, Dacca: Khoshroz Kitab Mahal, 1976.

Crow, Benjamin. *Sharing the Ganges: The Politics and Technology of River Development.* Thousand Oaks, CA: Sage Publications, 1994.

The Ganges-Brahmaputra Basin: Water Resource Cooperation Between Nepal, India, and Bangladesh. Austin, TX: Lyndon B. Johnson School of Public Affairs, 1992.

Islam, M. Rafiqul. *The Ganges Water Dispute: International Legal Aspects.* Dhaka: University Press, 1987.

Nazem, Nurul Islam. *Indo-Bangladesh Common Rivers and Water Diplomacy.* Dhaka: Bangladesh Institute of International and Strategic Studies, 1986.

Varghese, B. G. *Waters of Hope: Integrated Water Resource Development and Regional Cooperation within the Himalayan-Ganga- Brahmaputra- Barak-Basin.* New Delhi: Oxford University Press, 1990.

Water Resource Challenges in the Ganges-Brahmaputra Basin Austin, TX: University of Texas, 1993.

White Paper on the Ganges Water Dispute. Dacca: Government of the People's Republic of Bangladesh, 1976.

Bibliography

Bangladesh Agricultural Bibliography, 1983-1984. Dhaka: Bangladesh Agricultural Research Council, 1985.

Clay, Edward J. *A Select Bibliography on Agricultural Economics and Rural Development, with Special Reference to Bangladesh.* Dacca: Bangladesh Agricultural Research Council, 1978.

Goodland, Robert J. *Bibliography, Agriculture, and Ecology of Bangladesh.* Dacca: n.p., 1977.

Talukder, Alauddin. *Bangladesh Agricultural Economics: A Select Bibliography.* Dacca: Bangladesh Institute of Development Studies, 1975.

Economic Conditions

Abu Abdullah, ed. *Modernisation at Bay: Structure and Change in Bangladesh.* Dhaka: University Press, 1991.

Alamgir, Mohiuddin. *Bangladesh: A Case of Below Poverty Level Equilibrium Trap.* Dacca: Bangladesh Institute of Development Studies, 1978.

———. *Saving in Bangladesh: 1959/60 - 1969/70.* Dacca: Bangladesh Institute of Development Studies, 1974.

———. *Bangladesh: National Income and Expenditure: 1949/50 - 1969/70.* Dacca: Bangladesh Institute of Development Studies, 1974.

———. *An Analysis of National Accounts of Bangladesh: 1949/50 - 1968/69.* Dacca: Bangladesh Institute of Development Studies, 1972.

Chowdhury, A. K. M. Alauddin. *The Dynamics of Contemporary Famine*. Dacca: Ford Foundation, 1977.

Farouk, A. *Changes in the Economy of Bangladesh*. Dacca: University Press, 1982.

Habibullah, M. *Growth Problems of a Developing Economy*. Dhaka: Ruprekha Publishers, 1990.

Herbon, Dietmar. *The System of Exchange and Distribution in a Village in Bangladesh*. Gottingen: Herodot, 1985.

Huq, M. Nurul. *The Poor in Development: A Study on Bangladesh*. Bogra: Rural Development Academy, 1985.

Jack, James Charles. *The Economic Life of a Bengal District: A Study*. Delhi: Agam Prakashan, 1975.

Jansen, Eirik G. *Rural Bangladesh: Competition for Scarce Resources*. Oslo: Norwegian University Press, 1986.

Khan, Azizur Rahman. *The Economy of Bangladesh*. New York: St. Martin's Press, 1972.

Maloney, Clarence. *Behavior and Poverty in Bangladesh*. Dhaka: University Press, 1988.

Momin, M. A. *Rural Poverty and Agrarian Structure in Bangladesh*. New Delhi: Vikas, 1992.

Osmani, Siddiqur Rahman. *Economic Inequality and Group Welfare: A Theory of Comparison with Application to Bangladesh*. New York: Oxford University Press, 1982.

Rahim, A. M. A., ed. *Bangladesh Economy: Problems and Policies*. Dacca: Barnamala Press, 1980.

———, ed. *Current Issues of Bangladesh Economy*. Dacca: Bangladesh Books International, 1978.

———, ed. *Bangladesh Economy: Problems and Issues*. Dacca: University Press, 1977.

Rahman, Hossain Zillur, and Mahbub Hassan, eds. *Rethinking Rural Poverty: Bangladesh as a Case Study*. Thousand Oaks, CA: Sage Publications, 1994.

Rao, V. K. R. V., ed. *Bangla Desh Economy: Problems and Prospects*. Delhi: Vikas, 1972.

Schendel, Willem van. *Peasant Mobility: The Odds of Life in Rural Bangladesh*. Atlantic Highlands, NJ: Humanities Press, 1981.

Seth, Krishnan Lal. *Economic Prospects of Bangla Desh*. New Delhi: Trimurti Publications, 1972.

Siddiqui, Kamal. *The Political Economy of Rural Poverty in Bangladesh*. Dacca: National Institute of Local Government, 1982.

Sobhan, Rahman. *The Decade of Stagnation: The State of the Bangladesh Economy in the 1980s*. Dhaka: University Press, 1991.

Stepanek, Joseph F. *Bangladesh: Equitable Growth?* New York: Pergamon Press, 1979.

Vivekananda, Franklin, ed. *Bangladesh Economy: Some Selected Issues*. Stockholm: Bethany Books, 1986?

Who Gets What and Why: Resource Allocation in a Bangladesh Village. Dacca: Bangladesh Rural Advancement Committee, (1979?).

Bibliography

Talukder, Alauddin. *Bangladesh Economy: A Select Bibliography*. Dacca: Bangladesh Institute of Development Studies, 1976.

Economic History

Anisuzzaman. *Factory Correspondence and Other Bengali Documents in the India Office Library and Records: Supplementary to J. F. Blumhardt's Catalogue of the Bengali and Assamese MSS in the Library of the India Office (1924)*. London: India Office Library and Records, 1981.

Barui, Balai. *The Salt Industry of Bengal, 1757-1800: A Study in the Interaction of British Monopoly Control and Indigenous Enterprise*. Calcutta: K. P. Bagchi, 1985.

Bhattacharya, Sukumar. *The East India Company and the Economy of Bengal from 1704 to 1740*. London: Luzac, 1954.

Chakrabarty, Dipesh. *Rethinking Working-Class History: Bengal, 1890-1940*. Princeton, NJ: Princeton University Press, 1989.

Chowdhury, Benoy. *Growth of Commercial Agriculture in Bengal, 1757-1900*. Calcutta: R. K. Maitra, 1964.

Dutt, Romesh Chunder. *The Economic History of India in the Victorian Age*. London: K. Paul. Trench, Trubner, 1916.

Ghosal, Hari Ranjan. *Economic Transition in the Bengal Presidency, 1793-1833*. Calcutta: Firma K. L. Mukhopadhya, 1966.

Guha, Ranajit. *A Rule of Property for Bengal: An Essay on the Idea of Permanent Settlement*. Paris: Mouton, 1963.

Hossain, Hameeda. *The Company Weavers of Bengal: The East India Company and the Organization of Textile Production in Bengal, 1750-1813*. New York: Oxford University Press, 1988.

Huq, Mazharul. *The East India Company's Land Policy and Commerce in Bengal, 1698-1784*. Dacca: Asiatic Society of Pakistan, 1964.

Islam, M. Mufakharul. *Bengal Agriculture, 1920-1946: A Quantitative Study*. New York: Cambridge University Press, 1978.

Mitra, Debendra Bijoy. *Monetary System in the Bengal Presidency, 1757-1835*. Calcutta: K. P. Bagchi, 1991.

———. *The Cotton Weavers of Bengal, 1757-1833*. Calcutta: Firma KLM, 1978.

Mukerji, Karuna Moy. *The Problem of Land Transfer: A Study of Land Alienation in Bengal*. Shantiniketan: Bidyut Ranjan Basu, 1957.

Mukherjee, Radhakamal. *The Changing Face of Bengal: A Study in Riverine Economy*. Calcutta: University of Calcutta, 1938.

Ray, Ratnalekha. *Change in Bengal Agrarian Society, c.1760-1850*. New Delhi: Manohar, 1979.

Schendel, Willem van, and Aminul Haque Faraizi. *Rural Labourers in Bengal, 1880 to 1980*. Rotterdam: Comparative Asian Studies Program, Erasmus University, 1984.

Sen, Sunil Kumar. *Agrarian Struggle in Bengal, 1946-47*. New Delhi: People's Publishing House, 1972.

Sinha, Jogis Chandra. *Economic Annals of Bengal*. London: Macmillan, 1927.

Sinha, Narendra Krishna. *Economic History of Bengal,* 3 volumes. Calcutta: Firma K. L. Mukhopadhyay, 1956-70.

Tripathi, Amales. *Trade and Finance in the Bengal Presidency, 1793-1833*. Calcutta: Oxford University Press, 1979.

Economic Planning

Afsar, Rita. *Swanirvar as a Strategy for Endogenous Rural Development*. Dhaka: Bangladesh Institute for Development Studies, 1988.

Ahmed, Salahuddin. *Dualistic Economic Development in Bangladesh*. Dhaka: Parveen Ahmed, 1990.

———, ed. *Dimensions of Development in Islam*. Dhaka: Islamic Economics Research Bureau, 1991.

Alamgir, Mohiuddin Khan. *Development Strategy for Bangladesh*. Dacca: Centre for Social Studies, 1980.

Bangladesh: Promoting Higher Growth and Human Development Washington, DC World Bank, 1987.

Ejazul Huq, K. M. *Planning for Core Needs in Bangladesh: Basic Needs Approach*. Dhaka: University Press, 1984.

International Bank for Reconstruction and Development. *The World Bank and the Poorest Countries*. Washington, DC: World Bank, 1994.

Islam, Nurul. *Development Planning in Bangladesh: A Study in Political Economy*. New York: St. Martin's Press, 1977.

———. *Development Strategy of Bangladesh*, New York: Pergamon Press, 1978.

Khan, Azizur Rahman; and Mahabub Hossain. *The Strategy of Development in Bangladesh.* New York: St. Martin's Press, 1990.

Lovell, Catherine H. *Breaking the Cycle of Poverty: The BRAC Strategy.* West Hartford, CT: Kumarian Press, 1992.

Norbye, Ole David Koht, ed. *Bangladesh Faces the Future*. Dhaka: University Press, 1990.

Rahman, Sultan Hafeez. *Macroeconomic Performance, Stabilization, and Adjustment: The Experience of Bangladesh in the 1980s.* New Delhi: Indus Publishing Co., 1992.

Report of the Task Forces on Bangladesh Development Strategies for the 1990s. Dhaka: University Press, 1991.

Robinson, E.A.G, and Keith Griffin, eds. *The Economic Development of Bangladesh within a Socialist Framework.* London: Macmillan, 1974.

Samad, Abdus. *Bangladesh, Facing the Future*. Dhaka: Samad, 1983.

Sharif, M. Raihan. *Planning with Social Justice: The Bangladesh Case*. Dacca: Bangladesh Books International, 1979.

Sobhan, Rahman. *Rethinking the Role of the State in Development: Asian Perspectives*. Dhaka: University Press, 1993.

———, ed. *Structural Adjustment Policies in the Third World: Design and Experience*. Dhaka: University Press, 1991.

Streefland, Pieter, et al. *Different Ways to Support the Rural Poor: Effects of Two Development Approaches in Bangladesh*. Dhaka: Centre for Social Studies, University of Dhaka, 1986.

Bibliography

Sharma, Prakash C. *Rural and Economic Development Planning in Bangladesh (Formerly East Pakistan), 1950-1972: A Selected Research Bibliography*. Monticello, IL: Council of Planning Librarians, 1975.

Talukder, Alauddin. *Ten Years of BDS Articles and BIDS Publications: A Cumulative Index: Supplement, 1971-1989*. Dacca: Bangladesh Institute of Development Studies, 1980.

Economic Theory

Ahmad, Shamsuddin. *Dual Gap Analysis for Bangladesh*. Dhaka: Bureau of Economic Research, University of Dhaka, 1992.

Faaland, Just, and J. R. Parkinson. *Bangladesh: The Test Case of Development*. Boulder, CO: Westview Press, 1976.

Haque, Wahidul. *An Optional Macro-Economic Planning Model for the Bangladesh Economy: Strategies for Self-Reliant Development*. Dhaka: Bangladesh Institute of Development Studies, 1988.

Thomas, Winburn Townshed. *Bangladesh: Views on Development Planning*. Dhaka: Maleka Rahman, 1983.

Finance

Abedin, Zainul. *Commercial Banking in Bangladesh: A Study of Disparities of Regional and Sectoral Growth Trends (1846-1986)*. Dhaka: National Institute of Local Government, 1990.

Habibullah, M. *General Insurance Business in Bangladesh: An Appraisal of the Performance of Sadharan Bima Corporation*. Dhaka: Bureau of Business Research, University of Dhaka, 1989.

Hossain, Mahabub. *Credit for the Rural Poor: The Experience of the Grameen Bank in Bangladesh*. Dhaka: Bangladesh Institute of Development Economics, 1984.

Hussain, Motahar. *The System of Government Budgeting in Bangladesh*. Dhaka: Hasan Publishers, 1987.

Islamic Banking and Insurance: Proceedings of International Seminar Held in Dhaka, Bangladesh, on October 27, 1989. Dhaka: Islami Bank Bangladesh, 1990.

Patwary, S. U. *Financial Administration in Bangladesh*. Dhaka: Book Syndicate, 1983.

Ray, Jayanta Kumar. *To Chase a Miracle: A Study of the Grameen Bank of Bangladesh*. Dhaka: University Press, 1987.

Siddiqui, Kamal. *Fiscal Decentralization in Bangladesh*. Dhaka: National Institute of Local Government, 1991.

Taheruddin, M. *Essays on Banking and Development*. Dhaka: Academic Publishers, 1986.

The Grameen Reader: Training Materials for the International Replication of the Grameen Bank Financial System for Reduction of Rural Poverty. Dhaka: Grameen Bank, 1992.

Wahid, Abu N. M., ed. *The Grameen Bank: Poverty Relief in Bangladesh*. Boulder CO: Westview Press, 1993.

Watanabe, Tatsuya. *The Ponds and the Poor: The Story of the Grameen Bank's Initiative*. Dhaka: Grameen Bank, 1993.

Industry

Ahmad, Muzaffer. *State and Development: Essays on Public Enterprise*. Dhaka: University Press, 1987.

Ahmed, Hafizuddin. *Jute Spinning*. Dacca: Fatima Ahmed, 1967.

Ahmed, Momtaz Uddin. *The Financing of Small-Scale Industries: A Study of Bangladesh and Japan*. Dhaka: University of Dhaka, 1987.

Ahmed, Rakibuddin. *The Progress of the Jute Industry and Trade, 1855-1966*. Dacca: Pakistan Central Jute Committee, 1966.

Ali, Muhammad Raushan. *Achievement Motivation and Industrial Productivity in Bangladesh*. Dacca: University of Dacca, 1979.

Asaduzzaman, M. *Regional Cooperation in the Development of Energy in South Asia: A Bangladesh Perspective*. Dhaka: Bangladesh Institute of Development Studies, 1986.

DeLucia, Russell J. *Energy Planning for Developing Countries: A Study of Bangladesh*. Baltimore: Johns Hopkins University Press, 1982.

Habibullah, M. *Employee-Centered Supervision and Productivity in the Jute Industry*. Dacca: Bureau of Business Research, University of Dacca, 1980.

Haque, M. Shamsul. *Prices Policy, Accounting Methodology, and Corporate Financial Viability: An Empirical Study*. Dhaka: Institute of Business Administration, University of Dhaka, 1983.

Hoque, M. Jahirul. *Financial Planning and Control in Public Sector Industries in Bangladesh*. Chittagong: University of Chittagong, 1987.

Humphrey, Clare E. *Privatization in Bangladesh: Economic Transition in a Poor Country*. Boulder, CO: Westview Press, 1990.

Industry in Bangladesh. Dhaka: Ministry of Industries, 1986.

National Seminar on Productivity Movement in Bangladesh. Dhaka: National Productivity Organisation, 1990.

Nuclear Power Planning Study for Bangladesh. Vienna: International Atomic Energy Agency, 1975.

Reza, Sadrel, and Mizanur Rahman Shelley. *Privatizing Industrial Regulatory Functions in Bangladesh*. Dhaka: University Press, 1994.

Shamsul Islam. *Public Corporations in Bangladesh*. Dacca: Local Government Institute, 1975.

Siddiqi, Hafiz G. A. *Industrial Policies and Export Incentives*. Dhaka: Dana Prokashan, 1984.

———. *The Performance of the Nationalised Industries: Case of the U.K. Airlines and Biman-Bangladesh Airlines*. Dhaka: Institute of Business Administration, University of Dhaka, 1983.

Sobhan, Rahman and Muzaffar Ahmad. *Public Enterprise in an Intermediate Regime: A Study of the Political Economy of Bangladesh*. Dacca: Bangladesh Institute of Development Studies, 1980.

Yusuf, Fazlul Hassan. *Nationalisation of Industries in Bangladesh*. Dhaka: National Institute of Local Government, 1985.

International Economics

Ahmad, Shamsuddin. *Foreign Capital Inflow and Economic Growth in Bangladesh*. Dhaka: University of Dhaka, 1992.

Alam, Ahmed Fakhrul. *Problems of Export Financing in Bangladesh*. Dacca: Bureau of Economic Research, University of Dacca, 1974.

Bamberger, Michael, and G. Shabbir Cheema. *Case Studies of Project Sustainability: Implications for Policy and Operations from Asian Experience* Washington, DC: World Bank, 1990.

Barry, A. J. *Aid Co-ordination and Effectiveness: A Review of Country and Regional Experience*. Paris: Development Centre of the Organization for Economic Co-operation and Development, 1988.

Bhuyan, Ayubur Rahman *Non-Traditional Exports of Bangladesh: Trends, Performance, and Prospects*. Dacca: Bureau of Economic Research, Dacca University, 1982.

Cable, Vincent. *South Asia's Exports to the EEC: Obstacles and Opportunities*. London: Overseas Development Institute, 1979.

Chadha, I. S. *Managing Projects in Bangladesh: A Scenario Analysis of Institutional Environment for Development Projects*. Dhaka: University Press, 1989.

Choudhury, Khashruzzaman. *Foreign Aid, Government Sector, and Bangladesh*. Dhaka: National Institute of Local Government, 1990.

Chowdhury, Ashraf U. *Norway's Commodity Assistance and Import Support to Bangladesh*. Oslo: Royal Norwegian Ministry of Development Cooperation, 1986.

Ehrhardt, Roger. *Canadian Development Assistance to Bangladesh: An Independent Study*. Ottawa: North-South Institute, 1983.

Faaland, Just. *Aid and Influence: The Case of Bangladesh*. New York: St. Martin's Press, 1981.

Matin, K. M. *Bangladesh and the IMF: An Exploratory Study*. Dhaka: Bangladesh Institute of Development Studies, 1986.

Rahman, Mohammad Akhlaqur. *A Customs Union in South Asia: Prospects and Problems*. Dacca: Bangladesh Government Press, 1981.

———. *Foreign Aid and Self-Reliant Growth: The Case of Bangladesh*. Dhaka: Centre for Social Studies, Dhaka University, 1984.

———. *External Assistance, Saving, and Resource Mobilization in Bangladesh*. Dhaka: External Resources Division, Ministry of Finance and Planning, 1983.

———. *The Private Sector of East Pakistan: An Analysis of Lagged Development*. Karachi: United Bank, Ltd., 1970.

Rahman, M. Azizur. *Export and Economic Development of Bangladesh*. Dhaka: Bangladesh Young Economists' Association, 1993.

Reza, Sadrel. *Private Foreign Investment in Bangladesh*. Dhaka: University Press, 1987.

———. *Bangladesh in South Asian and ASEAN: A Study in Economic Cooperation*. Dhaka: Bangladesh Unnayan Parishad, 1984.

———. *The Export Trade of Bangladesh, 1950-1978* Dacca: University of Dacca, 1981.

Sobhan, Rahman. *The Crisis of External Dependence: The Political Economy of Foreign Aid to Bangladesh*. London: Zed Press, 1982.

———, ed. *From Aid Dependence to Self Reliance: Development Options for Bangladesh*. Dhaka: University Press, 1990.

Bibliography

Talukder, Alauddin. *Bangladesh International Economics: A Select Bibliography*. Dacca: Bangladesh Institute of Development Studies, 1975.

Labor

Ahmad, Alia. *Child Labour in Bangladesh*. Dhaka: Bangladesh Institute of Development Studies, 1991.

Ahmed, Salehuddin. *Rural Development and Employment Expansion in Bangladesh: Experiences from Ulashi*. Dacca: National Foundation for Research on Human Resource Development, 1982.

Farouk, A. *The Hardworking Poor: A Survey on How People Use Their Time in Bangladesh*. Dacca: Bureau of Economic Research, University of Dacca, 1975.

Gardner, Katy. *Global Migrants, Local Lives: Travel and Transformation in Rural Bangladesh*. New York: Oxford University Press, 1995.

Hossain, Hameeda. *No Better Option? Industrial Women Workers in Bangladesh*. Dhaka: University Press, 1990.

Islam, Rizwanul. *Export of Manpower from Bangladesh to the Middle-East Countries: The Impact of Remittance Money on Household Expenditure*. Dacca: National Foundation for Research on Human Resource Expenditure, 1980.

Jensen, Kurt Morck. *Non-agricultural Occupations in a Peasant Society: Weavers and Fishermen in Noakhali, Bangladesh*. Copenhagen: Centre for Development Research, 1987.

Khan, Muinuddin. *Labour Administration: Profile on Bangladesh*. Bangkok: International Labour Organization, 1987.

Mannan, M. A. *Workers' Participation in Managerial Decision-Making: A Study in a Developing Country.* Delhi: Daya Publishing House, 1987.

Trade Unions and SAARC. Colombo, Sri Lanka: Friedrich-Ebert Stiftung, 1989.

Land Development and Settlement

Alamgir, Mohiuddin Khan, ed. *Land Reform in Bangladesh.* Dacca: Centre for Social Studies, 1981.

Choudhury, A. K. M. Kalamuddin. *Land Use Planning in Bangladesh.* Dhaka: National Institute of Local Government, 1985.

Siddiqui, Kamal, ed. *Land Reforms and Land Management in Bangladesh and West Bengal: A Comparative Study.* Dhaka: University Press, 1988.

Shawkat Ali, A. M. M. *Politics and Land System in Bangladesh.* Dhaka: National Institute of Local Government, 1986.

Urban Land Management in Bangladesh. Dhaka: Ministry of Land, 1992.

Rural Development

The Academy at Comilla, an Introduction. Comilla: Bangladesh Academy for Rural Development, 1963.

Adnan, Shapan. *Annotation of Village Studies in Bangladesh and West Bengal: A Review of Socio-Economic Trends over 1942-88.* Comilla: Bangladesh Academy for Rural Development, 1990.

Ahmad, Nasiruddin. *Landlessness in Bangladesh.* Dhaka: University Press, 1988.

Ahmad, Razia. *Financing the Rural Poor: Obstacles and Realities,* Dhaka: University Press, 1983.

Ahmed, Jasimuddin. *Resource Use Pattern and Cost/Returns in Cooperative Boro Paddy Production in Bangladesh.* Dacca: National Foundation for Research on Human Resource Development, 1980.

Ahmed, Raisuddin, and Mahabub Hossain. *Developmental Impact of Rural Infrastructure in Bangladesh*. Washington, DC: International Food Policy Research Institute, 1990.

Akanda, Safar A., and Aminul Islam, eds. *Rural Poverty and Development Strategies in Bangladesh*. Rajshahi: Institute of Bangladesh Studies, Rajshahi University, 1991.

Akhunji, Syedul Haque. *The Role of Institutional Credit in Agricultural Development in Bangladesh*. Dacca: Integrated Rural Development Programme, 1982.

Alam, Mahmudul. *Capital Accumulation and Agrarian Structure in Bangladesh: A Study on Tubewell Irrigated Villages of Rajshahi and Comilla*. Dhaka: Centre for Social Studies, Dhaka University, 1984.

Ali, M. Hazrat. *Involvement of the Rural Poor in Development through Local Organizations: A Bangladesh Study*. Comilla: Bangladesh Academy for Rural Development, 1980.

Alim, Abdul. *Land Reforms in Bangladesh: Social Changes, Agricultural Development, and Eradication of Poverty*. Dacca: Samina, 1979.

———. *Agriculture Credit Financing in Bangladesh*. Dacca: Bangladesh Books International, 1981.

Ameer, K. M. *Rain and River*. Dhaka: Nabeela Books, 1991.

Anisuzzaman, M., ed. *Comilla Models of Rural Development: A Quarter Century of Experience*. Comilla: Bangladesh Academy for Rural Development, 1986.

Anisuzzaman, M., and Kirsten Westergaard, eds. *Growth and Development in Rural Bangladesh: A Critical Review*. Dhaka: University Press, 1993.

Barkat-e-Khuda. *Rural Development and Change: A Micro Study*. Dhaka: University Press, 1988.

Blair, Harry W. *The Elusiveness of Equity: Institutional Approaches to Rural Development in Bangladesh*. Ithaca, NY: Rural Development Committee, Center for International Studies, Cornell University, 1974.

Byrne, Jim. *The Savar Experiment: A Model for Village Technology.* Dacca: Lutheran World Federation, 1978.

Chashi, Mahbub Alam. *In Quest of Shawnirvar.* Dhaka: Shawnirvar Workers Trust, 1984.

Chowdhury, Anwarullah. *Agrarian Social Relations and Rural Development in Bangladesh.* Totowa NJ: Allenheld, Osmun Publishers, 1982.

Chowdhury, Pijush Kumar, M. Ameerul Huq, and Syed Aminur Rahman. *Cooperatives as Institutions for the Development of the Rural Poor.* Comilla: Bangladesh Academy for Rural Development, 1987.

Greeley, Michael, and Michael Howes, eds. *Rural Technology, Rural Institutions, and the Rural Poorest: Proceedings of a Workshop.* Comilla: CIRDAP, 1982.

Herbon, Dietmar. *Agrarian Reproduction in Bangladesh: Studies of Attempts to Ensure a Livelihood in a Rural Region.* Aachen: Alano/Herodot, 1992.

Hossain, Mohammad. *Rural Finance in Bangladesh.* Dhaka: National Institute of Local Government, 1991.

Hossain, Zillur Rahman, and Mahabub Hossain, eds. *Rethinking Rural Poverty.* Thousand Oaks, CA: Sage Publications, 1994.

Huq, M. Nurul. *Pioneers of Rural Development in Bangladesh: Their Programmes and Writings.* Bogra: Rural Development Academy, 1978.

———. *Village Development in Bangladesh: A Study of Monagram Village.* Comilla: Bangladesh Academy of Rural Development, 1973.

Integrated Rural Development in Bangladesh. London: Commonwealth Association of Surveying and Land Economy, 1981.

Islam, M. Rafiqul. *Human Resource Development in Rural Development in Bangladesh.* Dhaka: National Institute of Local Government, 1990.

Khan, Akhter Hameed. *The Works of Akhter Hameed Khan.* Comilla: Bangladesh Academy for Rural Development, 1983.

———. *Bengal Reminiscences.* Comilla: Bangladesh Academy for Rural Development, 1981.

Khan, Azizur Rahman, and Rahman Sobhan. *Trade, Planning, and Rural Development: Essays in Honor of Nurul Islam.* New York: St. Martin's Press, 1990.

Khan, Mohammad Mohabbat; and Habib Mohammad Zafrullah, eds. *Rural Development in Bangladesh: Trends and Issues.* Dacca: Centre for Administrative Studies, 1981.

Maloney, Clarence. *Rural Savings and Credit in Bangladesh.* Dhaka: University Press, 1988.

Mozammel Hossain, A. M. *Rural Development at the Cross Roads in Bangladesh.* Dhaka: Prottasha Prokashon, 1993.

Qudrat-i-Elahi, Khwaja. *Administration of Agricultural Credit in Bangladesh.* Mymensingh: Bangladesh Agricultural University, 1980.

Rahaman, Reza Shamsur. *A Praxis in Participatory Rural Development: Proshika with the Prisoners of Poverty.* Dhaka: Prokisha Manobik Unnayan Kendra, 1986.

Ray, Jayanta Kumar. *Organizing Villagers for Self-Reliance: A Study of Gonoshasthya Kendra in Bangladesh.* Calcutta: Orient Longman, 1986.

———. *Organizing Villagers for Self-Reliance: A Study of Deedar in Bangladesh.* Comilla: Bangladesh Academy for Rural Development, 1983.

Sabiha Sultana. *Rural Settlements in Bangladesh: Spatial Pattern and Development.* Dhaka: Graphosman, 1993.

Sattar, Muhammad Ghulam. *Rural Development through Self-help: A Study of the Self-help Ulashi-Jadunathpur Project in Jessore, Bangladesh.* Comilla: Bangladesh Academy for Rural Development, 1979.

———. *Co-operative Farming in Bangladesh.* Comilla: Bangladesh Academy for Rural Development, 1972.

Shahjahan, Mirza. *Agricultural Finance in East Pakistan* Dacca: n.p., 1968.

Shawkat Ali, A. M. M. *Agricultural Credit in Bangladesh, 1883-1986.* Dhaka: Centre for Development Research, Bangladesh, 1990.

Siddiqui, Kamal. *Implementation of Land Reform in Four Villages of Bangladesh*. Kuala Lumpur: Asian and Pacific Development Administration Centre, 1980.

Sobhan, Rahman, ed. *Public Allocative Strategies, Rural Development, and Poverty Alleviation: A Global Perspective*. Dhaka: University Press, 1991.

Socio-Economic Indicators for Monitoring and Evaluation of Agrarian Reform and Rural Development: Bangladesh. Dacca: Ministry of Planning, 1981.

Stevens, Robert D., Hamza Alavi, and Peter J. Bertocci, eds. *Rural Development in Bangladesh and Pakistan*. Honolulu: University Press of Hawaii, 1976.

Westergaard, Kirsten. *State and Rural Society in Bangladesh: A Study in Relationship*. London: Curzon Press, 1985.

Yousoof, M. A. *Agricultural Credit and Rural Financing in Bangladesh: Problems and Prospects*. Dhaka: Manju and Khosru, 1983.

Bibliography

Akhter, Nilufar. *Rural Development of Bangladesh: A Select Bibliography*. Dacca: Bangladesh Institute of Development Studies, 1981.

Cain, Mead. *Landlessness in India and Bangladesh: A Critical Review of Data Sources*. New York: Population Council, 1981.

Hye, Hasnat Abdul. *Village Studies in Bangladesh*. Comilla: Bangladesh Academy for Rural Development, 1985.

Schendel, Willem van. *Bangladesh: A Bibliography with Special Reference to the Peasantry*. Amsterdam: Antropologisch-Sociologisch Centrum, Universiteit Amsterdam, 1976.

Transportation

Jansen, Eirik G. *The Country Boats of Bangladesh*. Dhaka: University Press, 1989.

Urban Development

Atiqullah, Mohammad. *Growth of Dacca City: Population and Area, 1608-1981,* Dacca: Social Science Research Project, Department of Statistics, University of Dacca, 1965.

Farouk, A. *The Vagrants of Dacca City: A Socio-Economic Survey.* Dacca: Bureau of Economic Research, University of Dacca, 1978.

Qadir, Sayeeda. *Bastees of Dacca: A Study of Squatter Settlements.* Dacca: Local Government Institute, 1975.

Saqui, Q. M. Afsar Hossain. *Dacca Water Supply and Sewage Authority: An Enquiry into Selected Aspects.* Dacca: Local Government Institute, 1977.

Siddiqui, Kamal. *Social Formation in Dhaka City: A Study in Third World Urban Sociology.* Dhaka: University Press, 1990.

Slums in Dhaka City: A Socio-economic Survey for Feasibility of Slum Clearance and Urban Renewal Programme in Dhaka City. Dhaka: Centre for Urban Studies, 1983.

Bibliography

Islam, Nazrul. *Bibliography on Bangladesh Urbanization.* Dacca: Centre for Urban Studies, 1982.

Education

Ahmed, Salehuddin. *Primary Education Network in Bangladesh.* Dhaka: National Foundation for Research on Human Resource Development, 1983.

Alamgir, Mohiuddin. *A Long-Term Dynamic Model for Planning the Manpower and Educational System of Bangladesh.* Dacca: Bangladesh Institute of Development Economics, 1973.

Ali, Sheikh Neyamat, ed. *National Seminar on the Education of the Blind, First [Seminar], Dacca, Bangladesh.* Dacca: Department of Social Welfare, 1977.

Ara, Shawkat. *Ideology and Student Activism*. Rajshahi: University of Rajshahi, 1988.

Ayyub Ali, A. K. M. *History of Traditional Islamic Education in Bangladesh, Down to A.D. 1980* Dhaka: Islamic Foundation Bangladesh, 1983.

Bangladesh-UNESCO Operational Seminar. *Integrated Rural Development and the Role of Education*. Dacca: NFRHRD, 1979.

Choudhury, Azharul Huq. *Private Universities Facing the Future*. Dhaka: Quest, 1990.

Duza, Asfia, et al., eds. *Education and Gender Equity*. Dhaka: Women for Women, 1992.

Ferdouse Khan, Muhammad. *Mass Education in Bangladesh and the Role of Youth*. Dhaka: Professors World Peace Academy of Bangladesh, 1988.

Gustavsson, Styrbjorn. *Primary Education in Bangladesh: For Whom?* Dhaka: University Press, 1990.

Huq, A. K. M. Hedayetul, et al. *Sustainability of Primary Education Projects: A Case Study of Universal Primary Education in Bangladesh*. Dhaka: Bangladesh Public Administration Training Centre, 1989.

Huq, M. Shamsul, et al. *Higher Education and Employment in Bangladesh* Dhaka: University Press, 1983.

Ibrahimy, Sekander Ali, ed. *Reports on Islamic Education and Madrasah Education in Bengal, 1861-1977*. Dhaka: Islamic Foundation Bangladesh, 1990.

Institute of Education and Research. *Survey of Primary Schools and Evaluation of Primary School Agricultural Programme in Bangladesh: A Research Report*. Dacca: University of Dacca, 1979.

———. *Teachers in East Pakistan*. Karachi: Manager of Publications, 1972.

Islam, Rizwanul. *Background, Attitude, and Expectations of Students in the Higher Education System of Bangladesh*. Dacca: National

Foundation for Research on Human Resource Development, 1980.

Islam, Shamima. *Women's Education in Bangladesh: Needs and Issues*. Dacca: Foundation for Research on Educational Planning and Development, 1977.

Islam, Teherul. *An Analysis of Public Recurring Expenditure on Higher Education in Bangladesh*. Dacca: University Grants Commission, 1975.

———. *Social Justice and the Education System of Bangladesh*. Dacca: Bureau of Economic Research, University of Dacca, 1975.

National Foundation for Research on Human Resource Development. *Primary Education Network in Bangladesh: Capacity and Utilization*. Dacca: The Foundation, 1979.

Overviews on University Education and Research in Science in Bangladesh. Dacca: University Grants Commission, 1977.

Rahim, Muhammad Abdur. *The History of the University of Dacca*. Dacca: University of Dacca, 1981.

Report of the Universities Inquiry Commission, 1976-78. Dacca: Ministry of Education, 1979.

Sattar, Ellen. *Universal Primary Education in Bangladesh*. Dacca: University Press, 1982.

Shaidai, Shamsul Haque. *The Light of Other Days: A Teacher's Tale*. Dhaka: Pabna Samiti, 1988.

Women and Education, Bangladesh, 1978. Dacca: Women for Women, 1978.

Geography

Ahmad, Nafis. *A New Economic Geography of Bangladesh*. New Delhi: Vikas, 1976.

Ahmed, Noazesh. *Bangladesh*. Dacca: Bangladesh Books International, 1977.

Bhattacharyya, Amitabha. *Historical Geography of Ancient and Early Mediaeval Bengal*. Calcutta: Sanskrit Pustak Bandar, 1977.

Chatterjee, Shiba Prasad. *Bengal in Maps*. Bombay: Orient Longmans, 1949.

Das, Amal Kumar, Sankarananda Mukerji, and Manas Kamal Chowdhuri, eds. *A Focus on Sundarban*. Calcutta: Editions India, 1981.

De, Rathindranath. *The Sundarbans*. New York: Oxford University Press, 1990.

Hossain, Anwar. *A Journey Through Bangladesh*. Dhaka: Classic Books International, 1988.

Islam, M. Aminul, and M. Maniruzzaman Miah, general editors. *Bangladesh in Maps*. Dacca: University of Dacca, 1981.

Rashid, Haroun. *Geography of Bangladesh*. Dhaka: University Press, 1991.

Yeo, Dan. *Bangladesh: A Traveller's Guide*. Cambridge, MA: Bradt Enterprises, 1982.

Bibliography

Sukhwal, B. L. *A Systematic Geographic Bibliography on Bangla Desh*. Monticello, IL: Council of Planning Librarians, 1973.

History

General History

Ahmad, Kamruddin. *A Social History of Bengal*. Dhaka: Progoti Publishers, 1970.

Islam, Serajul, ed. *History of Bangladesh*. Dhaka: Asiatic Society of Bangladesh, 1992.

Majumdar, Romesh Chandra; and Jadunath Sarkar, eds. *The History of Bengal*. Dacca: University of Dacca, 1963.

Mondal, Sushila. *History of Bengal*. Calcutta: Prakash Mandir, 1970.

Rahim, Muhammad Abdur. *Social and Cultural History of Bengal.* Karachi: Pakistan Historical Society, 1963.

Sur, Atul Krishna. *History and Culture of Bengal.* Calcutta: Chuckervertti, Chatterjee, 1963.

Ancient, Buddhist, and Hindu Periods

Ali, Mohammed. *Archaeological Survey Report of Bogra District.* Dhaka: Directorate of Archaeology and Museums, 1986.

Bagchi, Jhunu. *The History and Culture of the Palas of Bengal and Bihar.* New Delhi: Abhinav, 1993.

Chakrabarti, Amita. *History of Bengal, c. A.D. 550 to c. A.D. 750.* Burdwan: University of Burdwan, 1991.

Choudhury, Pratap Chandra. *Assam-Bengal Relations from the Earliest Times to the Twelfth Century A.D.* Guwahati: United Publishers, 1988.

Chowdhury, Abdul Momin. *Dynastic History of Bengal.* Dacca: Asiatic Society of Pakistan, 1967.

Dani, Ahmad Hasan. *Bibliography of the Muslim Inscriptions of Bengal.* Dacca, n.p., 1957.

———. *Buddhist Sculptures in East Pakistan.* Karachi: Department of Archaeology, 1959.

———. *Prehistory and Protohistory of Eastern India, with a Detailed Account of the Neolithic Cultures in Mainland South East Asia.* Calcutta: Firma K. L. Mukhopadhyay, 1960.

Maitreya, Akshayakumara. *The Fall of the Pala Empire.* Rajarammohunpur, District Darjeeling: University of North Bengal, 1987.

Majumdar, Romesh Chandra. *History of Ancient Bengal.* Calcutta: G. Bharadwaj, 1971.

———. *History of Mediaeval Bengal.* Calcutta G. Bharadwaj, 1973.

Monahan, Francis John. *The Early History of Bengal.* Varanasi: Bhartiya Publishing House, 1974.

Mondal, Sushila. *History of Bengal.* Calcutta: Prakash Mandir, 1970ff.

Morrison, Barrie M. *Political Centers and Cultural Regions in Early Bengal.* Tucson: University of Arizona Press, 1970.

———. *Lalmai, A Cultural Center of Early Bengal: An Archaeological Report and Historical Analysis.* Seattle: University of Washington Press, 1974.

Nazimuddin Ahmad. *Mahasthan: A Preliminary Report on the Recent Archaeological Excavation at Mahasthangarh.* Karachi: Department of Archaeology and Museums, 1964.

Paul, Pramode Lal. *The Early History of Bengal, from the Earliest Times to the Muslim Conquest.* Calcutta: Indian Research Institute, 1939.

Roychoudhuri, Bani. *The Political History of Bengal to the Rise of the Pala Dynasty, c. 326 B.C. to A.D. 750.* Calcutta: Sanskrit Pustak Bhandar, 1990.

Shahanara Husain. *Everyday Life in the Pala Empire.* Dacca: Asiatic Society of Pakistan, 1968.

———. *The Social Life of Women in Early Medieval Bengal.* Dhaka: Asiatic Society of Bangladesh, 1985.

Tripathi, Ratikanta. *Social and Religious Aspects in Bengal Inscriptions.* Calcutta: Firma KLM, 1987.

Muslim Period

Akanda, Latifa. *Social History of Muslim Bengal.* Dhaka: Islamic Cultural Centre, 1981.

Ali, Muhammad Mohar. *History of the Muslims of Bengal.* Riyadh: Imam Muhammad ibn Sa'ud Islamic University, Department of Culture and Publications, 1988.

Azraf, Muhammad. *The Background of the Culture of Muslim Bengal.* Dacca: Society for Pakistan Studies, 1970.

Banerjee, Brajendra Nath. *Begams of Bengal.* Calcutta: S.K. Mitra and Brothers, 1942.

Chatterjee, Anjali. *Bengal in the Reign of Aurangzib, 1658-1707.* Calcutta: Progressive Publishers, 1967.

Chattopadhyay, Subhas Chandra. *Diwani in Bengal, 1765: Career of Nawab Najm-ud-daulah.* Varanasi: Vishwavidyalaya Prakashan, 1980.

Dani, Ahmad Hasan. *Muslim Architecture in Bengal.* Dacca: n.p., 1961.

Dasa Gupta, Yogendra-Natha. *Bengal in the Sixteenth Century A.D.* Calcutta: University of Calcutta, 1914.

Datta, Kalikinkar. *Alivardi and His Times* Calcutta: World Press, 1963.

———. *Studies in the History of the Bengal Subah.* Calcutta: University of Calcutta, 1936.

Eaton, Richard M. *The Rise of Islam and the Bengal Frontier, 1204-1760.* Berkeley: University of California Press, 1993.

Ghosh, Jamini Mohan. *Magh Raiders in Bengal.* Calcutta: Bookland, 1960.

Fuzli Rubbee, Khondkar. *The Origin of the Musalmans of Bengal.* Dacca: Society for Pakistan Studies, 1970.

Karim, Abdul. *History of Bengal: Mughal Period.* Rajshahi: Institute of Bangladesh Studies, University of Rajshahi, 1992.

———. *Social History of the Muslims in Bengal, Down to A.D. 1538.* Chittagong: Baitush Sharaf Islamic Research Institute, 1985.

———. *Murshid Quli Khan and His Times*, Dacca: Asiatic Society of Pakistan, 1963.

———. *Corpus of the Arabic and Persian Inscriptions of Bengal.* Dhaka: Asiatic Society of Bangladesh, 1992.

———. *The Provinces of Bihar and Bengal under Shahjahan.* Dacca: Asiatic Society of Bangladesh, 1974.

Raychaudhuri, Tapankumar. *Bengal under Akbar and Jehangir.* Calcutta: A. Mukherjee, 1953.

Roy, Atul Chandra. *History of Bengal: Turko-Afghan Period.* New Delhi: Kalyani Publishers, 1986.

———. *History of Bengal: Mughal Period, 1526-1765.* Calcutta: Nababharat Publishers, 1968.

———. *The Career of Mir Jafar Khan (1757-65 A.D.).* Calcutta: Das Gupta, 1953.

Saran, Parmatma. *The Provincial Government of the Mughals.* Allahabad: Kitabistan, 1941.

Sarkar, Jadu Nath, ed. and trans. *Bengal Nawabs, Containing Azad-al-Husaini's* Naubahar-i Murshid Quli Khani, *Karam 'Ali's* Muzaffarnamah, *and Yusuf 'Ali's* Ahwal-i-Mahabat Jang. Calcutta: Asiatic Society, 1985.

Sarkar, Jagadish Narayan. *Hindu-Muslim Relations in Bengal: Medieval Period.* Delhi: Idarah-i Adabiyat-i Delhi, 1985.

Srivastava, Ashirbadi Lal. *Shuja-ud-daulah.* Calcutta: S.N. Sarkar, 1939, 1945.

Stewart, Charles. *The History of Bengal from the First Mohammedan Invasion until the Virtual Conquest of that Country by the English, A.D. 1757.* Delhi: Oriental Publishers, 1971.

Tarafdar, Momtazur Rahman. *Husain Shahi Bengal, 1494-1538 A.D.: A Socio-Political Study.* Dacca: Asiatic Society of Pakistan, 1965.

British Period

Abdul Latif. *Autobiography and Other Writings of Nawab Abdul Latif Khan Bahadur.* Chittagong: Mehrub Publications, 1968.

Abdur Rab, A. S. M. *A.K. Fazlul Haq.* Lahore: Ferozsons, 1967.

Abul Hashim. *In Retrospection.* Dacca: Subarna Publishers, 1974.

Ahmad Khan, Muin-ud-din. *Muslim Struggle for Freedom in Bengal: From Plassey to Pakistan, A.D. 1757-1947.* Dhaka: Islamic Foundation of Bangladesh, 1982.

——. *Titu Mir and His Followers in British Indian Records, 1831-1833 A.D.* Dhaka: Islamic Foundation of Bangladesh, 1980.

Ahmed, Rafiuddin. *The Bengal Muslims, 1871-1906: A Quest for Identity*. New York: Oxford University Press, 1981.

Ahmed, A. F. Salahuddin. *Social Ideas and Social Change in Bengal, 1818-1835*. Leiden: E.J. Brill, 1965.

Ahmed, Sufia. *Muslim Community in Bengal, 1884-1912*. Dacca: Oxford University Press, 1974.

Akanda, S. A. ed. *Studies in Modern Bengal.* Rajshahi: Institute of Bangladesh Studies, University of Rajshahi, 1981.

Akhtar, Shirin. *The Role of the Zamindars in Bengal, 1707-1772*. Dacca: Asiatic Society of Bangladesh, 1982.

Banerjea, Surendranath. *A Nation in Making: Being the Reminiscences of Fifty Years of Public Life*. New York: Oxford University Press, 1925.

Banerjee, Tarasankar. *Various Bengal: Aspects of Modern History*. Calcutta: Ratna Prakashan, 1985.

Bence-Jones, Mark. *Clive of India*. London: Constable, 1974.

Bhattacharya, Bhabani. *Socio-Political Currents in Bengal: A Nineteenth Century Perspective*. New Delhi: Vikas, 1980.

Bose, Nemai Sadhan. *Indian Awakening and Bengal*. Calcutta: Firma KLM, 1976.

Broomfield, John H. *Mostly about Bengal: Essays in Modern South Asian History.* New Delhi: Manohar, 1982.

———. *Elite Conflict in a Plural Society: Twentieth Century Bengal.* Berkeley: University of California Press, 1968.

Buckland, Charles Edward. *Bengal Under the Lieutenant-Governors* Calcutta: K. Bose, 1902.

Campos, J. J. A. *History of the Portuguese in Bengal.* New York: AMS Press, 1975.

Chakravarty, Papia. *Hindu Response to Nationalist Ferment, 1909-1935.* Calcutta: Subarnarekha, 1992.

Chakravorty, Jagannath. *Studies in the Bengal Renaissance.* Calcutta: National Council of Education, 1977.

Chatterjee, Partha. *Bengal, 1920-1947: The Land Question.* Calcutta: K. P. Bagchi, 1984.

Chatterjee, Pranab Kumar. *Struggle and Strife in Urban Bengal, 1937-47: A Study of Calcutta-Based Urban Politics in Bengal.* Calcutta: Das Gupta, 1991.

Chatterjee, Shiba Prasad. *The Partition of Bengal: A Geographical Study with Maps and Diagrams.* Calcutta: D. R. Mitra, 1947.

Chatterji, Bhola. *Aspects of Bengal Politics in the Early Nineteen-thirties.* Calcutta: World Press, 1969.

Chatterji, Joya. *Bengal Divided: Hindu Communalism and Partition, 1932-1947.* New York: Cambridge University Press, 1964.

Chattopadhyay, Dilipkumar. *Dynamics of Social Change in Bengal, 1817-1851.* Calcutta: Punthi Pustak, 1990.

Chattopadhyay, Manju. *Petition to Agitation: Bengal, 1857-1885.* Calcutta: K. P. Bagchi, 1985.

Chattopadhyaya, Gautam. *Bengal Electoral Politics and the Freedom Struggle, 1862-1947.* New Delhi: Indian Council of Historical Research, 1984.

———, ed. *Awakening in Bengal in Early Nineteenth Century: Selected Documents.* Calcutta: Progressive Publishers, 1965.

Chaudhuri, K. N. *The English East India Company.* London: F. Cass, 1965.

Chaudhuri, Nirad C. *The Autobiography of an Unknown Indian.* London: Macmillan, 1951.

———. *Clive of India: A Political and Psychological Essay.* London: Barrie and Jenkins, 1975.

Cronin, Richard P. *British Policy and Administration in Bengal, 1905-1912: Partition and the New Province of Eastern Bengal and Assam.* Calcutta: Firma KLM, 1977.

Daly, F. C. *First Rebels: A Strictly Confidential Note on the Growth of the Revolutionary Movement in Bengal.* Calcutta: Riddhi-India, 1981.

Das, Binod Sankar. *Changing Profile of the Frontier Bengal, 1751-1833.* Delhi: Mittal Publications, 1984.

Das, Manmath Nath. *India Under Morley and Minto: Politics Behind Revolution.* London: G. Allen and Unwin, 1964.

Das, Tarakchandra. *Bengal Famine (1943) as Revealed in a Survey of the Destitutes in Calcutta.* Calcutta: University of Calcutta, 1949.

Datta, Kalikinkar. *The Dutch in Bengal and Bihar, 1740-1825 A.D.* Delhi: Motilal Banarsidas, 1968.

———. *The Santhal Insurrection of 1855-57.* Calcutta: University of Calcutta, 1989.

De, Amalendu. *Roots of Separatism in Nineteenth Century Bengal.* Calcutta: Ratna Prakashan, 1974.

De, Soumitra. *Nationalism and Separatism in Bengal: A Study of India's Partition.* New Delhi: Vikas, 1992.

Dutta, Abhijit. *Muslim Society in Revolt: Titu Meer's Revolt, 1831: A Study.* Calcutta: Minerva Associates, 1987.

Dutt, Kalpana. *Chittagong Armoury Raiders: Reminiscences.* Bombay: People's Publishing House, 1945.

Edwardes, Michael. *The Battle of Plassey and the Conquest of Bengal.* New York: Macmillan, 1963.

Forbes, Geraldine H. *Positivism in Bengal: A Case Study in the Transmission and Assimilation of an Ideology.* Calcutta: Minerva, 1975.

Fuller, Bampfylde. *Some Personal Experiences.* London: J. Murray, 1935.

Ghosh, Kali Charan. *Famines in Bengal, 1770-1943.* Calcutta: National Council of Education, 1987.

Ghosh, Niranjan. *The Role of Women in the Freedom Movement in Bengal, 1919-1947.* Calcutta: Firma KLM, 1988.

Ghosh, Suresh Chandra. *The Social Condition of the British Community in Bengal, 1757-1800*. Leiden: E. J. Brill, 1970.

Ghosha, Binayajibana. *Revolt of 1905 in Bengal*. Calcutta: G. A. E. Publishers, 1987.

Gordon, Leonard A. *Bengal: The Nationalist Movement, 1876-1940*. New York: Columbia University Press, 1973.

Greenough, Paul R. *Prosperity and Misery in Modern Bengal: The Famine of 1943-1944*. New York: Oxford University Press, 1982.

Guha, Ranajit. *An Indian Historiography of India: A Nineteenth-Century Agenda and Its Implications*. Calcutta: K. P. Bagchi, 1988.

Gupta, Brijen Kishore. *Sirajuddaullah and the East India Company, 1756-1757: Background to the Foundation of British Power in India*. Leiden: E. J. Brill, 1966.

Hamilton, Francis. *Francis Buchanan in Southeast Bengal, 1798: His Journey to Chittagong, Chittagong Hill Tracts, Noakhali, and Comilla*. Dhaka: University Press, 1992.

Haque, Enamul, comp. *Nawab Bahadur Abdul Latif: His Writings and Related Documents*. Dacca: Samudra Prokashani, 1968.

Harun-or-Rashid. *The Foreshadowing of Bangladesh: Bengal Muslim League and Muslim Politics, 1936-1947*. Dhaka: Asiatic Society of Bangladesh, 1987.

Hashmi, Taj ul-Islam. *Pakistan as a Peasant Utopia: The Communalization of Class Politics in East Bengal, 1920-1947*. Boulder, CO: Westview Press, 1992.

Hill, S. C. *Bengal in 1756-1757: A Selection of Papers Dealing with the Affairs of the British in Bengal during the Reign of Siraj-ud-Daula with Notes and Historical Introduction*. Delhi: Manas Publications, 1985.

Hunter, William Wilson. *Annals of Rural Bengal*. New York: Johnson Reprint Corp., 1970.

Islam, Sirajul. *Rural History of Bangladesh: A Source Study*. Dacca: Titot Islam, 1977.

———. *Bengal Land Tenure: The Origin and Growth of Intermediate Interests in the 19th Century*. Calcutta: K. P. Bagchi, 1988.

———. *Rent and Raiyat: Society and Economy of Eastern Bengal, 1859-1928*. Dhaka: Asiatic Society of Bangladesh, 1989.

———. *The Permanent Settlement in Bengal: A Study of Its Operation, 1790-1819*. Dacca: Bangla Academy, 1979.

Jones, Mary Evelyn Monckton. *Warren Hastings in Bengal, 1772-1774*. Oxford: Clarendon Press, 1918.

Kabeer, Rokeya Rahman. *Administrative Policy of the Government of Bengal, 1870-1890*. Dacca: National Institute of Public Administration, 1965.

Kabir, Humayun. *Muslim Politics, 1906-47, and Other Essays*. Calcutta: Firma K. L. Mukhopadhyay, 1969.

Kaviraj, Narahari. *Wahabi and Faraizi Rebels of Bengal*. New Delhi: People's Publishing House, 1982.

———. *A Peasant Uprising in Bengal, 1783: The First Formidable Peasant Uprising against the Rule of East India Company*. New Delhi: People's Publishing House 1972.

Kejariwal, O. P. *The Asiatic Society of Bengal and the Discovery of India's Past, 1784-1838*. New York: Oxford University Press, 1988.

Khan, Akbar Ali. *Some Aspects of Peasant Behaviour in Bengal, 1890-1914: A Neo-classical Analysis*. Dhaka: Asiatic Society of Bangladesh, 1982.

Khan, Abdul Majed. *The Transition of Bengal, 1756-1775: A Study of Seiyid Muhammad Reza Khan*. London: Cambridge University Press, 1969.

Khan, Bazlur Rahman. *Politics in Bengal, 1927-1936*. Dhaka: Asiatic Society of Bangladesh, 1987.

Kling, Blair. *The Blue Mutiny: The Indigo Disturbances in Bengal, 1859-1862*. Philadelphia: University of Pennsylvania Press, 1966.

———. *Partner in Empire: Dwarkanath Tagore and the Age of Enterprise in Eastern India*. Berkeley: University of California Press, 1976.

Kopf, David. *British Orientalism and the Bengal Renaissance*. Berkeley: University of California Press, 1969.

———. *The Brahmo Samaj and the Shaping of the Modern Indian Mind*. Princeton NJ: Princeton University Press, 1979.

Kopf, David, and Saifuddin Joarder, eds. *Seminar of Perspectives of the Bengal Renaissance*. Dacca: Bangladesh Books International, 1977.

Laushey, David M. *Bengal Terrorism and the Marxist Left: Aspects of Regional Nationalism in India, 1905-1943*. Calcutta: Firma KLM, 1975.

Madhok, Balraj. *Portrait of a Martyr: Biography of Dr. Shyama Prasad Mookerji*. Bombay: Jaico, 1969.

Mallikarjuna Sharma, I. *Easter Rebellion in India: The Chittagong Uprising*. Hyderabad, India: Marxist Study Forum: 1993.

Maitra, Jayanti. *Muslim Politics in Bengal, 1855-1906*. Calcutta: K. P. Bagchi, 1984.

Majumdar, Romesh Chandra. *The Revolutionary Movement in Bengal and the Role of Surya Sen*. Calcutta: University of Calcutta, 1978.

———. *Renascent India: First Phase*. Calcutta: G. Bharadwaj, 1976.

———. *Glimpses of Bengal in the Nineteenth Century*, Calcutta: Firma KLM, 1960.

Mazumdar, Durga Prasad. *Dimensions of Political Culture in Bengal, 1814-1857, with Special Reference to Raja Ram Mohan Roy*. Calcutta: Calcutta University, 1993.

Mallick, Azizur Rahman. *British Policy and the Muslims in Bengal, 1757-1856*, Dacca: Bangla Academy, 1977.

Mannan, Mohammad Siraj. *The Muslim Political Parties in Bengal, 1936-1947: A Study of Their Activities and Struggle for Freedom*. Dhaka: Islamic Foundation Bangladesh, 1987.

Marshall, Peter James. *Bengal—The British Bridgehead: Eastern India, 1740-1828.* New York: Cambridge University Press, 1987.

———. *East Indian Fortunes: The British in Bengal in the Eighteenth Century.* Oxford: Clarendon Press, 1976.

———. *The Impeachment of Warren Hastings.* London: Oxford University Press, 1965.

Mitra, Lalit Mohan. *The Danes in Bengal.* Calcutta: Prabartak Publishers, 1951.

Momen, Humaira. *Muslim Politics in Bengal: A Study of Krishak Praja Party and the Elections of 1937.* Dacca: Sunny House, 1972.

Mookerjee, Amalendu Prasad. *Social and Political Ideas of Bipin Chandra Pal.* Calcutta: Minerva, 1974.

Mukhopadhyay, Amar Kumar, ed. *The Bengali Intellectual Tradition, from Rammohun Roy to Dhirendranath Sen.* Calcutta: K. P. Bagchi, 1979.

Mukhopadhyaya, Amitabha. *Reform and Regeneration in Bengal, 1774-1823.* Calcutta: Rabindra Bharati University, 1968.

Neogy, Ajit K. *Partitions of Bengal.* Calcutta: A. Mukherjee & Co., 1987.

O'Malley, Lewis Sydney Steward. *History of Bengal, Bihar and Orissa under British Rule.* Calcutta: Bengal Secretariat Book Depot, 1925.

Palit, Chittabrata. *New Viewpoints on Nineteenth Century Bengal,* Calcutta: Progressive Publishers, 1980.

———. *Tensions in Bengal Rural Society: Landlords, Planters, and Colonial Rule, 1830-1860.* Calcutta: Progressive Publishers, 1975.

Poddara, Arabinda. *Renaissance in Bengal: Quests and Confrontations, 1800-1860.* Simla: Indian Institute of Advanced Study, 1970.

———. *Renaissance in Bengal: A Search for Identity* Simla: Indian Institute of Advanced Study, 1977.

Prakash, Om. *The Dutch East India Company and the Economy of Bengal, 1630-1720*. Princeton, NJ: Princeton University Press, 1985.

Rahim, Enayetur. *Provincial Autonomy in Bengal, 1937-1943*. Dhaka: University Press, 1981.

Rahman, Hossainur. *Hindu-Muslim Relations in Bengal, 1905-1947: A Study in Cultural Confrontation*. Bombay: Nachiketa Publications, 1974.

Ram Gopal. *How the British Occupied Bengal*. New York: Asia Publishing House, 1963.

Ray, Dalia. *The Bengal Revolutionaries and Freedom Movement*. New Delhi: Cosmo Publications, 1990.

Ray, Rajat Kanta. *Social Conflict and Political Unrest in Bengal, 1875-1927*. Delhi: Oxford University Press, 1984.

Raychaudri, Tapan. *Europe Reconsidered: Perceptions of the West in Nineteenth Century Bengal*. Delhi: Oxford University Press, 1988.

Rule, Pauline. *The Pursuit of Progress: A Study of the Intellectual Development of Romesh Chunder Dutt, 1848-1888*. Calcutta: Editions Indian, 1977.

Sanyal, Rajat. *Voluntary Associations and the Urban Public Life in Bengal, 1815-1876: An Aspect of Social History*. Calcutta: Riddhi-India, 1980.

Sarkar, Chandiprasad. *The Bengal Muslims: A Study in Their Politicization, 1912-1929*. Calcutta: K. P. Bagchi, 1991.

Sarkar, Kamala. *Bengal Politics, 1937-1947*. Calcutta: A. Mukherjee & Co., 1990.

Sarkar, Sumit: *The Swadeshi Movement in Bengal, 1903-1908*. New Delhi: People's Publishing House, 1973.

Sarkar, Tanika. *Bengal, 1928-1934: The Politics of Protest*. New York: Oxford University Press, 1987.

Saxena, Vinod Kumar, ed. *The Partition of Bengal, 1905-1911: Select Documents*. Delhi: Kanishka Publishing House, 1987.

Scrafton, Luke. *A History of Bengal Before and After Plassey, 739-1758*. Calcutta: Editions Indian, 1975.

Sen, Asoka Kumar. *The Popular Uprising and the Intelligentsia: Bengal between 1855-1873*. Calcutta: Firma KLM, 1992.

———. *The Educated Middle Class and Indian Nationalism: Bengal during the Pre-Congress Decades*. Calcutta: Progressive Publishers, 1988.

Sen, Ranjit. *New Elite and New Collaboration: A Study of Social Transformations in Bengal in the Eighteenth Century*. Calcutta: Papyrus, 1985.

Sen, Shila. *Muslim Politics in Bengal, 1937-1947*. New Delhi: Impex India, 1976.

Sen, Suranjit. *Metamorphosis of Bengal Polity, 1700-1793*. Calcutta: Rabindra Bharati University, 1987.

Sengupta, Kalyan Kumar. *Pabna Disturbances and the Politics of Rent, 1873-1885*. New Delhi: People's Publishing House, 1974.

Shan Muhammad. *The Right Honourable Syed Ameer Ali: Personality and Achievements*. New Delhi: Uppal House, 1991.

Sharma, Ram Suresh. *Bengal under John Peter Grant, 1859-1862*. Delhi: Captial Publishing House, 1989.

Sinha, Devi P. *The Educational Policy of the East India Company in Bengal to 1854*. Calcutta: Punthi Pustak, 1964.

Sinha, Narendra Krishna, ed. *The History of Bengal, 1757-1905*. Calcutta: University of Calcutta, 1967.

———. *Ashutosh Mookerjee: A Biographical Study*. Calcutta: Ashutosh Mookerjee Centenary Committee, 1966.

Sinha, Pradip. *Nineteenth Century Bengal: Aspects of Social History*. Calcutta: Firma K.L. Mukhopapdyay, 1965.

Scrafton, Luke. *A History of Bengal before and after Plassey, 1739-1758.* Calcutta: Firma KLM, 1975; reprint of London edition, 1763.

Sensarma, P. *The Military History of Bengal.* Calcutta: Naya Prokash, 1977.

Thankappan Nair, P. *British Beginnings in Bengal, 1600-1660.* Calcutta: Punthi Pustak, 1991.

Vansittart, Henry. *A Narrative of the Transactions in Bengal, 1760-1764.* Calcutta: K. P. Bagchi, 1976.

Wasti, Syed Razi. *Lord Minto and the Indian Nationalist Movement, 1905-1910.* Oxford: Clarendon Press, 1964.

Wilson, Charles Robert. *The Early Annals of the British in Bengal.* New Delhi: Bimla Publishing House, 1983.

Bibliography

Mamoon, Muntasir. *Index to Articles in* Bengal: Past and Present, *Volumes 1-85, 1907-1966.* Dhaka: Dhaka University Library, 1986.

Pakistan Period and War of Independence

Ahmad, Abul Mansur. *End of a Betrayal and Restoration of the Pakistan Resolution.* Dacca: Koshroz Kitab Mahal, 1975.

Ahmad, Kabir Uddin. *Breakup of Pakistan: Background and Prospects of Bangladesh.* London: Social Science Publishers, 1972.

Ahmed, Moudud. *Bangladesh: A Constitutional Quest for Autonomy.* Dacca: University Press, 1979.

Ahsan, Qamarul. *Politics and Personalities in Pakistan.* Dacca: Mohiuddin, 1969.

Akbar Khan, Mohammed. *The Mystery of the Debacle of Pakistan, 1971, and Myth of Exploitation since 1947, and Secret of the Covert War Unmasked.* Karachi: Islamic Military Science Association, 1972 or 1973.

Alama, Jagalula. *Emergence of Bangladesh and Big Power Role in 1971*. Dhaka: Progoti Prakashani, 1990.

Ayoob, Mohammed, et al. *Bangla Desh: A Struggle for Nationhood.* Delhi: Vikas, 1971.

Banerjee, Debendra Nath. *East Pakistan: A Case-Study in Muslim Politics*. Delhi: Vikas, 1969.

Bangladesh Documents. New Delhi: Ministry of External Affairs, 1971.

Bangladesh Establishment Illegal: A Legal Study by International Commission of Jurists. Lahore: Fazalsons, 1972.

The Bangla Desh Papers: The Recorded Statements of Z. A. Bhutto, Mujeeb-ur-Rahman, Gen. Yahya Khan, and Other Politicians of United Pakistan, 1969-1971 Lahore: Vanguard Books, 1978.

Bergsaker, Robert. *Storm over Bangla Desh.* Oslo: Filadelfiaforlaget, 1972.

Bhatnagar, Yatindra. *Bangladesh: Birth of a Nation.* Delhi: Publication Division, 1971.

———. *Mujib, the Architect of Bangla Desh: A Political Biography.* Delhi: Indian School Supply Depot, 1971.

Bhattacharjea, Ajit, comp. *Dateline Bangla Desh.* Bombay: Jaico Publishing House, 1971.

Bhuiyan, Muhammad Abdul Wadud. *Emergence of Bangladesh and Role of Awami League*. New Delhi: Vikas, 1982.

Bhutto, Zulfikar Ali. *The Great Tragedy*. Karachi: Pakistan People's Party, 1971.

Chakrabarti, S. K. *The Evolution of Politics in Bangladesh, 1947-1978*. New Delhi: Associated, 1978.

Chandra, Prabodh. *Bloodbath in Bangla esh*. New Delhi: Adarsh Publications, 1971.

Chatterjee, Sisir. *Bangladesh: The Birth of a Nation*. Calcutta: The Book Exchange, 1972.

Chaudhuri, Kalyan. *Genocide in Bangladesh*. Bombay: Orient Longman, 1972.

Choudhury, A. K. *The Independence of East Bengal: A Historical Process*. Dhaka: Jatiya Grantha Kendra, 1984.

Choudhury, G. W. *Constitutional Development in Pakistan*. Vancouver: Publications Centre, University of British Columbia, 1969.

———. *The Last Days of United Pakistan*. Bloomington, IN: Indiana University Press, 1974.

———. *Democracy in Pakistan*. Dacca: Green Book House, 1967.

Chowdhury, Hamidul Haq. *Memoirs*. Dhaka: Associated Printers, 1989.

Chowdhury, Namja. *The Legislative Process in Bangladesh: Politics and Functioning of the East Bengal Legislature, 1947-58*. Dacca: University of Dacca, 1980.

Das, Mitra. *From Nation to Nation: A Case Study of Bengali Independence*. Calcutta: Minerva, 1981.

Dasgupta, R. K. *Revolt in East Bengal*. Delhi: A. Dasgupta, 1971.

Dasgupta, Sukharanjan. *Midnight Massacre in Dacca*. New Delhi: Vikas, 1978.

Feldman, Herbert. *The End and the Beginning: Pakistan, 1969-1971*. London: Oxford University Press, 1975.

———. *From Crisis to Crisis: Pakistan, 1962-1969*. London: Oxford University Press, 1972.

Garg, S. K. *Spotlight: Freedom Fighters of Bangladesh: A New Outlook*. New Delhi: Allied, 1984.

Gandhi, Indira. *India and Bangladesh: Selected Speeches and Statements, March to December 1971*. New Delhi: Orient Longman, 1972.

Ghosh, Sucheta. *The Role of India in the Emergence of Bangladesh*. Calcutta: Minvera, 1983.

Harun, Shamsul Huda. *Parliamentary Behavior in a Multi-National State, 1947-58: Bangladesh Experience*. Dhaka: Asiatic Society of Bangladesh, 1984.

Hossain, Ishtiaq. *India and the War of Liberation in Bangladesh.* Dacca: Forum for International Affairs, 1978.

Huq, Ghaziul. *Bangla Desh Unchained.* Calcutta: Indian Associated Publishing Co., 1971.

Huq, M. Mahfuzul. *Electoral Problems in Pakistan*. Dacca: Asiatic Society of Pakistan, 1966.

Husain, Muhammad. *East Pakistan*. Lahore: Pakistan P.E.N. Centre, 1955.

Hussain, Syed Shabir. *The Death Dance*. Islamabad: Kamran Publishing House, 1979.

Ikramullah, Shaista Suhrawardy. *Huseyn Shaheed Suhrawardy, A Biography*. Karachi: Oxford University Press, 1991.

Imam, Jahanara. *Of Blood and Fire: The Untold Story of Bangladesh's War of Independence*. New Delhi: Sterling Publishers, 1989.

Islam, M. Rafiqul. *A Tale of Millions: Bangladesh Liberation War, 1971*. Dacca: Bangladesh Books International, 1981.

———. *The Bangladesh Liberation Movement: International Legal Implications.* Dhaka: University Press, 1987.

———, ed. *Genocide in Bangladesh: Harrowing Accounts of Some Eye-Witnesses and the Extracts from the Press*. Dhaka: Noman Brothers, 1991.

Jackson, Robert Victor. *South Asian Crisis: India, Pakistan, Bangla Desh*. London: Chatto and Windus, 1975.

Jafar, Abu. *Maulana Akram Khan: A Versatile Genius.* Dhaka: Islamic Foundation Bangladesh, 1984.

Jagdev Singh. *Dismemberment of Pakistan: 1971 Indo-Pak War*. New Delhi: Lancer, 1988.

Jahan, Rounaq. *Pakistan: Failure in National Integration*. New York: Columbia University Press, 1972.

Kamal, Kazi Ahmed. *Sheikh Mujibur Rahman: Man and Politician.* Dacca: Kazi Giasuddin Ahmed, 1970.

———. *Politicians and Inside Stories: A Glimpse Mainly into Lives of Fazlul Haq, Shaheed Suhrawardy, and Moulana Bhashani.* Dacca: Kazi Giasuddin Ahmed: 1970.

———. *Sheikh Mujibur Rahman and Birth of Bangladesh.* Dacca: Kazi Giasuddin Ahmed, 1972.

Karim, Nehal. *The Emergence of Nationalism in Bangladesh.* Dhaka: University of Dhaka, 1992.

Kashyap, Subhash C. *Bangla Desh: Background and Perspectives.* Delhi: National Publishing House, 1971.

Khan, Fazal Muqueem. *Pakistan's Crisis in Leadership.* Islamabad: National Book Foundation, 1973.

Khan, Rao Farman Ali. *How Pakistan Got Divided.* Lahore: Jang Publishers, 1992.

Khan, Zillur Rahman and A. T. R. Rahman. *Provincial Autonomy and Constitution Making: The Case of Bangladesh.* Dhaka: Green Book House, 1973.

Lachhman Singh. *Victory in Bangladesh.* Dehra Dun: Natraj Publishers, 1991.

———. *Indian Sword Strikes in East Pakistan.* New Delhi: Vikas, 1979.

Loshak, David. *Pakistan Crisis.* London: Heinemann, 1971.

Mahmood, Safdar. *The Deliberate Debacle.* Lahore: Sheikh Muhammad Ashraf, 1976.

———. *Pakistan Divided.* Lahore: Ferozsons, 1984.

Malik, Amita. *The Year of the Vulture.* New Delhi: Orient Longman, 1972.

Mankekar, D. R. *Pak Colonialism in East Bengal.* Bombay: Somaiya Publications, 1971.

Maniruzzaman, Talukder. *Group Interests and Political Change: Studies of Pakistan and Bangladesh*. New Delhi: South Asian Publishers, 1982.

———. *Radical Politics and the Emergence of Bangladesh*. Dacca: Bangladesh Books International, 1975.

Mascarenhas, Anthony. *The Rape of Bangla Desh*. Delhi: Vikas, 1971.

Maswani, A. M. K. *Subversion in East Pakistan*. Lahore: Amir Publications, 1979.

Mirza, Sarfaraz Hussain, comp. *Not the Whole Truth: East Pakistan Crisis, (March-December, 1971): The Foreign Press*. Lahore: Centre for South Asian Studies, University of Punjab, 1989.

Moraes, Dom. *The Tempest Within: An Account of East Pakistan*. Delhi: Vikas, 1971.

Muhith, A. M. A. *Bangladesh: Emergence of a Nation*. Dhaka: University Press, 1992.

Mujibur Rahman, Sheikh. *Bangladesh, My Bangladesh. Selected Speeches and Statements, October 28, 1970 to March 26, 1971*. New Delhi: Orient Longmans, 1972.

Nair, M. Bhaskaran. *Politics in Bangladesh: A Study of the Awami League, 1949-58*. New Delhi: Northern Book Centre, 1990.

Nicholas, Marta, and Philip Oldenburg. *Bangladesh: The Birth of a Nation: A Handbook of Background Information and Documentary Sources*. Madras: M. Seshachalam, 1972.

O'Connor, Noel G. *The Soldier is Afraid: An Account of Operation Sikander, Bangladesh War, 1971*. Bhopal: Services Publishing House, 1981.

Osmany, Shireen Hasan. *Bangladeshi Nationalism: History of Dialectics and Dimensions*. Dhaka: University Press, 1992.

Pakistan from 1947 to the Creation of Bangladesh. New York: Scribner, 1973. [From *Keesing's Archives*]

Payne, Robert. *Massacre*. New York: Macmillan, 1973.

Qutubuddin Aziz. *Blood and Tears.* Karachi: United Press of Pakistan, 1974.

Rahamana, Phajalura. *Culture Conflicts in East Pakistan, 1947-1971: A Study in the Attitude of Bengali Muslim Intelligentsia towards Bengali Literature and Islam.* Dhaka: Sejuty Prokashani, 1990.

Rahman, Choudhury Shamsur. *Life in East Pakistan.* Chittagong: Pakistan Cooperative Book Society, 1956.

Rahman, Matiur. *The Role of India and the Big Powers in the East Pakistan Crisis of 1971.* London: R. Rahman, 1984.

Rama, Sivalenka. *Role of India in Bangladesh Liberation Movement.* Hyderabad, India: Rama, 1978.

Ray, Jayanta Kumar. *Democracy and Nationalism on Trial: A Study of East Pakistan.* Simla: Indian Institute of Advanced Study, 1968.

Roy Chowdhury, Subrata. *The Genesis of Bangladesh: A Study in International Legal Norms and Permissive Conscience.* London: Asia Publishing House, 1972.

Rizvi, Hasan-Askari. *Internal Strife and External Intervention: India's Role in the Civil War in East Pakistan (Bangladesh).* Lahore: Progressive Publishers, 1981.

———. *The Military and Politics in Pakistan, 1947-86.* Lahore: Progressive Publishers, 1986.

Rushbrook Williams, L. F. *Pakistan Under Challenge.* London: Stacey International: 1975.

Saadullah Khan. *East Pakistan to Bangla Desh.* Lahore: Lahore Law Times Publications, 1975.

Salunke, S. P. *Pakistani POWs in India.* New Delhi: Vikas, 1977.

Sen Gupta, Jyoti. *Bangladesh in Blood and Tears.* Calcutta: Naya Prokash, 1981.

———. *History of Freedom Movement in Bangladesh, 1943-1973: Some Involvement.* Calcutta: Naya Prokash, 1974.

Sethi, Surinder Singh: *The Decisive War: Emergence of a New Nation.* New Delhi: Sagar Publications, 1972.

Sharma, Shri Ram. *Bangladesh Crisis and Indian Foreign Policy.* New Delhi: Young Asia, 1978.

Shelly [Shelley], Mizanur Rahman. *Emergence of a New Nation in a Multi-Polar World: Bangladesh.* Dacca: University Press, 1979.

Siddiq, Salik. *Witness to Surrender.* Karachi: Oxford University Press, 1977.

Siddiqui, Kalim. *Conflict, Crisis and War in Pakistan.* London: Macmillan, 1972.

Singh, Swaran. *Bangla Desh and Indo-Pak War: India Speaks at the U.N.* New Delhi: Publications Division, 1972.

Sisson, Richard; and Leo Rose. *War and Secession: Pakistan, India and the Creation of Bangladesh.* Berkeley: University of California Press, 1990.

Sodhi, Harinder Singh. *"Operation Windfall": Emergence of Bangladesh.* New Delhi: Allied, 1980.

Subrahmanyam, K. *Bangla Desh and India's Security.* Dehra Dun: Palit and Dutt, 1972.

Suhrawardy, Huseyn Shaheed. *Memoirs of Huseyn Shaheed Suhrawardy with a Brief Account of His Life and Work.* Dhaka: University Press, 1987.

Tiwary, I. N. *War of Independence in Bangla Desh: A Documentary Study with an Introduction.* Varanasi: Navachetna Prakashan: 1971.

Uban, Sujan Singh. *Phantoms of Chittagong: The "Fifth Army" in Bangladesh.* New Delhi: Allied Publishers, 1985.

Umar, Badruddin. *Politics and Society in East Pakistan and Bangladesh.* Dacca: Mowla Bros., 1974.

Wilcox, Wayne Ayres. *The Emergence of Bangladesh: Problems and Opportunities for a Redefined American Policy in South Asia.* Washington: American Enterprise Institute for Public Policy Research, 1973.

Zafar, S.M. *Through the Crisis.* Lahore: Book Centre, 1970.

Zaheer, Hasan. *The Separation of East Pakistan: The Rise and Realization of Bengali Muslim Nationalism*. New York: Oxford University Press, 1994.

Zaman, Hasan, comp. *East Pakistan Crisis and India*. Dacca: Pakistan Academy, 1971.

Local History

Ahmed, Sharif Uddin. *Dhaka: Past, Present, and Future*. Dhaka: Asiatic Society of Bangladesh, 1991.

———. *Dacca: A Study in Urban History and Development*. Riverdale, MD: Riverdale Co., 1986.

Akanda, S. A., ed. *The District of Rajshahi: Its Past and Present*. Rajshahi: Institute of Bangladesh Studies, University of Rajshahi, 1983.

Ali, Syed Murtaza. *History of Chittagong*. Dacca: Standard Publishers, 1964.

Dani, Ahmad Hasan. *Dacca: A Record of its Changing Fortunes* Dacca: Mrs. S. S. Dani: 1962.

D'Oyly, Charles, Sir. *Antiquities of Dacca*. London: J. Landseer, 1814-27.

Hasan, Sayed Mahmudul. *Dhaka: The City of Mosques*. Dacca: Islamic Foundation Bangladesh, 1981.

Hossain, Anwar. *Dhaka Portrait: 1967-1992: Images, Concept, Photographs, Designs and Layout* Dhaka: AB Publishers, 1992.

Hutchinson, Robert H. S. *An Account of the Chittagong Hill Tracts*. Calcutta: Bengal Secretariat Book Depot, 1906.

———. *Chittagong Hill Tracts*. Delhi: Vivek, 1978.

Islam, Sirajul, ed. *Bangladesh District Records: Dacca District*. Dacca: University of Dacca, 1981.

Kanunago, Suniti Bhushana. *A History of Chittagong*. Chittagong: Signet Library, 1988.

Karim, Abdul. *Dacca: The Mughal Capital*. Dacca: Asiatic Society of Pakistan, 1964.

Mohsin, K. M. *A Bengal District in Transition: Murshidabad, 1765-1793*. Dacca: Asiatic Society of Bangladesh, 1973.

Majumdar, Purna Chandra. *The Musnud of Murshidabad, 1704-1904: Being a Synopsis of the History of Murshidabad for the Last Two Centuries*. Murshidabad: Saroda Ray, 1905.

Mukherjee, Nilmani. *A Bengal Zamindar: Jaykrishna Mukherjee of Uttarpara and His Times, 1808-1888*. Calcutta: Firma KLM, 1975.

Taifoor, Syed Muhammed. *Glimpses of Old Dacca*. Dacca: S.M. Perwez, 1952.

Archaeology and Prehistory

Alam, A. K. M. Shamsul. *Mainamati*. Dhaka: Department of Archaeology, 1982.

Bangladesh: An Album of Archaeological Relics. Dhaka: Directorate of Archaeology and Museums, 1984.

Chakrabarti, Dilip K. *Ancient Bangladesh: A Study of the Archaeological Sources*. New York: Oxford University Press, 1992.

Chittagong University Museum. *Catalogue of Coins in the Cabinet of the Chittagong University Museum*. Chittagong: Chittagong University Museum, 1979.

Ghosh, Shankar Prosad. *Terracottas of Bengal, with Special Reference to Nadia*. New Delhi: D. K. Publishers, 1986.

Hasan, Sayed Mahmudul. *Muslim Monuments of Bangladesh*. Dhaka: Islamic Foundation Bangladesh, 1988.

———. *A Guide to Ancient Monuments of East Pakistan* Dacca: Society for Pakistan Studies, 1970.

———. *Sonargaon*. Dhaka: Bangladesh Folk Art and Crafts Foundation, 1982.

———. *Dacca: Gateway to the East*. Dacca: Research Centre for Islamic Art and Culture, 1982.

Khan, F. A. *Mainamati: Recent Archaeological Discoveries in East Pakistan*. Karachi: Pakistan Publications, 1955.

Majumdar, Nani Gopal, ed. *Inscriptions of Bengal,* volume 3. Rajshahi: Varendra Research Society, 1929.

Nazimuddin Ahmad. *Discover the Monuments of Bangladesh*. Dhaka: University Press, 1984.

Sen, Benoychandra. *Some Historical Aspects of the Inscriptions of Bengal: Pre-Muhammadan Epochs*. Calcutta: University of Calcutta, 1942.

Language

Azad, Humayun. *Pronominalization in Bengali*. Dhaka: University of Dhaka, 1983.

Chatterjee, Suniti Kumar. *The Origin and Development of the Bengali Language*. London: Allen and Unwin, 1970-72.

Gangopadhyay, Malaya. *The Noun Phrase in Bengali: Assignment of Role and the Karaka Theory*. Delhi: Motilal Banarsidas, 1990.

Haldar, Gopal. *A Comparative Grammar of East Bengal Dialects*. Calcutta: Puthipatra, 1986.

Jahan-Ara, Begum. *Pronominal Usage and Appellatives in Bangla*. Dhaka: Karim Book Corporation, 1991.

Khondkar, Abdur Rahim. *The Portuguese Contribution to Bengali Prose, Grammar, and Lexicography*. Dacca: Bangla Academy, 1976.

Morshed, Abul Kalam Manzur. *A Study of Standard Bengali and the Noakhali Dialect*. Dhaka: Bangla Academy, 1985.

Muhammad, Kazi Dina. *The Verbal Structure in Colloquial Bengali*. Dhaka: Bangla Academy, 1985.

Qayyum, Mohammad Abdul. *A Critical Study of the Early Bengali Grammars: Halhed to Haughton*. Dhaka: Asiatic Society of Bangladesh, 1982.

Sen, Sukuman. *Women's Dialect in Bengali*. Calcutta: Jijnasa: 1979.

Zbavitel, Dusan. *Non-finite Verbal Forms in Bengali*. Prague: Oriental Institute, 1970.

Literature

Ashraf, Syed Ali. *Muslim Traditions in Bengali Literature*. Dhaka: Islamic Foundation Bangladesh, 1983.

Bandhopadhyaya, Asitakumara. *History of Modern Bengali Literature: Nineteenth and Twentieth Centuries*. Calcutta: Modern Book Agency, 1986.

Bose, Amalendu. *Michael Madhusudan Dutt*. New Delhi: Sahitya Akademi, 1981.

Chakravarty, Basudha. *Kazi Nazrul Islam*. New Delhi: National Book Trust, India, 1968.

Chatterjee, Santa. *Tales of Bengal*. Thompson CT: Inter Culture Associates, 1979.

Chatterji, Suniti Kumar. *The Various "Matters" in New or Modern Indian Literature and the Romances of Medieval Bengal: Gauda Banga Ramya Katha*. Calcutta: Asiatic Society,, 1982.

De, Sushil Kumar. *History of Bengali Literature in the Nineteenth Century, 1800-1825*. Calcutta: University of Calcutta, 1919.

Gosvami, Karunamaya. *Aspects of Nazrul Songs*. Dhaka: Nazrul Institute, 1990.

Haldar, Gopal. *Kazi Nazrul Islam*. New Delhi: Sahitya Akademi, 1973.

Islam, Manu, ed. *Literary Personalities of Bangladesh*. Dhaka: Baktittya Prokashani, 1985.

Kripalani, Krishna. *Rabindranath Tagore: A Biography*. Calcutta: Visva-Bharati, 1980.

Krsndasa Kaviraja Gosvami. *Sri Sri Chaitanya Charitamrita.* English translation. Calcutta: Sri Sri Chaitanya-Charitamrita Karyalaya, 1954-1956.

Lago, Mary M. *Rabindranath Tagore*. Boston: Twayne Publishers, 1976.

Mahfuzullah, M. *The Distinctive Features of Our Literature*. Dacca: Society for Pakistan Studies, 1970.

Mostapha Kamala, Abu Hena. *The Bengali Press and Literary Writing, 1818-31*. Dacca: University Press, 1977.

Naravane, Vishwanath S. *Sarat Chandra Chatterji: An Introduction to His Life and Work*. Delhi: Macmillan, 1976.

Quader, Abedin, ed. *An Anthology of Modern Literature from Bangladesh*. Dhaka: Swaptapadi Publications, 1986.

Ramaswami Shastri, K. S. *Sir Rabindranath Tagore: His Life, Personality, and Genius*. Delhi: Akashdeep, 1988.

Rhys, Ernest. *Rabindranath Tagore: A Biographical Study*. New York: Haskell House, 1970.

Roy, Basanta Kumar. *Rabindranath Tagore: The Man and His Poetry*. Norwood PA: Norwood Editions, 1978.

Salkar, K. R. *Rabindranath Tagore: His Impact on Indian Education*. New Delhi: Sterling Publishers, 1990.

Sen, Dinesh Chandra. *History of Bengali Language and Literature*. Calcutta: University of Calcutta, 1911.

Sen, Sukumar. *History of Bengali Literature*. New Delhi: Sahitya Akademi, 1971.

Siddiqui, Zillur Rahman. *Literature of Bangladesh and Other Essays*. Dhaka: Bangladesh Books International, 1982.

Thompson, Edward John. *Rabindranath Tagore: Poet and Dramatist*. New York: Oxford University Press, 1991.

Zaman, Niaz Ali. *Animal Tales from Bangladesh*. Dhaka: Bangla Academy, 1985.

Fiction

Awwal, Mohammad Abdul. *The Prose Works of Mir Masarraf Hosen, 1869-1899*. Chittagong: University of Chittagong, 1975.

Samasujjamana, Abula Phajala. *The Trembling Flame (A Collection of Short Stories)*. Dhaka: Tribhuj Praksasani, 1992.

Poetry

Chandidas. *Love Songs of Chandidas, The Rebel Poet-Priest of Bengal*. New York: Grove Press, 1967.

Huda, Muhammad Nurul. *Flaming Flowers: Poets' Response to the Emergence of Bangladesh*. Dhaka: Bangla Academy, 1986.

Jasimuddin. *Selected Poems of Jasimuddin*. Dacca: Oxford University Press, 1975.

———. *Gipsy Wharf*. London: Allen and Unwin, 1969.

Lalon Shah. *Songs of Lalon Shah*. Dhaka: Bangla Academy, 1991.

———. *Songs of Lalon* Dhaka: University Press, 1987.

Nazrul Islam, Kazi. *The Morning Shinai: Twenty Poems of Kazi Nazrul Islam*. Dhaka: Nazrul Institute, 1991.

———. *A New Anthology*. Dhaka: Bangla Academy, 1990.

———. *The Rebel and Other Poems*. New Delhi: Sahitya Akademi, 1974.

———. *The Fiery Lyre of Nazrul Islam*. Dacca: Bangla Academy, 1974.

Rashid, M. Harunur, ed. *A Choice of Contemporary Verse from Bangladesh*. Dhaka: Bangla Academy, 1986.

Saif, Hayat and Mahbub Talukdar, eds. *A Selection of Contemporary Verse from Bangladesh*. Dhaka: Second Asian Poetry Festival, 1989.

Tofayell, Z. A. *Lalon Shah and Lyrics of the Padma.* Dacca: Ziaunnahar, 1968.

Philosophy and Religion

Bamladesa Hindu Bauddha Khrishtana Aikya Parishad. *Communal Persecution and Repression in Bangladesh, Some Facts.* Dhaka: Bangladesh Hindu Bouddha Christian Okhya Parishad, 1993.

Christianity

Ali, Muhammad Mohar. *The Bengali Reaction to Christian Missionary Activities, 1833-1857.* Chittagong: Mehrub Publications, 1965.

Dutta, Abhijit. *Nineteenth Century Bengal Society and Christian Missionaries.* Calcutta: Minerva Associates, 1992.

Hefley, James C. *Christ in Bangladesh.* New York: Harper and Row, 1973.

Lockerbie, Jeannie. *On Duty in Bangladesh.* Grand Rapids, MI: Zondervan, 1973.

———. *Write the Vision.* South Pasadena, CA: William Carey Library, 1989.

McKinley, Jim. *Death to Life, Bangladesh: The Experience of an American Missionary Family.* Dacca: Immanuel Baptist Church, 1979.

McNee, Peter. *Crucial Issues in Bangladesh: Making Missions More Effective in the Mosaic of Peoples.* South Pasadena, CA: William Carey Library, 1976.

Olsen, Viggo. *Daktar II.* Chicago: Moody Press, 1990.

Olsen, Viggo, and Jeannie Lockerbie. *Daktar: Diplomat in Bangladesh.* Chicago: Moody Press, 1973.

Soddy, Gordon. *Baptists in Bangladesh: An Historical Sketch of More than One Hundred Years' Work of the Baptist Missionary Society in Bengal.* Khulna: National Council of Churches, Bangladesh, 1987.

Walsh, Jay, and Patricia C. Oviatt. *Ripe Mangoes: Miracle Missionary Stories from Bangladesh*. Schaumburg IL: Regular Baptist Press, 1978.

Hinduism

Sastri, Sibnath. *History of the Brahmo Samaj*. Calcutta: Sadharan Brahmo Samaj, 1974.

Sen, Amiyakumar. *Tattwabodhini Sabha and the Bengal Renaissance*. Calcutta: Sadharan Brahmo Samaj, 1979.

Sen, Priyaranjan. *The Story of Chandidas: A Poetic Representation of the Fusion of Sakta and Vaishnava Cultures*. Calcutta: Indian Publications, 1963.

Islam

Ahmad Khan, Muin-ud-din. *History of the Fara'idi Movement in Bengal, 1818-1906*. Karachi: Pakistan Historical Society, 1965.

———. *Selections from Bengal Government Records on Wahhabi Trials (1863-1870)*. Dacca: n.p., 1961.

Ahmed, Rafiuddin, ed. *Islam in Bangladesh: Society, Culture, and Politics*. Dhaka: Elite Printing and Packages, 1983.

Ali, Syed Murtaza. *Saints of East Pakistan*. Dacca: Oxford University Press, Pakistan Branch, 1971.

Akramuzzaman. *A Sociological Profile of Islam*. Dacca: Islamic Foundation Bangladesh, 1979.

Ameer Ali, Syed. *Memoirs and Other Writings of Syed Ameer Ali*. Delhi: Renaissance Publishing House, 1985.

———. *The Spirit of Islam: A History of the Evolution and Ideals of Islam, with a Life of the Prophet*. London: Christophers, 1955.

Banu, U. A. B. Razia Akhter. *Islam in Bangladesh*. Leiden: Brill, 1991.

Ghazi, Shamsur Rahman. *Islamic Law as Administered in Bangladesh*. Dacca: Islamic Foundation Bangladesh, 1981.

Haq, Muhammad Enamul. *A History of Sufi-ism in Bengal.* Dacca: Asiatic Society of Bangladesh, 1975.

Haq, Muhammad Mazammil. *Some Aspects of the Principal Sufi Orders in India.* Dhaka: Islamic Foundation Bangladesh, 1985.

Jafar, Abu. *Muslim Festivals in Bangladesh.* Dacca: Islamic Foundation, 1980.

Latif, Abdul, Sheikh. *The Muslim Mystic Movement in Bengal, 1301-1550.* Calcutta: K. P. Bagchi, 1993.

Meerza, Delawar Hosaen Ahamed. *Muslim Modernism in Bengal: Selected Writings of Delawar Hosaen Ahamed Meerza, 1840-1913* Dacca: Centre for Social Studies, 1980.

Quasem, Abul. *Islam, Science, and Modern Thoughts.* Dacca: Islamic Foundation Bangladesh, 1980.

Roy, Asim. *The Islamic Syncretist Tradition in Bengal.* Princeton, NJ: Princeton University Press, 1983.

Sarkar, Jagadish Narayan. *Islam in Bengal (Thirteenth to Nineteenth Century).* Calcutta: Ratna Prakashan, 1972.

Bibliography

Ahmad Khan, Muin-ud-Din. *A Bibliographic Introduction to Modern Islamic Development in India and Pakistan, 1700-1955.* Dacca: n.p., 1959.

Politics and Government

Ahamed, Emajuddin. *Military Rule and the Myth of Democracy.* Dhaka: University Press, 1988.

———, ed. *Society and Politics in Bangladesh.* Dhaka: Academic Publishers, 1989.

Ahmed, Moudud. *Bangladesh: Era of Sheikh Mujibur Rahman.* Dhaka: University Press, 1983.

Ahmed, Rafiuddin, ed. *Religion, Nationalism, and Politics in Bangladesh.* New Delhi: South Asian Publishers, 1990.

Ali, A. F. Imam. *Hindu-Muslim Community in Bangladesh*. Delhi: Kanishka Publishing House, 1992.

Ali, S. M. *After the Dark Night: Problems of Sheikh Mujibur Rahman*. Delhi: Thompson Press, 1973.

Awami League Rule: Glimpses from the International Press. Dhaka: Oasis Press, 1992.

Badruddin Umar. *Towards the Emergency*. Dacca: Muktadhara, 1980.

Banerjee, Subrata. *Bangladesh*. New Delhi: National Book Trust, India, 1981.

Brace, Steve. *Bangladesh*. New York: Thompson Learning, 1995.

Dasgupta, Sukharanjan. *Midnight Massacre in Dacca*. New Delhi: Vikas, 1978.

Franda, Marcus F. *Bangladesh: The First Decade*. New Delhi: South Asian Publishers, 1982.

———. *Bangladesh Nationalism and Ziaur Rahman's Presidency*. Hanover, NH: American Universities Field Staff, 1981.

Hafiz, M. Abdul and Abdur Rob Khan, eds. *Nation Building in Bangladesh: Retrospect and Prospect*. Dhaka: Bangladesh Institute of International and Strategic Studies, 1986.

Hakim, Muhammad A. *Bangladesh Politics: The Shahabuddin Interregnum*. Dhaka: University Press, 1993.

Hakim, S. Abdul. *Begum Khaleda Zia of Bangladesh: A Political Biography*. New Delhi: Vikas, 1992.

Harun, Shamsul Huda. *Bangladesh Voting Behaviour: A Psephological Study, 1973*. Dhaka: Dhaka University, 1986.

Hasanuzzaman, al-Masud, ed. *Bangladesh: Crisis of Political Development*. Savar: Jahangirnagar University, 1988.

Hossain, Golam. *General Ziaur Rahman and the BNP: Political Transformation of a Military Regime*. Dhaka: University Press, 1988.

Huque, Kazi Anwarul. *Under Three Flags: Reminiscenses of a Public Servant*. Dhaka: Islamic Foundation, 1986.

Jahan, Rounaq. *Bangladesh Politics: Problems and Issues*. Dhaka: University Press, 1980.

Jahangir, Burhanuddin Khan. *Problematics of Nationalism in Bangladesh*. Dhaka: Centre for Social Studies, 1986.

Kabir, Muhammad Ghulam. *Minority Politics in Bangladesh*. New Delhi: Vikas, 1980.

Khan, Iqbal Ansari. *The Third Eye: Glimpses of the Politicos*. Dhaka: University Press, 1991.

Khan, M. Salimuddin, ed. *Politics and Stability in Bangladesh: Problems and Prospects*. Dhaka: Jahangirnagar University, 1985.

Khan, Mohammad Mohabbat, and Syed Anwarul Husain, eds. *Bangladesh Studies: Politics, Administration, Rural Development, and Foreign Policy*. Dhaka: Centre for Administrative Studies, University of Dhaka, 1985.

Khan, Zillur Rahman. *Leadership Crisis in Bangladesh: Martial Law to Martial Law*. Dhaka: University Press, 1983.

———. *Leadership in the Least Developed Nation: Bangladesh*. Syracuse, NY: Maxwell School of Citizenship and Public Affairs, 1983.

Kochanek, Stanley A. *Patron-Client Politics and Business in Bangladesh*. Thousand Oaks, CA: Sage Publications, 1993.

Lifschultz, Lawrence. *Bangladesh: The Unfinished Revolution*. London: Zed Press, 1979.

Maniruzzaman, Talukder. *The Bangladesh Revolution and Its Aftermath*. Dacca: Bangladesh Books International, 1980.

Mascarenhas, Anthony. *Bangladesh: A Legacy of Blood*. London: Hodder and Stoughton, 1986.

Momen, Nurul. *Bangladesh: The First Four Years (From 16 December 1971 to 15 December 1975).* Dacca: Bangladesh Institute of Law and International Affairs, 1980.

Nawaz, Mohammed. *Bangladesh through the Period of Turmoil and Reconstruction.* Lahore: Progressive Publishers, 1974.

Nurujjamana, Mohammada. *Prof. Ghulam Azam: A Profile of Struggle in the Cause of Allah.* Dhaka: Prachi Prakashani, 1992.

Puchkov, V. P. *Political Development of Bangladesh.* New Delhi: Patriot Publishers, 1989.

Rahman, Muhammad Anisur. *The Lost Moment: Dreams with a Nation Born through Fire: Papers on Political Economy of Bangladesh.* Dhaka: University Press, 1993.

Rahman, Matiur. *Bangladesh Today: An Indictment and a Lament.* London: News and Media, 1978.

Saha, B. P. *Liberation Struggle and After.* New Delhi: Vikas, 1985.

Sayem, Abusadat Mohammad. *At Bangabhaban: Last Phase.* Dhaka: Hakkani Publishers, 1988.

Sen, Achintya. *People, Power, Politics, 1972-1991.* Dhaka: Pinaki Das, 1991.

Sen, Rangalal. *Political Elites in Bangladesh.* Dhaka: University Press, 1986.

Shamsuddin, Abu Zafar. *Sociology of Bengal Politics and Other Essays.* Dacca: Bangla Academy, 1973.

Siddiqui, S. A. *The Pattern of Secularism in India and Bangladesh.* Chittagong: Siddiqui, 1974.

Sobhan, Rahman. *Bangladesh: Problems of Governance.* Delhi: Konark, 1993.

Ziring, Lawrence. *Bangladesh: From Mujib to Ershad: An Interpretive Study.* Karachi: Oxford University Press, 1992.

Bibliography

Zahiruddin, Habib Mohammad. *Government and Politics in Bangladesh: A Bibliographical Guide* Dacca: Centre for Administrative Studies, 1981.

Armed Forces

Ahmad, Borhanuddin. *The Generals of Pakistan and Bangladesh.* New Delhi: Vikas, 1993.

Hasanuzzaman. *Search for a New Dimension: Politico-Constitutional and Military Tangle in Bangladesh.* Dhaka: Bangladesh Book House, 1992.

Hossain, Golam. *Civil-Military Relations in Bangladesh.* Dhaka: Academic Publishers, 1991.

Defense

Buzan, Barry. *South Asian Insecurity and the Great Powers.* New York: St. Martin's Press, 1986.

Jain, B. M. *South Asian Security: Problems and Prospects.* New Delhi: Radiant Publishers, 1985.

Narain, Jai. *Economics of Defence: A Study of SAARC Countries.* New Delhi: Lancers Books, 1989.

Sinha, K. K. *Problems of Defence of South and East Asia* Bombay: Manaktalas, 1969.

Elections

Blair, Harry W. *Voting, Caste, Community, Society: Explorations in Aggregate Data Analysis in India and Bangladesh.* Delhi: Young Asia, 1979.

Chakravarty, S. R. *Bangladesh: The Nineteen Seventy-Nine Elections.* New Delhi: South Asian Publishers, 1988.

Coordinating Council for Human Rights in Bangladesh (CCHRB): *Parliamentary Election 1991: Observation Report.* Dhaka: The Council, 1991.

Kajal, Iftikhar. *National Parliament Election, 1991: Some Reflections.* Dhaka: Raktoreen, 1991.

International Relations

Abdur Razzak. *Foreign Powers and Bangladesh.* London: Bangladesh Krisak Sramik Awami League, 1977.

Ahamed, Emajuddin and Abul Kalam, eds. *Bangladesh, South Asia, and the World.* Dhaka: Academic Publishers, 1992.

Ahamed, Emajuddin, ed. *Foreign Policy of Bangladesh: A Small State's Imperative.* Dhaka: University Press, 1984.

Ahmad, Muzaffer, and Abul Kalam, eds. *Bangladesh Foreign Relations: Changes and Directions.* Dhaka: University Press, 1989.

Ayoob, Mohammed. *India, Pakistan and Bangladesh: Search for New Relationship.* New Delhi: Indian Council of World Affairs, 1975.

Bindra, Sukhwant Singh. *Indo-Bangladesh Relations.* New Delhi: Deep and Deep Publications, 1982.

Chakravarti, S. R. *Turmoil and Political Change in South Asia: Bangladesh, Sri Lanka, India, and Pakistan.* Jaipur: Aalekh Publishers, 1978.

Choudhury, Dilara. *Bangladesh and the South Asian International System.* Dhaka: Academic Publishers, 1992.

Choudhury, G. W. *India, Pakistan, Bangladesh, and the Major Powers: Politics of a Divided Subcontinent.* New York: Free Press, 1975.

Debbarma, P.K. *The Chakma Refugees in Tripura.* New Delhi: South Asian Publishers, 1993.

Gulati, Chandrika J. *Bangladesh: Liberation to Fundamentalism: A Study of Volatile Indo-Bangladesh Relations.* New Delhi: Commonwealth Publishers, 1988.

Haendel, Dan. *The Process of Policy Formulation: U.S. Foreign Policy in the Indo-Pakistan War of 1971*, Boulder, CO: Westview Press, 1977.

Islam, M. Rafiqul. *The Ganges Water Dispute: International Legal Aspects*. Dhaka: University Press, 1987.

Jain, Jagdish P. *China, Pakistan, and Bangladesh*. Delhi: Radiant Publishers, 1974-76.

Kabir, M.G. and Shaukat Hassan, eds. *Issues and Challenges Facing Bangladesh Foreign Policy*. Dhaka: Bangladesh Society for International Studies, 1989.

Khan, Ataur R. *India, Pakistan and Bangladesh: Conflict or Co-operation?* Dacca: Sindabad, 1976.

Khurshida Begum. *Tension over the Farakka Barrage: A Techno-Political Tangle in South Asia*. Dhaka: University Press, 1987.

Kuldeep Singh. *India and Bangladesh*. New Delhi: Anupama Publishers, 1987.

Lal, Shiv. *Bangla-Pak Polities*. New Delhi: Election Archives, 1985.

Momen, Nurul. *Bangladesh in the United Nations: A Study in Diplomacy*. Dhaka: University Press, 1987.

Narain, Virendra. *Foreign Policy of Bangladesh, 1971-1981: The Context of National Liberation Movement*. Jaipur: Aalekh Publishers, 1987.

Oliver, Thomas W. *The United Nations in Bangladesh*. Princeton, NJ: Princeton University Press, 1978.

Shamsul Huq, Muhammad. *Bangladesh International Politics: The Dilemmas of the Weak States*. New Delhi: Sterling Publishers, 1993.

Shashi Bhushan. *China's Shadow on India and Bangladesh*. New Delhi: Publications-India, 1973.

Tayyeb-ur Rahman, Syed. *Global Geo-strategy of Bangladesh, OIC, and Islamic Umma*. Dhaka: Islamic Foundation Bangladesh, 1985.

Wright, Denis. *Bangladesh: Origins and Indian Ocean Relations, 1971-1975*. New Delhi: Sterling Publishers, 1988.

Ziring, Lawrence. *The Subcontinent in World Politics: India, Its Neighbors, and the Great Powers*. New York: Praeger, 1982.

Law

Bhattacharya, Debesh Chandra. *Enemy (Vested) Property Laws in Bangladesh: Nature and Implications*. Dhaka: Chitra Bhattacharya, 1991.

Patwari, A. B. M. Mafizul Islam. *Legal System of Bangladesh*. Dhaka: Aligarh Library, 1991.

Rahman, Rafiqur. *Law of Evidence*. Dhaka: Nuruzzaman Choudhury, 1993.

Zahir, M. *Delay in Courts and Court Management*. Dhaka: Bangladesh Institute of Law and International Affairs, 1988.

Local Government

Abedin, Najmul. *Local Administration and Politics in Modernizing Societies: Bangladesh and Pakistan*. Dacca: Oxford University Press, 1973.

Ahmed, Tofail. *Decentralization and the Local State under Peripheral Capitalism: A Study in the Political Economy of Local Government in Bangladesh*. Dhaka: Academic Publishers, 1993.

Ali Ahmed. *Administration of Local Self-Government for Rural Areas in Bangladesh*. Dacca: Local Government Institute, 1979.

Ali, Qazi Azher. *District Administration in Bangladesh*. Dacca: National Institute of Public Administration, 1978.

Ali, Sheikh Maqsood. *Decentralization and People's Participation in Bangladesh*. Dhaka: National Institute of Local Government, 1983.

Aziz, Mohammed Abdul. *The Union Parishad in Bangladesh: An Analysis of Problems and Directions of Reform*. Dhaka: National Institute of Local Government, 1991.

Belal, Khalid, ed. *The Chittagong Hill Tracts: Falconry in the Hills*. Chittagong: Codec: 1992.

Chaudhuri, Muzaffar Ahmed. *Rural Government in East Pakistan*. Dacca: Puthighar. 1969.

Choudhury, Lutful Hoq. *Local Self-Government and its Reorganization in Bangladesh*. Dhaka: National Institute of Local Government, 1987.

Faizullah, Mohammad. *Development of Local Government in Bangladesh*. Dhaka: National Institute of Local Government, 1987.

Hasnat, Abdul Hye, ed. *Decentralization, Local Government Institutions and Resource Mobilization* Comilla: Bangladesh Academy. for Rural Development, 1985.

Huque, Ahmed Shafiqul. *Politics and Administration in Bangladesh: Problems of Participation*. Dhaka: University Press, 1988.

Karim, Muhammad Abdul. *Upazila System in Bangladesh: A Political and Administrative Analysis*. Dhaka: National Institute of Local Government, 1991.

Khandaker, Mushtaque Ahmad. *Paurashava (Municipal) Services: A Case Study of Narayanganj*. Dhaka: National Institute of Local Government, 1990.

Mey, Wolfgang, ed. *They Are Now Burning Village after Village: Genocide in the Chittagong Hill Tracts, Bangladesh*. Copenhagen: International Work Group for Indigenous Affairs, 1984.

Rahman, Atiur. *Rural Power Structure: A Study of the Local Level Leaders in Bangladesh*. Dacca: Bangladesh Books International, 1981.

Rahman, A. H. M. Aminur. *Politics of Rural Self-Government in Bangladesh*. Dhaka: University of Dhaka, 1990.

Rahman, Mohammad Shafiqur. *Planning and Development of Upazila in Bangladesh*. Dhaka: National Institute of Local Government, 1991.

Shamsul Hoque, A. N. *Subnational Administration in Bangladesh and its Role in Development: An Overview*. Rajshahi: Department of Political Science, Rajshahi University, 1982.

Shawkat Ali, A. M. M. *Politics, Development and Upazila*. Dhaka: National Institute of Local Government, 1986.

Shelley, Mizanur Rahman, ed. *The Chittagong Hills Tracts of Bangladesh: The Untold Story*. Dhaka: Centre for Development Research, Bangladesh, 1992.

Siddiqui, Kamal, ed. *Local Government in South Asia: A Comparative Study*. Dhaka: University Press, 1992.

———. *Local Government in Bangladesh*. Dhaka: National Institute of Local Government, 1984.

Bibliography

Aminuzzaman, Salahuddin M. *Local Government and Administration in Bangladesh: A Selected Bibliography*. Dacca: Centre for Administrative Studies, 1981.

Political Parties

Ahmad, Muzaffar. *The Communist Party of India and Its Formation Abroad*. Calcutta: National Book Agency, 1962.

Ghosh, Shyamali. *The Awami League, 1949-1971*. Dhaka: Academic Publishers, 1990.

Mohaimena, Mohammad Abdulla. *Awami League in the Politics of Bangladesh*. Dhaka: Pioneer Publications, 1990.

Shelley, Mizanur Rahman. *Pakistan, The Second Republic: Politics and Parties*. Dacca: Concept Publications, 1970.

Public Administration

Abedin, Mohammad Jainul. *Papers on Administration and Related Issues*. Dhaka: Academy for Planning and Development, 1991.

Ahamed, Emajuddin. *Development Administration*. Dhaka: Centre for Administrative Studies, 1981.

———. *Bureaucratic Elites in Pakistan and Bangladesh: Their Development Strategy*. New Delhi: Young Asia: 1985.

An Analysis of the Working of Basic Democracy Institutions in East Pakistan. Comilla: Bangladesh Academy for Rural Development, 1963.

Anisuzzaman, Mohammad. *Bangladesh Public Administration and Society.* Dhaka: Bangladesh Books International, 1979.

Chadha, I. S. *Managing Projects in Bangladesh: A Scenario Analysis of Institutional Environment for Development Projects.* Dhaka: University Press, 1990.

Giasuddin Ahmed, Syed. *Bangladesh Public Service Commission.* Dhaka: University of Dhaka, 1990.

———. *Public Personnel Administration in Bangladesh.* Dhaka: University of Dhaka, 1986.

———. *The Image of Public Service in Bangladesh: A Study of Attitudes of Students Towards Public Service and Public Employees in Bangladesh.* Dacca: Centre for Administrative Studies, Department of Public Administration, University of Dacca, 1975.

Hayadara, Iusupha. *Development, the Upazila Way.* Dhaka: Dhaka Prokashan, 1986.

Huda, A. T. M. Shamsul, ed. *Co-ordination in Public Administration in Bangladesh.* Dhaka: Bangladesh Public Administration Training Centre, 1987.

Huq, M. Enamul. *Readings on Policing.* Dhaka: Sumi, 1992.

Khan, Mohammad Mohabbat. *Politics of Administrative Reform: A Case Study of Bangladesh.* New Delhi: Ashish Publishing House, 1991.

Khan, Mohammad Mohabbat and Habib Mohammad Zafrullah, eds. *Politics and Bureaucracy in a New Nation: Bangladesh.* Dacca: Centre for Administrative Studies, 1980).

Kibria, A. B. M. G. *Police Administration in Bangladesh.* Dacca: Khoshroz Kitab Mahal, 1976.

Mamoon, Muntassir. *Inside Bureaucracy: Bangladesh.* Calcutta: Papyrus: 1987.

Muhith, A. M. A. *Thoughts on Development Administration.* Dacca: Sabia Muhith, 1981.

Rahman, M. Shamsur. *Administrative Elite in Bangladesh*. New Delhi: Manak Publications, 1991.

Seraj, Toufiq M. *The Role of Small Towns in Rural Development: A Case Study of Bangladesh*. Dhaka: National Institute of Local Government, 1989.

Shawkat Ali, A. M. M. *Field Administration and Rural Development in Bangladesh*. Dacca: Centre for Social Studies, 1982.

Shamsul Hoque, Abunasar. *Administrative Reform in Pakistan: An Analysis of Reform Commission Reports in the Light of United Nations Doctrine*. Dacca: National Institute of Public Administration, 1970.

Sirajuddin, Muhammad. *Institutional Support for Planning and Project Management*. Dhaka: Study Group, 1982.

Regional Associations

ASEAN Experiences of Regional and Inter-Regional Cooperation: Relevance for SAARC. Dhaka: Bangladesh Institute for International and Strategic Studies, 1988.

Ahamed, Emajuddin. *SARC: Seeds of Harmony*. Dhaka: University Press, 1985.

Ahsan, Abul. *SAARC: A Perspective*. Dhaka: University Press, 1992.

Anand, Ram Prakash. *South Asia in Search of a Regional Identity*. New Delhi: Banyan Publications, 1991.

Hafiz, M. Abdul, ed. *South Asian Regional Cooperation: A Socio-Economic Approach to Regional Stability*. Dhaka: Bangladesh Institute of International and Strategic Studies, 1985.

Mendis, Vernon L. B. *SAARC: Origins, Organization, and Prospects*. Perth, Western Australia: Indian Ocean Centre for Peace Studies, 1991.

Mishra, Pramod Kumar. *South-South Cooperation: A SAARC Perspective*. Calcutta: Chatterjee Publishers, 1990.

Nirmala Devi, T. *Regional Economic Cooperation in South Asia*. Allahabad: Chugh Publications, 1989.

Rahman, Atiur. *Political Economy of SARC*. Dhaka: Papari Prakasani, 1983.

Satyamurty, K. *South Asian Regional Cooperation*. Hyderabad, India: Booklinks, 1982.

Wadhva, Charan D., ed. *Regional Economic Cooperation in South Asia*. Ahmedabad: Allied Publishers, 1987.

Bibliography

Documentation on SAARC: Books and Documents, Addresses and Statements, Chronology of SAARC. Kathmandu: Tribuvan University, 1988.

Science and Technology

Biswas, Ahsan A., and M. O. Ghani, eds. *Directory of Scientists and Technologists in Bangladesh*. Dhaka: Bangladesh National Scientific and Technical Documentation Centre, 1989.

Farouk, A. *A Study of Occupations where Qualifications in Natural Sciences and Mathematics Are Required in East Pakistan*. Dacca: Bureau of Economic Research, 1970.

———. *Science Trained Manpower: A Study of Employment Problem in Bangladesh*. Dacca: Bureau of Economic Research 1972.

Harvey, W. G. *Birds in Bangladesh*. Dhaka: University Press, 1990.

Environmental Science

Anwar, Jamal. *Bangladesh: The State of the Environment.* Dhaka: Shahitya Prakash, 1993.

Elahi, K. Maudood, Sharif A. H. M. Raihan, and A. K. M. Abul Kalam, eds. *Bangladesh: Geography, Development, and Environment.* Dhaka: Bangladesh National Geographic Association, 1992.

Khan, Mohammad Ali Reza. *Wildlife of Bangladesh: A Checklist.* Dhaka: University of Dhaka, 1982.

Rahman, A. Atiq, et al., eds. *Environment and Development in Bangladesh.* Dhaka: University Press, 1994.

Seminar on Women and Environment (1991: Dhaka) Proceedings. Dhaka: Geographic Society, 1992.

Zaker Husain, Kazi. *An Introduction to the Wildlife of Bangladesh.* Dacca: F. Ahmed, 1974.

Bibliography

Siddiqi, N.A. *An Annotated Bibliography of the Wildlife of Bangladesh.* Chittagong: Forest Research Institute, 1979.

Public Health

Chen, Lincoln C. *Disaster in Bangladesh* New York: Oxford University Press, 1973.

ABOUT THE AUTHORS

CRAIG BAXTER (Ph.D., University of Pennsylvania) is professor of politics and history at Juniata College. He was an officer in the Foreign Service, 1956-1980, with several posts in South Asia. He was a visiting faculty member at the United States Military Academy, 1971-1974, on detail from the Foreign Service. He is the author of several books on South Asia including *Bangladesh: A New Nation in an Old Setting* (Westview Press, 1984) and *Bangladesh: From a Nation to a State* (Westview Press, forthcoming) and is the co-author of *Government and Politics in South Asia* (Westview Press, third edition, 1993). He has also published a number of articles and chapters in edited works. He has been president of the American Institute of Bangladesh Studies since 1989.

SYEDUR RAHMAN (Ph.D., Syracuse University) is coordinator of the Hubert H. Humphrey Fellowship Program and Research Associate at the Institute for Policy Research and Evaluation at the Pennsylvania State University. His articles on Bangladesh include "Political Boundary Building in Bangladesh," "Issues and Agenda for Regional Cooperation in South Asia" (with Robert LaPorte, Jr.), and "The Bangladesh Military and Economic Development" (with Craig Baxter). He has also served as a consultant with the United Nations Development Program on reform of the Bangladesh civil service and on local government. His research interests are in public administration, local government, and policy analysis and evaluation. He is treasurer of the American Institute of Bangladesh Studies.